TEMPORARY

ARCHITECTURE NOW!

IMPRINT

PROJECT MANAGEMENT
Florian Kobler, Cologne

COLLABORATION
Harriet Graham, Turin

PRODUCTION
Ute Wachendorf, Cologne

DESIGN
Sense/Net, Andy Disl
and Birgit Eichwede,
Cologne

GERMAN TRANSLATION
Kristina Brigitta Köper, Berlin

FRENCH TRANSLATION
Jacques Bosser, Paris

© VG BILD-KUNST
Bonn 2011, for the works of
Laurent Grasso, Jean
Nouvel, Rem Koolhaas, and
Ben van Berkel

PRINTED IN ITALY
ISBN 978–3–8365–2328–8

© 2011 TASCHEN GMBH
Hohenzollernring 53
D–50672 Cologne
www.taschen.com

TEMPORARY

ARCHITECTURE NOW!

TEMPORÄRE *Architektur heute!*
L'architecture ÉPHÉMÈRE *d'aujourd'hui!*
Philip Jodidio

TASCHEN

CONTENTS

INTRODUCTION

OUT, OUT, BRIEF CANDLE!

Always observe how ephemeral and worthless human things are. Pass then through this little space of time conformably to nature, and end thy journey in content, just as an olive falls off when it is ripe, blessing nature who produced it, and thanking the tree on which it grew. Marcus Aurelius, *Meditations*, Book 4, *c.* 170 A.D.

Marcus Aurelius (121–180 A.D.) was Emperor of Rome and wrote his *Meditations* in Greek as a series of thoughts and writings addressed to himself. In Greek, the word *ephemeros* means "lasting only one day." The word *temporary* is related to the Latin *temporarius* (of seasonal character, lasting a short time). What is temporary is the opposite of permanent. The ways in which these words can be applied to architecture are clearly broad and difficult to define. By essence, buildings are fundamentally temporary, even if centuries intervene before dust returns to dust. Architecture is by definition and nature temporary, but just how ephemeral it is depends naturally on the quality of its construction and a series of other factors ranging from location to the vagaries of climate. For want of better materials and methods, or because of nomadic lifestyles, much early architecture was no more than a wooden hut or a tent of sorts at the mercy of the winds. Obviously the purpose of a structure also dictates its solidity, as, too, might the way it is cared for. Japanese temples made of wood survive for centuries because they are sometimes rebuilt piece by piece, from generation to generation. Modern cities are subjected to constant remaking that challenges even the greatest architectural egos. What was once a symbol of power and constancy can be swept away to make room for a shopping center or a bowling alley. "Vanity of vanities, saith the Preacher, vanity of vanities; all *is* vanity."[1] But if architecture is inevitably temporary in some sense, and if modern lifestyles lead to an almost nomadic existence even in developed countries, might architects not accept the inevitable and build for the moment without worrying about posterity so much?

Modern methods allow materials such as plastics to be used in astonishing new ways, and even wood, the most ancient of building materials, can now be milled by computer-driven tools into unique forms not meant to last until the end of time. Purpose is essential—a fair stand, a stage design, or an exhibition pavilion usually have a predetermined and brief life span. Numerous architects have noticed that metal shipping containers, symbols of the global economy, are often abandoned even though they can easily be converted into shops or dwellings. Curiously, in this instance, objects that are meant to move can be anchored in the soil, where they may prove more solid and durable than more traditional architectural forms. Construction sites or archeological digs are the pretext or reason for a good deal of temporary architecture, but so too is art. An art show frequently requires a spatial design—architecture by any other name. Contemporary art that also courts the *ephemeral* may bring its own built environment close to the original Greek definition of the word.

TEMPORAL PERMANENCE

Even a cursory examination of contemporary architecture reveals a rise in the number of avowedly temporary structures completed in recent years. One reason for this may be economic constraints that favor a solution that usually costs less than a more solid building. The

other reason, perhaps more significant in the long run, is that there may be fewer clients who have the outright hubris to try to build something that will last "for centuries." Ours is obviously a culture of rapid consumption and architecture does not escape the overall trends. On a more positive note, rapidly conceived and executed structures may well permit architects to experiment and to invent the new forms that accompany the way we will live tomorrow.

Pavilions of various kinds form the core of temporary architecture, be it for individual events, or for large-scale international fairs and expositions. Though planned demolition is the rule in most of these cases, there are also exceptions, and these demonstrate the significance that "temporary" architecture can have. The Eiffel Tower was built as the entrance gate for the 1889 World's Fair and was originally due to stand for 20 years. It is still the most visited monument in the world requiring payment for entrance. Given its height, the Eiffel Tower had to be solidly constructed, whence perhaps its longevity, and yet this largely "useless" structure has in many ways become the symbol of Paris, if not of France. International exhibition of World's Fair architecture is still a motor for the design and construction of ambitious temporary buildings, as is demonstrated in this volume with a number of the national pavilions for the 2010 Shanghai Expo in China.

A MERMAID, A SPACESHIP, AND A CATHEDRAL FOR SEEDS

Although other national pavilions for Shanghai could well have been selected for this book, six structures are presented in detail here. The first of these was designed by Bjarke Ingels (BIG) for his native Denmark (page 92). Here an effort was made to distill some of the most typical Danish experiences, from bicycle riding to seeing the real Little Mermaid, a sculpture by Edward Eriksen that was placed on a rock in Copenhagen harbor in 1913. A well-known symbol of Denmark, it was moved from its location for the first time for Expo 2010. The Little Mermaid is a fairy tale by Hans Christian Andersen published in 1837 that recounts the willingness of a mermaid to give up her life in the sea for love of a human prince. The sculpture is set on a rock at the center of the white metal pavilion whose spiral form encloses a "harbor bath." While playing on the fairy-tale symbol of his country, Bjarke Ingels also seeks to embody its modernity for the Chinese who may be more familiar with the story of Hans Christian Andersen than they are with imagining Denmark as a creative, up-to-date place.

Designed by Buchner Bründler from Basel, the Swiss Pavilion (page 100) also seeks to distill a combination of contemporary design and symbolic or almost folkloric elements. With a plan that resembles a map of the country, the Swiss Pavilion featured a chairlift typical of the country's mountains, but also a high-tech open-net façade. The use of powerful concrete forms here also evokes a certain amount of modern and contemporary Swiss architecture for those who are even a bit familiar with this aspect of the culture. A green roof is at once a nod to ecologically oriented construction and a reminder of the natural beauty of the country.

The Spanish Pavilion (page 268) in Shanghai is the work of Benedetta Tagliabue (Miralles Tagliabue EMBT), and is a four-story steel structure whose most visible feature is a veritable cloud made of wickerwork. Wickerwork is selected as a typical example of Spanish handi-

2

crafts and the architects have also arranged the material so that Chinese characters evoking Spanish-Chinese friendship are formed. The concrete solidity of the interior of the Swiss Pavilion here gives way to a decidedly temporary appearance, in keeping with the nature of an event like Expo 2010, where the mixture of folklore, national pride, and decided modernity seems to shock no one. The city of Madrid is further represented by the Air Tree (page 136) designed by the group Ecosistema Urbano, a structure that is meant to create a comfortable environment in the midst of the heat of Shanghai in the summer. Here too, the goal is to create an attraction that gives visitors information about a place, but also insists on the modernity and inventiveness that the Chinese might not necessarily associate with a city like Madrid.

Though most countries have chosen their own nationals as architects, Egypt is an exception, represented with a structure designed by the noted architect Zaha Hadid (page 194). The magazine *Egypt Today* gave Hadid's design a rather tepid welcome, in an article entitled "Overplaying Egyptomania," writing: "Egypt's 1000-square-meter pavilion was designed as a gift by internationally renowned Iraqi architect Zaha Hadid. A bit stark with swirling black and white swooshes, it is apparently meant to combine modernity with antiquity, represented by the constellation-like graphic of three pyramids above the arched entrance. Indeed, the building looks like some lost spaceship which had landed in Shanghai by mistake and was now trying to avoid notice by disguising itself as a pavilion."[2] The magazine is obliged to admit that the pavilion attracted an average of 14 000 visitors per day who came to see the architecture as well as the pharaonic objects on display, the exhibition on Cairo, or perhaps to have their names written out in Egyptian hieroglyphs. Zaha Hadid is no stranger to controversy because her architecture does not fit into established categories or expectations about what a building should look like. What better place to challenge what the French call *idées recues* (received ideas) than in an international exhibition dedicated to the future.

Another pavilion that attracted a good deal of attention in Shanghai because of its unusual "hairy" appearance was that of the UK (page 200), designed by Thomas Heatherwick. This form, enclosing a space called the Seed Cathedral, is made up of 60 000 slender transparent fiber optic rods, each 7.5 meters in length and each encasing one or more seeds at its tip. It was designed in conjunction with Kew Gardens' Millennium Seed Bank, which plans to collect the seeds of 25% of the world's plant species by 2020. While certain countries clearly placed an emphasis on projecting an image of modernity in Shanghai, Great Britain and Heatherwick made a statement for ecological consciousness that might well be receivable in China as well as in the UK. The presence of this structure in Shanghai might also speak to the shift away from sleek modern forms toward a complex architecture that has other ambitions and goals than obvious aesthetics.

BLACK AND WHITE AND RED ALL OVER

Half a world away and in a very different context, the Serpentine Gallery located in London's Kensington Gardens celebrated its tenth year of summer pavilions (page 298). These pavilions, designed by such luminaries of the architecture world as Oscar Niemeyer, Toyo Ito, Frank O. Gehry, Álvaro Siza, and Eduardo Souto de Moura, are intended to last only for three months and are usually visited by over 200 000 people. The idea of Serpentine Director Julia Peyton-Jones was to select a well-known architect who had never built in the UK to design each of these structures. Her choice for 2010 was Jean Nouvel, who responded with a surprising 500-square-meter red structure intended for conferences or concerts, and including a café. In this case, as in that of the previous pavilions, the cost (£750 000 for Nouvel's building) was borne by sponsors eager to be associated with one of the most notable annual cultural events in London. Although the pavilions are sometimes sold and rebuilt elsewhere, as was the case for Frank Gehry's 2008 structure that now stands near Aix-en-Provence in France, the essence of these designs is to be temporary and to sum up something of the creativity of each architect. Given the public success of the Serpentine summer pavilions since 2000, there is no doubt that temporary architecture can and does attract substantial attention, often venturing into bold forms that might not have been appropriate for permanent buildings, especially in a protected context such as that of Hyde Park for example.

PURPLE HAZE AND ROBOTICS

Another interesting temporary building erected in 2010 was Coop Himmelb(l)au's 430-square-meter Pavilion 21 Mini Opera Space (page 124) installed on the Marstallplatz in Munich, Germany. Using computer-derived shapes linked in an unexpected way to the music of Jimi Hendrix (*Purple Haze*, "…'Scuse me while I kiss the sky…"), the architects created the building for an opera festival. Whatever its musical origins Pavilion 21 has the kind of spiky deconstructivist shape that is a familiar sign of the work of Coop Himmelb(l)au. Especially surrounded by the rather staid forms of Munich, this surprising eruption allowed opera-goers and passersby to sample a bit of contemporary architecture that would probably not have been so readily accepted on a permanent basis in this location. This again underlines a distinct advantage of temporary buildings, although some, like the Eiffel Tower, do manage to survive until public opinion catches up with their avant-garde design.

The House of Stone (Italy, page 326), designed by John Pawson in the context of the 2010 Milan Furniture Fair and more specifically for the Interni Think Tank on a site within the Università degli Studi, surely gave a good impression of minimalist solidity despite its ephemeral character. Pawson's design also points to another advantage of temporary architecture in that the structure made use of an innovative recycled stone material called Lithoverde whose only ingredient other than stone scrap is 1% natural resin. Again set in an architectural context that might not necessarily encourage modernity, the empty House of Stone with its strict, nearly funerary demeanor might have seemed more ancient than its surroundings.

Solid construction is not necessarily the hallmark of many contemporary pavilions, quite the contrary. Rendez-Vous (Tokyo, Japan, 2010, page 54), a 52-square-meter structure by the Tokyo firm Atelier Bow-Wow, was made in good part of bamboo and was intended to contrast with the strict solidity of the nearby building of the National Museum of Modern Art designed by Yoshiro Taniguchi. The young Japanese architects avowed that they wished "to ease this austere mood, while not letting go of the dignity of the place, but instead just slightly loosening up the atmosphere to turn it into a gentler space." Using the supple nature of bamboo to carry their idea even further, Atelier Bow-

Wow imagined the pavilion as a sort of giant animal emerging from the gardens of the Imperial Palace. This humoristic take on temporary architecture also represents a contrast to the dense urbanity of the surrounding city.

Another light structure was the ICD/ITKE Research Pavilion (page 206) designed by the University of Stuttgart's Institutes for Computational Design and of Building Structures and Structural Design in 2010. Made entirely with bent birch plywood strips, the building consisted in no less than 500 unique pieces made using computer-assisted design and manufacturing in the robotics laboratory of the University. Although birch could hardly be termed a "modern" material, its use in this instance calls on some of the most sophisticated design and cutting technologies available. Where an earlier generation of computer-designed buildings tended to rely more on curious shapes that broke out of the modernist grid, contemporary structures can develop along even more unexpected lines, particularly in the context of research work such as that of Stuttgart's ICD/ITKE.

STANDARDIZED AND STACKABLE

Although shipping containers seem to be a ubiquitous fixture of the modern port or urban landscape, they are a relatively recent invention, surely inspired by standard military containers of the sort developed by the United States Department of Defense in the 1950s. The International Organization for Standardization (ISO) based its own criteria for intermodal containers (able to be placed on ships or directly on trucks or trains, 1970) on the example of the US military. A typical container is made of corrugated steel and is either 20 feet (six meters) or 40 feet (12 meters) in length. Up to seven units can normally be stacked on each other using standardized fasteners. Although a steel box may not be the most obvious structure for a dwelling or building of other sorts, ISO containers were used for such purposes beginning in the 1980s.

Phillip Clark, the owner of a firm called Import Export & Overhaul in Miami, Florida, obtained US Patent Number 4 854 094 (filed: November 23, 1987; date of patent: August 8, 1989) for a: "Method for converting one or more steel shipping containers into a habitable building at a building site and the product thereof." Before that date (1985), the Australian architect Sean Godsell states that he began work on his Future Shack: "A mass-produced relocatable house for emergency and relief housing. Recycled shipping containers are used to form the main volume of the building. A parasol roof packs inside the container. When erected, the roof shades the container and reduces heat load on the building. Legs telescope from the container enabling it to be sited without excavation on uneven terrain."[3] Though the paternity of container architecture may not be entirely clear, it has emerged around the world as a solution for temporary or even permanent architecture. A number of recent examples of the reuse of ISO containers are published in this volume.

The Brazilian architects Bernades + Jacobsen, well-known for their luxurious seaside homes, have made frequent use of containers for ephemeral events such as a 2008 international video art exhibition in Villa Lobos Park in São Paulo. Their 1200-square-meter Container Art installation (page 84) was set up on the esplanade of the park on wooden bases and was made up of an orderly assemblage of six- and

3
*Adam Kalkin, illy Push Button House,
Venice, Italy, and other locations,
2007*

3

12-meter containers. They had already created a much larger installation with 250 containers for the stages, restrooms, and snack bars of the 2007 Tim Festival (Rio de Janeiro), a two-night music gathering. Most of the 40 000-square-meter facility took the form of a large wall. Twelve-meter containers were used as doorways, signaling access to the stages, entries, and exits of the event. In the form of a large, sinuous curve, open to the sea, the highest part of the wall hid the 15-meter-high tents used for concerts. Spaces between the containers were used for video projections and stages for performances set at different levels. The facilities were assembled beginning on September 16, 2007, and had been fully dismantled on November 18. More than 23 000 people attended the two nights of concerts. What containers lack in subtlety and formal flexibility, they clearly make up for in ease of transport and assembly.

The American architect Adam Kalkin has actually specialized in container architecture, as his 2008 book *Quik Build: Adam Kalkin's ABC of Container Architecture* attests. He has created a system he calls the Quik House (page 224) that makes use of recycled shipping containers to create houses that can be far more luxurious than their humble origin might suggest. These can be delivered within five months of the initial order and cost as little as $76 000, though various options proposed by Kalkin can also drive the price up considerably. His illy Push Button House (page 230) shown at the Venice Biennale in 2007 aims to show that a normal shipping container can convert itself into a real house in the space of just a few minutes by using hydraulic systems and clever design. Kalkin has also ventured into work with the US military in Afghanistan and a charitable foundation in Russia, showing the large number of uses that shipping containers can be put to.

The COP 15 Pavilion (page 258) designed by MAPT and located in the North Harbor of Copenhagen (Denmark, 2009–10), makes use of used shipping containers and other recycled materials. Placing an emphasis on the inexpensive and ecologically responsible aspects of such reuse, MAPT point out that shipping containers are considered so cheap that transport companies often judge it more economical to abandon them than to return them empty to their point of origin. This clearly offers a boon to willing designers such as this Danish firm.

The Italian group tamassociati created Emergency NGO housing (page 382) in the Salam Center for Cardiac Surgery (Soba, Khartoum, Sudan, 2009) using 95 six-meter containers for housing and seven 12-meter containers for a cafeteria. These containers had actually been left near the site during the construction of the larger Salam Center. Steel, of course, transmits heat or cold almost directly, which is one disadvantage in the use of containers for housing. The architects solved this problem with five-centimeter interior insulating panels and an insulated roof, together with a system of bamboo *brise-soleils* that ensure that direct sun does not actually touch the steel.

FAIR STANDS IN MARBLE, GLASS, AND WOOD

Fair stands have long been an area of experimentation in temporary architecture. The fact that these stands generally do not have to bear great loads or perform other functions of more traditional architecture allows them to strike out into new territory, or to set aside certain rules of the built form altogether. Nor are they always created by architects, since designers, sometimes specialized in the field, are equally

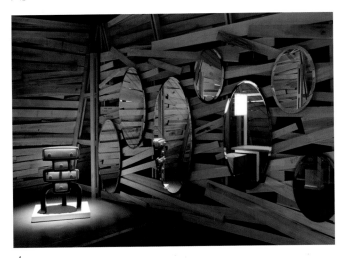

4
Established & Sons, "Established & Sons / Milan 2009", La Pelota, Milan, Italy, 2009

4

present. The Spanish architect Alberto Campo Baeza took a particularly architectural approach to the stand he designed for the Italian stone firm Piba Marbri at the 2009 Marmocacc Fair (Verona, Italy, page 112). His large black cube was entirely clad in white Carrara marble on the inside, creating a contrast of perception and volume that was heightened by a clever moving spotlight system that created the impression of changing sunlight inside the stand. Campo Baeza's strong, minimalist architecture is frequently concerned with such contrasts and with the play of the sun. What he did here was in some sense to translate his own design preoccupations into a form that was of interest to the firm concerned, and to visitors to the fair.

The Madrid architects Camila Aybar and Juan Jose Mateos have created fair stands for the glass manufacturer Vitro at IFEMA since 2006 (page 58). The 2006 stand used no less than 170 tons of glass assembled from 25 000 pieces recovered when larger panes were trimmed. The stacking technique used created effects compared by the architects to the work of artists such as Bill Viola or James Turrell. Indeed, where visual effects are concerned, this type of fair stand may be closer to art than it is to architecture in any traditional sense. This is surely a reason why this type of work interests architects. Their 2008 stand for Vitro used tiny red and black dots on ultra-clear glass to create space in which the color of the structure changed according to the location of viewers. Aybar and Mateos have used glass as a malleable and changing material that creates an artistic effect at the same time as it vaunts the merits of the client's products. Whether this is more specifically a work of design or of architecture might remain to be determined, but the more practical, hum-drum functions of normal architecture are certainly absent.

Though created only in 2005, the London firm Established & Sons has made a substantial reputation for itself in the production and sale of modern and contemporary furniture, in good part through the work of cofounders Alasdhair Willis and Sebastian Wrong, the Design Director. The company's stand at the 2009 Milan Furniture Fair (page 160), was an astonishing accumulation of 30 tons of untreated wood roughly arranged in stacked walls, creating spaces where 16 new designs were launched. Sebastian Wrong, who was responsible for the installation, spoke correctly of the "density and intensity" of the spaces that unusually contrasted with the modern furniture they enclosed.

Francesc Rifé's AB21 Stand (Hábitat Valencia 2009 Trade Fair, Spain, page 350) was intended for the display of rugs. He says quite openly that the "space was conceived like an art gallery." Indeed, with their bright colors and lighting, rugs do strongly resemble works of modern art, a fact that the client surely appreciated. The reason to call on a noted designer in such circumstances is surely to attract attention but also to elevate the products in some sense, and Rifé's stand accomplished that with brio.

SEEKING HIDDEN RHYTHMS
Perhaps because practicality is not always as important for temporary structures as it is for permanent ones, ephemeral architecture frequently approaches the domain of art, and indeed numerous artists cross over the unstated barrier between forms of expression to

5
*Cecil Balmond, "Element—Cecil
Balmond", Tokyo, Japan, 2010*

5

create what can resemble architecture. These distinctions become insignificant in the hands of a creator as inventive as Cecil Balmond. His "Element" exhibition (page 64), seen in Tokyo in 2010, has to do with his own career as an engineer who has worked with some of the best-known architects of the day. The show deals in part with what he calls "seeking hidden rhythms," or more specifically with "the underlying order and rhythm that resides within nature…" There can be little doubt that this kind of preoccupation also enters the reasoning of many artists, and as such there is no difference to be noted between such artists and an engineer at the level of Cecil Balmond.

Ammar Eloueini's design for the 2008 show "Le Tramway" at the Pavillon de l'Arsenal in Paris (page 146) made use of a polycarbonate skin that divided the space and allowed the route of the Paris tram line that circles the city to be played out within the exhibition. This type of use of light materials, seen also in retailing, exemplifies the capacity of the architect to conquer space in a way that artists often seek to do, occupying and transforming it, while leaving, in this instance, only a memory of their intervention once the show was finished. So, too, Philippe Rahm succeeded in transforming the cavernous 14 000-square-meter space of the Grand Palais in Paris (page 334) on the occasion of the art show "La Force de l'Art 02." Philippe Rahm explains that this white installation was "the opposite of exhibition design in the sense that it is not the work of art that fits into the architecture, but the architecture which yields to the demands of the work of art." The exhibits will work together to shape the landscape through the simultaneous play of pressure and checks and balances. The sense of a meeting between architecture and art was completed here by the surrounding early 20th-century form of the Grand Palais itself with its vast glazed roof.

UTOPIA OR OBLIVION

What might be called the love affair between art and architecture that is played out in temporary installations can be perceived equally well from the standpoint of architects or from that of artists. The young architects Florian Idenburg (born in 1975) and Jing Liu (born in 1980) took on the courtyard space of PS1 in Long Island City (New York, USA) in 2010 with their work Pole Dance (page 376), a lightweight combination of nine-meter-high poles, bungee cords, and open nets. With its brightly colored balls, a hammock, and a pool, this installation, designed to move in its entirety as any part was moved, could just as easily be called art as it might be qualified as the work of architects. Lightness, interdependence, and, indeed, an accentuated temporality combined here to give a real sense of what a relatively inexpensive installation can say about architecture, its future, and its possibilities.

Idenburg and Liu did not seem overly preoccupied with the practicality or usefulness of Pole Dance. The noted artist Tomas Saraceno, on the other hand, imagines his lightweight or levitating structures as a kind of template for the city and the architecture of the future. "I propose the concrete realization of cloud cities as proposed by R. Buckminster Fuller." Buckminster Fuller is, of course, a reference in the area of temporary architecture because of his largely theoretical "Cloud 9" concept, but also through any number of realized structures such as his inflatable domes. Buckminster Fuller imagined that a closed geodesic dome or sphere with a diameter of more than half a mile (805 meters) would have an air-to-structure weight ratio of 1000:1, meaning that the sunlight falling on it would raise interior air temperature

6
Solid Objectives—Idenburg Liu,
Pole Dance, PS1, Long Island City,
New York, USA, 2010

6

enough for the sphere to literally float in the air, along the lines of an inhabited, round hot-air balloon. Tomas Saraceno's allusion to Buckminster Fuller is thus evidence of a kind of thread through utopian theory to a real vision of what temporary architecture might become.

Saraceno's poetic works hide a secret practicality, or rather a dream that hopes to change architecture in the most fundamental sense, making it literally float in the air rather than taking root in the earth. "Such spheres," according to the artist, "could lift a considerable mass, and hence 'mini-cities' or airborne towns for thousands of people could be built in this way. These cloud cities could be tethered, or free-floating, or perhaps maneuverable so that they could 'migrate' in response to climatic and environmental conditions." Saraceno refers specifically here to R. Buckminster Fuller's 1969 book *Utopia or Oblivion: The Prospects for Humanity.* In the hands of Idenburg and Liu, and surely even more so in those of Tomas Saraceno, architecture takes on a poetic, artistic presence that reveals the true importance of temporary designs. Where weight is suspended and practical functions are obviated, architecture is left free to become a vehicle for dreams.

A BIGGER BANG

The word ephemeral in its original meaning, "lasting only one day," might best be applied to the architecture of events such as concerts or plays. The means and the scale of the performances of major rock groups place them in the forefront of this kind of design. One English designer, Mark Fisher, has been behind some of the most publicized stage designs of the Rolling Stones, U2, and Pink Floyd. Fisher, born in 1947, graduated from the Architectural Association School of Architecture in London in 1971, and was a Unit Master at the AA from 1973 to 1977. Amongst his more notable designs, the stage sets for the Rolling Stones *A Bigger Bang* world tour in 2005 (page 170) combined the idea of "decadent, picturesque fantasies of grand 19th-century opera house décor" with large high-resolution LED video screens and an innovative seating arrangement meant to recall opera boxes.

The 180-ton portable superstructure designed by Fisher for the U2 *360°* world tour (2009–11, page 178) encloses not only the stage but also several thousand spectators, while supporting 200 tons of technical equipment. Allowing, as its title suggests, for spectators to view the band from all angles, the structure had to be created in three copies in order to allow for the tour to change cities each day. Structurally, technically, and even musically innovative, this kind of temporary architecture may defy the ordinary classification of buildings or pavilions, but it is in some sense at the cutting edge of contemporary design. Mark Fisher also designed one of the most stunning elements of the Opening Ceremony of the 2008 Beijing Olympics, the "Dream Sphere" (page 174), a 19-meter globe set on a telescoping mast that supported the performance of 60 people, once again defying normal expectations of the use of space in such circumstances.

Stage sets of a more down-to-earth nature have long fascinated architects, and this volume, with its focus on recent work, includes the designs of Massimiliano and Doriana Fuksas for *Medea* and *Oedipus at Colonus* at the Greek theatre festival of Syracuse (Italy, 2009, page 182). Working with the concept of catharsis and the idea of the lost horizon of the first presentations of the plays of Euripides and Sophocles,

7
Mark Fisher, The Rolling Stones,
A Bigger Bang *world tour, 2005*

7

the architects imagined a "concave blade." This reduction to a pure and simple form is very much in keeping with the strength of the dramas played out on the stage, and yet it might be seen as contradictory with the more florid fantasies of ancient Greece that other designers might have proposed. Again, freed from the constraints of weightiness and strict function, architects like the Fuksas couple show what they are really capable of, breaking out of expected molds and reshaping space itself. This is in some sense the essence of temporary architecture.

BUBBLES AND BOOKS

While temporary architecture may indeed allow on some occasions for a freeing of architectural innovation from its usual constraints, other situations demand a careful attention to the element of practicality. The examples in this category published here vary from a rooftop restaurant to the largest object ever to orbit the earth, the International Space Station, which is admittedly in a class of its own. The inventive New York architects Diller Scofidio + Renfro, who once built a structure in the shape of a cloud (Blur Building, Expo '02, Yverdon-les-Bains, Switzerland, 2000–02), have proposed a temporary extension to Washington, D.C.'s Hirshhorn Museum in the shape of a malleable, inflatable bubble (page 130). This pneumatic membrane, intended to shelter up to 1000 people, would bulge out of the central courtyard of the modernist structure without touching its inner façades. The notion of an elastic space, particularly in the context of a rather strict modernist building, is a very contemporary one, and the inflatable structure is one of the clearest manifestations of ephemeral architecture.

In a very different style, the French multimedia artist Laurent Grasso and his brother, the architect Pascal Grasso, created a small (63 m^2) temporary restaurant that was assembled on the roof of the Palais de Tokyo in Paris and operated between April and June 2009. Called Nomiya (page 188), the 18-meter-long structure was built in two parts in a shipyard. The practical aspects of such a rooftop restaurant dictated much of its essence, but the architects certainly managed to create a chic, minimalist décor for this very popular venue. Again working within clear practical constraints, the Dutch designers Ira Koers and Roelof Mulder took on the complex task of creating a temporary décor for the University of Amsterdam library (page 234). With an area of 2300 square meters and 235 working posts, this project nonetheless had to be handled with a modest budget. Koers and Mulder associated bright colors (1105 red crates for books) with a functionality that earned the project a 2009 Great Indoors Award. Whereas some interesting temporary projects do escape the usual practical constraints of more durable architecture, both the Grasso brothers and the Koers Mulder team succeeded in forming ephemeral environments that were successful because of their appearance, but also because of the efficient ways in which they resolved practical issues of the functions concerned.

AROUND THE WORLD IN 90 MINUTES

Temporary structures clearly challenge the more limited definitions of just what constitutes architecture. Buildings by nature are rooted in the earth, though some people like Tomas Saraceno dream of having them float in the air. What of an astonishing structure like the International Space Station (page 286), currently taking on its final form even as the US Space Shuttle program grinds to a final halt. The work of the US (NASA), European (ESA), Russian (RKA), Japanese (JAXA), and Canadian (CSA) space agencies, the Station is the product of the progressive assembly of

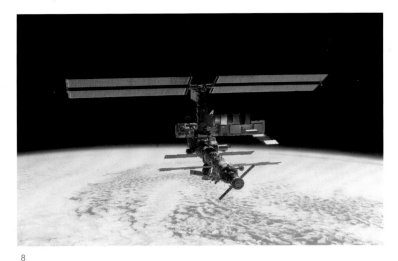

8

8
*National Aeronautics and Space
Administration (NASA), International
Space Station (ISS), 1998–2011
(ongoing)*

modules that have made a 370 000-kg (mass) orbiting structure unlike anything ever seen in space or on earth before. While most architecture can be questioned for aesthetic reasons, the ISS has a shape that is essentially influenced by the physics of low-earth orbit and human habitation. Some may find it curious in appearance, but this is a kind of architecture that largely escapes one the most fundamental forces, that of gravity.

In a sense, this is the ultimate expression of temporary architecture, floating in space, yet constrained by technicalities of a new sort. When Louis Sullivan coined the term "Form follows Function" at the end of the 19th century, he surely was not thinking of the ISS, yet that term defines the Space Station more fully than any architectural discourse. Certainly planes and ships have a kind of architecture of their own, but vehicles are generally excluded from the analysis of buildings. The ISS is a vehicle of sorts because it circles the earth 15.7 times a day, but it is also a laboratory and a hotel for astronauts. It is, for the first time, a piece of real temporary architecture in space, and undoubtedly the harbinger of forms to come. Indeed, one characteristic of temporary architecture in general is its lack of rootedness, its ability to move, where "permanent" forms tend to have concrete foundations, and await only demolition to disappear.

MODULAR, SUSTAINABLE, TRANSPORTABLE

For temporary architecture, as for its more permanent cousin, one of the most significant of functions is housing. Though some dream of houses made to last for centuries, modern times have brought more and more transient solutions to the fore, beginning with America's legions of mobile homes. The use of shipping containers to make homes that can be easily transported has already been evoked, but there are other categories of temporary housing that deserve notice. The German designer Werner Aisslinger, inventor of the Loftcube, a temporary residence intended for rooftop installation (2003), has more recently conceived the Fincube, a "modular, sustainable and transportable low-energy house" (2010, page 48). Minimum site preparation and durable, recyclable materials are the hallmark of this design, which responds to many questions about housing, including the increasingly nomadic ambitions of certain populations, even in developed countries.

Jennifer Siegal's Office of Mobile Design has specialized, as its name implies, in modular, transportable structures such as the Prefab Show House (page 312) and Taliesin Mod.Fab House published here (page 318). She has experimented with the use of shipping containers, as was the case in the Seatrain Residence (Los Angeles, California, USA), a custom residence composed of two pairs of stacked ISO shipping containers sheltered under a 15-meter steel-and-glass roof membrane. Her work also demonstrates the similarities between prefabricated housing and transportable units. Such residences were often equated with inexpensive construction and a relatively low level of quality, but Siegal imagined placing a luxurious Boffi kitchen in the middle of the Prefab Show House, showing that such structures have come a long way since the days of the Quonset Hut. It should be emphasized that many of today's initiatives in the area of easily transportable or assembled housing are related to the needs of the US military during World War II. Then, too, the mobile nature of the population of the United States beginning with the movement westward contributed to a state of mind that led many to imagine taking their homes with them. Inspired by the British Nissen hut developed by the British Royal Engineers during World War I to replace tents, a team working at Quonset Point, Rhode Is-

9
OBRA Architects, Red+Housing:
Architecture on the Edge of Survival,
Beijing, China, 2009

land, for the US Navy conceived the so-called Quonset Hut beginning in 1941 to respond to the pressing need for mass-produced, transportable, and easily assembled structures. Adapted in various ways, these semicylindrical shelters still inspire temporary architecture around the world, even if their summary design no longer meets the standards of comfort common in the developed world.

ONLY AN EXTREME FORM OF ARCHITECTURE

The New York–based architects OBRA created an emergency housing prototype (Red+Housing, page 306) for an exhibition in China one year after the devastating earthquake that occurred in Sichuan Province on May 12, 2008. Working with red parachute cloth and plywood, OBRA sought to demonstrate that "emergency housing, from the point of view of design, is only an extreme form of architecture." With a usable area of 45 square meters and a cost estimated at $5000, such housing would meet many requirements while also allowing contemporary architecture to contribute to real needs. Indeed, other architects, foremost amongst them Shigeru Ban, have contributed their time and efforts to creating affordable, easily assembled emergency housing.

Ban is the author of the Paper Log House (Nagata, Kobe, Japan, 1995, page 18) a one-story temporary residence with a floor area of 16 square meters. Designed between May and June of 1995, the year of the Great Hanshin Earthquake in Kobe, this house was inspired by the plight of a group of Vietnamese churchgoers who were still living in plastic-sheet tents months after the January 1995 earthquake. Shigeru Ban asked them why and they explained that government-provided housing was located too far away for easy transport and school registration for their children. He decided to create temporary houses for them. Shigeru Ban explains: "The design criteria called for a cheap structure that could be built by anyone, with reasonable insulated properties that was acceptably attractive in appearance. The solution was a foundation of sand-filled beer cases, walls of paper tubes (diameter 108 millimeters, 4 millimeters thick), and with the ceiling and roof made of membrane material. The design was a kind of log-house cabin. The beer cases were rented from the manufacturer and were also used to form steps during the construction process." The simplicity of this process and the fact that the paper tubes could be made on site met all of the criteria for solving difficult residence problems engendered by the earthquake. By the end of the summer of 1995, 27 of these houses had been built for both Vietnamese and Japanese users.

REFUGEES AND NOMADS

Ban went on to create a number of other shelters of this kind such as the Paper Emergency Shelters for the UNHCR (Byumba Refugee Camp, Rwanda, 1999, page 47). More recently, he has worked in Haiti and L'Aquila, Italy, though bureaucratic and practical barriers make earthquake-victim relief in such circumstances rather complex. On January 12, 2010, a 7.0-magnitude earthquake struck near Port-au-Prince. Over a million people lost their homes and more than half a million took refuge in hastily made tents. Shigeru Ban collaborated with professors and students from the Universidad Iberoamericana and Pontificia Universidad Católica Madre y Maestra (Dominican Republic) to build 100 shelters made of paper tubes and local materials for Haitian earthquake victims.

10
Shigeru Ban, Paper Log House, Naga-
ta, Kobe, Japan, 1995—here erected
in Bhuj, India, 2001

10

Clearly fascinated by the questions raised by temporary architecture, Shigeru Ban has worked extensively with shipping containers and paper tubes, and sometimes both in unison, as was the case in his Nomadic Museum (Pier 54, New York, 2005, page 33; Santa Monica, California, 2006; Tokyo, 2007), a 4180-square-meter structure intended to house "Ashes and Snow," an exhibition of large-scale photographs by Gregory Colbert. 205 meters long and 16 meters high, the building was made up essentially of ISO shipping containers and paper tubes fabricated from recycled paper. This was the first building to be made from shipping containers in New York, and it was reassembled later in California and Japan using locally available containers.

BURNING IN THE GULF, SINGING WITH BONO

The examples published here represent only a small fraction of the types of temporary architecture that can be seen around the world. Industrial facilities or military designs are not covered here for example, although they definitely are amongst the most common types of ephemeral structure. The catastrophe that involved the Deepwater Horizon semi-submersible offshore oil drilling rig in the Gulf of Mexico beginning in April 2010 demonstrates the ubiquity of large-scale and potentially dangerous forms of temporary industrial architecture. With forms, like those of the International Space Station, generated essentially by technical requirements, a floating structure like the Deepwater Horizon may not influence trends in contemporary architecture, nor indeed would it actually be the work of an architect at all. It is, nonetheless, a kind of temporary, moveable structure of which one should be aware.

There can be no doubt, finally, that all architecture is temporary, but some structures are meant to last longer than others, and it is in its conception that ephemeral architecture is most interesting. Temporary architecture is often freed of many of the constraints that weigh on the design of more permanent buildings and thus can allow architects a greater margin of creative freedom. As such, they are a potential source of inspiration for the rest of architecture. Temporary structures can also flirt more easily with the boundaries between art and architecture, tempting both artists and architects to cross the line from opposite directions. Transportable residences, event spaces, and emergency disaster relief housing are all part of the mandate of temporary architecture now. So are the 360° stage of the world straddling rock group U2, and the nets and poles that made up the PS1 courtyard installation of Idenburg and Liu in 2010. *Temporary Architecture Now!* is even more fluid and dynamic than its more staid and solid cousins. In many ways, these are the most fascinating and inventive structures of the moment.

[1] Ecclesiastes, 1:2
[2] http://www.egypttoday.com/article.aspx?ArticleID=9064 (accessed on August 14, 2010)
[3] http://www.seangodsell.com/future-shack (accessed on August 15, 2010)

EINLEITUNG

AUS! KLEINES LICHT![1]

Denn alles Menschliche ist nichtig und vorübergehend [...] Darum nutze das Heute so wie du sollst, dann scheidet's sich leicht: wie die Olive, wenn sie reif geworden abfällt – preisend den Zweig, an dem sie hing, dankend dem Baum, der sie hervorgebracht!
Marc Aurel, *Selbstbetrachtungen*, Viertes Buch, um 170 n. Chr.[2]

Die auf griechisch verfassten *Selbstbetrachtungen* Marc Aurels (121–180 n. Chr.) sind eine Sammlung von Gedanken und Schriften, die der römische Kaiser an sich selbst gerichtet hatte. Der griechische Begriff *ephemeros* (im Zitat mit „vorübergehend" übersetzt) bedeutet „für einen Tag". Der Begriff *temporär* hingegen leitet sich vom Lateinischen *temporarius* ab („auf eine gewisse Zeit beschränkt, eine Zeitlang dauernd"): temporär – das Gegenteil von permanent. Die Anwendung dieser beiden Begriffe auf die Architektur ist fraglos ein weites Feld und nicht leicht zu definieren. Natürlich sind Bauwerke als solche und grundsätzlich temporärer Natur, selbst wenn es manchmal Jahrhunderte dauert, bevor Staub wieder zu Staub wird. Architektur ist also per definitionem und von Natur aus temporär – wie flüchtig sie jedoch im Einzelfall ist, hängt selbstredend von ihrer baulichen Qualität und einer Reihe weiterer Faktoren ab, die vom Standort bis hin zu Wechselfällen des Klimas reichen. Mangels besserer Baumaterialien und -methoden oder aufgrund nomadischer Lebensformen war ein Großteil frühzeitlicher Architektur nicht viel mehr als eine Hütte aus Holz oder eine Art Zelt im Wind. Zweifellos hängt die Dauerhaftigkeit eines Bauwerks auch von seiner Nutzung sowie von seiner Pflege ab. Japanische Holztempel überdauern auch deshalb ganze Jahrhunderte, weil sie bisweilen Stück für Stück, von Generation zu Generation erneuert werden. Unterdessen sind moderne Städte einem permanenten Erneuerungsprozess unterworfen, der selbst für die selbstbewusstesten Architekten eine Herausforderung ist. Was früher Symbol für Macht und Unveränderlichkeit war, muss heute vielleicht einem Einkaufszentrum oder einer Bowlingbahn weichen. „Vergeblich und vergänglich! Alles ist vergebliche Mühe!" lautet ein berühmtes Zitat aus dem Buch des Predigers.[3] Doch wenn Architektur unweigerlich auf die eine oder andere Weise temporär ist, wenn moderne Lebensstile selbst in Industrieländern zu einer geradezu nomadenhaften Existenz führen, sollten Architekten sich dann nicht in das Unvermeidliche schicken und für den Moment bauen, ohne sich allzu viele Gedanken um die Zukunft zu machen?

Dank moderner Technologien ist es heute möglich, Kunststoffe auf die erstaunlichste Art und Weise einzusetzen. Selbst Holz, das älteste aller Baumaterialien, lässt sich inzwischen mit computergesteuerten Maschinen zu einzigartigen Formen fräsen, die erst gar nicht darauf angelegt sind, bis ans Ende der Zeit zu überdauern. Entscheidend ist vielmehr der Zweck – ein Messestand, ein Bühnenbild oder ein Ausstellungspavillon sind üblicherweise von vornherein nur für eine bestimmte, kurze Lebensdauer geplant. Viele Architekten haben inzwischen entdeckt, dass Seefrachtcontainer aus Metall – Symbole der globalen Wirtschaft – oftmals ausrangiert werden, obwohl sie leicht als Laden- oder Wohnraum umnutzbar sind. Interessanterweise werden hierbei Objekte, die eigentlich auf Mobilität ausgelegt sind, im Boden verankert und erweisen sich als stabiler und dauerhafter als so manch traditionelle Bauform. Insbesondere Baustellen und archäologische Grabungsstätten sind häufig Vorwand oder Grund für einen Großteil temporärer Architektur. Doch auch die Kunst braucht solche Bauten.

Oft erfordern Ausstellungen räumliches Design (wie Architektur mitunter genannt wird). Und so sorgt die zeitgenössische Kunst durch ihr Liebäugeln mit dem Ephemeren dafür, ihren baulichen Kontext wieder in die Nähe der ursprünglichen griechischen Definition dieses Begriffs zu rücken.

TEMPORÄRE PERMANENZ

Bereits eine oberflächliche Auseinandersetzung mit zeitgenössischer Architektur belegt eine Zunahme an erklärtermaßen temporären Bauten in den letzten Jahren. Grund hierfür mögen finanzielle Einschränkungen sein, die dazu führen, einer Lösung den Vorzug zu geben, die in der Regel weniger kostet als langlebigere Konstruktionen. Ein weiterer, langfristig vermutlich bedeutsamerer Grund ist, dass es inzwischen weniger Auftraggeber geben dürfte, die unverhohlen die Hybris besitzen, etwas bauen zu wollen, das „die Jahrhunderte überdauert". Unsere Kultur ist eindeutig von schnellem Konsum geprägt, und auch die Architektur wird sich diesen allgemeinen Tendenzen nicht entziehen können. Positiv gesehen erlauben rasch entworfene und realisierte Bauten Architekten, zu experimentieren und neue Formen zu entwickeln, die der Art und Weise entsprechen, wie wir morgen leben werden.

Pavillons der verschiedensten Art sind ein zentrales Phänomen temporärer Architektur – sei es für einmalige Veranstaltungen oder groß angelegte internationale Messen und Ausstellungen. Obwohl der Abriss in den meisten Fällen bereits eingeplant wird, gibt es Ausnahmen, die belegen, von welcher Tragweite „temporäre" Architektur sein kann. Der Eiffelturm, als Tor zur Weltausstellung 1889 erbaut, sollte ursprünglich nur zwanzig Jahre lang stehen. Noch heute ist er das meistbesuchte kostenpflichtige Baudenkmal der Welt. Wegen seiner Höhe musste der Eiffelturm konstruktiv besonders belastbar sein – eine Tatsache, der er womöglich seine Langlebigkeit verdankt. Letztendlich wurde dieses primär „zweckfreie" Bauwerk zum Wahrzeichen für Paris, wenn nicht gar für ganz Frankreich. Die internationale Bühne, die Weltausstellungen Architektur bieten, ist nach wie vor Anreiz, ehrgeizige temporäre Bauten zu entwerfen und zu realisieren, wie auch dieser Band mit einer Auswahl verschiedener Länderpavillons der Expo 2010 in Shanghai belegt.

EINE MEERJUNGFRAU, EIN RAUMSCHIFF UND EINE KATHEDRALE FÜR SAATGUT

Sicher hätten auch andere Länderpavillons für Shanghai in die Auswahl dieses Bandes kommen können, doch werden hier nun sechs Bauten detailliert vorgestellt. Der erste dieser Pavillons ist ein Entwurf von Bjarke Ingels (BIG) für sein Heimatland Dänemark (Seite 92). Ingels ging es darum, einige der typischsten Aspekte des dänischen Lebensstils herauszuarbeiten – vom Fahrradfahren bis hin zur (echten) Kleinen Meerjungfrau, einer Skulptur von Edward Eriksen, die seit 1913 auf einem Felsen im Hafen von Kopenhagen zu sehen ist. Dieses bekannte dänische Wahrzeichen wurde für die Expo 2010 erstmals von seinem Standort bewegt. Inspiriert wurde das Werk von Hans Christian Andersens Märchen *Die kleine Meerjungfrau* (1837), der Geschichte einer Meerjungfrau, die ihr Leben im Meer schließlich der Liebe zu einem menschlichen Prinzen opferte. In Shanghai ruht die Skulptur im Herzen des spiralförmigen, weißen Metallpavillons auf einem Felsen in einem mit Hafenwasser gefüllten Becken. Doch obwohl Bjarke Ingels mit dem Märchen spielt, das zum Symbol seines Landes geworden ist, geht es

11
Buchner Bründler Architekten, Swiss Pavilion, Expo 2010, Shanghai, China, 2010

11

ihm auch darum, dem chinesischen Publikum (das vermutlich eher das Märchen von Hans Christian Andersen kennt, als eine Vorstellung von einem kreativen, zeitgemäßen Dänemark zu haben) ein modernes Land zu vermitteln.

Auch der Schweizer Pavillon, ein Entwurf des Büros Buchner Bründler Architekten aus Basel (Seite 100), ist der Versuch, zeitgenössisches Design mit symbolischen, fast folkloristischen Elementen zu verbinden. Der Grundriss des Pavillons zeichnet die Konturen der Schweizer Landkarte nach; Highlights sind ein für die Schweizer Berge typischer Sessellift sowie eine technisch aufwendige, offene Netzfassade. Die markanten Formen aus Beton wecken zugleich Assoziationen an einen Großteil moderner und zeitgenössischer Schweizer Architektur – vermutlich selbst bei jenen, die diesen Aspekt der Schweizer Kultur nur ansatzweise kennen. Das begrünte Dach des Pavillons ist ebenso eine Anspielung auf ökologisches Bauen wie ein Hinweis auf die Naturschönheit des Landes.

Der spanische Pavillon (Seite 268) in Shanghai, ein Entwurf von Benedetta Tagliabue (Miralles Tagliabue EMBT), ist eine vierstöckige Stahlkonstruktion, deren auffälligstes Merkmal eine wahre Wolke aus Korbflechtwerk ist. Einerseits gilt das Material als typisches Beispiel für spanisches Kunsthandwerk, andererseits ordneten die Architekten die Korbelemente so an, dass sie die chinesischen Schriftzeichen für spanisch-chinesische Freundschaft nachempfanden. Statt der Massivität des betondominierten Innenraums im Schweizer Pavillon begegnet einem hier eine dezidiert zeitgenössische Optik. Dies erklärt sich in gewisser Weise aus der Natur eines Ereignisses wie der Expo 2010, bei dem eine Mischung aus Folklore, Nationalstolz und ausgeprägter Modernität niemanden zu schockieren scheint. Neben dem spanischen Landespavillon ist auch Madrid mit dem Air Tree (Seite 136) von Ecosistema Urbano vertreten, eine Konstruktion, die ein angenehmes klimatisches Umfeld bietet. Auch hier war es Ziel, eine Attraktion zu schaffen, die den Besuchern Wissen über einen Ort vermittelt und zugleich das Moderne und Innovative herausstreicht, das man in China vielleicht nicht mit einer Stadt wie Madrid assoziiert.

Während die meisten Länder ihre Architekten aus den eigenen Reihen wählten, ist Ägypten eine Ausnahme und präsentiert sich mit einem Entwurf der namhaften Architektin Zaha Hadid (Seite 194). Die Zeitschrift *Egypt Today* begrüßte Hadids Entwurf eher verhalten. In ihrem Artikel „Overplaying Egyptomania" heißt es: „Der 1000 m² große ägyptische Pavillon wurde von der international renommierten, irakischen Architektin Zaha Hadid als Geschenk entworfen. Der eher strenge Bau mit seinen wirbelnden schwarzen und weißen Schwüngen soll augenscheinlich Moderne und Antike – repräsentiert durch die grafische Andeutung dreier Pyramiden über dem Eingang – verbinden. Tatsächlich wirkt das Bauwerk eher wie ein versehentlich in Shanghai gestandetes Raumschiff, das unentdeckt zu bleiben versucht, indem es sich als Pavillon tarnt."[4] Immerhin konnte die Zeitschrift nicht umhin zuzugeben, dass der Pavillon täglich 14 000 Besucher anzog, die ebenso sehr an der Architektur wie an den dort präsentierten pharaonischen Kunstwerken, der Ausstellung über Kairo oder daran interessiert waren, ihren Namen in ägyptischen Hieroglyphen schreiben zu lassen. Für Zaha Hadid sind Kontroversen nichts Unbekanntes, schließlich entzieht sich ihre Architektur den üblichen Kategorien und Erwartungen dessen, wie Gebäude auszusehen haben. Welch besseren Ort könnte es geben, um überkommene Vorstellungen zu hinterfragen, als eine zukunftsorientierte Weltausstellung?

Ein weiterer Pavillon, der Dank seiner „haarigen" Erscheinung in Shanghai große Aufmerksamkeit auf sich gezogen hat, ist der englische Pavillon (Seite 200), ein Entwurf von Thomas Heatherwick. Die Konstruktionshülle umfängt die sogenannte Seed Cathedral (Saatgut-Kathedrale) und besteht aus 60 000 schlanken transparenten Glasfaserstäben. Diese sind jeweils 7,5 m lang; in ihren Spitzen befinden sich je ein oder mehrere Pflanzensamen. Der Entwurf entstand in Zusammenarbeit mit der Millenium Seedbank von Kew Gardens, deren Ziel es ist, bis 2020 das Saatgut von 25 % sämtlicher Pflanzenarten weltweit zusammenzutragen. Während es manchen Ländern offensichtlich darum ging, in Shanghai vor allem ein modernes Image zu vermitteln, entschied sich das vereinigte Königreich mit Heatherwick, Stellung für ökologisches Bewusstsein zu beziehen, was in China ebenso auf Zuspruch treffen dürfte wie in Großbritannien. Dass eine solche Konstruktion in Shanghai vertreten ist, mag auch für einen neuen Trend sprechen: weg von glatten modernen Formen, hin zu einer komplexeren Architektur, die für andere Ambitionen und Ziele steht als für augenfällige Ästhetik.

SCHWARZ UND WEISS UND ROT VON KOPF BIS FUSS

Eine halbe Weltreise entfernt, und in vollkommen anderem Kontext, feierte die Serpentine Gallery in den Londoner Kensington Gardens das zehnjährige Jubiläum ihrer Sommerpavillons (Seite 298). Die Pavillons, gestaltet von so namhaften Architekturkoryphäen wie Oscar Niemeyer, Toyo Ito, Frank O. Gehry, Álvaro Siza und Eduardo Souto de Moura, sind jeweils für drei Monate konzipiert und werden im Schnitt von über 200 000 Besuchern besichtigt. Ausgangspunkt des Projekts war die Idee der Direktorin der Serpentine Gallery, Julia Peyton-Jones, für den Bau der Pavillons je einen renommierten Architekten auszuwählen, der nie zuvor in Großbritannien gebaut hatte. 2010 fiel ihre Wahl auf Jean Nouvel, der mit dem Entwurf eines erstaunlichen 500 m² großen Bauwerks reagierte, in dem Tagungen und Konzerte stattfinden sollten und zu dem darüber hinaus ein Café gehörte. Die Kosten (750 000 Pfund für Nouvels Entwurf) wurden, wie schon bei früheren Pavillons, von Sponsoren übernommen, die nur zu gern mit einem der prestigeträchtigsten Kulturereignisse in London in Verbindung gebracht werden. Obwohl die Pavillons teils verkauft und an anderer Stelle wieder aufgebaut wurden, wie etwa Frank Gehrys Bau (2008), der inzwischen in Aix-en-Provence steht, sind diese Entwürfe vom Kern her temporär und darauf angelegt, das kreative Profil des jeweiligen Architekten zu repräsentieren. Angesichts des öffentlichen Erfolgs der Serpentine Sommerpavillons seit 2000 kann kein Zweifel bestehen, dass temporäre Architektur erhebliche Aufmerksamkeit erregen kann und dies auch tut. Oftmals zeigt sie sich in gewagten Formen, die für dauerhafte Bauten sicher nicht in Frage kämen – gerade in einem geschützten Umfeld wie dem Hyde Park.

PURPLE HAZE UND ROBOTIK

Ein weiterer, 2010 errichteter temporärer Entwurf war der Pavillon 21 Mini Opera Space (Seite 124) von Coop Himmelb(l)au auf dem Münchner Marstallplatz, ein 430 m² großer Bau. Mit computergenerierten Formen, die erstaunlicherweise auf Musik von Jimi Hendrix Bezug nahmen (*Purple Haze*, „…'Scuse me while I kiss the sky…"), realisierten die Architekten ein Gebäude für die Opernfestspiele. Doch ganz abgesehen von den musikalischen Ursprüngen des Pavillon 21 weist der Bau jene spitzen dekonstruktivistischen Formen auf, die im Werk von Coop Himmelb(l)au ein so vertrautes Merkmal sind. Gerade inmitten der eher konservativen Formensprache Münchens vermittelte dieser er-

12
Coop Himmelb(l)au, Pavilion 21 Mini
Opera Space, Munich, Germany,
2008–10

12

staunliche architektonische Ausbruch Opernbesuchern und Passanten einen Eindruck von zeitgenössischer Architektur. Vermutlich hätte man sie nicht so bereitwillig akzeptiert, wäre sie als permanenter Bau an diesem Standort geplant gewesen. Auch dies unterstreicht einen ausgesprochenen Vorteil temporärer Bauten – ungeachtet dessen, dass es einigen, wie etwa dem Eiffelturm, gelingt zu überleben, nachdem sich die öffentliche Meinung mit ihrem Avantgarde-Design angefreundet hat.

Das House of Stone (Italien, Seite 326) wurde von John Pawson im Rahmen der Mailänder Möbelmesse 2010, genauer gesagt für den Interni Think Tank, entworfen. Standort des Bauwerks war die Università degli Studi. Trotz seiner ephemeren Natur wirkte der Bau ebenso minimalistisch wie massiv. Pawsons Design verweist darüber hinaus auf einen weiteren Vorteil temporärer Architektur: Der Bau wurde aus Lithoverde, einem innovativen, recycelten Mauerstein errichtet, der abgesehen von Steinabfällen ausschließlich aus 1 % natürlichem Harz besteht. Auch das House of Stone ist in einen architektonischen Kontext eingeschrieben, der nicht gerade angetan ist, moderne Formen anzuregen; dabei wirkt das vollkommen leere Bauwerk mit seiner strengen, fast mausoleenhaften Anmutung beinahe älter als sein Umfeld.

Dennoch sind massive Bauweisen nicht eben typisch für zeitgenössische Pavillons, ganz im Gegenteil. Rendez-Vous (Tokio, Japan, 2010, Seite 54), eine 52 m² Installation des Tokioter Büros Atelier Bow-Wow, war in erster Linie aus Bambus gefertigt und darauf angelegt, einen Kontrast zur strengen Massivität des nahe gelegenen Nationalmuseums für Moderne Kunst von Yoshiro Taniguchi zu bilden. Die jungen japanischen Architekten betonen, es ginge ihnen darum, „die strenge Atmosphäre aufzuhellen, ohne die Würde des Ortes anzutasten, vielmehr die Atmosphäre aufzulockern und dem Ort sanftere Seiten abzugewinnen." Atelier Bow-Wow nutzte die Biegsamkeit des Bambusmaterials, um diese Idee noch stärker herauszuarbeiten, und gestaltete den Pavillon wie eine Art übergroßes Tier, das sich aus dem Garten des Kaiserlichen Palastes heranpirscht. Eine solch humoristische Interpretation temporärer Architektur kontrastiert zugleich mit der dichten urbanen Bebauung der angrenzenden Stadt.

Eine weitere Leichtbaukonstruktion war der ICD/ITKE-Forschungspavillon (2010, Seite 206), ein gemeinsamer Entwurf des Instituts für Computerbasiertes Entwerfen (ICD) und des Instituts für Tragkonstruktionen und Konstruktives Entwerfen (ITKE) der Universität Stuttgart. Das vollständig aus gebogenen Birkensperrholzstreifen errichtete Bauwerk bestand aus nicht weniger als 500 individuell geformten Einzelteilen, die computergesteuert entworfen und in der universitätseigenen robotischen Fertigungsanlage gefräst wurden. Obwohl man Birkenholz kaum ein „modernes" Material nennen kann, erfordert es in diesem Fall einige der anspruchsvollsten Konstruktions- und Fertigungsmethoden, die zur Zeit verfügbar sind. Während sich frühere Generationen von computergestützt entworfenen Bauten stärker auf ausgefallene Formen verließen, die mit der Formensprache der Moderne brachen, können sich zeitgenössische Konstruktionen heute weitaus überraschender entwickeln – gerade in einem Forschungskontext wie beim Stuttgarter ICD/ITKE-Pavillon.

13

STANDARDISIERT UND STAPELBAR

Obwohl Seefrachtcontainer zu einem allgegenwärtigen Phänomen in den modernen Häfen unserer urbanen Landschaft geworden sind, sind sie doch eine vergleichsweise junge Erfindung. Sicherlich wurde sie auch von jenen standardisierten Militärcontainern beeinflusst, die das US-amerikanische Verteidigungsministerium in den 1950er Jahren entwickelt hatte. Die International Organization for Standardization (ISO) lehnte ihre eigenen Kriterien für Container im kombinierten Verkehr (verladefähig auf Schiffe, LKWs oder Züge, 1970) an das Vorbild des amerikanischen Militärs an. Ein typischer Standardcontainer besteht aus Trapezblech und ist in der Regel 20 oder 40 Fuß (6 oder 12 m) lang. Üblicherweise lassen sich bis zu sieben Container mithilfe standardisierter Riegel stapeln. Obwohl Kisten aus Stahl nicht das naheliegendste Bauelement für Wohn- oder andere Bauten sein mögen, fing man bereits Anfang der 1980er Jahre an, sie für derlei Zwecke einzusetzen.

Phillip Clark, Eigentümer der Firma Import Export & Overhaul in Miami, Florida, sicherte sich das US-amerikanische Patent Nummer 4 854 094 (eingereicht: 23. November 1987; Patentbewilligung: 8. August 1989) für eine „Methode, einen oder mehrere Seefrachtcontainer aus Stahl als bewohnbares Gebäude auf Baustellen umzuwandeln, sowie für das daraus resultierende Produkt". Der australische Architekt Sean Godsell gibt an, bereits zuvor (1985) die Arbeiten an seiner Future Shack aufgenommen zu haben: „Ein massenproduzierbares, transportierbares Haus, nutzbar als Not- oder Flüchtlingsunterkunft. Recycelte Seefrachtcontainer dienen als Hauptbaukörper der Unterkunft. Ein Schirmdach lässt sich zusammenfalten und im Container verstauen. Montiert bietet das Dach dem Container Schatten und reduziert die Wärmelasten auf dem Haus. Dank Teleskopstützen lässt sich der Container selbst ohne Aushub auf unebenem Terrain errichten."[5] Selbst wenn sich nicht zweifelsfrei klären lässt, wer die Containerarchitektur erfunden hat, so hat sie sich doch weltweit als Lösungsansatz für temporäre und dauerhafte Architektur etabliert. Eine Reihe aktueller Beispiele umgenutzter ISO-Container werden in diesem Band präsentiert.

Die brasilianischen Architekten Bernades + Jacobsen, bekannt für ihre luxuriösen Villen am Meer, haben bei temporären Veranstaltungen bereits häufig mit Containern gearbeitet. So auch 2008 bei einer internationalen Ausstellung für Videokunst im Villa-Lobos-Park von São Paulo. Das 1200 m² große Projekt Container Art (Seite 84) wurde auf Holzpodesten auf einer Promenade im Park errichtet und bestand aus einer systematischen Anordnung von 20- und 40-Fuß-Containern. Für das Tim Festival 2007 (Rio de Janeiro), einem zweitägigen Musikfestival, hatten die Architekten bereits eine wesentlich größere Installation mit 250 Containern realisiert – die Bühnenbauten, sanitäre Einrichtungen und Snackbars umfasste. Ein Großteil des 40 000 m² großen Festivalgeländes bestand aus einer großen Wand. 40-Fuß-Container dienten als Tore und markierten die Bühnenzugänge sowie die Ein- und Ausgänge zum Gelände. Hinter dem höchsten Punkt der zu einem sinnlichen Bogen angeordneten Containerwand, die sich zum Meer hin öffnete, verbargen sich die 15 m hohen Konzertzelte. Die Container-Zwischenräume auf verschiedenen Ebenen wurden für Videoprojektionen sowie als Kleinbühnen genutzt. Der Aufbau des Geländes hatte am 16. September 2007 begonnen; am 18. November war bereits alles vollständig demontiert. Über 23 000 Zuschauer hatten die Konzerte an zwei Nächten besucht. Was Container an Subtilität und formaler Flexibilität vermissen lassen, machen sie zweifelsohne durch problemlosen Transport und Montage wett.

Der amerikanische Architekt Adam Kalkin hat sich auf Containerarchitektur spezialisiert, wie sein 2008 erschienenes Buch *Quik Build: Adam Kalkin's ABC of Container Architecture* belegt. Das von ihm entwickelte System Quik House (Seite 224) nutzt recycelte Frachtcontainer für den Bau von Häusern, die wesentlich luxuriöser sind, als ihr bescheidener Ursprung vermuten ließe. Solche Hausbauten können bereits fünf Monate nach Auftrag geliefert werden und kosten lediglich 76 000 US Dollar, obwohl zahlreiche Sonderausstattungen, die laut Kalkin möglich sind, den Preis gegebenenfalls erheblich in die Höhe treiben. Sein 2007 auf der Biennale in Venedig vorgestelltes illy Push Button House (Seite 230) will unter Beweis stellen, dass sich ein normaler Frachtcontainer dank hydraulischer Systeme und gelungenen Designs innerhalb weniger Minuten in ein echtes Haus verwandeln kann. Kalkin arbeitete zudem an Projekten mit dem amerikanischen Militär in Afghanistan und einer Hilfsorganisation in Russland und zeigt, auf wie vielfältige Weise sich Frachtcontainer nutzen lassen.

Der COP 15 Pavilion (Seite 258), entworfen vom Architekturbüro MAPT, lag im Nordhafen von Kopenhagen (Dänemark, 2009–10) und bestand aus alten Schiffscontainern und weiteren recycelten Materialien. MAPT betont besonders die kostensparenden und ökologisch verantwortlichen Aspekte einer solchen Umnutzung und weist darauf hin, dass Container für Speditionen so günstig sind, dass es häufig wirtschaftlicher ist, sie abzugeben, als sie ohne Ladung an ihren Ursprungsort zurückzuverfrachten. Für interessierte Gestalter wie das dänische Büro erweist sich dies als Segen.

2009 realisierte das italienische Architektenteam tamassociati eine Wohnsiedlung für die NGO Emergency (Seite 382) auf dem Gelände des Salam Center für Herzchirurgie (Soba, Khartum, Sudan). Hierbei kamen 95 20-Fuß-Container für Wohnunterkünfte und sieben 40-Fuß-Container für eine Cafeteria zum Einsatz. Die Container waren während der Bauarbeiten des Salam Center unweit des Geländes zurückgelassen worden. Stahl leitet Hitze und Kälte fast ungefiltert, was bei der Nutzung von Containern als Wohnbauten natürlich ein Nachteil ist. Die Architekten lösten dieses Problem mithilfe 5 cm starker Dämmplatten im Innenraum und einem gedämmten Dach sowie einem System aus Bambus-*brise-soleils*, die direkte Sonneneinstrahlung auf die Stahloberfläche verhindern.

MESSESTÄNDE AUS MARMOR, GLAS UND HOLZ

Messestände sind schon lange ein Experimentierfeld für temporäre Architektur. Der Umstand, dass sie in der Regel keine großen Lasten tragen oder andere Funktionen regulärer Architektur erfüllen müssen, erlaubt ihnen, Neuland zu erobern, ja bestimmte Gesetzmäßigkeiten des Bauens gänzlich außer Acht zu lassen. Hinzu kommt, dass sie nicht zwingend von Architekten entworfen werden, da auch spezialisierte Designer im Messebau vertreten sind. Der spanische Architekt Alberto Campo Baeza verfolgte jedoch einen dezidiert architektonischen Ansatz bei seinem Messestand, den er für den italienischen Steinhändler Piba Marbri auf der Marmocacc-Messe 2009 entwarf (Verona, Italien, Seite 112). Der große schwarze Kubus war innen vollständig mit weißem Carrara-Marmor ausgekleidet. Die optischen und physischen Kontraste des Baukörpers wurden durch ein ausgeklügeltes, dynamisches Spotlichtsystem unterstrichen, das den Eindruck entstehen ließ, Sonnenlicht wandere durch den Stand. Campo Baezas strenge, minimalistische Architektur beschäftigt sich häufig mit solchen Kontrasten und dem Spiel

14

des Sonnenlichts. Was er hier tat, war im Grunde die Umsetzung seiner eigenen gestalterischen Themen in eine Form, die ebenso für die fragliche Firma als auch für die Messebesucher reizvoll war.

Die Architekten Camila Aybar und Juan Jose Mateos aus Madrid gestalten seit 2006 Messestände für den Glashersteller Vitro auf der IFEMA (Seite 58). Für den Stand 2006 wurden nicht weniger als 170 t Glas verwendet, insgesamt 25 000 Teile, die beim Zuschnitt größerer Glasplatten abfielen. Die eingesetzte Stapeltechnik erzeugte Effekte, die die Architekten mit dem Werk von Künstlern wie Bill Viola oder James Turrell verglichen. Tatsächlich sind solche Messestände im Hinblick auf visuelle Effekte enger mit der Kunst als mit Architektur im traditionellen Sinne verwandt, was sicherlich einer der Gründe ist, warum sie für Architekten interessant sind. Für den Vitro-Stand 2008 arbeitete das Team mit ultra-klarem Glas mit winzigen roten und schwarzen Punkten. So entstand ein Raum, in dem der Farbeindruck je nach Standpunkt des Besuchers variiert. Aybar und Mateos nutzen Glas als formbares und wandelbares Material, das sowohl künstlerische Wirkung besitzt als auch den Produkten des Auftraggebers schmeichelt. Ob dies nun Design oder Architektur ist, mag strittig sein, doch die eher praktischen, profanen Funktionen „üblicher" Architektur sucht man hier sicher vergebens.

Obwohl erst 2005 gegründet, hat sich das Londoner Unternehmen Established & Sons einen beeindruckenden Ruf mit der Herstellung und dem Vertrieb moderner und zeitgenössischer Möbel erarbeitet, was zu einem guten Teil das Verdienst der Gründer Alasdhair Willis und Sebastian Wrong ist, dem Design Director der Firma. Der Stand des Unternehmens auf der Mailänder Möbelmesse 2009 in La Pelota (Seite 160) war eine überraschende Installation aus 30 t unbehandeltem Holz, das grob zu Wänden übereinandergeschichtet wurde. So entstanden Räume, in denen 16 neue Möbelentwürfe präsentiert wurden. Sebastian Wrong, der für die Installation verantwortlich zeichnete, sprach treffend von der „Dichte und Intensität" der Räume, die überwiegend mit den so umbauten, modernen Möbeln kontrastierten.

Der von Francesc Rifé entworfene Messestand für AB21 (Hábitat Valencia 2009, Valencia, Spanien, Seite 350) war auf die Präsentation von Teppichen zugeschnitten. Rifé sagt ganz offen, er habe „den Raum wie eine Galerie gestaltet". Und tatsächlich wirken die Teppiche mit ihren kräftigen Farben und entsprechender Beleuchtung auffällig wie moderne Kunst – ein Effekt, der dem Auftraggeber gefallen haben dürfte. Ein Grund, für solche Zwecke renommierte Architekten hinzuzuziehen, ist sicherlich der Wunsch, Aufmerksamkeit zu erregen, doch ebenso, die Produkte auf die eine oder andere Weise zu überhöhen. Rifés Stand wurde dieser Aufgabe mit Elan gerecht.

DEN GEHEIMEN RHYTHMUS FINDEN

Dass ephemere Architektur sich häufig in den Bereich der Kunst vorwagt, mag daran liegen, dass Praktikabilität bei temporären Bauten nicht so wichtig ist wie bei dauerhaften Bauten. Tatsächlich überschreiten viele Künstler die diffuse Grenze zwischen den verschiedenen Disziplinen und schaffen Werke, die an Architektur erinnern. Doch solche Unterscheidungen sind in den Händen eines so innovativen Gestalters wie Cecil Balmond nicht länger relevant. Seine Ausstellung *Element* (Tokio, 2010, Seite 64) knüpfte an seine Tätigkeit als Ingenieur an –

15
Francesc Rifé, AB21 Stand,
Hábitat Valencia 2009 Trade Fair,
Valencia, Spain, 2009

15

Balmond hat mit einigen der bekanntesten Architekten der Gegenwart zusammengearbeitet. Doch seine Ausstellung war auch eine Auseinandersetzung mit etwas, das er „den geheimen Rhythmus finden" nennt, „das Grundordnungsprinzip und den Rhythmus, der der Natur innewohnt ..." Es besteht wohl kaum Zweifel daran, dass Überlegungen dieser Art auch in das Denken zahlreicher Künstler einfließen. So gesehen lassen sich keine Unterschiede zwischen Künstlern und einem Ingenieur auf dem Niveau eines Cecil Balmond ausmachen.

Bei seiner Ausstellungsarchitektur für die Schau *Le Tramway* im Pavillon de l'Arsenal in Paris (2008, Seite 146) arbeitete Ammar Eloueini mit einer Haut aus Polycarbonat, die den Raum gliederte. Hier konnte die neue Straßenbahnlinie, die als Ring um Paris verläuft, präsentiert werden. Der Einsatz leichter Materialien, die auch im Einzelhandel zu finden sind, ist beispielhaft für die Fähigkeit des Architekten, den Raum auf eine Weise zu erobern, wie es Künstler oft tun, ihn zu besetzen und zu transformieren. Beim Verlassen des Raums, in diesem Fall nach Ende der Ausstellung, bleibt nichts zurück als eine Erinnerung an die Intervention. Auch dem jungen französisch-schweizerischen Architekten Philippe Rahm gelang die Transformation eines Raums, genauer des 14 000 m² großen Grand Palais in Paris (Seite 334). Anlass war die Kunstausstellung *La Force de l'Art 02*. Philippe Rahm erklärt, seine weiße Installation sei „das Gegenteil von Ausstellungsarchitektur, in dem Sinne, dass es hier nicht das Kunstwerk ist, das sich der Architektur anpasst, sondern die Architektur vielmehr den Anforderungen des Kunstwerks gerecht wird." Gemeinsam definieren die Exponate durch das simultane Zusammenspiel von Druck, Barrieren und Gegendruck eine Landschaft. Der Eindruck eines Zusammentreffens von Architektur und Kunst wurde hier durch die Formensprache des Grand Palais selbst verstärkt, einem Bau des frühen 20. Jahrhunderts mit einem monumentalen Glasdach.

KONKRETE UTOPIE

Das, was man die Liebesgeschichte von Kunst und Architektur nennen könnte und sich in zeitgenössischen Installationen zeigt, ist aus dem Blickwinkel von Architekten ebenso wahrnehmbar wie aus dem der Künstler. Die jungen Architekten Florian Idenburg (1975 geboren) und Jing Liu (1980 geboren) bespielten den Hof des PS1 in Long Island City (New York, USA) 2010 mit ihrer Arbeit *Pole Dance* (Seite 376), einer Leichtbaukonstruktion aus 9 m hohen Pfählen, Bungeeseilen und Netzen. Die Installation mit ihren leuchtend bunten Bällen, einer Hängematte und einem kleinen Pool geriet in Bewegung, sobald ein Teil des Ganzen angestoßen wurde. Sie könnte ebenso als Kunstwerk wie als Werk von Architekten durchgehen. Leichtigkeit, Interdependenz und ein hier besonders stark ausgeprägter temporärer Charakter vermitteln eindrücklich, was eine vergleichsweise kostengünstige Installation über Architektur, deren Zukunft und Möglichkeiten auszusagen vermag.

Idenburg und Liu schien es eher weniger um die Praktikabilität oder den Nutzen von *Pole Dance* zu gehen. Der namhafte Künstler Tomas Saraceno hingegen versteht leichte oder schwebende Konstruktionen als eine Art Parameter für die Stadt und die Architektur der Zukunft. „Ich schlage die konkrete Schaffung von ‚Cloud'-Städten vor, wie R. Buckminster Fuller sie geplant hatte." Natürlich ist Buckminster Fuller ein Referenzpunkt für die temporäre Architektur, einerseits wegen seines weitgehend utopischen „Cloud 9"-Konzepts, andererseits wegen zahlreicher realisierter Konstruktionen, darunter auch aufblasbarer Kuppeln. Buckminster Fuller nahm an, dass eine geschlossene

16

16
*Mark Fisher, U2, 360° world tour,
2009–11*

geodätische Kuppel beziehungsweise Kugel mit einem Durchmesser von über einer halben Meile (805 m) eine Luft-Konstruktions-Gewichts-ratio von 1000 zu 1 aufweisen würde, wodurch sich die Lufttemperatur im Innern der Kugel durch Sonneneinstrahlung ausreichend erwärmen würde, um buchstäblich zu schweben – wie ein bewohnter, runder Heißluftballon. Tomas Saracenos Anspielung auf Buckminster Fuller verweist also auf einen roten Faden, der sich von utopischen Theorien bis hin zu realen Visionen dessen, was temporäre Architektur einmal sein könnte, zieht.

Saracenos poetische Arbeiten überspielen ihre verborgene Praktikabilität, oder vielmehr den Traum, Architektur so fundamental wie nur möglich zu verändern – sie buchstäblich schweben, statt im Boden ankern zu lassen. „Solche Kugeln", meint der Künstler, „könnten ein erhebliches Gewicht tragen, weshalb man auf diese Weise ganze ‚Mini-Städte' oder fliegende Städte für Tausende von Menschen bauen könnte. Diese ‚Cloud'-Städte könnten am Boden fixiert oder gänzlich frei schwebend sein, oder vielleicht sogar manövrierbar, sodass sie auf klimatische oder Umweltbedingungen reagieren und entsprechend ‚wandern' könnten." Saraceno bezieht sich hier insbesondere auf Buckminster Fullers Buch *Konkrete Utopie. Die Krise der Menschheit und ihre Chance zu überleben* (1969, dt. 1974). Bei Idenburg und Liu, und sicherlich noch stärker bei Tomas Saraceno, gewinnt Architektur eine poetische, künstlerische Präsenz, durch die die wahre Bedeutung temporärer Bauten deutlich wird. Wo Lasten außer Kraft gesetzt und praktische Funktionen nicht zählen, gewinnt Architektur die Freiheit, zum Vehikel für Träume zu werden.

A BIGGER BANG

In seiner ursprünglichen Bedeutung lässt sich der Begriff *ephemer* („für einen Tag") wohl am ehesten auf die Architektur von Veranstaltungen wie Konzerten oder Theaterstücken anwenden. Dank finanzieller Mittel und einer entsprechenden Größenordnung konnten sich die Tourbühnen großer Bands an die Spitze dieser Art von Architektur spielen. Der englische Architekt Mark Fisher zeichnet verantwortlich für einige der meist publizierten Bühnen der Rolling Stones, U2 und Pink Floyd. Fisher, geboren 1947, schloss sein Studium 1971 an der Architectural Association School of Architecture in London ab, wo er von 1973 bis 1977 Unit Master war. Zu seinen bemerkenswertesten Entwürfen zählen die Szenografie für die Rolling-Stones-Tour *A Bigger Bang* (2005, Seite 170), wo Fisher „dekadente, malerische Vorstellungen von großartiger Opernhausopulenz des 19. Jahrhunderts" mit großformatigen, hochauflösenden LED-Videowänden und einem innovativen Bestuhlungsplan kombinierte, der an Opernlogen erinnern sollte.

Die transportfähigen, 180 t schweren Aufbauten, die Fisher für die *360°*-Worldtour von U2 entwarf (2009–11, Seite 178), rahmen nicht nur die Bühne selbst, sondern mehrere Tausend Konzertbesucher ein, und tragen darüber hinaus 200 t Technik. Die Konstruktion erlaubte den Zuschauern, wie schon der Tour-Titel sagt, die Band von allen Seiten zu sehen. Die Bühne wurde in dreifacher Ausfertigung realisiert, um den täglichen Wechsel der Tour-Orte zu ermöglichen. Diese Art temporärer Architektur mag die üblichen Kategorien von Bauten und Pavillons sprengen. Nichtsdestotrotz zählt sie in gewisser Weise zur Avantgarde zeitgenössischer Architektur. Mark Fisher hat zudem eines der beeindruckendsten Elemente für die Eröffnungsfeier der Olympiade in Peking 2008 entworfen, die sogennante „Dream Sphere" (Seite 174), eine Kugel mit einem Durchmesser von 19 m, die auf einem Teleskopmast montiert war und auf der 60 Akrobaten auftraten. Auch hier wurden die in einem solchen Rahmen üblichen Erwartungen von Raumnutzung außer Kraft gesetzt.

Bescheidenere Bühnenbilder faszinieren Architekten ebenfalls seit langem, und so enthält dieser Band neben zumeist sehr aktuellen Projekten auch eine Kulisse, die Massimiliano und Doriana Fuksas für *Medea* und *Ödipus auf Kolonos* beim griechischen Theaterfestival in Syrakus (Italien, 2009, Seite 182) gestaltet haben. Für die Premiere der beiden Dramen von Euripides und Sophokles entwarfen sie eine „konkave Klinge" – Ausgangspunkt war das Konzept der Katharsis und die Vorstellung eines verlorenen Horizonts. Die Reduktion auf eine reine, einfache Form bildet ein stimmiges Pendant zu den sich auf der Bühne entfaltenden, ausdrucksstarken Tragödien. Nichtsdestotrotz mögen manche diese Konzept als Widerspruch zu blumigeren Ansätzen empfunden haben, die andere Architekten vielleicht entwickelt hätten. Befreit von solchen Einschränkungen wie Schwere und strenger Funktionalität, zeigen die beiden Partner von Fuksas hier, wozu sie wirklich fähig sind, brechen mit konventionellen Erwartungen und gestalten den Raum auf neuartige Weise. In mancher Hinsicht ist genau dies das Herzstück temporärer Architektur.

BLASEN UND BÜCHER

Obwohl temporäre Architektur in manchen Fällen tatsächlich erlaubt, architektonische Innovation von üblichen Einengungen zu lösen, erfordern andere Umstände die besonders sorgfältige Beachtung praktischer Gesichtspunkte. Die unter dieser Überschrift versammelten Beispiele reichen von einem Dachrestaurant bis hin zum größten Flugobjekt der Erdumlaufbahn: die internationale Raumstation (ISS), zugegebenermaßen eine Klasse für sich. Die innovativen New Yorker Architekten Diller Scofidio + Renfro, realisierten bereits ein Gebäude in Form einer Wolke (Blur Building, Expo '02, Yverdon-les-Bains, Schweiz, 2000–02), und legten jüngst den Entwurf für einen temporären Erweiterungsbau des Hirshhorn Museums in Washington vor: eine formbare, aufpumpbare Blase (Seite 130). Die pneumatische Membran soll über 1000 Menschen Raum bieten und aus dem zentralen Innenhof des modernistischen Gebäudes heraustreten, ohne seine Innenfassade zu berühren. Das Konzept eines elastischen Raums, gerade im Kontext eines eher strengen modernistischen Bauwerks, ist ausgesprochen zeitgenössisch. Die aufblasbare Konstruktion ist damit eine der auffälligsten Manifestationen ephemerer Architektur.

Der französische Multimediakünstler Laurent Grasso und sein Bruder, der Architekt Pascal Grasso, verfolgen einen völlig anderen Stil. Sie entwarfen ein kleines temporäres Restaurant (63 m²), das auf dem Dach des Palais de Tokyo in Paris installiert wurde und von April bis Juni 2009 in Betrieb war. Das 18 m lange Restaurant Nomiya (Seite 188) wurde in einer Werft in zwei Einzelteilen gebaut. Die praktischen Aspekte eines solchen Dachrestaurants diktierten einen Großteil des Entwurfs; dennoch gelang es den Architekten fraglos, das Interieur des überaus populären Restaurants chic und minimalistisch zu gestalten. Auch die niederländischen Architekten Ira Koers und Roelof Mulder arbeiteten nach klaren praktischen Vorgaben und entwarfen eine temporäre Innenarchitektur für die Universitätsbibliothek Amsterdam (Seite

17
*Office of Mobile Design, Taliesin
Mod.Fab, Frank Lloyd Wright School
of Architecture, Taliesin West,
Scottsdale, Arizona, USA, 2009*

17

234). Trotz einer Fläche von 2300 m² und insgesamt 235 Lernplätzen musste das Projekt mit einem bescheidenen Budget auskommen. Koers und Mulder gestalteten temporäre Räume, die nicht nur dank ihres Erscheinungsbilds, sondern auch wegen der effizienten Lösung praktischer, funktionaler Anforderungen gelungen sind.

IN 90 MINUTEN UM DIE WELT

Temporäre Bauten hinterfragen offensichtlich allzu enge Definitionen dessen, was Architektur ist. Es liegt in der Natur von Bauwerken, im Boden zu gründen, auch wenn Menschen wie Tomas Saraceno davon träumen, sie schweben zu lassen. Was ist also von einer so erstaunlichen Konstruktion wie der Internationalen Raumstation (ISS, Seite 286) zu halten, die zur Zeit letzte Form annimmt, obwohl sich das amerikanische Space-Shuttle-Programm seinem Ende nähert. Die Raumstation, ein Gemeinschaftsprojekt verschiedener Raumfahrtbehörden, darunter die amerikanischen (NASA), europäischen (ESA), russischen (RKA), japanischen (JAXA) und kanadischen (CSA) Agenturen, ist das Resultat einer in Stufen vollzogenen Montage von Modulen. So entsteht eine erdumkreisende Konstruktion mit einer Masse von 370 000 kg – etwas weder auf der Erde noch im Weltraum je Dagewesenes. Während sich die meisten Bauten auch ästhetisch infrage stellen lassen müssen, wird die Form der ISS primär von physikalischen Anforderungen diktiert, die sich aus einer niedrigen Erdumlaufbahn und permanenter Bemannung ergeben. Manche mögen ihr Aussehen merkwürdig finden, dennoch ist es eine Architektur, die sich fast gänzlich einer der fundamentalsten Kräfte überhaupt entzieht: der Schwerkraft.

In gewisser Weise ist diese im Raum schwebende Konstruktion der ultimative Ausdruck temporärer Architektur. Doch zugleich muss sie technischen Anforderungen völlig neuer Art gerecht werden. Als Louis Sullivan gegen Ende des 19. Jahrhunderts die Maxime „Form follows function" formulierte, dachte er zweifellos nicht an die ISS. Dennoch prägt diese Vorgabe die Raumstation stärker als jeder architektonische Diskurs. Sicherlich haben Flugzeuge und Schiffe eine eigene Art von Architektur. Und doch werden bei der Analyse von Bauten Fahrzeuge normalerweise nicht berücksichtigt. Die ISS ist eine Art Fahrzeug, denn sie umrundet die Erde 15,7 Mal am Tag; zugleich ist sie Labor und zugleich ein Hotel für Astronauten. Mit ihr ist erstmals eine reale, temporäre Architektur im All, ohne Frage ein Vorbote zukünftiger Bauformen. Tatsächlich ist eines der elementarsten Merkmale temporärer Architektur der Verzicht auf Verwurzelung, ihre Fähigkeit zur Mobilität – während dauerhafte Bauten in der Regel Betonfundamente besitzen und letztlich nur durch einen Abriss verschwinden.

MODULAR, NACHHALTIG, TRANSPORTABEL

Eine der wichtigsten Nutzungsformen temporärer Architektur ist – ebenso wie bei ihren dauerhafteren Verwandten – der Wohnbau. Zwar mögen manche von Häusern träumen, die Jahrhunderte überdauern, doch unsere modernen Zeiten haben kurzfristige Lösungen mehr und mehr in den Vordergrund rücken lassen – angefangen bei den für Amerika so typischen Mobilheimen. Auf den Einsatz von Frachtcontainern als Wohnbauten, die leicht transportierbar sind, wurde bereits hingewiesen. Allerdings gibt es weitere Kategorien temporärer Wohnbauten, die Aufmerksamkeit verdienen. Der deutsche Architekt Werner Aisslinger, Erfinder des Loftcube, einer temporären Wohneinheit, die auf

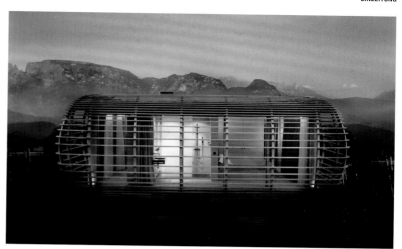

18
Werner Aisslinger, Fincube, Winterinn,
Ritten, South Tyrol, Italy, 2010

18

Dächern installiert werden kann (2003), hat in jüngster Zeit den Fincube entworfen, ein „modulares, nachhaltiges und transportables Niedrig-energiehaus" (2010, Seite 48). Zentrale Charakteristika des Designs sind minimale Baugrundvorbereitung und langlebige und recycelbare Materialien, womit es auf zahlreiche Fragen des Wohnens reagiert, darunter die zunehmend nomadenhaften Tendenzen bestimmter Bevölke-rungsgruppen, auch in modernen Industrieländern.

Jennifer Siegals Office of Mobile Design ist, wie schon der Name vermuten lässt, auf transportable Modulbauten spezialisiert, wie etwa das Prefab Show House (Seite 312) oder das Taliesin Mod.Fab House (Seite 318). Siegal experimentierte mit Seefrachtcontainern, etwa bei der Seatrain Residence (Los Angeles, Kalifornien, USA), einem nach Kundenwünschen gestalteten Wohnhaus aus zweimal zwei aufeinander-gestapelten ISO-Containern, geschützt von einer 15 m langen Dachmembran aus Stahl und Glas. Ihre Projekte belegten zudem die Verwandt-schaft von Fertighäusern und transportablen Wohneinheiten. Häuser dieser Art wurden bisher oft mit billiger Bauweise und geringen Quali-tätsstandards assoziiert, doch Siegal sah vor, in ihrem Prefab Show House als Herzstück eine luxuriöse Boffi-Küche zu installieren und signalisierte damit, dass sich Wohnbauten wie diese seit den Tagen der Quonset Hut erheblich weiterentwickelt haben.

Zahlreiche leicht transportierbare und montierbare Wohnbauten haben ihre Ursprünge in Projekten, die auf Anforderung des amerikani-schen Militärs im Zweiten Weltkrieg entstanden. Schon damals hatte die Mobilität der amerikanischen Bevölkerung, die ihre Wurzeln in den Trecks nach Westen hatte, zu einem Selbstverständnis geführt, das manche wünschen ließ, ihr Heim nach Bedarf mitnehmen zu können. Ab 1941 entwickelte ein Team der US Navy in Quonset Point, Rhode Island, die sogenannte Quonset Hut – inspiriert von der britischen Nissen Hut, die königlich-britische Ingenieure im Ersten Weltkrieg als Alternative zu Zelten entwickelt hatten. Es war eine Reaktion auf den immer dringenderen Bedarf an massenproduzierbaren, transportablen und leicht zu montierenden Bauten. Die auf verschiedene Weise abgewandel-ten, halbrunden Notunterkünfte inspirieren nach wie vor temporäre Architektur in aller Welt, auch wenn ihr Einheitsdesign den Komfortstan-dards der industrialisierten Welt nicht länger entspricht.

NICHTS WEITER ALS EINE EXTREME FORM VON ARCHITEKTUR

Ein Jahr nach dem verheerenden Erdbeben in der Provinz Sichuan am 12. Mai 2008 entwarfen die Architekten OBRA aus New York für eine Ausstellung in China einen Prototyp für Notunterkünfte (Red+Housing, Seite 306). OBRA arbeitete mit roter Fallschirmseide und Sperr-holz und stellte unter Beweis, dass „Notunterkünfte aus gestalterische Sicht nichts weiter als eine extreme Form von Architektur sind". Mit einer Nutzfläche von 45 m² und geschätzten Kosten von 5000 US Dollar erfüllen solche Unterkünfte zahlreiche Anforderungen und sind zu-dem eine Chance für die zeitgenössische Architektur, in realen Notsituationen zu helfen. In der Tat haben auch andere Architekten, an erster Stelle Shigeru Ban, Zeit und Mühen investiert, um erschwingliche, leicht zu montierende Notunterkünfte zu entwerfen.

So gestaltete Ban das Paper Log House (Nagata, Kobe, Japan, 1995, Seite 18), einen einstöckigen temporären Wohnbau mit einer Nutzfläche von 16 m². Das zwischen Mai und Juni 1995, im Jahr des großen Erdbebens von Kobe, geplante Haus wurde vom Schicksal vietnamesischer Kirchgänger angeregt, die noch Monate nach dem Erdbeben im Januar 1995 in Zelten aus Plastikplanen lebten. Als Shigeru Ban sie nach dem Grund fragte, erklärten sie ihm, die von der Regierung zur Verfügung gestellten Notunterkünfte lägen zu weit ab von Verkehrsmitteln und außerhalb des Schuleinzugsgebiets ihrer Kinder. Ban beschloss, temporäre Häuser für sie zu bauen. Er führt aus: „Die Kriterien für den Entwurf waren: eine kostengünstige Konstruktion zu entwickeln, die jedermann aufbauen konnte, mit akzeptablen Dämmeigenschaften und außerdem einigermaßen attraktiv. Die Lösung war ein Fundament aus sandgefüllten Bierkästen, Wänden aus Pappröhren (Durchmesser 108 mm bei 4 mm Stärke) und Decken und einem Dach aus Textilmembran. Der Entwurf ähnelte einer Blockhütte. Die Bierkästen wurden vom Getränkehersteller gemietet und dienten während der Bauphase außerdem als Tritte." Die Einfachheit des Verfahrens und die Tatsache, dass die Pappröhren vor Ort angefertigt werden konnten, wurden der problematischen Lage gerecht, die durch den Wohnraummangel nach dem Erdbeben entstanden war. Bis Ende Sommer 1995 konnten 27 dieser Häuser für vietnamesische und japanische Bewohner erbaut werden.

FLÜCHTLINGE UND NOMADEN

Ban entwarf auch weiterhin eine ganze Reihe ähnlicher Wohnbauten wie etwa die Notunterkünfte aus Papier für die UNHCR (Flüchtlingslager Byumba, Ruanda, 1999, Seite 47). In jüngster Zeit arbeitete er in Haiti und L'Aquila, Italien, obwohl bürokratische und praktische Hürden die Erdbebenhilfe unter solchen Bedingungen komplex gestalten. Am 12. Januar 2010 erschütterte ein Erbeben der Stärke 7,0 die Gegend um Port-au-Prince. Über eine Million Menschen verloren ihr Zuhause – mehr als eine halbe Million von ihnen fand Zuflucht in hastig errichteten Zelten. Shigeru Ban kooperierte mit Professoren und Studenten der Universidad Iberoamericana sowie der Pontificia Universidad Católica Madre y Maestra (Dominikanische Republik), um 100 Notunterkünfte aus Pappröhren und lokal vorhandenen Materialien für die Erdbebenopfer von Haiti zu bauen.

Ganz offensichtlich fasziniert von Fragen, die die temporäre Architektur aufwirft, arbeitete Shigeru Ban ausgiebig mit Schiffscontainern und Pappröhren – mitunter in Kombination, wie etwa bei seinem Nomadic Museum (Pier 54, New York, 2005, Seite 33; Santa Monica, Kalifornien, 2006; Tokio, 2007), einem 4180 m² großen Bauwerk, das für die Ausstellung *Ashes and Snow* gebaut wurde, die großformatige Fotografien des Fotografen Gregory Colbert präsentierte. Das nicht weniger als 205 m lange, 16 m hohe, rechteckige Gebäude bestand in erster Linie aus ISO-Containern und Pappröhren aus recyceltem Papier. Es war das erste Gebäude in New York, das aus Containern realisiert wurde. Anschließend wurde der Bau in Santa Monica, Kalifornien, sowie in Japan mit örtlich verfügbaren Containern wieder errichtet.

FEUER IM GOLF, KONZERTE MIT BONO

Die hier publizierten Beispiele sind nur ein Bruchteil der weltweit vertretenen Typen temporärer Architektur. Ausgenommen sind beispielsweise Industrie- oder auch militärische Bauten, obwohl sie zweifellos zu den meist verbreiteten Typen ephemerer Konstruktionen

19
Shigeru Ban, Nomadic Museum,
Pier 54, New York, 2005

19

zählen. Die Katastrophe um die Deepwater Horizon, eine Halbtaucherbohrinsel im Golf von Mexiko, die sich Anfang April 2010 ereignete, ist ein Beispiel für die weite Verbreitung monumentaler und potenziell gefährlicher Formen temporärer Architektur. Bauformen wie die Internationale Raumstation werden in der Regel von technischen Anforderungen diktiert, weshalb schwimmende Bauten wie die Deepwater Horizon wohl kaum Einfluss auf zukünftige Trends der zeitgenössischen Architektur haben dürften; tatsächlich sind sie erst gar nicht das Werk von Architekten. Nichtsdestotrotz sollte man sich solcher Konstruktionen, die sowohl temporär als auch mobil sind, bewusst sein.

Letztendlich ist sicherlich jede Form von Architektur temporär – auch wenn manche Bauten länger leben als andere. Dennoch ist das Konzept ephemerer Architektur überaus faszinierend. Temporäre Bauten sind häufig frei von Einschränkungen, die den Entwurf dauerhafterer Entwürfe belasten: Aus diesem Grunde bieten sie Architekten mehr Spielraum für kreative Freiheiten und sind zugleich eine potenzielle Inspirationsquelle für alle anderen Formen von Architektur. Hinzu kommt, dass temporäre Bauten unbeschwerter mit den fließenden Grenzen von Kunst und Architektur spielen können. Sie reizen Künstler ebenso wie Architekten, Grenzen zu überschreiten. Transportable Wohnbauten, Eventlocations und auch Notunterkünfte fallen allesamt in das Spektrum temporärer Architektur heute. Dasselbe gilt für die 360°-Bühne der internationalen Rockband U2 oder die Netze und Pfosten der Hofinstallation am PS1 von Idenburg und Liu. *Temporary Architecture Now!* ist dynamischer und fließender als seine gesetzeren und klarer definierten Schwesterpublikationen. In vielerlei Hinsicht zählen die hier vorgestellten Bauten zu den faszinierendsten und innovativsten unserer Zeit.

[1] William Shakespeare, *Macbeth*, 5. Aufzug, 5. Szene.
[2] Prediger 1:2.
[3] http://www.egypttoday.com/article.aspx?ArticleID=9064, Zugriff am 14. August 2010.
[4] http://www.seangodsell.com/future-shack, Zugriff am 15. August 2010.

INTRODUCTION

ÉTEINS-TOI, ÉTEINS-TOI, PETITE CHANDELLE ! [1]

Considère toujours toute chose humaine comme éphémère et de peu de prix. On doit vivre cet imperceptible moment de la durée du temps conformément à la nature et quitter la vie avec sérénité, comme une olive mûre tombe en remerciant la terre qui l'a produite et rend grâce à l'arbre qui l'a portée.

Marc-Aurèle, *Pensées pour moi-même*, livre 4, vers 170 av. J.-C.

L'empereur romain Marc-Aurèle (121–180 av. J.-C.) rédigea en langue grecque son ouvrage de méditation, *Pensées pour moi-même*. En grec, le mot *ephemeros* signifie « qui ne dure qu'un jour ». Temporaire vient du latin *temporarius* (de caractère saisonnier, durant peu de temps). Le temporaire est l'opposé du permanent. La manière dont ces termes peuvent s'appliquer à l'architecture est évidement aussi différenciée que difficile à définir. Par essence, toute construction est temporaire, même si des siècles peuvent s'écouler avant qu'elle ne retourne en poussière. L'architecture est donc par définition et par nature temporaire, mais ce caractère éphémère dépend naturellement de la qualité de la construction et de divers facteurs qui vont de l'emplacement aux variations climatiques. Par manque de matériaux, insuffisance des techniques, ou du fait de styles de vie nomade, une grande partie de l'architecture des premiers temps de l'histoire consistait surtout en des huttes ou des tentes toujours à la merci des vents. La fonction d'une structure architecturale dicte également sa solidité, de même que la façon dont elle est entretenue. Les temples japonais en bois ont survécu parce qu'ils sont régulièrement reconstruits par segment, de génération en génération. Les villes modernes sont l'objet d'une reconstruction permanente qui n'hésite pas à s'attaquer aux égos architecturaux. Un symbole du pouvoir et de la permanence peut être effacé en quelques jours pour laisser la place à un centre commercial ou un bowling. « Vanité des vanités, tout est vanité », dit l'*Ecclésiaste* [2]. Mais si l'architecture est en un sens forcément temporaire et si le style de vie moderne pousse à une existence presque nomade, y compris dans les pays développés, les architectes ne pourraient-ils accepter l'inévitable et construire pour l'instant qui vient, sans trop de préoccuper de la postérité ?

Les techniques modernes permettent aujourd'hui de recourir à des matériaux nouveaux comme les plastiques aux utilisations étonnantes, ou traditionnels comme le bois (le plus ancien des matériaux de construction), grâce à des machines-outils à pilotage numérique donnant la possibilité d'élaborer des structures qui ne sont pas prévues pour durer jusqu'à la fin des temps. C'est l'usage qui prime ici : un stand de foire, un décor de scène ou un pavillon d'exposition ne possèdent généralement qu'une durée de vie brève et prédéterminée. De nombreux architectes ont réalisé que les symboles de l'économie que sont les conteneurs de transport sont souvent abandonnés, alors qu'ils peuvent être facilement transformés en boutiques ou en logements. C'est ainsi que des objets censés être nomades sont ancrés dans le sol, où ils se révèlent plus résistants et durables que des réalisations plus traditionnelles. Les sites de chantiers de construction ou de fouilles archéologiques sont eux aussi prétextes à de nombreuses architectures temporaires, de même que l'univers de la création artistique. Une exposition tend souvent de nos jours à prendre une forme spatiale, ou, autrement dit, architecturale. L'art contemporain, qui flirte aussi volontiers avec l'éphémère, peut ainsi conduire à des constructions proches de la définition originale du mot grec : « qui ne dure qu'un jour ».

20
Miralles Tagliabue EMBT, Spanish Pavilion, Expo 2010, Shanghai, China, 2010

PERMANENCE TEMPORAIRE ?

Un examen même rapide de la production architecturale contemporaine montre l'augmentation du nombre de structures résolument temporaires au cours de ces dernières années. Une des premières raisons tient peut-être aux contraintes économiques qui facilitent des solutions au coût généralement inférieur à celui de constructions plus pérennes. L'autre raison, peut-être plus significative à long terme, est que l'on trouve aujourd'hui moins de clients suffisamment audacieux pour tenter de construire quelque chose « qui durera des siècles ». Notre culture est à l'évidence vouée à la consommation rapide et l'architecture n'échappe pas aux tendances de son temps. Sur un plan plus positif, des constructions rapidement conçues et exécutées peuvent permettre aux architectes d'expérimenter et d'inventer des formes nouvelles qui accompagneront la façon dont nous vivrons demain.

Les pavillons de toutes sortes forment le noyau de cette architecture temporaire, qu'ils soient destinés à des événements uniques ou à de grandes foires ou expositions internationales. Si la démolition planifiée est de règle dans la plupart de ces cas, on trouve également des exceptions qui illustrent le caractère « temporaire » spécifique de ces projets. La tour Eiffel a été édifiée pour la porte d'entrée de l'Exposition universelle de 1889, et ne devait rester en place que vingt ans. Elle est encore aujourd'hui le monument payant le plus visité au monde. Étant donnée sa hauteur, elle devait être solidement construite, d'où peut-être sa longévité. Cette structure en grande partie « inutile » est même devenue l'un des symboles de Paris, si ce n'est de la France. Les expositions universelles ou foires internationales restent un des catalyseurs de la conception et de la construction de bâtiments temporaires ambitieux, comme l'ont encore illustré récemment un certain nombre de pavillons nationaux pour l'Expo 2010 de Shanghaï.

LA SIRÈNE, LE VAISSEAU SPATIAL ET LA CATHÉDRALE DES SEMENCES

Parmi les pavillons nationaux de Shanghaï qui auraient pu être sélectionnés pour cet ouvrage, six sont présentés ici en détail. Le premier est celui de Bjarke Ingels (BIG) pour son Danemark natal (page 92). Il a voulu traduire quelques traits caractéristiques de son pays, de la bicyclette à *La Petite Sirène*, sculpture d'Edward Eriksen posée sur un rocher dans le port de Copenhague en 1913. Célèbre symbole du royaume, elle a, pour la première fois de son existence, quitté la capitale danoise pour un bref séjour à Shanghaï. *La Petite Sirène* est aussi un conte d'Hans Christian Andersen publié en 1837, qui raconte comment une sirène accepta d'abandonner son existence aquatique pour l'amour d'un prince bien terrestre. La sculpture a été déposée sur un rocher au centre d'un pavillon de métal blanc, dont la forme en spirale entoure un « bassin de port ». Tout en jouant avec le symbole de son pays, Bjarke Ingels a cherché à incarner sa modernité pour des Chinois sans doute plus familiers du conte d'Andersen que de la vision d'un Danemark créateur, à la pointe de son temps.

Conçu par l'agence Buchner Bründler de Bâle, le Pavillon suisse (page 100) a cherché, lui aussi, à distiller un mélange de création contemporaine et d'éléments symboliques ou presque folkloriques. Organisé selon un plan qui rappelle la carte de son pays, ce pavillon se distinguait par un télésiège typique des montagnes suisses, mais aussi par une façade en treillis d'aluminium qui fait appel à des technologies d'avant-garde. Ses formes puissantes réalisées en béton évoquaient également à leur façon l'architecture suisse moderne et contemporaine pour les connaisseurs. Son toit végétalisé était à la fois le signe des principes de construction écologiques appliqués et le rappel de la beauté naturelle du pays.

Œuvre de Benedetta Tagliabue (agence Miralles Tagliabue EMBT), le Pavillon espagnol (page 268) était une structure en acier de quatre niveaux, mais qui se présentait sous la forme d'un nuage d'osier tressé. La vannerie est un artisanat espagnol typique et les architectes ont fait en sorte que les formes choisies reprennent celle des caractères chinois évoquant l'amitié sino-espagnole. La massivité interne en béton du Pavillon suisse laissait place dans ce cas à un sentiment d'éphémère conforme à l'esprit d'un événement comme Expo 2010, où le mélange de folklore, de fierté nationale et de modernité résolue n'a semblé choquer personne. La ville de Madrid était par ailleurs représentée par l'Air Tree (page 136) conçu par Ecosistema Urbano, structure censée créer un environnement physique agréable au cœur de la chaleur tropicale que connaît Shanghaï en été. Là encore, l'objectif était de créer une attraction offrant aux visiteurs des informations sur le lieu, tout en mettant en valeur une modernité et une inventivité que les Chinois n'associent pas forcément à une ville comme Madrid.

Si la plupart des pays ont choisi un architecte national pour concevoir leur pavillon, l'Égypte a fait exception en confiant son projet à la célèbre Zaha Hadid (page 194). Le magazine *Egypt Today* lui a réservé un accueil assez tiède dans un article intitulé « Surjouer l'égyptomanie », qui expliquait : « Le pavillon de l'Égypte, de 1000 mètres carrés, est à l'origine un cadeau de l'architecte iranienne de notoriété internationale, Zaha Hadid. Un peu raide, marqué d'accents noir et blanc, il veut apparemment combiner la modernité et l'Antiquité que représente une symbolisation graphique en constellation de trois grandes pyramides au-dessus de la voûte d'entrée. En fait, le bâtiment fait penser à une sorte de vaisseau spatial égaré qui aurait atterri à Shanghaï par erreur, et qui essaierait d'éviter de se faire remarquer en se déguisant en pavillon. » [3] Cependant, le magazine a été obligé d'admettre que ce pavillon a attiré en moyenne 14 000 visiteurs par jour venus admirer tout autant l'architecture que les objets antiques ou l'exposition sur le Caire, ou peut-être encore avoir leur nom écrit en hiéroglyphes égyptiens. Zaha Hadid, dont l'architecture ne se range pas dans des catégories établies et ne répond pas davantage à ce que l'on attend généralement du projet demandé, est habituée aux controverses. Quel meilleur endroit pour défier ce que les Français appellent « les idées reçues » qu'une exposition universelle dédiée au futur ?

Un autre pavillon qui a beaucoup attiré l'attention à Shanghaï par son curieux aspect « hirsute » était celui du Royaume-Uni (page 200), conçu par Thomas Heatherwick. Cette structure qui contient un espace appelé la « Cathédrale des semences », a été réalisée à partir de 60 000 tiges de fibre optique souple et transparente de 7,5 mètres de long, chacune enfermant une ou plusieurs graines végétales à son extrémité. Elle avait été conçue en collaboration avec la Millennium Seed Bank des Kew Gardens, qui a pour objectif de réunir des échantillons de 25 % des semences mondiales d'ici 2020. Alors que certains pays ont ciblé la mise en avant de leur modernité, l'Angleterre, avec Heatherwick, a opté pour un parti pris écologique aussi recevable en Chine qu'au Royaume-Uni. La présence de cette structure à Shanghaï a

21
Zaha Hadid, "Egypt—Mother of the World, " Egyptian Pavilion, Expo 2010, Shanghai, China, 2010

pu également exprimer un glissement des formes modernistes lisses vers une architecture complexe qui affiche d'autres objectifs que la seule ambition esthétique.

LE ROUGE EST MIS

De retour en Europe et dans un contexte très différent, la Serpentine Gallery, située dans les jardins de Kensington à Londres, célébrait en 2010 la dixième année de son projet de Pavillons d'été (page 298). Ces pavillons, dessinés par quelques gloires de l'architecture internationale comme Oscar Niemeyer, Toyo Ito, Frank Gehry, Álvaro Siza et Edouardo Souto de Moura sont prévus pour ne durer que trois mois et reçoivent généralement plus de 200 000 visiteurs. Le concept de la directrice de la Serpentine, Julia Peyton-Jones, est de sélectionner un architecte très connu qui n'a jamais encore construit au Royaume-Uni pour édifier un pavillon temporaire. En 2010, son choix s'est porté sur Jean Nouvel, qui a envoyé un projet destiné à abriter sur 500 mètres carrés des conférences, des concerts et, bien sûr, un café. Il est entièrement de couleur rouge. Comme les années précédentes, le coût (750 000 livres sterling pour le projet Nouvel) a été pris en charge par des sponsors toujours prêts à soutenir l'une des manifestations culturelles les plus médiatisées de Londres. Bien que ces pavillons aient été parfois vendus et reconstruits ailleurs – comme celui de Frank Gehry (2008) dressé aujourd'hui près d'Aix-en-Provence –, l'idée essentielle est qu'ils soient temporaires et illustrent la créativité de l'architecte choisi. Étant donné le succès de ces pavillons depuis 2000, on constate que l'architecture temporaire attire réellement l'attention du public quand elle s'aventure vers des formes souvent audacieuses qui n'auraient sans doute pas été acceptées pour des constructions permanentes, en particulier dans un site aussi protégé que celui de Hyde Park.

PURPLE HAZE ET ROBOTIQUE

Autre construction temporaire intéressante érigée en 2010, le Pavillon 21 MINI Opera Space de Coop Himmelb(l)au de 430 mètres carrés, érigé sur la Marstallplatz à Munich (page 124). C'est grâce à divers calculs informatiques liés à une composition musicale de Jimmy Hendrix (*Purple Haze*, « …'Scuse me while I kiss the sky… ») que les architectes ont créé cette petite structure destinée à un festival d'opéra. Malgré ces origines musicales, le Pavillon 21 arbore le style déconstructiviste hérissé des œuvres de Coop Himmelb(l)au. Dans un environnement munichois assez terne, cette explosion formelle a offert aux amateurs d'opéra et aux passants des morceaux choisis d'une architecture contemporaine, qui n'aurait probablement pas été acceptée en ces lieux sous une forme permanente. C'est une fois encore un exemple de l'intérêt des constructions temporaires, même si certaines, comme la tour Eiffel, ont réussi à se maintenir jusqu'à ce que le public s'habitue à leur conception révolutionnaire.

La maison de pierre (House of Stone, Italie, page 326), conçue par John Pawson dans le cadre de la Foire du meuble de Milan en 2010, et plus spécialement pour le Think Tank d'Interni sur un terrain de l'Université degli Studi, donnait une impression de solidité minimaliste, malgré son caractère éphémère. Le projet de Pawson mettait également le doigt sur une autre caractéristique de l'architecture temporaire, à savoir que son bâtiment avait pu utiliser un matériau nouveau, appelé Lithoverde, à base de pierre recyclée et de 1 % de résine natu-

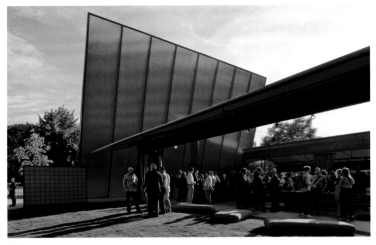

22

22
Jean Nouvel, Serpentine Pavilion,
Kensington Gardens, London, UK,
2010

relle. Dans un contexte architectural qui n'est pas vraiment ouvert à la modernité, cette maison de pierre vide, austère et aux résonances presque funèbres, semblait presque plus ancienne que son environnement.

Construire en dur n'est pas le passage obligé pour de nombreux pavillons contemporains, bien au contraire. Rendez-Vous (Tokyo, 2010, page 54), une petite construction de 52 mètres carrés signée par l'agence Atelier Bow-Wow, a été réalisée en grande partie en bambou, un matériau qui contraste avec la solidité et la rigueur du Musée national d'art moderne voisin édifié par Yoshiro Taniguchi. Ces jeunes architectes japonais souhaitaient « adoucir cette austérité, tout en conservant la dignité du lieu, mais en allégeant un peu l'atmosphère pour en faire un endroit plus agréable ». Mettant à profit la souplesse du bambou pour pousser leur idée encore plus loin, ils ont imaginé un pavillon qui serait une sorte d'animal géant émergeant des jardins du palais impérial. Cette approche humoristique de l'architecture temporaire contraste aussi avec la forte densité urbaine de la capitale nippone.

Le pavillon de recherche de l'ICD/ITKE (page 206), conçu par l'Institut de design informatique (ICD) et l'Institut de construction et de design de structures (ITKE) de l'université de Stuttgart en 2010, a été entièrement réalisé en lattes de contreplaqué de bouleau cintrées. Il se composait de 500 pièces de bois de dimensions uniques, dessinées et fabriquées à l'aide d'outils de conception et de fabrication assistés par ordinateur dans les laboratoires de robotique de l'université. Bien que le bouleau ne puisse être qualifié de matériau « moderne », son utilisation repose ici sur des technologies de design et de découpe de pointe. Alors que la génération précédente de constructions conçues par ordinateur s'intéressait davantage à des formes curieuses rompant avec la trame moderniste, les réalisations actuelles s'orientent vers des approches encore plus inattendues, en particulier dans le contexte de travaux de recherche, comme ceux menés à l'ICD/ITKE de Stuttgart.

STANDARDISÉS ET EMPILABLES

Si les conteneurs de transport sont omniprésents dans les ports et le paysage urbain, ils ne sont qu'une invention relativement récente, inspirée des conteneurs militaires standardisés mis au point par l'armée américaine dans les années 1950. L'Organisation internationale de normalisation (ISO) a d'ailleurs basé ses normes pour conteneurs intermodaux (capables d'être transportés aussi bien par bateau que par train ou camion, 1970) sur celles des militaires américains. Un conteneur standard est en tôle d'acier ondulé et mesure 20 ou 40 pieds (6 ou 12 mètres) de long. On peut en empiler jusqu'à 7 à l'aide de fixations normalisées. Aussi étrange que cela puisse paraître, les conteneurs ISO ont commencé à être utilisés pour l'habitat et la construction dès les années 1980.

Phillip Clark, propriétaire de la firme Import Export & Overhaul de Miami, obtint le brevet américain n° 4 854 094 (déposé le 23 novembre 1987, date du brevet 8 août 1989) pour « une méthode de conversion d'un ou plusieurs conteneurs d'expédition en acier en bâtiments habitables sur un site de construction et leur production ». Avant cette date (1985), l'architecte australien Sean Godsell avait commencé à travailler sur son projet intitulé « Future Shack » décrit comme une « maison transportable produite en série pour des situations de logements d'urgence et de refuge. Des conteneurs d'expédition recyclés constituent le volume principal du bâtiment. Un toit-parasol est installé dans le conteneur. Une fois érigé, il protège le conteneur et réduit la charge thermique sur le bâtiment. Des pieds télescopiques soutiennent le conteneur et permettent son installation sans creusement ni même aplanissement du terrain ». [4] Si la paternité de l'architecture de conteneurs n'est pas entièrement claire, elle est apparue néanmoins rapidement comme une solution valable pour des constructions temporaires voire permanentes. Un certain nombre d'exemples récents de réutilisation de conteneurs ISO sont présentés dans ce volume.

Les architectes brésiliens Bernades + Jacobsen, bien connus pour leurs luxueuses résidences en bord de mer, ont fréquemment utilisé des conteneurs pour des manifestations ponctuelles telle l'exposition internationale d'art vidéo qui s'est déroulée en 2008 dans le parc Villa-Lobos à São Paulo. Leur installation de « Container Art » de 1200 mètres carrés (page 84), dressée sur une esplanade sur des supports en bois, se composait d'un assemblage ordonné de conteneurs de 6 et 12 mètres. Ils avaient déjà créé une installation beaucoup plus importante, composée de 250 conteneurs servant de scènes, snack-bars ou sanitaires, pour les deux nuits de concerts du Tim Festival (Rio de Janeiro, 2007). L'ensemble de cette installation de 40 000 mètres carrés avait pris la forme d'un grand mur. Des conteneurs de 12 mètres servaient de passages d'entrée signalant l'accès aux scènes, aux entrées et aux sorties. La partie du mur la plus étendue, qui suivait une longue courbe sinueuse orientée vers la mer, dissimulait les tentes de 15 mètres de haut utilisées pour les concerts. À différents niveaux, des vides entre les conteneurs étaient aménagés en espaces pour projections vidéo ou petites scènes de spectacle. L'ensemble, assemblé à partir du 16 septembre 2007, fut entièrement démonté le 18 novembre. Plus de 23 000 personnes assistèrent aux concerts. Le manque de subtilité et de flexibilité formelles des conteneurs a pour contrepartie de faciliter leur assemblage et leur transport.

L'architecte américain Adam Kalkin s'est spécialisé dans l'architecture à base de conteneurs, comme le montre son livre paru en 2008, *Quik Build: Adam Kalkin's ABC of Container Architecture*. Il a créé un système nommé Quik House (page 224) qui utilise des conteneurs recyclés pour construire des maisons parfois beaucoup plus luxueuses que leur humble origine pourrait le laisser supposer. Elles peuvent être livrées cinq mois après la commande et ne coûter que 76 000 dollars, bien que diverses options puissent considérablement alourdir leur prix. Sa maison illy Push Button (page 230), présentée à la Biennale de Venise en 2007, voulait montrer qu'un conteneur d'exposition banal pouvait se transformer en vrai logement en quelques minutes, grâce à des systèmes hydrauliques et une conception intelligente. Kalkin s'est également lancé dans une collaboration avec l'armée américaine en Afghanistan et une fondation charitable en Russie pour développer les multiples usages possibles de ces conteneurs.

Le pavillon COP 15 (page 258), conçu par l'agence d'architecture MAPT et installé dans le port nord de Copenhague (2009–10), utilise de vieux conteneurs et d'autres matériaux recyclés. Insistant sur les aspects économiques et écologiques de ce type de réutilisation, MAPT fait remarquer que ces conteneurs sont si peu chers que les compagnies de transport préfèrent souvent les abandonner plutôt que de les renvoyer vides à leur point de départ. C'est alors une aubaine pour des créateurs comme cette agence danoise.

23

Le groupe italien tamassociati a créé Emergency ONG housing (« logements d'urgence pour Organisations non gouvernementales », (page 382) pour le Centre Salam de chirurgie cardiaque de Soba (Khartoum, Soudan, 2009), à partir de quatre-vingt-quinze conteneurs de 6 mètres pour les logements et de sept conteneurs de 12 mètres pour une cafétéria. Ils avaient été abandonnés à proximité lors de la construction du Centre Salam. L'acier est un conducteur direct du froid et de la chaleur, ce qui est un inconvénient lorsqu'on utilise ces conteneurs pour le logement. Les architectes ont résolu le problème à l'aide de panneaux isolants intérieurs de 5 centimètres d'épaisseur et d'une isolation du toit, tout en mettant en place un système de brise-soleil en bambou qui évite toute action directe du soleil sur le métal.

STANDS DE FOIRE EN MARBRE, VERRE ET BOIS

Les stands de foire ont longtemps été un terrain d'expérimentations pour l'architecture temporaire. Le fait qu'ils ne doivent généralement ni supporter de fortes charges ni répondre aux fonctions traditionnelles leur permet de s'aventurer dans des territoires nouveaux et de s'abstraire de certaines règles du bâti. Des designers, souvent spécialisés dans ce domaine précis, entrent fréquemment en concurrence avec les architectes pour les construire. L'architecte espagnol Alberto Campo Baeza a choisi une approche particulièrement architecturée pour le stand de la société d'exploitation de pierre italienne Piba Marbri à la Foire Marmocacc (Vérone, Italie, 2009, page 112). Son grand cube noir entièrement habillé à l'intérieur de marbre de Carrare blanc créait un contraste de perceptions et de volume souligné par un habile système de spots d'éclairage donnant l'impression de variations de la lumière naturelle à l'intérieur du stand. Puissante et minimaliste, l'architecture de Campo Baeza utilise souvent les contrastes provoqués par l'éclairage solaire. D'une certaine façon, il a ici traduit ses préoccupations conceptuelles en une forme liée aux produits de l'exposant et capable d'intéresser les visiteurs de la foire.

Les architectes madrilènes Camila Aybar et Juan Jose Mateos créent les stands de foire du verrier Vitro à l'IFEMA depuis 2006 (page 58). Cette année-là, leur stand n'utilisait pas moins de 170 tonnes de verre sous forme de 25 000 petits morceaux pris entre des panneaux de verre. Cet empilement provoquait des effets comparés par les architectes à des œuvres d'artistes comme Bill Viola ou James Turrell. En termes d'effets visuels, ce type de stand est sans doute plus proche de l'art que de l'architecture au sens traditionnel. C'est certainement pour cela que ce type d'intervention intéresse les architectes. Leur stand de 2008, toujours pour Vitro, mettait en scène de petites pastilles rouges et blanches posées sur des panneaux de verre ultra-clair, pour créer un espace dans lequel la couleur de la structure changeait en fonction de l'angle de vue du spectateur. Aybar et Mateos ont considéré le verre comme un matériau malléable et changeant, et créé des effets artistiques qui vantent néanmoins les caractéristiques des produits du client. Il reste à voir s'il s'agit d'un travail de design ou d'architecture, mais les fonctions pratiques ou de base de l'architecture ne tenaient guère de place dans ces projets.

Fondée en 2005 seulement, la société londonienne Established & Sons s'est déjà assurée une réputation substantielle en produisant et commercialisant des meubles modernes et contemporains qui sont en grande partie l'œuvre de ses cofondateurs, Alasdhair Willis et Sebastian Wrong, ce dernier étant directeur de design. Leur stand au Salon international du meuble de Milan en 2009 (page 160), à La Pelota, était une étonnante accumulation de 30 tonnes de pièces de bois non traité négligemment empilées pour constituer des murs, créant des espaces de présentation pour leurs seize nouveaux projets. Sebastian Wrong, responsable de cette installation, a insisté sur la « densité et l'intensité » de ces espaces qui contrastaient avec le mobilier ainsi mis en valeur.

Le stand AB21 de Francesc Rifé (Foire de Valence, Espagne, 2009, page 350) était, lui, consacré à une exposition de tapis. L'architecte explique sans détour que « l'espace a été conçu comme une galerie d'art ». Les tapis de couleurs vives brillamment éclairés font en effet penser à des œuvres artistiques, ce qu'apprécient certainement les clients. La raison de faire appel à un designer connu dans ces circonstances est certes d'attirer l'attention, mais aussi, en un sens, de sublimer le produit, objectif atteint avec brio par le stand de Rifé.

À LA RECHERCHE DES RYTHMES CACHÉS

Parce que les aspects pratiques ne sont pas toujours aussi importants pour les structures temporaires que pour les constructions permanentes, l'architecture éphémère se rapproche fréquemment du domaine de l'art, et de nombreux artistes ont d'ailleurs franchi les barrières tacites qui les séparent pour créer ce qui pourrait ressembler à de l'architecture. Ces distinctions peuvent même devenir insignifiantes entre les mains d'un créateur aussi inventif que Cecil Balmond. Son exposition « Element » (page 64), organisée à Tokyo en 2010, illustre la carrière d'un ingénieur ayant collaboré avec certains des architectes les plus célèbres du moment. L'exposition traitait en partie de ce qu'il appelle « la recherche des rythmes cachés », ou plus spécifiquement de « l'ordre et du rythme sous-jacent qui résident dans la nature… » Il n'y a guère de doute que ce type de préoccupation relève aussi du mode de raisonnement de nombreux artistes, et il n'y a que peu de différence entre de tels artistes et un ingénieur du niveau de Cecil Balmond.

Le projet d'Ammar Eloueini pour le spectacle « Le Tramway » au Pavillon de l'Arsenal à Paris en 2008 (page 146) faisait appel à une peau en polycarbonate qui divisait l'espace en reproduisant le trajet de la ligne de tramway prévue pour faire le tour de la capitale. Ce type de matériaux légers est un exemple de la capacité des architectes à conquérir l'espace à la manière des artistes, l'occuper et le transformer, et ne laisser, comme ici, qu'un souvenir de leur intervention une fois celle-ci terminée. Ainsi, le jeune architecte franco-suisse Philippe Rahm a-t-il réussi à transformer le vaste espace de 14 000 mètres carrés du Grand Palais à Paris (page 334) pour l'exposition d'art contemporain « La Force de l'art 02 ». Pour Philippe Rahm « c'est là […] un appareil muséographique inversé qui est proposé, en ce sens que ce n'est pas l'œuvre d'art qui s'adapte à l'architecture, mais l'architecture qui se plie aux exigences de l'œuvre d'art ». Les pièces exposées œuvreront à mettre en forme un paysage par les jeux simultanés de pressions, de temps d'arrêt, et d'équilibres. La forte présence du bâtiment du Grand Palais et de son immense verrière du début du XXe siècle complétait ici le sentiment d'une rencontre entre l'architecture et l'art.

24
Ammar Eloueini, "Le Tramway,"
Pavilion de l'Arsenal, Paris,
France, 2008

UTOPIE OU OUBLI

Ce que l'on pourrait prendre pour une histoire d'amour entre l'art et l'architecture à travers ces installations temporaires peut se constater aussi bien du point de vue des architectes que de celui des artistes. Les jeunes architectes Florian Idenburg, né en 1975, et Jing Liu, né en 1980, se sont emparés en 2010 de la cour de PS1 à Long Island City (New York) pour leur installation intitulée *Pole Dance* (page 376), une combinaison légère de poteaux de 9 mètres de haut, de cordes élastiques et de filets. Avec ses boules de couleurs vives, son hamac et son bassin, cette installation, conçue pour être en permanence en mouvement puisque chacun de ses composants l'était, pouvait tout aussi bien être regardée comme une œuvre d'art que comme une œuvre architecturale. Sa légèreté, l'interdépendance de ses composants et sa forte impression de temporalité donnaient à comprendre ce qu'une installation de coût relativement réduit peut aussi exprimer sur l'architecture, ses possibilités et son futur.

Idenburg et Liu ne semblent pas s'être beaucoup préoccupés de l'utilité ou des aspects pratiques de leur *Pole Dance*. Par ailleurs, un artiste connu, Tomas Saraceno, imagine des structures légères ou en lévitation, sortes de modèles de la ville et de l'architecture du futur. « Je propose la réalisation concrète de cités-nuages, comme proposées par R. Buckminster Fuller. Ce dernier est, bien entendu, l'une des grandes références de l'architecture temporaire à travers son concept largement théorique de "Cloud 9", mais aussi grâce à un certain nombre de structures réalisées comme ses dômes gonflables. Buckminster Fuller avait calculé qu'un dôme géodésique fermé, ou une sphère de plus de 805 mètres de diamètre, présente un rapport air/structure de 1 pour 1000, et donc que la chaleur solaire pourrait faire monter la température intérieure suffisamment pour que la sphère se déplace dans les airs comme un ballon à air chaud. L'allusion de Tomas Saraceno à Buckminster Fuller met ainsi en évidence une sorte de continuité théorique utopique sur le futur de l'architecture temporaire.

Les œuvres poétiques de Saraceno dissimulent des qualités pratiques ou plutôt le rêve d'espérer modifier l'architecture dans son sens le plus fondamental, en la faisant littéralement flotter dans les airs au lieu de l'enraciner dans le sol. « De telles sphères, poursuit-il, pourraient soulever une masse considérable, ce qui permettrait d'édifier des minicités ou des villes aéroportées de milliers d'habitants. Ces cités-nuages pourraient être arrimées, ou flotter librement, voire même être manœuvrées pour pouvoir "migrer" en réponse aux conditions climatiques et environnementales. » Saraceno se réfère spécifiquement ici au livre de Richard Buckminster Fuller publié en 1969, *Utopia or Oblivion : The Prospects for Humanity*. Chez Idenburg et Liu, et encore plus chez Tomas Saraceno, l'architecture affirme une présence poétique et artistique qui révèle l'importance que peuvent prendre les projets temporaires. Lorsque ce qui pèse en vient à être suspendu et que les fonctions principales sont contournées, l'architecture peut alors librement devenir le véhicule de nos rêves.

A BIGGER BANG

Le terme « éphémère », dans son sens original « qui ne dure qu'un jour », s'applique particulièrement bien à l'architecture d'événements tels que des concerts ou des pièces de théâtre. Les moyens mis en jeu et l'échelle des spectacles des plus importants groupes de rock

25
Philippe Rahm, White Geology, Grand Palais, Paris, France, 2009

25

les placent au premier rang de ce type de projets. Un designer britannique, Mark Fisher, est l'auteur de certains des dispositifs scéniques les plus remarqués des Rolling Stones, de U2 et des Pink Floyd. Né en 1947 et diplômé de l'école de l'Architectural Association de Londres, Fisher a été responsable d'unité à l'AA de 1973 à 1977. Parmi ses projets les plus célèbres, le décor de scène de *A Bigger Bang* – la tournée internationale des Rolling Stones en 2005 (page 170) – combinait l'idée « d'un décor d'opéra décadent et pittoresque du XIXᵉ siècle » avec des écrans DEL haute définition et une disposition originale des sièges rappelant les loges d'opéra.

La superstructure transportable de 180 tonnes conçue par Fisher pour la tournée mondiale *360°* de U2 (2009–11, page 178) ne comprend pas seulement la scène, mais intègre également la place pour plusieurs milliers de spectateurs, et sert de support à 200 tonnes d'équipements techniques. Novatrice sur les plans structurel, technique et même musical, ce type d'architecture temporaire défie la typologie ordinaire des bâtiments, pavillons compris, et se retrouve d'une certaine façon à l'avant-garde de la conception plastique contemporaine. Mark Fisher a également conçu l'un des éléments les plus étonnants de la cérémonie d'ouverture des Jeux olympiques de Pékin 2008, la « Dream Sphere » (page 174), un globe de 19 mètres de diamètre au sommet d'un mât télescopique accueillant soixante personnes et révolutionnant l'utilisation de l'espace dans ce type de manifestations.

Des décors de scène de nature plus banale ont longtemps fasciné les architectes et ce volume présente ceux de Massimiliano et Doriana Fuksas pour *Médée* et *Œdipe à Colone* réalisés pour le festival de théâtre grec de Syracuse (Italie, 2009, page 182). Travaillant sur le concept de catharsis et l'idée que nous avons perdu la perception des premières représentations des pièces d'Euripide et de Sophocle en leur temps, les architectes ont imaginé une « lame concave ». Cette réduction du concept à une forme simple et pure exprime parfaitement bien la puissance de ces drames, tout en s'éloignant des représentations flamboyantes de la Grèce antique, que d'autres designers auraient pu proposer. En se libérant des contraintes du poids et de la stricte fonction, des architectes comme les Fuksas sont capables de redonner forme à l'espace même et de rompre avec les moules classiques, ce qui relève aussi de l'essence de l'architecture temporaire.

DES BULLES ET DES LIVRES

Si l'architecture temporaire peut permettre de libérer l'innovation architecturale de ses contraintes habituelles, d'autres situations réclament une attention plus soutenue aux aspects pratiques. Les exemples de cette catégorie publiés ici vont d'un restaurant au sommet d'un immeuble au plus important objet jamais mis en orbite autour de la terre, la Station spatiale internationale (ISS), qui forme une catégorie en soi. Les très créatifs architectes new-yorkais Diller Scofidio + Renfro, auteurs d'une construction en forme de nuage (Blur Building, Expo '02, Yverdon-les-Bains, Suisse, 2000–02), ont proposé une extension temporaire du musée Hirshhorn de Washington en forme de bulle gonflable malléable (page 130). Cette membrane pneumatique pour mille personnes se développerait à partir de la cour centrale du bâtiment d'origine, de style moderniste, sans toucher ses façades. Cette notion d'espace élastique, en particulier dans le contexte d'un bâtiment strictement moderniste, est très contemporaine et les structures gonflables sont une expression évidente de l'architecture éphémère.

26
*Mark Fisher, Beijing Olympics 2008
Opening Ceremony, "Dream Sphere,"
Beijing, China, 2008*

Dans un style très différent, l'artiste multimédia français Laurent Grasso et son frère, l'architecte Pascal Grasso, ont créé un petit restaurant temporaire de 63 mètres carrés sur la toiture en terrasse du Palais de Tokyo à Paris, qui a fonctionné d'avril à juin 2009. Appelée Nomiya (page 188), cette structure de 18 mètres de long a été construite en deux parties dans un chantier naval. Les aspects pratiques de la présence d'un restaurant en toiture ont dicté une grande partie de sa conception, mais les architectes a réussi à créer un décor minimaliste chic pour ce lieu très recherché. Soumis eux aussi à des contraintes pratiques évidentes, les designers néerlandais Ira Koers et Roelof Mulder ont été chargés de la tâche complexe de concevoir un décor temporaire pour la bibliothèque de l'université d'Amsterdam (page 234). Cet important projet de 2300 mètres carrés pour 235 postes de travail a été réalisé avec un budget modeste. Les couleurs vives (1105 cadres de rangement rouges pour les livres) et le fonctionnalisme de l'ensemble a rapporté aux architectes le prix Great Indoors 2009. Alors que certains projets temporaires s'efforcent d'échapper aux contraintes pratiques de constructions plus permanentes, les frères Grasso comme Koers et Mulder sont parvenus à constituer des environnements éphémères réussis non seulement pour leur apparence, mais aussi pour la manière efficace dont ils ont résolu les aspects pratiques des fonctions concernées.

LE TOUR DU MONDE EN 90 MINUTES

À l'évidence, les structures temporaires remettent en cause les définitions étroites de ce qui constitue l'architecture. Par nature, les constructions sont enracinées dans le sol, même si certains, comme Tomás Saraceno, rêvent de les voir flotter dans les airs. Mais où placer une structure aussi étonnante que la Station spatiale internationale (page 286), qui est en phase de formalisation finale bien que le programme de la navette spatiale américaine approche de sa fin ? Travail collaboratif des agences spatiales suivantes : NASA (États-Unis), ASE (Europe), RKA (Russie), JAXA (Japon) et ASC (Canada), cette station est constituée de l'assemblage par étapes de modules pour aboutir à la mise en orbite d'un objet de 370 000 kilos, un événement unique dans l'histoire de l'espace et de la terre. Si toute création architecturale peut être critiquée pour des raisons esthétiques, l'ISS présente une forme essentiellement influencée par les contraintes liées à la physique des orbites basses et de l'habitat humain. On peut trouver son aspect curieux, mais c'est un type d'architecture qui échappe largement à l'une des forces les plus fondamentales, la gravité.

En un sens, il s'agit là de l'expression ultime d'une architecture temporaire flottant dans l'espace et soumise à des contraintes techniques d'un type nouveau. Lorsque Louis Sullivan lança son fameux « la forme suit la fonction » à la fin du XIXᵉ siècle, il ne pensait certainement pas à l'ISS, mais définissait en même temps cette station spatiale mieux que n'importe quel discours d'architecte. Les avions et les bateaux relèvent d'une architecture particulière, même si les véhicules sont généralement exclus de l'analyse de l'art de construire. L'ISS en est un, car il fait le tour de la terre 15,7 fois par jour, mais c'est aussi un laboratoire et un hôtel pour astronautes. Elle constitue, pour la première fois, une œuvre d'architecture temporaire bien réelle dans l'espace. Elle annonce sans aucun doute des formes nouvelles à venir, car l'une des caractéristiques de l'architecture contemporaine en général est son indépendance par rapport au sol, sa capacité au déplacement, alors que les structures « permanentes » tendent à reposer sur des fondations en béton et ne disparaissent qu'en cas de démolition.

27
Laurent Grasso & Pascal Grasso,
Nomiya, Palais de Tokyo, Paris,
France, 2009

27

MODULAIRE, DURABLE, TRANSPORTABLE

Pour l'architecture temporaire comme pour ses cousines plus permanentes, l'une des plus importantes fonctions à remplir est le logement. Bien que certains rêvent encore de maisons faites pour durer des siècles, l'époque moderne a vu apparaître des solutions de plus en plus transitoires, à commencer par les nombreux mobile homes américains. Le recours aux conteneurs d'expédition pour en faire des maisons facilement transportables a déjà été évoqué ici, mais une autre catégorie mérite l'attention. Le designer allemand Werner Aisslinger, inventeur du Loftcube, résidence temporaire à implanter en toiture (2003), a plus récemment conçu le Fincube, « une maison modulaire, durable et transportable, à faible consommation d'énergie » (2010, page 48). Ce projet se distingue par une préparation minimale du terrain, et le recours à des matériaux durables et recyclables. Il répond à de multiples problèmes posés par le logement en général, y compris la tendance croissante au nomadisme de certaines populations, même dans les pays développés.

Comme son nom l'exprime, l'Office of Mobile Design de Jennifer Siegal s'est spécialisé dans les structures modulaires transportables comme sa Prefab Show House (« Maison d'exposition préfabriquée », page 312) ou sa Taliesin Mod.Fab House (« Maison modèle préfabriquée Taliesin », page 318). Siegal s'était déjà intéressée aux conteneurs à l'occasion de son projet de Seatrain Residence à Los Angeles, petite maison privée composée de deux paires de conteneurs empilés réunis sous un toit de verre et d'acier. Son travail illustre également les similarités entre le logement préfabriqué et les logements transportables, souvent synonymes de faible coût de revient et d'un niveau de qualité relativement bas. Siegal a cependant choisi d'implanter une luxueuse cuisine Boffi au milieu de sa Prefab Show House, montrant du coup que ces structures ont accompli de grands progrès depuis l'époque de la Quonset Hut.

Il faut savoir, en effet, que nombre des initiatives actuelles dans le domaine des logements aisément transportables ou assemblables trouvent leur origine dans les recherches de l'armée américaine réalisées pendant la Seconde Guerre mondiale. Inspirée de l'abri Nissen britannique mis au point par le Corps royal britannique des ingénieurs pendant la Première Guerre mondiale pour remplacer la tente, une équipe travaillant à Quonset Point, dans l'État du Rhode Island, pour la marine américaine, conçut en 1941 la Quonset Hut, pour répondre aux besoins pressants d'abris transportables, faciles à monter et à produire en série. Dans ces différentes adaptations, ces abris semi-cylindriques inspirent encore aujourd'hui l'architecture temporaire partout dans le monde, même si leur conception sommaire ne correspond plus aux standards de confort du monde développé. Par ailleurs, l'esprit des pionniers américains partant vers l'Ouest avec tous leurs biens rassemblés dans un chariot, a sans doute contribué à cet état d'esprit favorable à la mobilité résidentielle.

JUSTE UNE FORME EXTRÊME D'ARCHITECTURE

L'agence new-yorkaise OBRA a créé un prototype de logement d'urgence (Red + Housing, page 306) pour une exposition qui s'est tenue en Chine, un an après le tremblement de terre dévastateur qui a touché la province du Sichuan, le 12 mai 2008. À l'aide de toile de parachute rouge et de contreplaqué, OBRA a cherché à démontrer que « du point de vue de la conception, le logement d'urgence n'est

28
Ira Koers, Roelof Mulder, Library
of the University of Amsterdam,
Amsterdam, The Netherlands, 2009

28

qu'une forme extrême d'architecture ». D'une surface de 45 mètres carrés pour un coût estimé à 5000 dollars, ce type de logement pourrait répondre à de nombreuses contraintes, tout en donnant l'occasion à l'architecture contemporaine de répondre à des demandes très concrètes. D'autres architectes, en particulier Shigeru Ban, ont ainsi consacré leur temps et leurs efforts à créer des abris d'urgence facilement montables sur place et d'un coût accessible.

Ban est l'auteur de la Paper Log House (« Maison en rondins de papier », Nagata, Kobe, Japon, 1995, page 18), petite construction de 16 mètres carrés d'un seul niveau. Conçue entre mai et juin 1995, l'année du grand tremblement de terre de Hanshin à Kobe, elle a été inspirée à l'architecte par la détresse d'un groupe de Vietnamiens qui vivaient toujours sous des tentes en plastique dix mois après le séisme. Shigeru Ban les avait interrogés sur leur situation et ils lui avaient expliqué que les logements proposés par l'administration étaient trop éloignés de leur lieu de travail, sans moyens de transport faciles et loin des écoles de leurs enfants. Il décida alors de créer pour eux ces abris temporaires : « L'objectif du projet était d'arriver à une construction bon marché que n'importe qui pouvait réaliser, d'aspect acceptable, et raisonnablement isolée de la température extérieure. La solution passait par des fondations faites de caisses de bière remplies de sable, des murs en tubes de carton (108 mm de diamètre, 4 mm d'épaisseur), un plafond et un toit en film plastique. Le projet se rapprochait d'une sorte de cabane en rondins. Les caisses de bière empruntées à un fabricant servaient également de marchepieds pendant le chantier. » La simplicité de ce procédé et le fait que les tubes en carton pouvaient être fabriqués sur place répondaient à tous les critères de résolution des problèmes de logement provoqués par le séisme. À la fin de l'été 1995, vingt-sept maisons de ce type avaient été construites pour des familles vietnamiennes et japonaises.

RÉFUGIÉS ET NOMADES

Ban a continué à créer divers abris de ce type comme ses Paper Emergency Shelters (« Abris d'urgence en papier ») pour le Haut Commissariat des Nations Unies pour les réfugiés (Camp de réfugiés de Byumba, Rwanda, 1999, page 47). Plus récemment, il a travaillé pour Haïti et la ville de L'Aquila (Italie), bien que les obstacles pratiques et administratifs aient rendu l'aide aux victimes de tremblements de terre, dans de telles circonstances, assez complexe. Le 12 janvier 2010, un séisme de magnitude 7 a frappé Port-au-Prince. Plus d'un million de personnes ont perdu leur foyer et plus d'un demi-million ont trouvé refuge dans des tentes montées à la hâte. Shigeru Ban a collaboré avec des enseignants et des étudiants de l'Universidad Iberoamericana et de la Pontificia Universidad Católica Madre y Maestra (République dominicaine) pour construire cent abris en tubes de carton et matériaux locaux.

Fasciné à l'évidence par les questions soulevées par l'architecture contemporaine, Shigeru Ban a beaucoup travaillé sur les utilisations des conteneurs et des tubes de carton, parfois en associant les deux, comme dans le cas avec son Nomadic Museum (Pier 54, New York, 2005, page 33 ; Santa Monica, Californie, 2006 ; Tokyo, 2007), une structure de 4800 mètres carrés destinée à abriter « Ashes and Snow » (Cendres et neige), une exposition de photographies grand format de Gregory Colbert. D'une longueur de 205 mètres pour 16 mètres de

29
Shigeru Ban, Paper Emergency
Shelters for the UNHCR, Byumba
Refugee Camp, Rwanda, 1999

29

hauteur, elle faisait essentiellement appel à des conteneurs ISO et à des tubes de carton en papier recyclé. Ce fut le premier bâtiment réalisé à New York à partir de conteneurs. Il a été réassemblé par la suite en Californie et au Japon à l'aide de conteneurs trouvés sur place.

CATASTROPHE DANS LE GOLFE, CONCERT AVEC BONO

Les exemples publiés dans ces pages ne représentent qu'une faible fraction des formes d'architecture temporaire observables dans le monde. Par exemple, les installations industrielles ou militaires n'ont pas été abordées, bien qu'elles fassent partie des types de structures éphémères les plus communes. La catastrophe de la plate-forme pétrolière Deepwater Horizon, qui s'est produite dans le golfe du Mexique en avril 2010, illustre l'ubiquité des réalisations de l'architecture industrielle temporaire à grande échelle et potentiellement dangereuses. À travers ses plans, en grande partie dictés, comme pour la Station spatiale internationale, par des considérations techniques, une structure flottante telle que Deepwater Horizon n'exerce pas plus d'influence sur les tendances de l'architecture contemporaine qu'elle n'a été l'œuvre d'un architecte. Elle constitue néanmoins une sorte de structure temporaire déplaçable, ce qui ne doit pas être oublié.

Finalement, toute architecture est temporaire, mais certaines structures sont censées durer plus longtemps que d'autres, et c'est au niveau de sa conception que l'architecture éphémère est la plus intéressante. Souvent libérée de bon nombre des contraintes qui pèsent sur la conception de bâtiments « permanents », elle offre, pour cette raison, une marge de liberté beaucoup plus grande aux architectes. En tant que telle, elle est une source potentielle d'inspiration pour le reste de l'architecture et peut jouer davantage sur les frontières entre l'art et l'architecture, ce qui incite à la fois les artistes et les architectes à franchir les lignes qui séparent leurs disciplines. Les résidences mobiles, les espaces événementiels et les logements pour réfugiés font tous partie du champ de l'architecture temporaire d'aujourd'hui. C'est le cas de la scène à 360° de la tournée internationale du groupe de rock U2, comme des filets et des poteaux qui constituent l'installation d'Idenburg et de Liu dans la cour du PS1 en 2010. *Temporary Architecture Now!* est le panorama d'une création encore plus fluide et dynamique que celle que l'on peut trouver dans d'autres volumes de la collection consacrés à des réalisations plus « solides » et moins originales. À de nombreux égards, c'est l'architecture la plus fascinante et la plus inventive du moment.

---

[1] William Shakespeare, Macbeth, acte V, scène v.
[2] L'Ecclésiaste 1:2.
[3] http://www.egypttoday.com/article.aspx?ArticleID=9064, consulté le 14 août 2010.
[4] http://www.seangodsell.com/future-shack, consulté le 15 août 2010.

WERNER AISSLINGER

Studio Aisslinger
Heidestr. 46–52
10557 Berlin
Germany

Tel: +49 30 31 50 54 00
Fax: +49 30 31 50 54 01
E-mail: studio@aisslinger.de
Web: www.aisslinger.de

WERNER AISSLINGER was born in Nördlingen, Germany, in 1964. He studied design at the University of Arts (Hochschule der Künste, 1987–91), Berlin. From 1989 to 1992, he freelanced with the offices of Jasper Morrison and Ron Arad in London and at the Studio de Lucchi in Milan. In 1993, he founded Studio Aisslinger in Berlin, focusing on product design, design concepts, and brand architecture. From 1998 to 2005, he was a Professor of Product Design at the Design College (Hochschule für Gestaltung) in Karlsruhe (Department of Product Design). He has developed furniture with Italian brands such as Cappellini and Zanotta and office furniture with Vitra in Switzerland. He works on product designs and architectural projects with brands like Interlübke, Mercedes-Benz, Adidas, and Hugo Boss. In 2003, he designed the Loftcube, a temporary residence intended for rooftop installation (Berlin), which would appear to have a conceptual relation to the Fincube (Ritten, Italy, 2010) published here.

WERNER AISSLINGER wurde 1964 in Nördlingen geboren und studierte Design an der Hochschule der Künste Berlin (1987–91). Zwischen 1989 und 1992 arbeitete er als freier Mitarbeiter für die Büros von Jasper Morrison und Ron Arad in London sowie für das Studio de Lucchi in Mailand. 1993 gründete er das Studio Aisslinger in Berlin, das sich auf Produktdesign, Designkonzepte und Markenarchitektur spezialisiert hat. Von 1998 bis 2005 war Aisslinger Professor für Produktdesign an der Hochschule für Gestaltung in Karlsruhe. Er entwickelte Möbel für italienische Hersteller wie Cappellini und Zanotta sowie Büromöbel für Vitra in der Schweiz. Aisslinger arbeitet an Produktentwürfen für Firmen wie Interlübke, Mercedes-Benz, Adidas und Hugo Boss. 2003 entwarf er den Loftcube, eine temporäre Wohneinheit, die sich auf Dächern installieren lässt (Berlin) und vom Konzept her erkennbar mit dem hier vorgestellten Fincube (Ritten, Italien, 2010) verwandt ist.

WERNER AISSLINGER, né à Nördlingen (Allemagne) en 1964, a étudié le design à l'Université des arts de Berlin (Hochschule der Künste,1987–91). De 1989 à 1992, il collabore en free-lance avec les agences de Jasper Morrison et Ron Arad à Londres et le Studio de Lucchi à Milan. En 1993, il fonde le Studio Aisslinger à Berlin, qui se consacre au design produit, aux concepts de design et à l'architecture de marques. De 1998 à 2005, il a été professeur de design produit à l'École supérieure de Design de Karlsruhe (Hochschule für Gestaltung). Il a créé des meubles pour des marques italiennes comme Cappellini et Zanotta, et du mobilier de bureau pour Vitra en Suisse. Il travaille aussi bien sur des projets de design que d'architecture pour des marques comme Interlübke, Mercedes-Benz, Adidas ou Hugo Boss. En 2003, il a conçu le Loftcube, résidence temporaire destinée à une toiture berlinoise, projet non sans lien conceptuel avec son Fincube (Ritten, Italie, 2010), publié ici.

FINCUBE

Winterinn, Ritten, South Tyrol, Italy, 2010

Area: 47 m². Client: Josef Innerhofter, Fincube. Cost: €150 000 (basic version).
Collaboration: Tina Bunyaprasit (Studio Aisslinger, Interior Design), Markus Lobis (Interior Wood Structure),
Matthias Prast (Finishes)

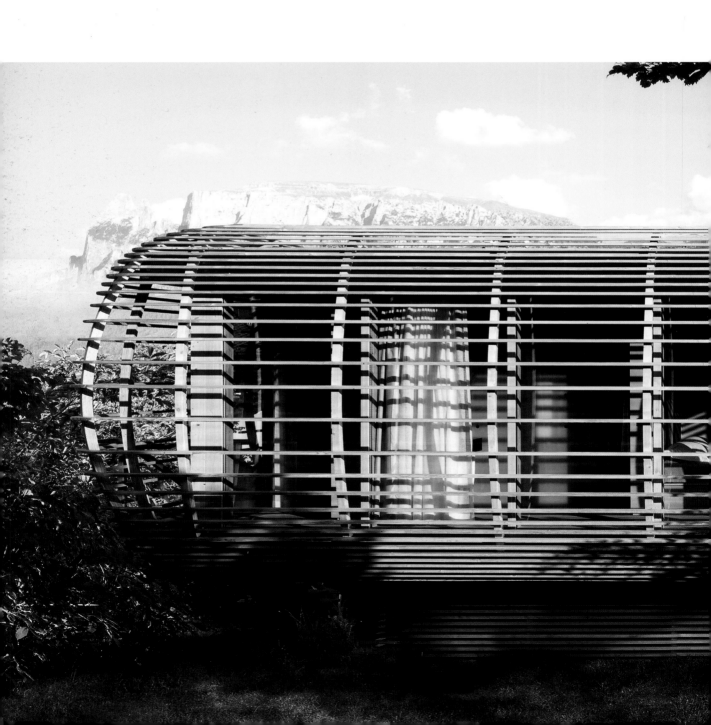

The extensive use of locally harvested larch and a double skin assures that this easily transportable house is also ecologically sound.

Dank der Nutzung lokaler Lärchenholzbestände und einer doppelten Außenhaut ist das transportable Haus auch ökologisch nachhaltig.

Le recours intensif au mélèze local et la double peau assurent à cette maison facilement transportable de réelles qualités écologiques.

According to the designer: "Natural high tech is the concept of this new modular, sustainable, and transportable low-energy house." The structure was installed at an altitude of 1200 meters above sea level in the South Tyrol and made with local collaboration. Built with locally harvested larch, the structure employs "long-lasting and recyclable materials," and so the **FINCUBE** can be dismantled and reassembled on another site. Triple glazing and a double façade are formed into a "unique overall mushroom-like monoshape." The client has envisaged placing a group of these residences in temporary locations, given that minimum preparation of the site is required.

Der Designer erklärt: „Das Konzept dieses neuen modularen, nachhaltigen und transportablen Niedrigenergiehauses ist naturverbundenes Hightech." Der Bau wurde in Tirol auf einer Höhe von 1200 m über N.N. errichtet und in Zusammenarbeit mit lokalen Firmen realisiert. Die Konstruktion aus regional geschlagenem Lärchenholz nutzt „langlebige und recycelbare Materialien", weshalb sich der **FINCUBE** demontieren und an anderen Standorten wieder errichten lässt. Dreifachverglasung und Doppelfassade sind zu einem „außergewöhnlichen, pilzähnlichen fließenden Gesamtkörper" geformt. Da der Baugrund nur minimal vorbereitet werden muss, plant der Auftraggeber, eine ganze Gruppe dieser Wohnbauten vor Ort zu errichten.

Selon le designer : « Le concept de cette nouvelle maison modulaire, durable, transportable, à faible consommation d'énergie est le high-tech naturel. » Cette structure en « cube » a été installée à une altitude de 1200 m dans le Tyrol du Sud en collaboration avec des entreprises locales. Réalisé en mélèze de la région, il fait appel à « des matériaux de longue durabilité et recyclables ». Le **FINCUBE** peut être démonté et réassemblé ailleurs. Sa double façade à triple vitrage présente une « forme monocoque originale de champignon ». Intéressé par le faible coût de préparation du terrain, le client a envisagé de réaliser un groupe de ces résidences destinées à la location temporaire.

Despite its double skin, the house remains quite open to its environment, as seen in the image above.

Trotz seiner doppelten Außenhaut öffnet sich das Haus zur Umgebung, wie die Aufnahme oben belegt.

Malgré sa double peau, la maison reste ouverte sur son environnement, comme le montre l'image ci-dessus.

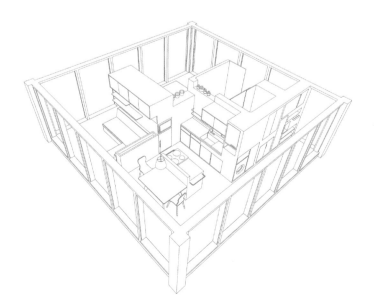

Renderings show the way the volume of the house sits above the site. An axonometric of the interior renders explicit the compact, square design. Above, a walkway behind the larch outer frame, and an interior view.

Renderings verdeutlichen die minimale Bodenversiegelung durch den Baukörper. Eine Axonometrie des Innenraums bietet Einblicke in den kompakten Entwurf auf quadratischem Grundriss. Oben eine hinter dem äußeren Lärchenrahmen verlaufende Holzgalerie sowie eine Innenaufnahme.

Ces deux images de synthèse montrent comment la maison repose sur son terrain. La vue axonométrique de l'intérieur précise la compacité des aménagements à l'intérieur de la forme carrée. En haut, une coursive entre les deux peaux et une vue de l'intérieur.

ATELIER BOW-WOW

Atelier Bow-Wow
8–79 Suga-Cho
Shinjuku-ku
Tokyo 160–0018
Japan

Tel: +81 3 3226 5336
E-mail: info@bow-wow.jp

Atelier Bow-Wow was established in 1992 by **YOSHIHARU TSUKAMOTO** and **MOMOYO KAIJIMA**. Yoshiharu Tsukamoto was born in 1965 in Tokyo and graduated from the Tokyo Institute of Technology (Doctorate in Engineering, 1987). He also studied at the École d'architecture (Paris, Belleville, UP8, 1987–88). He was a Visiting Associate Professor at UCLA (2007–08). Momoyo Kaijima was born in 1969 in Tokyo; she graduated from Japan Women's University (1991) and the Graduate School of the Tokyo Institute of Technology (1994) and studied at the ETH (Zurich, 1996–97). Their work includes the Hanamidori Cultural Center (Tokyo, 2005); the House and Atelier Bow-Wow (Tokyo, 2005); Mado Building (Tokyo, 2006); Pony Garden (Kanagawa, 2008); Machiya Guesthouse (Kanazawa, 2008); Mountain House (Nevada, USA, 2008); Four Boxes Gallery (Skive, Denmark, 2009); Machiya Tower (Tokyo, 2010); the installation Rendez-Vous, National Museum of Modern Art Tokyo (Tokyo, 2010, published here); and housing on the Rue Rebière (Paris, France, under construction, 2011), all in Japan unless stated otherwise.

1992 gründeten **YOSHIHARU TSUKAMOTO** und **MOMOYO KAIJIMA** ihr Büro Atelier Bow-Wow. Yoshiharu Tsukamoto, 1965 in Tokio geboren, schloss sein Studium am Tokyo Institute of Technology mit einer Promotion im Bauingenieurwesen ab (1987). Darüber hinaus studierte er an der École d'Architecture (Paris, Belleville, UP8, 1987–88) und war außerordentlicher Gastprofessor an der UCLA (2007–08). Momoyo Kaijima wurde 1969 in Tokio geboren und absolvierte ihr Studium an der Japan Women's University (1991), der Graduiertenfakultät des Tokyo Institute of Technology (1994) sowie der ETH Zürich (1996–97). Zu ihren Projekten zählen das Hanamidori Cultural Center (Tokio, 2005), das Haus und Atelier Bow-Wow (Tokio, 2005), das Mado Building (Tokio, 2006), der Pony Garden (Kanagawa, 2008), das Machiya Gästehaus (Kanazawa, 2008), das Mountain House (Nevada, USA, 2008), die Four Boxes Gallery (Skive, Dänemark, 2009), der Machiya Tower (Tokio, 2010), die Installation Rendez-Vous, National Museum of Modern Art in Tokio (2010, hier vorgestellt) sowie ein Wohnbauprojekt an der Rue Rebière (Paris, Frankreich, im Bau, 2011), alle in Japan, sofern nicht anders angegeben.

L'Atelier Bow-Wow a été fondé en 1992 par **YOSHIHARU TSUKAMOTO** et **MOMOYO KAIJIMA**. Yoshiharu Tsukamoto, né en 1965 à Tokyo, est diplômé de l'Institut de technologie de Tokyo (docteur en ingénierie, 1987). Il a également étudié à l'École d'architecture de Paris-Belleville (UP8, 1987–88) et a été professeur associé invité à UCLA (2007–08). Momoyo Kaijima, née en 1969 à Tokyo, est diplômée de l'Université féminine du Japon (1991), de l'École supérieure de l'Institut de technologie de Tokyo (1994) et a étudié à l'ETH (Zurich, 1996–97). Parmi leurs principales réalisations : le centre culturel Hanamidori (Tokyo, 2005) ; la maison-atelier Bow-Wow (Tokyo, 2005) ; l'immeuble Mado (Tokyo, 2006) ; Pony Garden (Kanagawa, 2008) ; la maison d'hôtes Machiya (Kanazawa, 2008) ; le chalet de montagne (Mountain House, Nevada, 2008) ; la galerie Four Boxes (Skive, Danemark, 2009) ; la tour Machiya (Tokyo, 2010) ; l'installation Rendez-Vous au Musée national d'art moderne de Tokyo (2010, publiée ici) et un projet d'immeuble de logements à Paris, rue Rebière (en construction, 2011).

RENDEZ-VOUS

National Museum of Modern Art Tokyo, Tokyo, Japan, 2010

Area: 52 m². Client: The National Museum of Modern Art Tokyo. Cost: not disclosed.
Collaboration: Yuki Chida, Reika Tatekawa

Designed between November 2009 and March 2010, this installation was placed in the forecourt of Yoshiro Taniguchi's National Museum of Modern Art Tokyo from April 29 to August 8, 2010. It was made of bamboo, steel, and reinforced concrete. Sensing the reticence of visitors to step onto the lawn of this rather strict space, Atelier Bow-Wow attempted "to ease this austere mood, while not letting go of the dignity of the place, but instead just slightly loosening up the atmosphere to turn it into a gentler space." Inspiring themselves from the name of the closest subway station (Takebashi, meaning "bamboo bridge"), they decided to work with bamboo. "Placing so-called architecture in the face of an architectural work by Yoshiro Taniguchi is not a good idea, as our construction is an ephemeral one after all and would therefore pale before the permanent structure." They imagined "some gigantic animal striding across" the wooded gardens of the nearby Imperial Palace. "The result," they wrote, "would be a mixing of human and animal, almost as if the two were meeting up in the forecourt of the museum." They conclude: "The main interest of Atelier Bow-Wow is to create spaces imbued with tolerance and generosity, fully aware of the interactive nature of architecture as a form of common cultural capital, or creative commons in public and shared platforms. This focus remains unchanged, whether the architecture in question is housing, a public space, or an installation for an art exhibition."

Die zwischen November 2009 und März 2010 entworfene Installation war vom 29. April bis 8. August 2010 im Vorhof des National Museum of Modern Art in Tokio zu sehen, einem Bau von Yoshiro Taniguchi. Die Konstruktion bestand aus Bambus, Stahl und Stahlbeton. Atelier Bow-Wow hatte den Eindruck, dass die Besucher zögerten, den Rasen des eher strengen Museumsgeländes zu betreten, und versuchten, „die strenge Atmosphäre aufzuhellen, ohne die Würde des Ortes anzutasten, vielmehr die Atmosphäre aufzulockern und dem Ort sanftere Seiten abzugewinnen." Angeregt durch den Namen der nächstgelegenen U-Bahnstation (Takebashi, „Bambusbrücke"), beschlossen sie, mit Bambus zu arbeiten. „Es schien keine gute Idee, etwas Architektonisches direkt neben einer Architektur von Yoshiro Taniguchi zu platzieren; schließlich wirkt unsere Konstruktion eher ephemer und wäre neben dem permanenten Bau verblasst." So erfanden sie ein „riesiges Tier", das sich durch die waldigen Gärten des nahe gelegenen Kaiserlichen Palastes „heranpirscht". „Das Resultat", schreiben sie, „war eine Kreuzung aus Mensch und Tier, fast so, als würden sich die beiden im Vorhof des Museum begegnen." Das Team fasst zusammen: „Das zentrale Interesse von Atelier Bow-Wow ist es, Räume zu schaffen, die von Toleranz und Großzügigkeit geprägt sind. Dabei sind wir uns zutiefst bewusst, dass Architektur interaktiv ist – im Sinne eines gemeinschaftlichen kulturellen Kapitals beziehungsweise eines Creative Commons (CC, dt. gemeinfreie Werke), das auf öffentlichen und gemeinschaftlich genutzten Plattformen präsent ist. Dieses zentrale Anliegen bleibt unverändert, ob es sich bei der fraglichen Architektur nun um Wohnbauten, öffentlichen Raum oder eine Installation für eine Kunstausstellung handelt."

Conçue entre novembre 2009 et mars 2010, cette installation en bambou, acier et béton armé, a été mise en place dans l'avant-cour du Musée national d'art moderne de Tokyo (Yoshiro Taniguchi architecte) du 29 avril au 8 août 2010. Conscient des réticences des visiteurs à marcher sur la pelouse de cet espace très formel, l'Atelier Bow-Wow a tenté « d'adoucir l'austérité de cette ambiance, sans rien perdre pour autant de la dignité du lieu, juste en détendant légèrement l'atmosphère pour en faire un espace plus aimable ». S'inspirant du nom d'une station de métro proche, Takebashi (« pont de bambou » en japonais), les architectes ont décidé d'opter pour le bambou. « Faire ce que l'on appelle de l'architecture face à une œuvre architecturale de Yoshiro Taniguchi n'est pas une bonne idée, mais notre projet qui pourrait faire pâle figure devant cette structure permanente n'est après tout qu'éphémère. » Ils ont imaginé « une sorte de gigantesque animal se déplaçant par grandes enjambées » dans les jardins boisés du palais impérial tout proche. « Il en résulte un mélange d'humain et d'animal, un peu comme si les deux se rencontraient dans cette avant-cour du musée… La principale préoccupation de l'Atelier Bow-Wow est de créer des espaces pénétrés de tolérance et de générosité, pleinement conscients de la nature interactive de l'architecture qui appartient au patrimoine culturel commun, des espaces communautaires créatifs dans des lieux publics et de partage. Cet objectif reste inchangé, que l'architecture en question soit des logements, un lieu public ou une installation pour une exposition artistique. »

The curious animal forms chosen for the installation by the architects clearly attracted passersby and others to explore the structures.

Ganz offensichtlich wirkt die ungewöhnliche Formgebung der Installation, die an ein Tier erinnert, einladend auf Passanten und Besucher und regt zum Entdecken an.

Les formes animalières voulues par les architectes attirent visiblement les passants et invitent à l'exploration.

Visitors are picnicking under the arching forms of the Rendez-Vous installation, fully justifying its title.

Besucher beim Picknick unter den Bögen der Installation, die ihrem Titel Rendez-Vous alle Ehre macht.

Des visiteurs piqueniquent sous les arches de l'installation Rendez-vous, qui justifie ainsi son titre.

AYBAR MATEOS

Aybar Mateos Arquitectos
Ibiza 17 2° derecha
Madrid 28009
Spain

Tel/Fax: +34 91 754 55 61
E-mail: estudio@aybar-mateos.com
Web: www.aybar-mateos.com

Aybar Mateos Arquitectos is directed by **CAMILA AYBAR** (born in Buenos Aires in 1976) and **JUAN JOSÉ MATEOS** (born in Madrid in 1976). They both studied at the ETSA Madrid and respectively at Columbia University and the Bartlett School. They have completed a number of buildings but have also worked on temporary exhibition stands, such as those for the glass manufacturer Vitro (2006 and 2008, published here). Their recent work includes the Capsicum Restaurant (Torrelodones, Madrid, 2009); JL House (Torrelodones, Madrid, 2010); Vitro Pavilion 2010 (IFEMA, Madrid, 2010); Espartales Norte, public housing (Madrid, 2006–11); the CIB Pavilion, Spanish Ministry of Science (Madrid, 2011); Aguas Vivas, public housing (Guadalajara, Spain, 2006–ongoing); and the refurbishment and extension of Torrelavega Town Hall (Torrelavega, Cantabria, 2009–ongoing), all in Spain.

Aybar Mateos Arquitectos arbeitet unter der Leitung von **CAMILA AYBAR** (geboren 1976 in Buenos Aires) und **JUAN JOSÉ MATEOS** (geboren 1976 in Madrid). Beide studierten an der ETSA Madrid sowie an der Columbia University beziehungsweise der Bartlett School of Architecture. Gemeinsam realisierten sie eine Reihe von Bauten und arbeiteten an temporären Messeständen, etwa für den Glashersteller Vitro (2006 und 2008, hier vorgestellt). Zu ihren aktuelleren Projekten zählen das Capsicum Restaurant (Torrelodones, Madrid, 2009), das JL House (Torrelodones, Madrid, 2010), der Vitro-Pavillon 2010 (IFEMA, Madrid, 2010), eine städtische Wohnanlage in Espartales Norte (Madrid, 2006–11), der CIB-Pavillon für das spanische Wissenschaftsministerium (Madrid, 2011), eine städtische Wohnanlage in Aguas Vivas (Guadalajara, 2006–andauernd) sowie die Sanierung und Erweiterung des Rathauses in Torrelavega (Torrelavega, Cantabria, 2009–andauernd), alle in Spanien.

L'agence Aybar Mateos Arquitectos est dirigée par **CAMILA AYBAR**, née à Buenos Aires en 1976, et **JUAN JOSÉ MATEOS**, né à Madrid en 1976. Tous deux ont étudié à l'ETSA de Madrid et respectivement à l'université Columbia et à la Bartlett School. Ils ont réalisé un certain nombre d'immeubles, mais ont également travaillé sur des projets de stands d'expositions temporaires comme ceux du verrier Vitro (2006 et 2008, publié ici). Parmi leurs réalisations récentes, toutes en Espagne : le restaurant Capsicum (Torrelodones, Madrid, 2009) ; la maison JL (Torrelodones, Madrid, 2010) ; le pavillon 2010 Vitro (IFEMA, Madrid, 2010) ; des logements sociaux Espartales Norte (Madrid, 2006–11) ; le pavillon CIB, ministère espagnol de la Science (Madrid, 2011) ; les logements sociaux Aguas Vivas (Guadalajara, 2006–en cours) et la rénovation et extension de l'Hôtel de Ville de Torrelavega (Cantabrie, 2009–en cours).

VITRO PAVILIONS

IFEMA, Madrid, Spain, 2006, 2008

Area: 200 m² and 320 m² respectively. Client: Vitro Cristalglass.
Cost: €75 000 (excluding glass) and €200 000 respectively

The 2006 **VITRO PAVILION** for the Madrid fair IFEMA was built with no less than 170 tons of glass. Assembled from 25 000 pieces, the structure was destroyed after the event. "We built just with glass, waste glass, extracted from other buildings," state the architects. "When glass sheets are cut there are always some un-used left-overs; we stored these pieces and recycled them in the pavilion." They made an orthogonal, flat exterior form with an "amorphous" interior. Dark glass was used on the bottom of the pavilion and the clearest varieties on top. The architects refer to the work of James Turrell and Bill Viola to describe the impressions created. Aybar Mateos describes the 2008 Pavilion as a "work in progress." Double-faced serigraphy with red and black dots individually invisible to the human eye was employed on ultra-clear glass, causing the apparent color of the glass to vary from red to black according to the position of visitors.

Der **VITRO-PAVILLON** für die IFEMA 2006 in Madrid wurde aus nicht weniger als 170 t Glas gebaut. Die aus 25 000 Einzelteilen errichtete Konstruktion wurde nach der Veranstaltung zerstört. „Wir bauten ganz einfach mit Glas, mit Glasabfällen anderer Bauten," erklären die Architekten. „Wenn Glasplatten zugeschnitten werden, fällt immer ungenutzter Verschnitt an. Diese Abfälle sammelten wir und recycelten sie für den Pavillon." Das Team entwarf einen rechtwinkligen Außenbau mit flachen Oberflächen und einen „amorphen" Innenraum. Im unteren Bereich des Pavillons wurde dunkles Glas, nach oben hin die hellsten Glassorten verbaut. Um die so geschaffenen Effekte zu beschreiben, stellten die Architekten Bezüge zu Arbeiten von James Turrell und Bill Viola her. Den Pavillon von 2008 bezeichnen Aybar Mateos als „work in progress". Hierfür wurde ultraklares Glas beidseitig mit einem Siebdruckmuster aus roten und schwarzen Punkten versehen, die einzeln für das bloße Auge nicht sichtbar sind. Je nach Position des Betrachters entsteht ein variierender Farbeindruck zwischen rot und schwarz.

Réalisé pour la foire madrilène IFEMA, le **PAVILLON VITRO** a nécessité pas moins de 170 tonnes de verre. Assemblée à partir de 25 000 morceaux de ce matériau, la structure a été détruite après la manifestation. « Nous avons uniquement utilisé du verre, du verre de recyclage, tiré d'autres bâtiments », expliquent les architectes. « Lorsque les panneaux de verre sont découpés, il reste toujours des déchets non utilisés. Nous les avons récupérés et recyclés dans le pavillon. » L'extérieur est de forme orthogonale et l'intérieur « amorphe ». Le verre le plus foncé a été utilisé en partie basse, le plus clair en partie haute. Les architectes se réfèrent aux œuvres de James Turrell et de Bill Viola pour décrire l'impression ainsi donnée. Aybar et Mateos décrivent également leur pavillon de 2008 comme une « œuvre en chantier ». Des panneaux de verre ultraclair ont été sérigraphiés de pastilles rouges et noires, chacune ne pouvant être perçue par l'œil. La couleur du verre semble alors varier entre le rouge et le noir, selon le point de vue du visiteur.

Above, the 2008 installation for Vitro at the IFEMA show in Madrid. Another view of this structure is shown on the right page (bottom).

Oben die Installation für Vitro auf der IFEMA 2008 in Madrid. Eine weitere Ansicht der Konstruktion rechts unten.

Ci-dessus, stand Vitro pour le salon IFEMA à Madrid. Page de droite en bas, une autre vue du projet.

Above, the 2006 Vitro stand created
by Aybar Mateos with no less than
170 tons of stacked glass sheets.

Oben der Vitro-Messestand 2006 von
Aybar Mateos. Der Entwurf bestand
aus nicht weniger als 170 t gestapelten Glasplatten.

Ci-dessus : le stand Vitro 2006 conçu
par Aybar Mateos n'utilisait pas
moins de 170 tonnes de plaques de
verre empilées.

Two images (above) show the solidity and translucency obtained by the architects with their idea of a massive quantity of stacked glass in the 2006 stand. Right page (top), an acoustic installation in the stand.

Die beiden Aufnahmen oben belegen, dass es den Architekten gelungen ist, sowohl Massivität als auch Translu-zenz zu vermitteln, indem sie für den Messestand 2006 Glasplatten in gro-ßen Mengen übereinander stapelten. Rechts oben eine Audioinstallation.

Deux images (à droite et à gauche) montrent la solidité et la translucidité obtenues par l'architecte à partir de l'empilement massif de plaques de verre dans le stand de 2006. Page de droite (en haut), installation acousti-que dans le stand.

On the right page, two views of the seating area in the stand, where the architects play on the reflections and coloring imposed on the impression given to visitors by the glass.

Auf der rechten Seite zwei Ansichten der Sitzbereiche auf dem Stand. Die Architekten spielen mit den Spiegel- und Farbeffekten, die durch das Glas erzeugt werden.

Page de droite, deux vues des zones de réception du stand. L'architecte joue sur les reflets et les couleurs produits par l'empilement du verre.

CECIL BALMOND

Balmond Studio / Unit 9
190a New North Road / London N1 7BJ / UK

Tel: +44 20 70 43 06 51
E-mail: info@balmondstudio.com
Web: www.balmondstudio.com

Born and educated in Sri Lanka, **CECIL BALMOND** came to London for postgraduate studies and joined Arup in 1968. He is an internationally recognized designer, structural engineer, and author, and Deputy Chairman of the multidisciplinary engineering firm Arup since 2004, where he founded the Advanced Geometry Unit (AGU). His notable books include *Number 9: The Search for the Sigma Code* (Prestel, 1998) and *Informal* (Prestel, 2002), which explores structure as catalyst in architecture. He is an external examiner at the Architectural Association in London and Senior Design Fellow at the London School of Economics. He has collaborated successfully with a number of major international architects, for example, with Rem Koolhaas on the Kunsthal (Rotterdam, the Netherlands, 1994); Grand Palais (Lille, France, 1994); Seattle Central Library (Seattle, Washington, USA, 2004); Casa da Música (Porto, Portugal, 2005); and the Serpentine Pavilion (London, UK, 2006); with Álvaro Siza on the Portuguese National Pavilion for Expo '98 in Lisbon (Portugal); with Daniel Libeskind on the latter's ill-fated World Trade Center projects (New York); and with the artist Anish Kapoor on the sculpture *Marsyas*, presented in London's Tate Modern in 2002. Other projects include the redevelopment of Battersea Power Station (London, UK, since 1999); Coimbra Footbridge (Coimbra, Portugal, 2006); the CCTV Headquarters building in Beijing (China, 2005–08, with OMA/Rem Koolhaas); *Tenemos*, the first of the Tees Valley Giants sculptures, with Anish Kapoor (Middlehaven, UK, 2008–09); UPENN Weave Bridge (Philadelphia, Pennsylvania, USA, 2008–09); and the design of the new Centre Pompidou-Metz (Metz, France, 2006–10, with Shigeru Ban).

CECIL BALMOND, geboren und ausgebildet in Sri Lanka, kam zu weiterführenden Studien nach London und schloss sich 1968 dem Büro Arup an. Balmond ist ein international bekannter Designer, Bauingenieur und Autor und seit 2004 stellvertretender Vorsitzender des multidisziplinären Ingenieurbüros Arup, wo er die Advanced Geometry Unit (AGU) gründete. Zu seinen wichtigsten Büchern gehören *Number 9: The Search for the Sigma Code* (Prestel, 1998) oder *Informal* (Prestel, 2002), in dem er sich mit Baukonstruktion als Katalysator in der Architektur beschäftigt. Er ist externer Prüfer an der Architectural Association in London und Honorarprofessor für Design an der London School of Economics. Er kooperierte erfolgreich mit zahlreichen international bedeutenden Architekten, etwa mit Rem Koolhaas an der Kunsthal Rotterdam (Niederlande, 1994), dem Grand Palais in Lille (Frankreich, 1994), der Seattle Central Library (Washington, USA, 2004), der Casa da Música in Porto (Portugal, 2005) und dem Serpentine Pavilion in London (2006), mit Álvaro Siza am Portugiesischen Pavillon für die Expo '98 in Lissabon, mit Daniel Libeskind an dessen vom Unglück verfolgten Plänen für das World Trade Center (New York), mit dem Künstler Anish Kapoor an der 2002 in der Tate Modern präsentierten Skulptur *Marsyas*. Weitere Projekte sind die Umgestaltung der Battersea Power Station in London (seit 1999), eine Fußgängerbrücke in Coimbra (Portugal, 2006), die CCTV-Zentrale in Peking (China, 2005–08, mit OMA/Rem Koolhaas), *Tenemos* (mit Anish Kapoor), der erste Beitrag für das Skulpturenprojekt Tees Valley Giants (Middlehaven, Großbritannien, 2008–09), die UPENN Weave Bridge in Philadelphia (Pennsylvania, USA, 2008–09) und die Planung des neuen Centre Pompidou-Metz (Frankreich, 2006–10, mit Shigeru Ban).

Né et formé au Sri-Lanka, **CECIL BALMOND** est venu à Londres pour y poursuivre des études supérieures et a rejoint l'agence Arup en 1968. Concepteur, ingénieur structurel et auteur de notoriété internationale, il est depuis 2004 vice-président de l'agence d'ingénierie multidisciplinaire Arup, au sein de laquelle il a fondé une Unité de géométrie avancée (AGU). Parmi ses écrits les plus importants figurent *Number 9, The Search for the Sigma Code* (Prestel, 1998) et *Informal* (Prestel, 2002) qui explorent la structure catalysatrice de l'architecture. Il est examinateur invité à l'Architectural Association de Londres et Senior Design Fellow de la London School of Economics. Son intérêt pour l'architecture et la conception l'a conduit à des collaborations remarquées avec quelques-uns des plus grands architectes mondiaux, par exemple avec l'architecte néerlandais Rem Koolhaas sur le Kunsthal de Rotterdam (1994) ; Lille Grand Palais (1994) ; la bibliothèque centrale de Seattle (Washington, 2004) ; la Casa da Música à Porto (2005) et le Pavillon 2006 de la Serpentine à Londres (2006). Il a aussi travaillé avec Álvaro Siza sur le projet du Pavillon national portugais pour Expo '98 à Lisbonne, avec Daniel Libeskind sur des projets malheureusement inaboutis pour le World Trade Center à New York, et a assisté l'artiste Anish Kapoor pour la sculpture *Marsyas* installée à la Tate Modern à Londres, en 2002. Parmi ses autres réalisations figurent la restructuration de la centrale électrique de Battersea à Londres (depuis 1999) ; la passerelle de Coimbra (Coimbra, Portugal, 2006) ; le siège de la chaîne de télévision chinoise CCTV à Pékin (2005–08, avec OMA/Rem Koolhaas) ; *Tenemos*, la première des sculptures des Géants de la Tees Valley avec Anish Kapoor (Middlehaven, Grande-Bretagne, 2008–09) ; le pont UPENN (Philadelphie, Pennsylvanie, 2008–09) et la conception du Centre Pompidou-Metz (2006–10, avec Shigeru Ban).

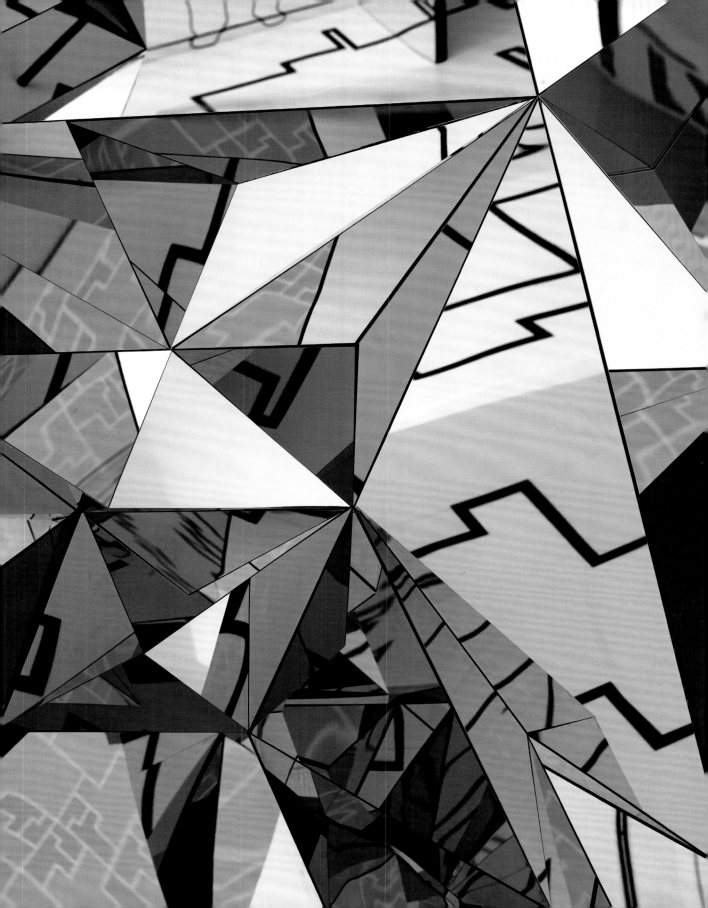

"ELEMENT—CECIL BALMOND"

Tokyo, Japan, 2010

Area: 1200 m². Client: Tokyo Opera City Art Gallery.
Cost: not disclosed

This exhibition on the work of Cecil Balmond, divided in three sections, was held in Tokyo from January 16 to March 22, 2010. The first part of the show, designed by the engineer, was called "Seeking Hidden Rhythms," and dealt with "the underlying order and rhythm that resides within nature…" The second section of the exhibition dealt with the "underlying mechanisms" of architecture. The point of this part of the show was to pose "the question of whether it is possible to create rich architecture that appears to grow naturally of its own accord, responding flexibly to complex factors and conditions, as opposed to rigid architecture consisting of pillars and beams in rigid horizontal and vertical planes." Two large works, called *H_edge*, made up of H-shaped aluminum plates, and *Danzer*, made up of four different types of tetrahedrons, were set in this part of the show. The final part of "**ELEMENT**" explained Balmond's ongoing collaboration with architects through photographs, drawings, and text.

Die Ausstellung zum Werk von Cecil Balmond gliederte sich in drei Teile und war vom 16. Januar bis 22. März 2010 in Tokio zu sehen. Der erste Teil der von Balmond persönlich gestalteten Ausstellung war mit dem Leitmotiv „den geheimen Rhythmus finden" überschrieben und war eine Auseinandersetzung mit „dem Grundordnungsprinzip und dem Rhythmus, der der Natur innewohnt …" Der zweite Abschnitt der Ausstellung befasste sich mit den „Grundmechanismen" der Architektur. Anliegen dieses Abschnitts war es, „die Frage zu stellen, ob es möglich ist, eine facettenreiche Architektur zu gestalten, die aus sich selbst heraus zu wachsen scheint und dabei flexibel auf komplexe Faktoren und Bedingungen reagiert, ganz anders als eine starre Architektur aus Stützen und Trägern in starren horizontalen und vertikalen Ebenen". In diesem Ausstellungsabschnitt befanden sich zwei raumgreifende Arbeiten: *H_edge*, ein Werk aus H-förmigen Elementen aus Aluminiumblech und *Danzer*, eine Arbeit aus vier verschieden geformten Tetraedern. Der abschließende Teil von **ELEMENT** dokumentierte Balmonds andauernde Kollaboration mit Architekten anhand von Fotografien, Zeichnungen und Texten.

Cette exposition sur l'œuvre de Cecil Balmond, divisée en trois sections, s'est tenue à Tokyo du 16 janvier au 22 mars 2010. La première partie, conçue par l'ingénieur, était intitulée « À la recherche des rythmes cachés » et traitait « de l'ordre et du rythme sous-jacents qui résident dans la nature… ». La seconde section abordait les « mécanismes sous-jacents » de l'architecture. Elle posait « la question de savoir s'il est possible de créer une architecture riche qui semble se développer naturellement d'elle-même, en répondant en souplesse à des conditions et des facteurs complexes, par opposition à une architecture rigide de poteaux et poutres déterminant des plans horizontaux et verticaux tout aussi rigides ». Deux œuvres de grandes dimensions, *H_edge* en panneaux d'aluminium en forme de H et *Danzer*, composée de quatre types de tétraèdres, étaient présentées dans cette section. La partie finale d'**ELEMENT** expliquait les nombreuses collaborations de Balmond avec des architectes sous forme de photographies, de dessins et de textes.

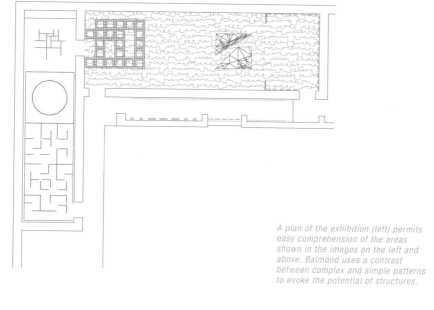

Der Grundriss (links) veranschaulicht die Lage der einzelnen Ausstellungsbereiche (links und oben). Balmond arbeitet mit dem Kontrast von komplexen und einfachen Mustern und visualisiert auf diese Weise das Potenzial bautechnischer Prozesse.

Le plan de l'exposition (à gauche) permet de mieux comprendre le fonctionnement des zones représentées à gauche et ci-dessus. Balmond utilise le contraste entre des motifs simples ou complexes pour évoquer le potentiel des structures.

A plan of the exhibition (left) permits easy comprehension of the areas shown in the images on the left and above. Balmond uses a contrast between complex and simple patterns to evoke the potential of structures.

Based entirely on his knowledge of engineering, "Element" comes across almost more like an art show than one related strictly to structural issues—thus, a point made is that when it is related to nature, engineering can be beautiful.

Balmonds Ausstellung „Element" beruht auf seinen Kenntnissen als Ingenieur, wirkt jedoch wie eine Kunstschau – und belegt unter anderem, dass bautechnische Planung von großer Schönheit sein kann, wo sie Bezüge zur Natur sucht.

Reposant entièrement sur la maîtrise de l'ingénieur, « Element » se présente davantage comme une œuvre artistique qu'une réflexion sur la structure. En se rapprochant de la nature, le travail de l'ingénieur touche à la beauté.

SHIGERU BAN

Shigeru Ban Architects
5–2–4 Matsubara
Setagaya-ku
Tokyo 156–0043
Japan

Tel: +81 3 3324 6760
Fax: +81 3 3324 6789
E-mail: tokyo@shigerubanarchitects.com
Web: www.shigerubanarchitects.com

Born in 1957 in Tokyo, **SHIGERU BAN** studied at SCI-Arc from 1977 to 1980. He then attended the Cooper Union School of Architecture, where he studied under John Hejduk (1980–82). He worked in the office of Arata Isozaki (1982–83), before founding his own firm in Tokyo in 1985. He has designed ephemeral structures such as his Paper Refugee Shelter made with plastic sheets and paper tubes for the United Nations High Commissioner for Refugees (UNHCR). He designed the Japanese Pavilion at Expo 2000 in Hanover. He installed his Paper Temporary Studio on top of the Centre Pompidou in Paris to work on the new Centre Pompidou-Metz (Metz, France, 2006–10). Other recent work includes the Papertainer Museum (Seoul Olympic Park, Songpa-Gu, South Korea, 2003–06); the Nicolas G. Hayek Center (Tokyo, 2005–07); the Takatori Church (Kobe, Hyogo, 2005–07), the last two in Japan; the disaster relief Post-Tsunami Rehabilitation Houses (Kirinda, Hambantota, Sri Lanka, 2005–07); the Paper Teahouse (London, UK, 2008); the Metal Shutter Houses on West 19th Street in New York (New York, USA, 2009); and the Paper Tube Tower (London, UK, 2009, published here).

SHIGERU BAN, 1957 in Tokio geboren, studierte von 1977 bis 1980 am Southern California Institute of Architecture (SCI-Arc). Anschließend besuchte er die Cooper Union School of Architecture, wo er bei John Hejduk studierte (1980–82). Bevor er 1985 sein eigenes Büro in Tokio gründete, arbeitete er bei Arata Isozaki (1982–83). Ban entwarf temporäre Bauten, so etwa Flüchtlingsquartiere aus Papier, die er aus Plastikplanen und Pappröhren für das UN-Flüchtlingskommissariat (UNHCR) realisierte. Für die Expo 2000 in Hannover entwarf er den Japanischen Pavillon. Auf dem Dach des Centre Pompidou in Paris hatte Ban ein temporäres Atelier aus Papier eingerichtet, um dort am neuen Centre Pompidou-Metz (2006–10) zu arbeiten. Andere jüngere Arbeiten sind u.a. das Papertainer Museum (Olympiapark Seoul, Songpa-Gu, Südkorea, 2003–06), das Nicolas G. Hayek Center (Tokio, 2005–07) und die Takatori-Kirche (Kobe, Hyogo, 2005–07), beide in Japan, sowie Einrichtungen für die Katastrophenhilfe nach dem großen Tsunami (Kirinda, Hambantota, Sri Lanka, 2005–07), das Paper Teahouse (London, 2008), die Metal Shutter Houses, West 19th Street (New York, 2009) sowie der Paper Tube Tower (London, 2009, hier vorgestellt).

Né en 1957 à Tokyo, **SHIGERU BAN** a étudié au SCI-Arc de 1977 à 1980 et à l'École d'architecture de la Cooper Union, auprès de John Hejduk (1980–82). Il a travaillé dans l'agence d'Arata Isozaki (1982–83) avant de fonder la sienne à Tokyo en 1985. Il a conçu des structures éphémères comme son abri en carton pour réfugiés fait de films en plastique et de tubes de carton pour le Haut Commissariat des Nations Unies pour les réfugiés (HCR). Il est l'auteur du Pavillon japonais pour Expo 2000 à Hanovre. Son atelier temporaire de papier a été installé au sommet du Centre Pompidou à Paris pour servir d'annexe à son agence pendant la construction du Centre Pompidou-Metz (2004–09). Parmi ses autres réalisations récentes : le Papertainer Museum (Séoul, Parc olympique, Songpa-Gu, Corée du Sud, 2003–06) ; le Nicolas G. Hayek Center (Tokyo, 2005–07) ; l'église de Takatori (Kobé, Hyogo, 2005–07) ; les maisons de la reconstruction post-tsunami (Kirinda, Hambantota, Sri Lanka, 2005–07) ; la maison de thé en carton (Paper Teahouse, Londres, 2008) ; les maisons à volets de métal (Metal Shutter Houses, West 19th Street, New York, 2009) et la tour en tubes de carton (Londres, 2009, publiée ici).

PAPER TUBE TOWER

London, UK, 2009

Area: 110 m². Client: London Design Festival. Cost: €80 000.
Collaboration: Jean de Gastines (Partner); Marc Ferrand, Alessandro Boldrini (Shigeru Ban Architects);
Mitsuhiro Kanada, Christian Dercks (Ove Arup)

This temporary structure was a 22-meter-high cone-shaped tower made up of four diameters of paper tubes connected by steel nodes. The paper tubes, each with a steel rod in its center designed to keep the connectors in compression, were dipped in resin to make them water-resistant, while the topmost cone was made of galvanized steel. The construction required six days on the South Bank Center site in London. The architect explains: "The foundations for the London Design Festival site were made with concrete blocks; but this could also be done with wooden boxes filled with sand for future programs."

Bei diesem temporären Bauwerk handelte es sich um einen 22 m hohen, kegelförmigen Turm aus Pappröhren. Die Röhren mit vier unterschiedlichen Durchmessern waren mit Stahlknotenpunkten verbunden. Durch ein Tauchbad in Harz waren sie wasserfest; innen waren sie mit einem Stahlstab verstärkt, der die Knotenpunkte unter Spannung hielt. Die abschließende Kegelspitze bestand aus verzinktem Stahl. Der Aufbau des Turms an seinem Standort am South Bank Center in London dauerte sechs Tage. Der Architekt führt aus: „Das Fundament des Turms für das London Design Festival bestand aus Betonblöcken. Bei weiteren Umsetzungen in der Zukunft ließe sich dies auch mit sandgefüllten Holzkisten realisieren."

Cette construction temporaire de forme conique de 22 m de haut a été réalisée à partir de tubes de carton de quatre diamètres différents, réunis pas des nœuds en acier. Chaque tube, renforcé par une tige d'acier centrale pour maintenir les connexions en compression, avait été plongé dans une résine pour l'imperméabiliser. Le sommet du cône était en acier galvanisé. Le chantier de construction sur le terrain du South Bank Center à Londres a duré six jours. L'architecte a expliqué que « les fondations utilisées pour le terrain du Design Festival de Londres étaient en béton, mais pourront, à l'avenir, être faites de caisses de bois remplies de sable ».

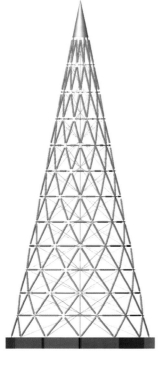

As is often the case, Shigeru Ban has made use of simple materials and elaborated an unusual form with the use of basic geometry, as can be seen in plan and elevation.

Wie so häufig arbeitet Shigeru Ban mit einfachen Materialien. Grundriss und Aufriss illustrieren, wie er ausgehend von einfachen geometrischen Elementen ungewöhnliche Formen entwickelt.

Comme souvent, Shigeru Ban a recours à des matériaux et des principes géométriques de base pour élaborer une forme étonnante, comme le montrent le plan et l'élévation.

TASCHEN FRANKFURT BOOK FAIR STAND

Frankfurt am Main, Germany, 2010

Area: 100 m². Client: TASCHEN. Cost: not disclosed.

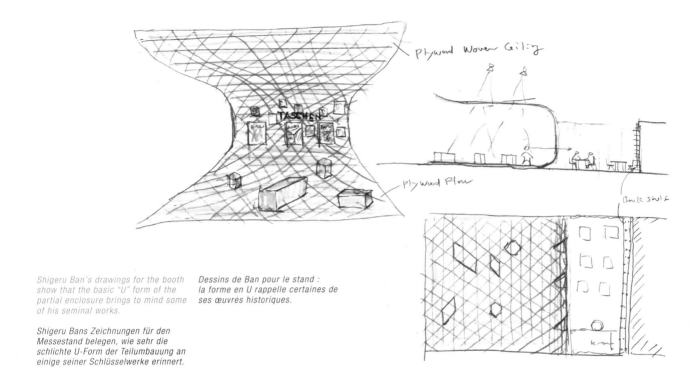

Shigeru Ban's drawings for the booth show that the basic "U" form of the partial enclosure brings to mind some of his seminal works.

Dessins de Ban pour le stand : la forme en U rappelle certaines de ses œuvres historiques.

Shigeru Bans Zeichnungen für den Messestand belegen, wie sehr die schlichte U-Form der Teilumbauung an einige seiner Schlüsselwerke erinnert.

The **TASCHEN STAND** at the 2010 Frankfurt Book Fair was designed specifically for the occasion by Shigeru Ban, the architect of the Centre Pompidou-Metz and the object of a recently published Taschen monograph. Indeed, the Metz project has a direct bearing on the ideas of the architect for Frankfurt. As he states: "The roof, wall, and floor were made using the same geometry—hexagon and triangle—that were used for the timber roof of the Centre Pompidou-Metz. This structure gives a warm and translucent atmosphere." Adhering to the principle of his works, such as the Wall-less House (Karuizawa, Nagano, Japan, 1996–97), the stand adopts a minimal structure, with no support on three sides. The tables or stands for the books were also designed according to the same geometric principles, originally derived by Shigeru Ban from the form of a Chinese hat he bought in Paris. The system selected allows the stand to be adjusted in size for use at other fairs in the future. In this instance, as in many others, Shigeru Ban has shown his interest in temporary structures and his openness to issues related to the commercial exploitation of architectural space.

Der **TASCHEN-STAND** auf der Frankfurter Buchmesse 2010 wurde eigens zu diesem Zweck von Shigeru Ban entworfen; Taschen widmete dem Architekten des Centre Pompidou-Metz kürzlich auch eine Monografie. Tatsächlich gibt es unmittelbare Bezüge zwischen dem Metzer Projekt und dem Konzept, das der Architekt für den Frankfurter Stand entwickelte. Ban erklärt: „Decke, Wände und Boden basieren auf denselben Geometrien – Hexagon und Dreieck – die sich auch in der Holzdachkonstruktion des Centre Pompidou-Metz finden. Die Struktur strahlt Wärme aus und ist lichtdurchlässig." Der Stand greift ein Prinzip auf, das schon andere Projekte Bans prägte, etwa das Wall-less House (Karuizawa, Nagano, Japan, 1996–97), und kommt mit minimaler baulicher Struktur aus: Drei Seiten der Konstruktion sind stützenfrei. Dasselbe geometrische Muster, zu dem Ban ursprünglich durch einen in Paris gekauften chinesischen Bambushut inspiriert wurde, findet sich auch in den Tischen und Pulten für die Bücher wieder. Das System ist flexibel und lässt sich für die Nutzung auf zukünftigen Messen modifizieren. Hier wie in vielen anderen Fällen zeigt sich Bans Interesse an temporären Bauten, jedoch auch seine Offenheit für die Nutzung von Architektur für gewerbliche Zwecke.

Le **STAND TASCHEN** à la Foire du livre de Francfort 2010 a été spécialement conçu pour cette manifestation par Shigeru Ban, l'architecte du Centre Pompidou-Metz, sujet par ailleurs d'une monographie publiée par Taschen. Le projet de Metz a exercé une influence directe sur les idées de l'architecte pour Francfort. « Le toit, le mur et le sol utilisent la même géométrie – hexagones et triangles – que celle de la toiture en bois de Metz. Cette structure crée une atmosphère lumineuse et chaleureuse », explique Ban. Proche du concept de réalisations comme la maison sans mur (Karuizawa, Nagano, Japon, 1996–97), le stand reposait sur une structure minimaliste sans support sur trois côtés. Les tables ou présentoirs de livres ont été conçus sur les mêmes principes géométriques, issus au départ de la forme d'un chapeau chinois que Ban avait trouvé à Paris. Le système permet également de modifier le stand pour l'adapter à d'autres foires dans le futur. Ici, comme souvent, Shigeru Ban montre son intérêt pour les structures temporaires et son ouverture d'esprit envers les contraintes de l'exploitation commerciale de l'espace architectural.

The basic floor plan is square, while the web-grid structure that forms the ceiling and back wall wrap around the floor and display space.

Der schlichte Grundriss basiert auf einem Quadrat, während die an ein Korbgeflecht erinnernde Konstruktion, die Decke und Rückwand bildet, auch Boden und Ausstellungsfläche umfängt.

À partir d'un plan au sol carré, la structure tramée qui constitue le mur du fond et le plafond semble envelopper l'espace d'exposition des livres.

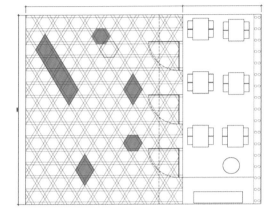

The stand is completely open on three sides, encouraging visitors to come and discover all the books, for example in the Architecture Now! series.

Der Stand ist an drei Seiten vollständig offen und lädt Besucher ein, das Verlagsprogramm zu entdecken, einschließlich der Architecture Now!-Reihe.

Le stand est entièrement ouvert sur trois côtés, ce qui facilite la découverte des livres par les visiteurs y compris la série Architecture Now!.

PAPER TEMPORARY SHELTERS IN HAITI

Port-au-Prince, Haiti, 2010–11

Area: 16 m² per shelter. Client: Voluntary Architects' Network (VAN). Cost: $300 per unit; total cost $30,000 for 50 units.
Collaboration: Universidad Iberoamericana (UNIBE), Santo Domingo, Dominican Republic

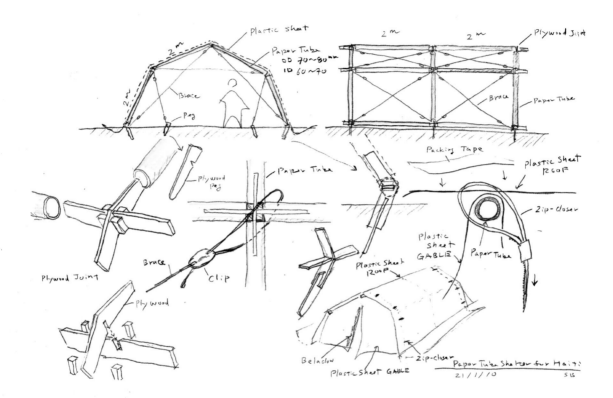

Shigeru Ban has worked on numerous structures destined to relief projects in earthquake or disaster zones, including his native Japan, Turkey, Sri Lanka, Sichuan, or L'Aquila, Italy. He has created a personal NGO called Voluntary Architects' Network for these projects. Subsequent to the earthquake that struck Haiti on January 12, 2010, he began an effort to provide temporary housing for some of the 500,000 people left without homes. He arrived in Port-au-Prince on February 14, 2010 with students and professors from the Universidad Iberoamericana (UNIBE) located in Santo Domingo. Working on a site near the U.S. Embassy, and working with the local population, he erected 37 hand-built shelters using polyurethane coated paper tubes, plywood joints and plastic tarps.

Shigeru Ban realisierte bereits zahlreiche Bauvorhaben für Flüchtlingsprojekte in Erdbeben- oder anderen Katastrophengebieten – in seinem Heimatland Japan ebenso wie in der Türkei, in Sri Lanka, Sichuan oder im italienischen L'Aquila. Zu diesem Zweck gründete er eigens eine NGO, das sogenannte Voluntary Architects' Network. Nach dem Erdbeben in Haiti vom 12. Januar 2010 machte er sich daran, Notunterkünfte für einige der rund 500 000 obdachlos gewordenen Menschen zu planen. Am 14. Februar 2010 erreichte er Port-au-Prince, zusammen mit Studierenden und Professoren der Universidad Iberoamericana (UNIBE) aus Santo Domingo. Auf einem Gelände unweit der U.S.-amerikanischen Botschaft errichtete er gemeinsam mit Anwohnern 37 Notunterkünfte von Hand, die aus polyurethanbeschichteten Pappröhren, Sperrholz-Steckverbindungen und Plastikplanen bestanden.

Shigeru Ban a travaillé sur de nombreux projets de structures de secours temporaires utilisables lors de tremblements de terre ou de désastres naturels, que ce soit pour son pays natal, le Japon, mais aussi pour la Turquie, le Sri Lanka, le Sichuan et la ville de L'Aquila en Italie. Il a fondé une ONG, Voluntary Architects' Network, pour mettre en œuvre ces projets. Arrivé à Port-au-Prince le 14 février 2010 accompagné d'étudiants et de professeurs de l'Université Ibéro-américaine (UNIBE) de Saint-Domingue, il a lancé un programme de logements temporaires pour 500 000 personnes victimes du tremblement de terre qui avait frappé Haïti le 12 janvier. Travaillant sur un terrain proche de l'ambassade américaine et à l'aide de la population locale, il a érigé 37 abris montés à la main en tubes de carton enduits de polyuréthane, d'articulations en contreplaqué et de bâches en plastique.

Images showing local residents participating in the construction of the Paper Shelters designed by Shigeru Ban for Haiti after the earthquake.

Anwohner beteiligen sich am Aufbau der Paper Shelters, die Shigeru Ban nach dem Erdbeben in Haiti entworfen hatte.

Images montrant des habitants participant à la construction des abris en carton conçus par Shigeru Ban pour Haïti, après le séisme.

Tents using a simple paper tube
structure and plastic sheeting are
erected in Haiti.

Aufbau der Zelte mit einer einfachen
Konstruktion aus Pappröhren und
Plastikplanen in Haiti.

Montage de tentes faites d'une simple ossature en tubes de carton et
d'une bâche de plastique.

Below, shelters being assembled with
an easy-to-install system that provides some protection from the elements and privacy.

Notunterkünfte werden errichtet (unten). Das einfache, von Hand montierbare System bietet zumindest etwas
Schutz vor der Witterung und ein
gewisses Maß an Privatsphäre.

Ci-dessous, construction des abris
faciles à monter. Ils offrent un certain
niveau d'intimité et de protection
contre les éléments.

BERNARDES + JACOBSEN ARQUITETURA

Bernardes + Jacobsen Arquitetura
Rua Corcovado 250
Jardim Botânico
22460–050 Rio de Janeiro, RJ
Brazil

Tel/Fax: +55 21 2512 7743
E-mail: bjrj@bja.com.br
Web: www.bja.com.br

THIAGO BERNARDES was born in Rio de Janeiro in 1974. The office of Bernardes + Jacobsen was created in 1980 by his father, **CLAUDIO BERNARDES**, and **PAULO JACOBSEN**, pioneers of a new type of residential architecture based on an effort to combine contemporary design and Brazilian culture. Thiago Bernardes worked in his father's office from 1991 to 1996, when he left to create his own firm, working on more than 30 residential projects between that date and 2001. With the death of his father, Thiago Bernardes reintegrated the firm and began to work with Paulo Jacobsen, who was born in 1954 in Rio. Jacobsen studied photography in London before graduating from the Bennett Methodist Institute in 1979. The office of Bernardes + Jacobsen currently employs approximately 50 people in Rio de Janeiro and São Paulo and they work on roughly 40 projects per year. Some of their significant projects include the Gerdau Headquarters (Santa Catarina, 2005); FW House (Guaruja, 2005); and the MPM Agency Main Office (São Paulo, 2006). Recent work includes the JH House (São Paulo, 2008); the JZ House (Bahia, 2008); RW House (Búzios, Rio de Janeiro, 2009); and the FN and DB Houses (both in São Paulo, 2009), all in Brazil. Published here is Container Art of 2008 (São Paulo, Brazil).

THIAGO BERNARDES wurde 1974 in Rio de Janeiro geboren. Schon 1980 gründete sein Vater **CLAUDIO BERNARDES** mit **PAULO JACOBSEN** das Büro Bernardes + Jacobsen. Die beiden Partner waren Pioniere einer neuartigen Wohnbauarchitektur, die zeitgenössische Gestaltung und brasilianische Kultur miteinander vereinte. Von 1991 bis 1996 war Thiago Bernardes im Büro seines Vaters tätig, und gründete anschließend sein eigenes Büro, mit dem er zwischen 1996 und 2001 über 30 Wohnbauprojekte realisierte. Nach dem Tod seines Vaters führte Thiago Bernardes die beiden Firmen zusammen und begann seine Zusammenarbeit mit Paulo Jacobsen, der 1954 in Rio geboren wurde. Jacobsen studierte Fotografie in London, bevor er sein Studium 1979 am Bennett Methodist Institute abschloss. Bernardes + Jacobsen beschäftigt derzeit rund 50 Mitarbeiter in Rio de Janeiro und São Paulo und arbeitet an etwa 40 Projekten pro Jahr. Ausgewählte Schlüsselprojekte sind u.a. die Gerdau-Zentrale (Santa Catarina, 2005), das FW House (Guaruja, 2005) sowie die Hauptniederlassung der Agentur MPM (São Paulo, 2006). Neuere Projekte sind u.a. das JH House (São Paulo, 2008), das JZ House (Bahia, 2008), das RW House (Búzios, Rio de Janeiro, 2009) sowie das FN House und das DB House (beide in São Paulo, 2009), alle in Brasilien. Hier vorgestellt wird ihr Projekt Container Art (São Paulo, 2008).

THIAGO BERNARDES est né à Rio de Janeiro en 1974. L'agence Bernardes + Jacobsen a été fondée en 1980 par son père, **CLAUDIO BERNARDES**, et **PAULO JACOBSEN**, pionniers d'un nouveau type d'architecture résidentielle qui voulait associer un'e conception contemporaine à la culture brésilienne. Thiago Bernardes a travaillé dans l'agence paternelle de 1991 à 1996, puis a créé sa propre structure, réalisant plus de 30 projets résidentiels jusqu'en 2001. Après le décès de son père, il a réintégré l'agence de celui-ci et commencé à collaborer avec Paulo Jacobsen, né en 1954 à Rio de Janeiro. Jacobsen avait également étudié la photographie à Londres, avant d'être diplômé du Bennett Methodist Institute en 1979. L'agence Bernardes + Jacobsen emploie actuellement environ 50 personnes à Rio de Janeiro et São Paulo, et travaille sur une quarantaine de projets environ chaque année. Parmi leurs réalisations les plus significatives : le siège de Gerdau (Santa Catarina, 2005) ; la maison FW (Guaruja, 2005) et le siège de l'agence MPM (São Paulo, 2006). Parmi leurs travaux actuels : les maisons JH (Sao Paulo, 2008), JZ (Bahia, 2008), RW (Búzios, Rio de Janeiro, 2009), FN et DB (São Paulo, 2009) ainsi que le projet Container Art (São Paulo, 2008, publié ici).

CONTAINER ART

São Paulo, Brazil, 2008

Area: 1200 m². Client: not disclosed. Cost: not disclosed

On the concrete esplanade of the Villa Lobos Park in São Paulo the architects used shipping containers to temporarily house an international video art exhibition. The mobility and also the modular nature of the containers were key elements in the design; however, the fact that they were rented for the event meant that structural modifications were not possible. Protective wooden squares assured that the containers did not damage the existing esplanade. 20 and 40 ft containers were used. Careful attention was paid to the existing visual axes and the architects adopted a 2.1.1.2.1 rhythm in their arrangement of the metal containers. They state: "The composition, treated as a great installation inside the park, could be seen from the street of its main access, creating a subtle counterpoint in the predominantly green and organic landscape, merging full volumes and empty spaces, inviting the users."

Die Architekten arbeiteten mit alten Frachtcontainern, um eine temporäre, internationale Ausstellung für Videokunst auf einer Betonesplanade im Villa-Lobos-Park in São Paulo zu präsentieren. Mobilität und Modulhaftigkeit der Container waren Schlüsselaspekte des Entwurfs. Da sie für die Veranstaltung jedoch nur angemietet wurden, konnten keine konstruktiven Modifikationen vorgenommen werden. Schützende quadratische Holzplatten sorgten dafür, dass die Esplanade nicht von den Containern beschädigt wurde. Zum Einsatz kamen 20- und 40-Fuß-Container. Besonders berücksichtigt wurden bestehende Sichtachsen. Bei der Anordnung der Stahlcontainer entschieden sich die Architekten für einen 2.1.1.2.1-Rhythmus. Sie führen aus: „Die Komposition wurde wie eine Großinstallation im Park interpretiert. Sie war durch den Hauptzugang schon von der Straße aus sichtbar und bildete einen subtilen Kontrapunkt inmitten der überwiegend grünen, organischen Landschaft. Hier verschmolzen massive Volumina und leere Räume zu einem Ganzen und luden die Besucher ein."

C'est sur l'esplanade en béton du parc Villa-Lobos à São Paulo que les architectes ont réalisé cette construction temporaire faite de conteneurs d'expédition pour une exposition internationale d'art vidéo. La mobilité et la modularité des conteneurs sont parmi les éléments clés de ce projet, bien que le fait qu'ils aient été loués interdisait de les modifier structurellement. Des cadres de bois posés au sol évitaient aux conteneurs de 20 et 40 pieds de long d'endommager l'esplanade. Une attention particulière a été portée aux alignements pour lesquels les architectes ont adopté un rythme d'implantation de 2.1.1.2.1 des conteneurs en métal. « La composition, traitée comme une installation de grandes dimensions, était visible de l'accès principal et offrait un contrepoint subtil à un environnement essentiellement vert et organique. Il associait des volumes pleins et des espaces vides, et incitait les visiteurs à entrer », ont expliqué les architectes.

By alternating types of containers and their placement, the architects achieve a rather powerful form that is of course entirely temporary. Their essentially "blind" nature is well suited to the projection of video art.

Durch verschiedene, im Wechsel angeordnete Containertypen gelingt den Architekten eine ausdrucksstarke Bauform, die naturgemäß temporär ist. Die im Grunde „blinden" Boxen eignen sich ideal für die Präsentation von Videokunst.

En alternant les types de conteneurs et leur mise en place, les architectes obtiennent un ensemble d'aspect assez solide, qui reste bien sûr entièrement temporaire. Leur fermeture quasi totale est bien adaptée à la présentation d'œuvres d'art vidéo.

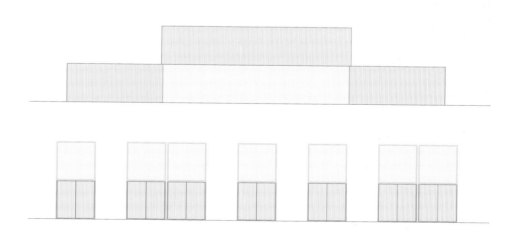

Since the containers themselves are conceived along modular lines, they are well adapted to a stacked grid system of placement.

Die modular konzipierten Container bieten sich für rasterförmige Stapel-konfigurationen an.

Conçus dans un esprit modulaire, les conteneurs se prêtent bien à un empilement selon une trame.

A site plan shows the park and the placement of the containers with a red square. Images make clear how some containers are lifted off the ground, and (right, below) how they are used for the projection of videos.

Ein Lageplan des Parks mit der rot eingezeichneten Containerkonstruktion. Die Aufnahmen illustrieren, dass manche Container scheinbar über dem Boden schweben und wie sie für die Präsentation der Videos genutzt werden (rechts unten).

Un plan du site montre le parc et l'emplacement des conteneurs (carré rouge). Les images représentent les conteneurs en passerelle, utilisés comme cabine vidéo.

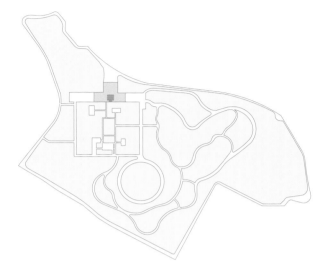

BIG

BIG
Bjarke Ingels Group
Nørrebrogade 66d, 2nd floor
2200 Copenhagen N
Denmark

Tel: +45 72 21 72 27
Fax: +45 35 12 72 27
E-mail: big@big.dk
Web: www.big.dk

BJARKE INGELS was born in 1974 in Copenhagen. He graduated from the Royal Academy of Arts School of Architecture (Copenhagen, 1999) and attended the ETSAB School of Architecture (Barcelona). He created his own office in 2005 under the name Bjarke Ingels Group (BIG), after having cofounded PLOT Architects in 2001 and collaborated with Rem Koolhaas at OMA (Rotterdam). In 2004 he was awarded the Golden Lion at the Venice Biennale for the Stavanger Concert House. One of his latest completed projects, the Mountain (Copenhagen, Denmark, 2006–08), has received numerous awards including the World Architecture Festival Housing Award, Forum Aid Award, and the MIPIM Residential Development Award. BIG has recently undertaken the design of the National Library of Astana (Kazakhstan) and Tallin Town Hall (Estonia). Their Danish Pavilion for Expo 2010 (Shanghai, China, published here) and the Danish Maritime Museum (Elsinore, Denmark, 2011) are amongst numerous projects that make BIG one of the most carefully watched young architecture firms in the world.

BJARKE INGELS wurde 1974 in Kopenhagen geboren. Er schloss sein Studium an der Fakultät für Architektur der Royal Academy of Arts ab (Kopenhagen, 1999) und besuchte die Architekturfakultät der ETSAB in Barcelona. 2005 gründete er sein eigenes Büro Bjarke Ingels Group (BIG), nachdem er 2001 bereits PLOT Architects mitbegründet und mit Rem Koolhaas/OMA (Rotterdam) zusammengearbeitet hatte. Für seinen Entwurf des Konzerthauses in Stavanger erhielt er 2004 auf der Biennale in Venedig den Goldenen Löwen. Eines seiner aktuellsten Projekte, Mountain (Kopenhagen, Dänemark, 2006–08), wurde mit zahlreichen Preisen ausgezeichnet, darunter dem World Architecture Festival Housing Award, dem Forum Aid Award und dem MIPIM Residential Development Award. In jüngster Zeit übernahm BIG den Entwurf der Nationalbibliothek in Astana (Kasachstan) sowie des Rathauses in Tallin (Estland). Der Dänische Pavillon für die Expo 2010 (Shanghai, China, hier vorgestellt) und das Dänische Handels- und Seefahrtsmuseum (Elsinore, Dänemark, 2011) sind nur einige der zahlreichen Projekte, die BIG zu einem mit größter Aufmerksamkeit beobachteten jungen Architekturbüro der Welt machen.

BJARKE INGELS, né en 1974 à Copenhague, est diplômé de l'École d'architecture de l'Académie royale des arts (Copenhague, 1999) et a également étudié à l'ETSAB de Barcelone. Il a créé son agence en 2005 sous le nom de Bjarke Ingels Group (BIG), après avoir participé à la fondation de PLOT Architects en 2001 et collaboré avec Rem Koolhaas à OMA (Rotterdam). En 2004, il a reçu le Lion d'or de la Biennale de Venise pour la salle de concerts de Stavanger. L'une de ses dernières réalisations, Mountain (Copenhague, 2006–08), a reçu de nombreux prix dont le World Architecture Festival Housing Award, le Forum Aid Award et le MIPIM Residential Development Award. L'agence a récemment entrepris la construction de la Bibliothèque nationale d'Astana (Kazakhstan) et de l'Hôtel de Ville de Tallin (Estonie). Le Pavillon danois pour Expo 2010 (Shanghaï, Chine, publié ici) et le Musée maritime danois (Elsinore, Danemark, 2011) sont parmi les nombreux projets qui font de BIG l'une des jeunes agences les plus remarquées sur le marché mondial de l'architecture.

DANISH PAVILION

Expo 2010, Shanghai, China, 2009–10

Area: 3000 m². Client: EBST. Cost: $9 million.
Collaboration: 2+1, Arup AGU, Arup Shanghai, Tongji Design Institute, Ai Wei Wei,
Jeppe Hein, Martin De Thurah, Peter Funch

Bjarke Ingels states: "When we visited the World Exhibition in Saragossa, we were stunned by the artificial content. State propaganda in papier-mâché. The **DANISH EXPO PAVILION** 2010 is the real deal, and not just endless talking. You can ride the city bike, take a swim in the harbor bath, and see the real Little Mermaid." Three hundred city bicycles were provided for visitors to use in the "traffic loop" of the pavilion. The monolithic steel structure was painted white to reduce heat gain in the summer. The Little Mermaid was presented in Shanghai because the Hans Christian Andersen fable on which the sculpture is based is well known in China. A multimedia artwork by Ai Wei Wei, including a live broadcast of the sculpture in China, was used to replace the landmark in Copenhagen.

Bjarke Ingels berichtet: „Als wir die Expo in Saragossa besuchten, waren wir schockiert von der Künstlichkeit der Exponate. Staatspropaganda aus Pappmaché. Der **DÄNISCHE PAVILLON** für die Expo 2010 ist etwas Echtes statt leerer Worthülsen. Man kann hier auf einem Stadtrad fahren, im Hafenbecken schwimmen und die echte Kleine Meerjungfrau sehen." Dreihundert Stadträder wurden für die Besucher bereitgestellt, um die „Verkehrsschleife" des Pavillons befahren zu können. Der Stahlbaumonolith wurde weiß gestrichen, um den Wärmegewinn im Sommer zu reduzieren. Die Kleine Meerjungfrau sollte auch deshalb in Shanghai gezeigt werden, weil das gleichnamige Märchen von Hans Christian Andersen in China weithin bekannt ist. Eine Multimediaarbeit von Ai Wei Wei, inklusive einer Liveschaltung zur Skulptur in China, ersetzte unterdessen das Wahrzeichen in Kopenhagen.

Comme l'explique Bjarke Ingels : « Lorsque nous avons visité l'Exposition internationale de Saragosse, nous avons été surpris par le côté artificiel de son contenu. C'était de la propagande officielle en papier mâché. Le **PAVILLON DANOIS** pour l'Exposition de 2010 est quelque chose de réel, pas un vague discours. Vous pouvez emprunter un vélo, vous baigner dans le bassin du port et voir *La Petite Sirène*, la vraie. » Trois cents vélos urbains ont été mis à la disposition des visiteurs pour parcourir la « boucle de circulation » du pavillon. Sa structure monolithique en acier était peinte en blanc pour réduire le gain thermique en été. *La Petite Sirène* a été présentée à Shanghaï parce que le conte d'Andersen qui l'a inspirée est bien connu en Chine. Pendant ce temps, à Copenhague, une œuvre multimédia d'Ai Wei Wei, qui comprenait une vision en direct de la sculpture transportée en Chine, avait pris la place du petit monument danois.

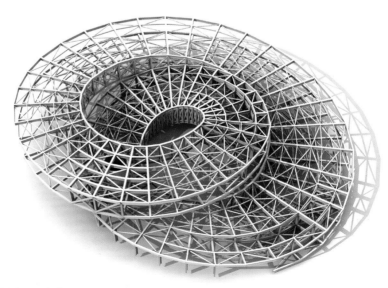

The basic shape of the pavilion is an ascending spiral with walkways that allow visitors to reach the uppermost level.

Die Grundform des Pavillons ist eine aufsteigende Spirale mit Rampen, über die Besucher die oberste Ebene erreichen.

La forme du pavillon est une spirale ascendante entourée d'une coursive permettant aux visiteurs d'atteindre son sommet.

The entire concept of the pavilion is related to the exhibition of the Little Mermaid brought specially to Shanghai from the harbor of Copenhagen where it is normally sited.

Der Pavillon wurde konzeptionell auf die Kleine Meerjungfrau abgestimmt, die eigens aus dem Kopenhagener Hafen nach Shanghai transportiert wurde, um dort präsentiert zu werden.

Tout le concept du pavillon repose sur la mise en scène de La Petite Sirène spécialement transportée pour l'occasion du port de Copenhague à Shanghaï.

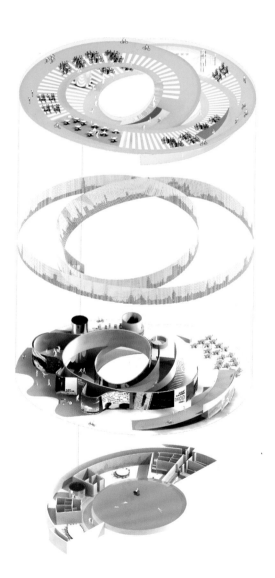

The spiral shape allows different moods and activities to be introduced into a continuous experience for visitors, again centered around the Little Mermaid statue.

Durch die Spiralform entstehen Bereiche unterschiedlicher Stimmung und Funktion – für die Besucher ein fließendes Gesamterlebnis, dessen Mittelpunkt wiederum die Kleine Meerjungfrau ist.

La forme en spirale permet de créer diverses ambiances et activités le long du parcours de la visite, centrée sur La Petite Sirène.

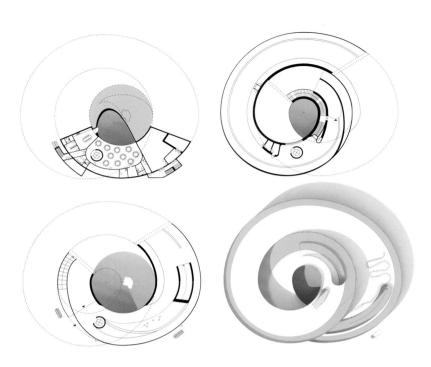

The sweeping curves of the pavilion
envelope the statue and create a sur-
prisingly dynamic, yet solemn space.

Die ausgreifenden, geschwungenen
Formen des Pavillons umfangen die
Statue. Es entsteht ein überraschend
dynamischer und dennoch kontempla-
tiver Raum.

Les courbes enveloppantes du pavillon se lovent autour de la statue en
créant un espace plein de solennité,
mais étonnement dynamique.

The architects use the generous spaces within the spiral structure to selectively filter natural light, generating a series of spatial surprises within the outwardly simple shape of the building.

Die Architekten interpretieren die großzügigen Flächen im spiralförmigen Bau durch die selektive Filterung von Tageslicht und sorgen so immer wieder für räumliche Überraschungen in der nach außen so schlicht wirkenden Gebäudeform.

Les généreux volumes sont éclairés par la lumière naturelle filtrée sélectivement pour ménager des surprises spatiales à l'intérieur de la forme extrêmement simple.

BUCHNER BRÜNDLER ARCHITEKTEN

Buchner Bründler Architekten
Utengasse 19
4858 Basel
Switzerland

Tel: +41 61 381 81 11
Fax: +41 61 383 97 78
E-mail: mail@bbarc.ch
Web: www.bbarc.ch

Buchner Bründler Architects was established by **DANIEL BUCHNER** and **ANDREAS BRÜNDLER** in Basel in 1997. Born in Berneck, Switzerland, in 1967, Daniel Buchner graduated from the University of Applied Sciences in Basel in 1993 and worked for Morger & Degelo Architects in Basel before creating the present firm. He was a Guest Professor at the École Polytechnique Fédérale de Lausanne (EPFL) in 2008 and Guest Lecturer at the ETH in Zurich in 2010. Andreas Bründler was born in 1967 in Sins, Switzerland. He graduated from the University of Applied Sciences in Basel in 1993 as well, working with Miller & Maranta Architects in Basel prior to establishing the current partnership with Buchner. He was also a Guest Lecturer at the ETH in Zurich in 2010. They have built houses in Büren (2000–02); Blonay (2001–02); and Aesch (2003–04); and the Set & Sekt Retail Store and Bar (Basel, 2007), all in Switzerland. The pair participated in artist Ai Wei Wei's scheme for a public park in Jinhua (China, 2006–07) and also in his Ordos project (Ordos, Mongolia), and is currently working on houses in Berzona, Ticino, and Ettingen, in Switzerland. They designed the Swiss Pavilion for Expo 2010 in Shanghai (China, published here).

Buchner Bründler Architekten wurde 1997 von **DANIEL BUCHNER** und **ANDREAS BRÜNDLER** in Basel gegründet. Daniel Buchner, geboren 1967 in Berneck, Schweiz, absolvierte seinen Abschluss 1993 an der Ingenieurschule beider Basel und arbeitete vor der Gründung des eigenen Büros für Morger & Degelo Architekten, ebenfalls in Basel. 2008 war er Gastprofessor an der École Polytechnique Fédérale de Lausanne (EPFL) und 2010 Gastdozent an der ETH Zürich. Andreas Bründler wurde 1967 in Sins, Schweiz, geboren. Auch er schloss sein Studium 1993 an der Ingenieurschule beider Basel ab und arbeitete für Miller & Maranta Architekten in Basel, ehe er seine Partnerschaft mit Buchner aufnahm. Auch er war 2010 Gastdozent an der ETH Zürich. Das Team baute Häuser in Büren (2000–02), Blonay (2001–02) und Aesch (2003–04) sowie Set & Sekt, Laden und Bar (Basel, 2007), alle in der Schweiz. Die beiden waren zudem an zwei Projekten des Künstlers Ai Wei Wei beteiligt, dem Entwurf eines öffentlichen Parks in Jinhua (China, 2006–07) sowie dem Ordos-Projekt (Ordos, Mongolei). Aktuell arbeiten sie an Häusern in Berzona, Tessin, und Ettingen, Schweiz. Sie entwarfen den Schweizer Pavillon für die Expo 2010 in Shanghai (China, hier vorgestellt).

L'agence Buchner Bründler Architekten a été fondée par **DANIEL BUCHNER** et **ANDREAS BRÜNDLER** à Bâle en 1997. Né à Berneck (Suisse) en 1967, Daniel Buchner est diplômé de l'Université des sciences appliquées de Bâle (1993) et a travaillé pour l'agence Morger & Degelo à Bâle avant de créer son agence actuelle. Il a été professeur invité à l'École Polytechnique Fédérale de Lausanne (EPFL) en 2008 et conférencier invité de l'ETH de Zurich en 2010. Andreas Bründler, né en 1967 à Sins (Suisse), est également diplômé de l'Université des sciences appliquées de Bâle (1993) et a travaillé pour les architectes Miller & Maranta à Bâle avant de s'associer avec Buchner. Il a été également conférencier invité à l'ETH de Zurich en 2010. En Suisse, ils ont construit des maisons à Büren (2000–02), Blonay (2001–02), Aesch (2003–04) et le magasin et bar Set & Sekt (Bâle, 2007). Les deux architectes ont participé au projet de l'artiste Ai Wei Wei d'un parc public à Jinhua (Chine, 2006–07) ainsi qu'à son projet Ordos (Ordos, Mongolie) et travaillent actuellement sur des projets de maisons à Berzona (Tessin) et Ettingen, toujours en Suisse. Ils ont conçu le Pavillon suisse pour l'Expo 2010 à Shanghaï (Chine, publié ici).

SWISS PAVILION

Expo 2010, Shanghai, China, 2010

Area: 2400 m². Client: Federal Department of Foreign Affairs FDFA General Secretariat GS-FDFA with Presence Switzerland, Berne, Switzerland. Cost: €8 million. Collaboration: Stefan Oehy, Friederike Kluge, Jonas Staehelin, Xu Zhang, Florian Rink, Magdalena Falska, Nick Waldmeier (Competition), Bülend Yigin (Competition)

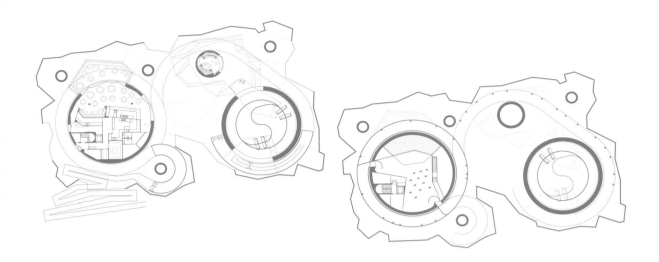

The external net with LED lights gives the façade a particularly permeable presence, much more inviting to visitors than a more traditional, closed building.

Durch ein mit LEDs besetztes Netz wirkt die Fassade besonders durchlässig und auf Besucher wesentlich einladender als ein konventionelleres, geschlosseneres Gebäude.

Le filet extérieur à éclairages DEL rend la façade particulièrement perméable. Elle est plus accueillante que celle d'un bâtiment traditionnel fermé.

Plans show how the architects used an abstract map of Switzerland to place the functions of the pavilion within essentially circular volumes.

Grundrisse illustrieren, wie die Architekten die Funktionen des Pavillons in runden Baukörpern untergebracht und diese in eine abstrahierte Landkarte der Schweiz eingeschrieben haben.

Les plans montrent comment les architectes ont réparti les zones fonctionnelles dans des volumes circulaires à l'intérieur d'une carte stylisée de la Suisse.

Intended for 20 000 visitors per day or 3.6 million visitors total, the **SWISS PAVILION** was one of the outstanding public successes of Expo 2010. The architects describe their structure as a "hybrid" between nature and technical structure. A chairlift like those used so frequently in the Swiss Alps connected the ground level to a "green meadow in the abstract shape of the country." An exhibition space, a restaurant, and a shop occupy the building, intended to illustrate the Expo theme, which was "Better City, Better Life." A façade made up of air-permeable net has round "energy collectors" that power LED lights. The architects collaborated on the exhibition area of this project with the designer Andreas Hunckeler and his firm Element and with the landscape architects Fontana Landschaftsarchitektur, Basel.

Der für 20 000 Besucher täglich – beziehungsweise 3,6 Millionen Besucher insgesamt – geplante **SCHWEIZER PAVILLON** war einer der großen Erfolge der Expo 2010. Die Architekten bezeichnen ihren Bau als „Hybrid" zwischen Natur und Technik. Eine Sesselbahn, wie sie in den Schweizer Alpen oft im Einsatz ist, verband das Erdgeschoss des Pavillons mit einer „grünen Wiese in Form einer abstrahierten Landkarte" der Schweiz. Das Bauwerk beherbergt Ausstellungsflächen, ein Restaurant und einen Shop, um das Expo-Thema „Bessere Stadt, besseres Leben" zu beleuchten. Die Fassade aus einer durchlässigen Netzstruktur ist mit runden „Energiekollektoren" ausgestattet, die LED-Leuchten mit Strom versorgen. Auf dem Gelände des Pavillons arbeiteten die Architekten mit dem Designer Andreas Hunckeler und dessen Büro Element sowie dem Baseler Büro Fontana Landschaftsarchitektur zusammen.

Conçu pour recevoir 20 000 visiteurs par jour – soit 3,6 millions au total –, le **PAVILLON SUISSE** a été l'une des grandes attractions d'Expo 2010. Les architectes décrivent leur projet comme un « hybride » entre nature et structure technique. Un télésiège, d'un type fréquent dans les Alpes suisses, partait du rez-de-chaussée vers « une prairie verte reprenant de façon abstraite la forme du pays ». Un espace d'expositions, un restaurant et une boutique occupaient le bâtiment qui illustrait le thème de l'Expo : « Une ville meilleure, une vie meilleure. » La façade en filet perméable à l'air était bardée de « collecteurs d'énergie » de forme ronde qui alimentaient des éclairages en DEL. Les architectes ont collaboré sur la partie exposition du projet avec le designer Andreas Hunckeler et son agence Element, ainsi qu'avec les architectes paysagistes bâlois Fontana Landschaftsarchitektur.

Despite some technical difficulties, one of the most popular features of the Swiss Pavilion was the chairlift system inspired directly by those used in the Alps.

Trotz verschiedener technischer Schwierigkeiten war eine der größten Attraktionen des Schweizer Pavillons eine Schwebebahn, inspiriert von Seilbahnen aus den Alpen.

Malgré des difficultés techniques, l'une des attractions les plus populaires du pavillon était son télésiège, directement inspiré des modèles utilisés dans les stations de ski.

Generous interior spaces are located below the "Alpine garden" on the roof, seen as a green mass in the sections below.

Unterhalb des „Alpengartens" auf dem Dach – auf den Querschnitten unten hellgrün markiert – verbergen sich großzügige Räume.

De généreux volumes intérieurs étaient aménagés sous le Jardin alpin en toiture, représenté par le triangle vert dans les coupes ci-dessous.

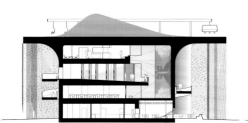

ALBERTO CAMPO BAEZA

Estudio Arquitectura Campo Baeza
C/ Almirante 9, 2 izq
28004 Madrid
Spain

Tel: +34 91 701 06 95
Fax: +34 91 521 70 61
E-mail: estudio@campobaeza.com
Web: www.campobaeza.com

Born in Valladolid, Spain, in 1946, **ALBERTO CAMPO BAEZA** studied in Madrid where he obtained his Ph.D. in 1982 (ETSAM). He has taught in Madrid, at the ETH in Zurich (1989–90), at Cornell University, at the University of Pennsylvania (1986 and 1999), and at ETSAM, where he has served as Head Professor of Design. His work includes the Fene Town Hall (1980); S. Fermin Public School (Madrid, 1985); and the BIT Center in Mallorca (1998); as well as a number of private houses, such as the Belvedere, De Blas House (Sevilla de la Nueva, Madrid, 2000). In 2001, he completed what he considers his most representative building, the Headquarters of the Caja General de Ahorros de Granada. In 2002, he finished an office building for the Consejería de Salud de la Junta de Andalucía in Almería and the SM Editorial building in Madrid. More recent work includes the NMAC Museum (Cádiz, 2006); Montecarmelo Public School (Madrid, 2006); Olnik Spanu House (Garrison, New York, 2005–07); Falla Square Housing (Cádiz, 2007); Centro de Interpretación Salinas de Janubio (Lanzarote, 2008); San Sebastián Castle (Cádiz, 2008); and Offices for Benetton (Samara, Russia, 2009), all in Spain unless stated otherwise.

ALBERTO CAMPO BAEZA, 1946 in Valladolid geboren, studierte in Madrid, wo er 1982 promovierte (ETSAM). Er lehrte in Madrid, an der ETH Zürich (1989–90), der Cornell University, der University of Pennsylvania (1986 und 1999) und der ETSAM, wo er als Professor den Bereich Entwerfen leitete. Zu seinen Projekten zählen das Rathaus in Fene (1980), die Schule S. Fermin (Madrid, 1985), das BIT Center in Mallorca (1998) sowie eine Reihe privater Wohnbauten, darunter das Belvedere, De Blas House (Sevilla de la Nueva, Madrid, 2000). 2001 konnte er das in seinen Augen bisher repräsentativste Projekt fertigstellen: die Zentrale der Caja General de Ahorros de Granada. 2002 wurde ein Bürogebäude für die Consejería de Salud de la Junta de Andalucía in Almería fertiggestellt sowie ein Gebäude für SM Editorial in Madrid. Jüngere Projekte sind u.a. das NMAC Museum (Cádiz, 2006), die Montecarmelo-Schule (Madrid, 2006), das Olnik Spanu House (Garrison, New York, 2005–07), ein Wohnkomplex an der Plaza de Falla (Cádiz, 2007), das Centro de Interpretación Salinas de Janubio (Lanzarote, 2008), das Kastell San Sebastián (Cádiz, 2008) sowie Büros für Benetton (Samara, Russland, 2009), alle in Spanien, sofern nicht anders angegeben.

ALBERTO CAMPO BAEZA, né à Valladolid en 1946, a étudié l'architecture à Madrid. Il est docteur de l'Escuela Tecnica Superior de Arquitectura de Madrid (ETSAM, 1982). Il a enseigné à Madrid, à l'ETH de Zurich (1989–90), à la Cornell University, à l'université de Pennsylvanie (1986 et 1989) et à l'ETSAM où il a été professeur principal de conception. Parmi ses réalisations figurent l'Hôtel de Ville de Fene (1980) ; l'école San Fermin (Madrid, 1985) ; le BIT Center de Mallorca (1998) et un certain nombre de résidences privées, comme la maison belvédère De Blas (Sevilla de la Nueva, Madrid, 2000). Il a achevé, en 2001, ce qu'il considère être son œuvre la plus représentative, le siège de la Caja General de Ahorros de Granada. En 2002, il a réalisé un immeuble de bureaux pour la Consejería de Salud de la Junta de Andalucía à Almería et l'immeuble des éditions SM à Madrid. Plus récemment, il a construit le musée NMAC (Cádix, 2006) ; l'école publique de Montecarmelo (Madrid, 2006) ; la maison Olnik Spanu (Garrison, New York, 2005–07) ; l'immeuble de logements de la place Falla (Cádix, 2007) ; le Centre d'interprétation Salinas de Janubio (Lanzarote, 2008) ; le château de San Sebastián (Cádix, 2008) et des bureaux pour Benetton (Samara, Russie, 2009).

BETWEEN CATHEDRALS

Cádiz, Spain, 2009

Area: 1000 m². Client: City of Cádiz. Cost: €1.475 million

Alberto Campo Baeza is a master of minimal architecture, as the image below, the temporary platform of the Between Cathedrals installation, demonstrates.

Alberto Campo Baeza ist ein Meister der minimalistischen Architektur, wie die Ansicht unten belegt: Sie zeigt die temporäre Plattform Entre Catedrales (Zwischen den Kathedralen).

Alberto Campo Baeza est un maître de l'architecture minimaliste, comme cette image de la plate-forme temporaire de l'installation « Entre les cathédrales » le démontre.

The temporary structure was erected over an archeological site between the old and new cathedrals of Cádiz, facing the sea. The light, white platform was meant to protect the dig, while creating a public area high enough (2.5 meters above the ground) to give a clear view, without being encumbered by the sight of the access road below. Skylights in the platform allowed visitors to peer down on the archeological site. An awning provided partial protection from the sun or rain while a stone face to the rear gave continuity with the existing buildings. Campo Baeza likens the base of the platform to ship design, while the metal awning on eight six-meter-high poles is reminiscent of "religious processions." White painted steel, and white Macael marble are the main structural elements. The architect concludes: "In all, we want to offer a simple and effective project that, on the one hand, shows its light and ethereal nature clearly and, on the other, reveals the beauty and wonders of this place and the city in which it is incorporated."

Die temporäre Konstruktion wurde über einer archäologischen Grabungsstätte zwischen der Alten und der Neuen Kathedrale von Cádiz mit Blick auf das Meer errichtet. Die leichte weiße Plattform sollte die Grabungsstätte schützen und zugleich einen öffentlichen Bereich schaffen, der hoch genug lag (2,5 m über dem Boden), um unverstellte Sicht zu bieten, ohne die darunter liegende Zufahrtsstraße im Blick zu haben. In die Plattform integrierte Oberlichter erlaubten den Besuchern den Blick hinunter auf die archäologische Stätte. Ein Markisendach bot für einen Teilbereich Schutz vor Sonne oder Regen, während die rückwärtige Steinmauer an die bestehende Bebauung anknüpfte. Campo Baeza vergleicht die Plattform mit einem Schiff, die auf sechs Meter hohen Pfählen ruhende Metallmarkise hingegen erinnere an „religiöse Prozessionen". Hauptbauelemente der Konstruktion sind weiß gestrichener Stahl und weißer Marmor aus Macael. Der Architekt fasst zusammen: „Alles in allem ging es uns darum, ein einfaches und effektives Projekt zu gestalten, das einerseits unmissverständlich seine Leichtigkeit und Flüchtigkeit, andererseits die Schönheit und Wunder des Standorts und der Stadt zur Schau stellt, in die es eingebettet ist."

Cette structure temporaire a été édifiée sur un terrain de fouilles archéologiques entre l'ancienne et la nouvelle cathédrale de Cádix, face à la mer. Blanche et aérienne, cette plate-forme d'observation avait pour fonction de protéger les fouilles tout en créant un espace public suffisamment relevé (2,5 m au-dessus du niveau du sol) pour donner une meilleure vision du chantier, sans être perturbée par la vue de la voie d'accès en contrebas. Des verrières percées dans la plate-forme permettaient aux visiteurs de regarder les fouilles. Un auvent protégeait en partie du soleil ou de la pluie, tandis qu'à l'arrière, un mur paré de pierres faisait le lien entre les deux cathédrales. Campo Baeza compare la base de sa plate-forme à un bateau et l'auvent en métal posé sur des piliers de 6 m de haut à des « processions religieuses ». L'acier laqué blanc et le marbre blanc de Macael sont les principaux matériaux structurels. En conclusion, explique l'architecte : « Au total, nous voulions un projet simple et efficace qui, d'un côté, affiche clairement son caractère léger et éthéré, et de l'autre révèle la beauté et la magie de cette place et de la cité qui l'entoure. »

With its light design, the platform appears to float between the older structures and in no way interferes with their more mineral appearance.

Dank ihrer Leichtigkeit scheint die Plattform zwischen den älteren Bauten zu schweben und stört deren steinerne Präsenz in keiner Weise.

De conception légère, la plate-forme semble flotter entre les constructions anciennes sans interférer en rien avec leur nature minérale.

As the architect's sketch (below) implies, the space on top of the platform offers an exceptionally pure and uninterrupted view of the sea.

Wie in der Skizze des Architekten (unten) angedeutet, bietet sich von der oberen Ebene der Plattform ein ungewöhnlich klarer, unverstellter Blick auf das Meer.

Comme le montre un premier croquis de l'architecte (en bas), le plan supérieur de la plate-forme offre une vue totalement dégagée sur la mer à l'infini.

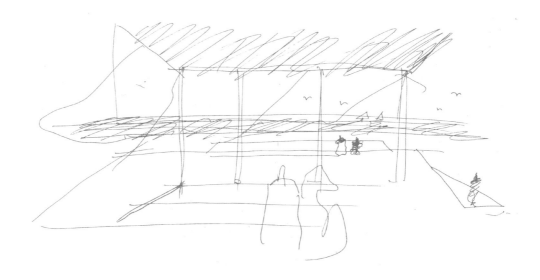

PIBA MARBRI PAVILION

Verona, Italy, 2009

Area: 36 m². Client: Piba Marbri. Cost: not disclosed

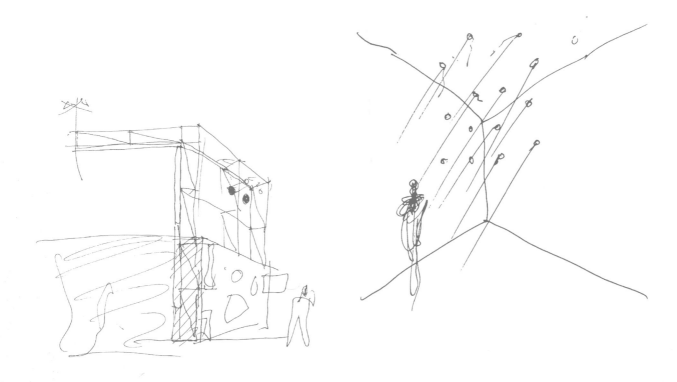

This stand was designed for the 2009 Marmocacc Fair for the Italian marble company **PIBA MARBRI**. The architect created a large black cubic form with white plaster reproductions on the exterior, mixed with marble pieces manufactured by Piba Marbi. The interior of the 6 x 6 x 6-meter cube was clad in white Carrara marble. Ten circular openings above this space allowed light to penetrate from a moving spotlight that was intended to imitate the light of the sun. "Once again," says the architect referring to his other projects, this is "a work of architecture in which light is the protagonist of the space—in this case, sunlight in motion over the white marble of Carrara."

Der Messestand wurde für den Marmorhersteller **PIBA MARBRI** auf der Marmocacc 2009 geplant. Der Architekt entwarf einen großen schwarzen Kubus, an dem außen weiße Gipsabgüsse und Marmorobjekte aus dem Programm von Piba Marbri angebracht waren. Der Innenraum des 6 x 6 x 6 m großen Kubus war mit weißem Carrara-Marmor verblendet. Zehn kreisrunde Öffnungen in der Dachplatte ermöglichten Lichteinfall von oben: Ein beweglicher Spot simulierte Sonnenlicht. „Wieder einmal", so der Architekt in Bezugnahme auf andere eigene Projekte, ist dies „ein Architekturprojekt, in dem das Licht die Hauptrolle spielt – in diesem das Fall Sonnenlicht, das über den weißen Cararra-Marmor wandert."

Ce stand a été conçu à l'occasion de l'édition 2009 de la Foire Marmocacc pour la société de marbres italiens **PIBA MARBRI**. Alberto Campo Baeza a dessiné une grande forme cubique noire dont les parois extérieures servaient de cimaises à des reproductions en plâtre et des pièces de marbre fabriquées par Piba Marbri. L'intérieur était doublé de marbre de Carrare blanc. Dix ouvertures circulaires zénithales laissaient pénétrer un éclairage fourni par un projecteur mobile dont les effets imitaient la présence du soleil. « Une fois encore », a précisé l'architecte en se référant à certains de ses projets, « c'est une œuvre d'architecture dans laquelle la lumière devient le protagoniste de l'espace, en l'occurrence les rayons du soleil se déplaçant sur du marbre de Carrare blanc. »

Sketches by Alberto Campo Baeza deal with issues of scale, but mainly with the effects of light coming into the closed space of the stand.

Alberto Campo Baezas Skizzen thematisieren die Maßstäblichkeit des Messestands, jedoch insbesondere die Effekte des Lichts, das in den umbauten Innenraum einfällt.

Des croquis d'Alberto Campo Baeza abordent le problème de l'échelle mais surtout les effets de la lumière tombant dans l'espace fermé du stand.

By daring to create a nearly empty and abstract space, the architect focuses the attention of visitors on light and the marble of the company concerned.

Dank der durchaus gewagten Entscheidung, einen fast leeren, abstrakten Raum zu entwerfen, lenkt der Architekt die Aufmerksamkeit der Besucher auf das Licht und die Marmorprodukte der Firma.

En osant créer un volume abstrait quasi vide, l'architecte concentre l'attention des visiteurs sur la lumière et le marbre, c'est-à-dire le produit à mettre en valeur.

CARMODY GROARKE

Carmody Groarke
25 Denmark Street
London WC2H 8NJ
UK

Tel: +44 20 78 36 23 33
Fax: +44 20 78 36 23 34
E-mail: studio@carmodygroarke.com
Web: www.carmodygroarke.com

KEVIN CARMODY was born in 1974 in Canberra, Australia. He worked in the office of David Chipperfield in London, before participating in the creation of **CARMODY GROARKE** in 2006. Andrew Groarke is also a Director of the firm and was born in 1971 in Manchester (UK). He also worked in the office of David Chipperfield, and with Haworth Tomkinds Architects in London prior to 2006. Their completed work includes the NLA Skywalk Pavilion, the British Museum (London, 2008); the Architecture Foundation Headquarters (London, 2009); 7 July Memorial, Hyde Park (London, 2009); Regents Place Pavilion (London, 2010); and Studio East Dining (London, 2010, published here). Work in progress includes the Sheffield Festival Center (Sheffield); a renovation and extension of the Peer Gallery (London); and the Tsunami Memorial, Natural History Museum (London), all in the UK.

KEVIN CARMODY wurde 1974 in Canberra, Australien, geboren. Er arbeitete im Büro von David Chipperfield in London, bevor er 2006 Carmody Groarke mitbegründete. **ANDREW GROARKE** ist zweiter Direktor des Büros und wurde 1971 in Manchester (Großbritannien) geboren. Vor 2006 arbeitete er ebenfalls im Büro von David Chipperfield sowie für Haworth Tomkinds Architects, beide London. Realisierte Projekte des Teams sind u.a. der NLA Skywalk Pavilion am British Museum (London, 2008) die Zentrale der Architecture Foundation (London, 2009) die Gedenkstätte für den 7. Juli im Hyde Park (London, 2009), der Regents Place Pavilion (London, 2010) und das Studio East Dining (London, 2010, hier vorgestellt). Derzeit in Arbeit sind das Sheffield Festival Center (Sheffield), die Sanierung und Erweiterung der Peer Gallery (London) sowie die Tsunami-Gedenkstätte am Natural History Museum (London), alle in Großbritannien.

Né en 1974 à Canberra (Australie), **KEVIN CARMODY** a travaillé dans l'agence de David Chipperfield à Londres, avant de fonder Carmody Groarke en 2006. **ANDREW GROARKE**, codirecteur de l'agence, est né en 1971 à Manchester (GB). Il a également travaillé chez David Chipperfield, puis chez Haworth Tomkinds Architects à Londres avant 2006. Ils ont réalisé le pavillon NLA Skywalk (British Museum, Londres, 2008) ; le siège de la Fondation d'architecture (Londres, 2009) ; le mémorial du 7 juillet (Hyde Park, Londres, 2009) ; le pavillon de Regents Place (Londres, 2010) et le restaurant *Studio East Dining* (Londres, 2010, publié ici). Actuellement, ils travaillent sur les projets du Centre des festivals de Sheffield (Sheffield) ; la rénovation et l'extension de la Peer Gallery (Londres) et le mémorial du tsunami (Musée d'histoire naturelle, Londres).

STUDIO EAST DINING

Stratford City Westfield, London, UK, 2010

Area: 800 m². Client: Westfield Bistrotheque. Cost: not disclosed.
Collaboration: Lewis Kinneir (Carmody Groarke)

Designed in just six weeks (March–April 2010) and erected in four weeks in May 2010 this temporary restaurant was set on the 35-meter-high roof of a construction site overlooking the 2012 Olympic Park and Zaha Hadid's Aquatics Center. It was made of scaffolding and boards from the construction site as well as recyclable industrial grade heat retractable polyethylene sheeting. The life span of the project was only three weeks and a total of 2000 clients were served. The architects collaborated closely with the client to allow for efficient service and use of the space. The architects explain: "The roof of the pavilion structure is designed to be seen from all directions; a series of flying roofs, tilting toward key views forming a playful roofscape. The spaces beneath this roof consist of a number of interlocking ceilings creating a radiating series of spaces, from the central dining area with its grand piano to each of the external views."

Das temporäre Restaurant, entworfen in nur sechs Wochen (März–April 2010) und erbaut in nur vier Wochen im Mai 2010, befand sich auf dem 35 m hohen Dach einer Baustelle mit Blick auf den Olympischen Park und das Aquatics Center von Zaha Hadid für die Olympiade 2012. Realisiert wurde die Konstruktion aus Baugerüsten und Brettern von der Baustelle sowie aus hochbelastbarer und recycelbarer PE-Schrumpffolie. Die Lebensspanne des Projekts belief sich auf gerade einmal drei Wochen, in denen 2000 Gäste bewirtet wurden. Die Architekten arbeiteten eng mit dem Auftraggeber zusammen, um effizienten Service und Raumnutzung zu gewährleisten. Die Architekten erklären: „Das Dach der Pavillonkonstruktion war so angelegt, das es von allen Seiten aus sichtbar war – als eine Serie von fliegenden Dächern, die sich zu zentralen Aussichtspunkten orientierten und so eine spielerische Dachlandschaft ergaben. Die Räume unterhalb des Dachs wiederum bestanden aus mehreren ineinandergreifenden Deckenabschnitten, sodass verschiedene Räume wie die Speichen eines Rads vom zentralen Hauptspeisebereich mit seinem Flügel ausstrahlten und sich zum jeweiligen Panorama hin öffneten."

Conçu en six semaines (mars–avril 2010) et monté en trente jours en mai de la même année, ce restaurant temporaire a été installé au sommet d'un immeuble en chantier dominant de 35 m le parc des Jeux olympiques de 2012 et le centre aquatique de Zaha Hadid. Il a été fabriqué en planches, pièces d'échafaudage prises sur le chantier et film de polyéthylène rétractable et recyclable de qualité industrielle. Sa durée de vie n'a été que de trois semaines, mais 2000 clients ont été servis. Les architectes ont collaboré avec leur commanditaire pour l'utilisation de l'espace et l'organisation du service : « La couverture du pavillon était conçue pour être vue de toutes les directions ; une série de toits suspendus, inclinés vers les perspectives les plus intéressantes, formaient une composition animée. Les espaces se développpaient sous cette toiture en une imbrication complexe de plafonds, qui créait une série de volumes partant de l'espace central (doté d'un piano à queue) vers les baies ouvertes sur l'extérieur. »

Using materials from construction sites, the architects created a restaurant on a roof in London in 2010. Although they are not the first to imagine such a setting, their work is original and striking.

Mit Baustellenmaterial gestalteten die Architekten 2010 ein Dachrestaurant in London. Obwohl sie zweifellos nicht die ersten waren, die einen solchen Standort wählten, ist ihr Entwurf doch unverwechselbar und markant.

À partir de matériaux récupérés sur des chantiers, les architectes ont créé ce restaurant sur le toit d'un bâtiment à Londres en 2010. S'ils n'ont pas été les premiers à imaginer ce type d'implantation, leur projet était original et surprenant.

Using scaffolding and a refined sense of lighting, the designers created a space that bears comparison to stage sets, but here takes on something of the drama of the construction of the 2012 Olympics site.

Mithilfe von Gerüsten und einem ausgeprägten Sinn für Lichtführung gestalteten die Architekten einen Raum, der an Bühnenbilder erinnert. Zugleich vermittelt er etwas von der Dramatik der Bauarbeiten für die Olympiade 2012.

Des éléments d'échafaudage et un sens raffiné de la lumière ont permis aux architectes de créer un espace qui évoque un décor de théâtre, mais traduit aussi à sa façon l'esprit des travaux préparatoires aux Jeux olympiques de 2012.

By filtering light and massing the me-
tallic tubing of the scaffolding or the
solid wooden blocks, this realization
demonstrates the advantages that
temporary structures can have over
more permanent ones.

Die Umsetzung des Entwurfs mit ge-
filtertem Licht, der Bündelung von
Gerüststangen aus Metall sowie den
massiv wirkenden Holzblöcken macht
deutlich, welche Vorteile temporäre
Bauten gegenüber permanenteren
Konstruktionen bieten können.

Articulation des tubes métalliques et
des habillages de bois, filtrage de la
lumière par des voiles : cette réalisation montre la souplesse des structures temporaires par rapport aux
permanentes.

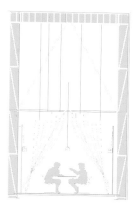

SANTIAGO CIRUGEDA

Santiago Cirugeda Parejo
C/ Joaquín Costa 7
41002 Seville
Spain

Tel: +34 670 79 44 09
Fax: +34 954 90 45 81
E-mail: sc@recetasurbanas.net
Web: www.recetasurbanas.net

SANTIAGO CIRUGEDA was born in Seville, Spain, in 1971 and studied architecture at the ETSA in his native city. He calls himself an "artist with the title of architect." His work has consisted in the production of a number of temporary, usually parasitic, structures that call into question the very nature of architecture and its materials. He has participated extensively in debates, workshops, and exhibitions. He has frequently flirted with illegality in the realization of these projects, again questioning the rules that govern construction and urban development. He refers to a number of his projects as "strategies for subversive occupation." He participated in the 2003 Venice Biennale. His work includes House Enlargement with Scaffolding (Seville, 1998); Institutional Prosthesis (Seville, 1998–99); Puzzle House, the Closet Strategy (Seville, 2002–03); and Trenches, Malaga Faculty of Fine Arts (Malaga, 2005). More recent projects are the Recycling of a High-Voltage Equipment Building (Olmeda de la Cuesta, Cuenca, 2009); Trucks, Containers, Collectives (various locations, 2007–10, published here); Extension 2010 + Chill-Out for Zanfoña Aldana (Coca Piñera, Seville, 2010); Rooftop Housing (Madrid, 2010); and Cement Recycling (Maimona Saints, Badajoz, 2010), all in Spain.

SANTIAGO CIRUGEDA wurde 1971 in Sevilla, Spanien, geboren und studierte Architektur an der ETSA seiner Heimatstadt. Er bezeichnet sich selbst als „Künstler mit dem Titel Architekt". Sein Werk besteht aus einer Folge temporärer, zumeist parasitärer Konstruktionen, mit denen er die Architektur und ihre Materialien in Frage stellt. Cirugeda beteiligt sich umfassend an Debatten, Workshops und Ausstellungen. Bei der Umsetzung seiner Projekte kokettiert er häufig mit der Illegalität und hinterfragt immer wieder die Spielregeln von Bauerschließung und Stadtentwicklung. Eine Reihe seiner Projekte nannte er „Strategien für subversive Besetzung". 2003 nahm er an der Biennale von Venedig teil. Zu seinen Arbeiten zählen „Hausanbau mit Baugerüsten" (Sevilla, 1998), „Institutionsprothese" (Sevilla, 1998–99), „Puzzle-Haus, ein Kabinettstückchen" (Seville, 2002–03) und „Schützengräben" an der Fakultät für Bildende Kunst in Malaga (2005). Aktuellere Projekte sind „Recycling eines Lagergebäudes für Hochspannungselemente" (Olmeda de la Cuesta, Cuenca, 2009), „Trucks, Container, Kollektive" (verschiedene Standorte, 2007–10, hier vorgestellt), „Erweiterungsbau 2010 + Chill-Out für Zanfoña Aldana" (Coca Piñera, Sevilla, 2010), ein Haus auf einem Dach (Madrid, 2010) und eine Anlage für Zementrecycling (Maimona Saints, Badajoz, 2010), alle in Spanien.

SANTIAGO CIRUGEDA, né à Séville (Espagne) en 1971, a étudié l'architecture à l'ETSA de sa ville natale. Il se qualifie lui-même « d'artiste qui possède un titre d'architecte ». Son travail consiste à produire un certain nombre de structures temporaires, généralement parasites, qui remettent en question la nature même de l'architecture et de ses matériaux. Il participe à de multiples débats, ateliers et expositions. Il se met fréquemment en marge de la légalité pour réaliser des projets qui remettent souvent en question les réglementations de la construction et de l'urbanisme. Il utilise souvent l'expression de « stratégies d'occupation subversive » pour expliquer ses projets. Il a participé à la Biennale de Venise en 2003. Parmi ses réalisations, toutes en Espagne : un agrandissement de maison par échafaudages (Séville, 1998) ; une Prothèse institutionnelle (Séville, 1998–99) ; la maison Puzzle, la Stratégie du placard (Séville, 2002–03), et des tranchées pour la faculté des beaux-arts de Malaga (2005). Plus récemment, il a proposé le recyclage d'un immeuble d'équipements haute tension (Olmeda de la Cuesta, Cuenca, 2009) ; l'action « Camions, Conteneurs, Collectifs » (divers lieux, 2007–10, publié ici) ; Extension 2010 + Chill-Out pour Zanfoña Aldana (Coca Piñera, Séville, 2010) ; un logement en toiture (Madrid, 2010) et un recyclage de ciment (Maimona Saints, Badajoz, 2010).

TRUCKS, CONTAINERS, COLLECTIVES

Various locations in Spain, 2007–10

Area: 15 m² to 150 m². Client: Collectives.
Cost: €30/m² to €440/m²

Santiago Cirugeda took advantage of the use of a series of 42-square-meter container-like housing modules granted by the Municipal Society for Urban Rehabilitation of the City of Saragossa. Thirteen activist groups (collectives) were involved. Under the civil responsibility of Cirugeda, a construction site equipped with concrete mixers was set up near the Church of Santa Lucía (Seville) to create prefabricated elements for the project between September and November 2009. Self-managed and built, the containers were installed on land that the participants managed to garner without costs. The project was subjected to vandalism in 2009, when one project called the Künstainer was burnt in its city park location in Tarragona. Cirugeda concludes: "**TRUCKS, CONTAINERS, COLLECTIVES** has... showed us different management and funding protocols, mechanisms for occupying sites or buildings, ways of operating as collectives, associations, cooperatives, as well as self-criticism and evaluation tools... Our greatest challenge now is to work together to create a digital collaborative system which supports this and other networks by providing information, facilitating exchange and connections, and offering new formulas. Our short-term goal is to achieve transnational cooperation and to extend our scope and field of action."

Santiago Cirugeda nutzte eine Anzahl 42 m² großer, containerähnlicher Wohnmodule, die die Städtische Gesellschaft für urbane Rückgewinnung von Saragossa zur Verfügung gestellt hatte. Beteiligt am Projekt waren 13 Aktivistengruppen (Kollektive). Unter Leitung von Cirugeda wurde eine Baustelle unweit der Kirche Santa Lucía (Sevilla) mit Betonmischern ausgestattet, um zwischen September und November 2009 Fertigbauelemente für das Projekt herzustellen. Die selbst verwalteten und gebauten Containerbauten wurden auf Grundstücken errichtet, die die Beteiligten kostenfrei organisieren konnten. 2009 wurde das Projekt Opfer von Vandalismus, als einer der Bauten, der sogenannte Künstainer, an seinem Standort im Stadtpark von Tarragona in Brand gesteckt wurde. Cirugeda fasst zusammen: „**LASTWAGEN, CONTAINER, KOLLEKTIVE** haben uns ... verschiedene Management- und Finanzierungsprotokolle erschlossen, verschiedene Mechanismen für die Besetzung von Grundstücken oder Gebäuden, verschiedene Arten, als Kollektive, Verbände und Kooperativen zusammenzuarbeiten, sowie Selbstkritik und Instrumente zur Evaluation gelehrt ... Unsere größte Herausforderung ist es nun, gemeinsam darauf hin zu arbeiten, ein digitales Kollaborationssystem zu schaffen, das dieses und andere Netzwerke mit Information versorgt, Austausch und Verknüpfungen erleichtert und neue Vorgehensweisen erschließt. Unser kurzfristiges Ziel sind transnationale Kooperationen und die Ausweitung unseres Aktionsbereichs und -radius'."

La Société municipale de réhabilitation urbaine de la ville de Saragosse a confié à Santiago Cirugeda un ensemble de modules de logement en forme de conteneurs de 42 m². Treize groupes d'action (collectifs) participaient à ce projet. Sous la responsabilité civile de Cirugeda, un chantier de construction équipé de bétonnières a été installé près de l'église de Santa Lucia à Séville pour créer les éléments préfabriqués du projet de septembre à novembre 2009. Les conteneurs construits et gérés en autogestion furent installés sur des terrains que les participants avaient réussi à occuper gratuitement. Le projet fut victime de vandalisme en 2009 et l'un des conteneurs, le Künstainer, fut incendié dans un parc de Tarragone. Pour Cirugeda : « **CAMIONS, CONTENEURS, COLLECTIFS** nous a montré ... comment pouvaient fonctionner différents protocoles de gestion et de financement, mécanismes d'occupation des sols ou de construction, façons d'intervenir en tant que collectifs, associations, coopératives, ainsi que l'intérêt de l'autocritique et des outils d'évaluation... Notre plus grand défi, aujourd'hui, est de travailler ensemble à créer un système collaboratif numérique en appui de ce réseau et d'autres systèmes pour fournir de l'information, faciliter les échanges et les connexions et offrir de nouvelles formules. Notre objectif à court terme est de parvenir à une coopération transnationale et de développer nos ambitions et nos champs d'action. »

Santiago Cirugeda is known for his radical approach to design and construction, making use not only of available materials, but also of loopholes in the laws and surveillance of urban rules.

Santiago Cirugeda ist bekannt für seine radikale Herangehensweise an Entwurf und Bauen: Er arbeitet nicht nur mit vorhandenen Materialien, sondern nutzt auch Schlupflöcher in der Gesetzgebung und städtischen Bauvorgaben.

Santiago Cirugeda est connu pour son approche radicale de la conception et de la construction. Il se sert à la fois des matériaux disponibles sur place et des lacunes de la loi et des règles d'urbanisme.

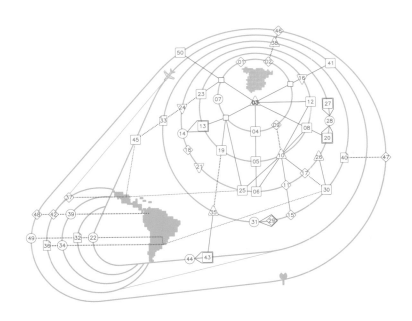

Temporary housing or shelters were conceived with recuperated materials and with the collaboration of various citizens' organizations.

In Kollaboration mit Bürgerorganisationen wurden temporäre Wohnbauten und Unterkünfte aus recycelten und umgenutzten Materialien realisiert.

Ces logements temporaires, ou abris, ont été conçus avec la collaboration d'association d'habitants, à partir de matériaux de récupération.

COOP HIMMELB(L)AU

Coop Himmelb(l)au
Wolf D. Prix / W. Dreibholz & Partner ZT GmbH
Spengergasse 37 / 1050 Vienna / Austria
Tel: +43 1 546 60 / Fax: +43 1 54 66 06 00
E-mail: office@coop-himmelblau.at / Web: www.coop-himmelblau.at

COOP HIMMELB(L)AU was founded by **WOLF D. PRIX**, Helmut Swiczinsky, and Michael Holzer in Vienna, Austria, in 1968. In 1988, a second studio was opened in Los Angeles, USA. Today the studio is directed by Wolf D. Prix, Wolfdieter Dreibholz, Harald Krieger, Karolin Schmidbaur, and project partners. It currently employs 150 team members from 19 nations. Wolf D. Prix was born in 1942 in Vienna, and educated at the Technical University, Vienna; at SCI-Arc; and at the Architectural Association (AA), London. Since 1993 he has been a Professor of Architecture at the University of Applied Arts in Vienna. Since 2003 he has been Head of the Institute for Architecture, the Head of Studio Prix, and serves as Vice-Rector of the University. Wolfdieter Dreibholz was born in Vienna in 1941 and received a degree in engineering and architecture from the Technical University, Vienna, in 1966. He became CEO of Coop Himmelb(l)au Wolf D. Prix / W. Dreibholz & Partner ZT GmbH in 2004. Completed projects of the group include the master plan for Melun-Sénart (France, 1986–87); the rooftop remodeling Falkestrasse (Vienna, 1983/1987–88); the East Pavilion of the Groninger Museum (Groningen, The Netherlands, 1990–94); remodeling of the Austrian Pavilion in the Giardini (Venice, Italy, 1995); the UFA Cinema Center (Dresden, Germany, 1993–98); the SEG Apartment Tower (Vienna, 1994–98); and Expo '02, Forum Arteplage (Biel, Switzerland, 1999–2002). Recent and current work includes the Academy of Fine Arts (Munich, Germany, 1992/2002–05); the Akron Art Museum (Akron, Ohio, USA, 2001–07); BMW-Welt (Munich, Germany, 2001–07); the Central Los Angeles Area High School #9 for the Visual and Performing Arts (Los Angeles, California, USA, 2002–08); the Busan Cinema Center (Busan, South Korea, 2005–11); the Dalian International Conference Center (Dalian, China, 2008–11); the Musée des Confluences (Lyon, France, 2001–13); and the European Central Bank (Frankfurt, Germany, 2003–14).

COOP HIMMELB(L)AU wurde 1968 von **WOLF D. PRIX**, Helmut Swiczinsky und Michael Holzer in Wien gegründet. 1988 wurde ein zweites Studio in Los Angeles eröffnet. Gegenwärtig wird das Studio von Wolf D. Prix, Wolfdieter Dreibholz, Harald Krieger, Karolin Schmidbaur und Projektpartnern geleitete und beschäftigt 150 Team-mitglieder aus 19 Nationen. Wolf D. Prix wurde 1942 in Wien geboren und studierte an der Technischen Universität Wien, am SCI-Arc und der Architectural Association (AA) London. Seit 1993 ist er Professor für Architektur an der Universität für Angewandte Kunst in Wien, wo er seit 2003 zudem Vorstand am Institut für Architektur sowie Leiter des Studio Prix und Vizerektor der Universität ist. Wolfdieter Dreibholz wurde 1941 in Wien geboren und schloss sein Studium der Architektur und Bauingenieurwissen-schaften 1966 an der TU Wien ab. 2004 wurde er Geschäftsführer bei Coop Himmelb(l)au Wolf D. Prix / W. Dreibholz & Partner ZT GmbH. Gebaute Projekte der Gruppe sind u.a. der Masterplan für Melun-Sénart (Frankreich, 1986–87), der Dachausbau Falkestraße (Wien, 1983/1987–88), der Ostpavillon des Museums Groningen (Groningen, Niederlande, 1990–94), der Umbau des Österreichischen Pavillons in den Giardini (Venedig, 1995), das UFA-Kinocenter (Dresden, 1993–98), das SEG Apartmenthochhaus (Wien, 1994–98) sowie das Forum Arteplage, EXPO '02 (Biel, Schweiz, 1999–2002). Jüngere Arbeiten sind u.a. die Akademie der Bildenden Künste (München, 1992/2002–05), das Akron Art Museum (Akron, Ohio, USA, 2001–07), die BMW-Welt (München, 2001–07) und die Central Los Angeles Area High School #9 für Bildende und Darstellende Künste (Los Angeles, Kalifornien, USA, 2002–08), ein Kinocenter in Busan (Busan, Südkorea, 2005–11), das Internationale Konferenzzentrum in Dalian (Dalian, China, 2008–10), das Musée des Confluences (Lyon, Frankreich, 2001–13) und die Europäische Zentralbank (Frankfurt am Main, 2003–14).

L'agence Coop Himmelb(l)au a été fondée par **WOLF D. PRIX**, Helmut Swiczinsky et Michael Holzer à Vienne en 1968. En 1988, une seconde agence à Los Angeles est ouverte. Actuellement, Coop Himmelb(l)blau est dirigé par Wolf D. Prix, Wolfdieter Dreibholz, Harald Krieger, Karolin Schmidbaur et d'autres partenaires et a une équipe de 150 collaborateurs originaires de 19 pays. Wolf D. Prix, né à Vienne en 1942, a étudié à la TU de Vienne, au SCI-Arc et à l'AA de Londres. Professeur d'architecture à l'Université des arts appliqués de Vienne depuis 1993, il dirige l'Institut d'architecture et le Studio Prix depuis 2003 et occupe le poste de vice-recteur de l'université. Wolfdieter Dreibholz, né à Vienne en 1941, est diplômé en ingénierie et en architecture de la TU de Vienne (1966). Il prend la direction de Coop Himmelb(l)au Wolf D. Prix / W. Dreibholz & Partner ZT GmbH, en 2004. Parmi les réalisations du groupe : le plan directeur de Melun-Sénart (France, 1986–87) ; l'aménagement d'un penthouse en toiture Falkestrasse à Vienne (1983/1987–88) ; le pavillon Est du musée de Groningue (Pays-Bas, 1990–94) ; la rénovation du pavillon autrichien dans les Giardini (Venise, 1995) ; le Centre du cinéma UFA (Dresde, 1993–98) ; la tour d'appartements SEG (Vienne, 1994–98) et le forum Arteplage d'Expo '02, (Biel, Suisse, 1999–2002). Plus récem-ment : l'Académie des beaux-arts (Munich, 1992/2002–05) ; l'Akron Art Museum (Akron, Ohio, 2001–07) ; BMW-Welt (Munich, 2001–07) ; le Collège Central #9 de Los Angeles pour les arts visuels et de la scène (Los Angeles, 2002–08) ; le Centre du cinéma de Busan (Busan, Corée du Sud, 2005–11) ; le Centre de conférences internatio-nal Dalian (Dalian, Chine 2008–11) ; le musée des Confluences (Lyon, France, 2001–13) et la Banque centrale européenne (Francfort-sur-le-Main, 2003–14).

PAVILION 21 MINI OPERA SPACE

Munich, Germany, 2008–10

Area: 430 m². Client: the State of Bavaria represented by the Bavarian State Opera Munich, Germany.
Cost: €2.1 million

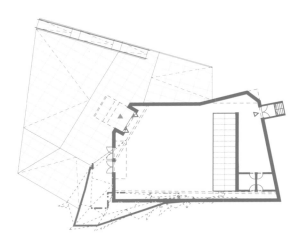 

This temporary mobile performance space was intended for use during the annual Opera Festival by 300 people and was installed on the Marstallplatz in Munich. The structure is due to travel to other locations. The architects state: "The design approach studies the impact of physical influences on our hearing perception and how to apply soundscape effects to alter our sensation through transforming and adopting building volumes and their material specifications." Reducing apparent noise to create a "zone of silence" was one design goal. The concept also sought to "materialize music into architecture." More specifically, the architects used part of the music of Jimi Hendrix—*Purple Haze* "…'Scuse me while I kiss the sky…"—to generate exterior forms. Interior space measures 21 meters in length by 17 meters in width, with careful attention paid to the acoustics that were handled by Arup London. The structure was inaugurated in June 2010.

Der temporäre mobile Bühnenraum war entworfen worden, um bei den jährlichen Opernfestspielen 300 Besuchern Platz zu bieten und wurde auf dem Münchner Marstallplatz errichtet. Geplant ist, den Bau auch an anderen Standorten einzusetzen. Die Architekten erklären: „Der gestalterische Ansatz ist eine Auseinandersetzung mit den Auswirkungen physischer Einflüsse auf unser Hörempfinden sowie die Frage, wie sich Soundscape-Effekte nutzen lassen, um unser Erleben zu verändern, indem man bauliche Volumina und deren materielle Beschaffenheit verändert und anpasst." Ein Ziel war es, Raumgeräusche zu reduzieren und eine „Zone der Stille" zu schaffen. Darüber hinaus sollte das Konzept, „Musik in Gestalt von Architektur materialisieren". Insbesondere arbeiteten die Architekten mit einem Ausschnitt aus Jimi Hendrix' *Purple Haze* „… 'Scuse me while I kiss the sky…", um die Formen des Außenbaus zu generieren. Der Innenraum ist 21 m lang und 17 m breit. Besondere Aufmerksamkeit galt der Akkustik, die vom Büro Arup in London geplant wurde. Eingeweiht wurde der Bau im Juni 2010.

Inaugurée en juin 2010, cette structure mobile pour performances a été conçue pour accueillir 300 spectateurs pendant la durée d'un festival annuel d'opéra. Elle a été installée sur la Marstallplatz à Munich, mais pourrait être remontée ailleurs. Selon les architectes : « Notre approche conceptuelle étudie l'impact des influences physiques sur notre perception auditive et sur la façon d'appliquer certains effets de l'environnement sonore pour modifier nos sensations en transformant et adaptant le volume de la construction et ses caractéristiques matérielles. » Un des objectifs était de réduire le bruit ressenti pour créer une « zone de silence ». Le concept cherchait également à « matérialiser la musique en architecture ». Plus spécifiquement, les architectes ont utilisé en partie un morceau de Jimi Hendrix, *Purple Haze*, « 'Scuse me while I kiss the sky… », pour générer la forme extérieure. L'espace intérieur mesure 21 m de long par 17 de large. Les études acoustiques ont été assurées par l'Agence Arup London.

A sketch by the architect shows the freely conceived form that is resolved into a more formal spiked design that is meant to have a direct relationship to music.

Eine Skizze des Architekten zeigt die freie Grundform, die zu einem strengeren, spitzzackigen Entwurf entwickelt wurde, der konzeptionell an musikalische Formen anknüpft.

Ce croquis de l'architecte montre la forme libre qui débouchera sur un plan plus formel, anguleux, d'allure hérissée, en relation directe avec la musique.

Contrasting rather strongly with its built environment, the pavilion created a feeling of dynamic action for the Opera Festival in Munich.

Der Pavillon, ein auffälliger Kontrast zum baulichen Umfeld, signalisiert dynamische Impulse für die Münchner Opernfestspiele.

Contrastant fortement avec son environnement bâti, le pavillon crée un geste dynamique adapté au cadre du festival de l'opéra de Munich.

A section drawing (below) gives a feeling for the way in which the architect has resolved the spiked exterior form into a usable interior space.

Ein Querschnitt (unten) macht deutlich, wie der Architekt den spitzwinkligen Außenbau zu einem nutzbaren Innenraum aufzulösen verstand.

Une coupe (ci-dessous) montre comment l'architecte a réussi à tirer parti de l'extérieur d'apparence hérissée pour en faire un volume intérieur utilisable.

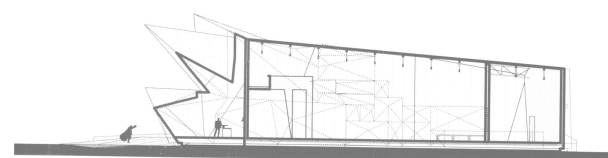

DILLER SCOFIDIO + RENFRO

Diller Scofidio + Renfro
601 West 26th Street, 1815 / New York, NY 10001 / USA

Tel: +1 212 260 7971
Fax: +1 212 260 7924
E-mail: disco@dsrny.com
Web: www.dsrny.com

ELIZABETH DILLER was born in Lodz, Poland, in 1954. She received her B.Arch degree from Cooper Union School of Arts in 1979. She is a Professor of Architecture at Princeton University. **RICARDO SCOFIDIO** was born in New York in 1935. He graduated from Cooper Union School of Architecture and Columbia University, where he is currently a Professor of Architecture. They founded Diller+Scofidio in 1979. **CHARLES RENFRO** became a partner in 2004. Renfro was born in Houston in 1964 and graduated from Rice University and Columbia. They completed the Brasserie Restaurant in the Seagram Building (New York, New York, 1998–99); the Blur Building (Expo '02, Yverdon-les-Bains, Switzerland, 2000–02); the Viewing Platforms at Ground Zero in Manhattan (New York, 2001); and the Institute of Contemporary Art in Boston (Massachusetts, 2004–06). Further recently completed work counts the Lincoln Center projects in New York including the expansion of the Juilliard School of Music (2009), the renovation of Alice Tully Hall (2006–09), and the Hypar Restaurant (2010); the conversion of the High Line, a 2.4-kilometer stretch of elevated railroad into a New York City park (2009); and the Creative Arts Center at Brown University (Providence, Rhode Island, 2010). Among current and ongoing work are the Museum of Image and Sound (Rio de Janeiro, Brazil, 2012); the Broad Museum (Los Angeles, California, 2013); UC Berkeley Art Museum/Pacific Film Archive (Berkeley, California, 2014); and the Columbia Business School (New York, New York), all in the USA unless stated otherwise. Published here is the Bubble, an inflatable event space (Washington, D.C., USA, 2010–12).

ELIZABETH DILLER wurde 1954 in Lodz, Polen, geboren. 1979 schloss sie ihr Studium an der Cooper Union School of Arts mit einem B.Arch ab. Sie ist Professorin für Architektur an der Universität Princeton. **RICARDO SCOFIDIO** wurde 1935 in New York geboren. Er absolvierte sein Studium an der Cooper Union School of Architecture und der Columbia University, wo er derzeit Professor für Architektur ist. Gemeinsam gründeten sie 1979 Diller+Scofidio. **CHARLES RENFRO** wurde 2004 Partner des Büros. Renfro wurde 1964 in Houston geboren und absolvierte sein Studium an der Rice University und der Columbia University. Abgeschlossene Projekte sind u.a. das Brasserie Restaurant im Seagram Building (New York, 1998–99), das Blur Building (Expo '02, Yverdon-les-Bains, Schweiz, 2000–02), die Aussichtsplattformen für Ground Zero in Manhattan (New York, 2001) sowie das Institute of Contemporary Art in Boston (Massachusetts, 2004–06). Unlängst fertig gestellt wurden außerdem die Projekte am Lincoln Center in New York, einschließlich der Erweiterung der Juilliard School of Music (2009), die Sanierung der Alice Tully Hall (2006–09) und das Hypar Restaurant (2010), die Umnutzung der High Line, einem 2,4 km langen ehemaligen Hochbahnabschnitt, als Parkanlage (New York, 2009) und das Creative Arts Center an der Brown University (Providence, Rhode Island, 2010). Aktuelle Projekte sind u.a. das Museum of Image and Sound (Rio de Janeiro, Brasilien, 2012), das Broad Museum (Los Angeles, Kalifornien, 2013) das UC Berkeley Art Museum/Pacific Film Archive (Berkeley, Kalifornien, 2014) sowie die Colombia Business School (New York), alle in den USA, sofern nicht anders angegeben. Hier vorgestellt ist Bubble, ein aufblasbarer Veranstaltungsraum (Washington, D.C., USA, 2010–12).

Née à Lodz (Pologne) en 1954, **ELIZABETH DILLER** est diplômée B. Arch de l'École d'art de la Cooper Union (1979). Elle est professeure d'architecture à Princeton University. **RICARDO SCOFIDIO**, né à New York en 1935, est diplômé de l'École d'architecture de la Cooper Union et de l'université Columbia où il enseigne actuellement l'architecture. Ils ont fondé leur agence en 1979. **CHARLES RENFRO** est devenu partenaire en 2004. Né à Houston en 1964, il est diplômé de la Rice University et de l'université Columbia. Ils ont réalisé, entre autres, le brasserie-restaurant du Seagram Building (New York, 1998–99) ; le Blur Building à Expo '02 (Yverdon-les-Bains, Suisse, 2000–02) ; les plates-formes d'observation pour Ground Zero à Manhattan (New York, 2001) et l'Institut d'art contemporain de Boston (2004–06). Parmi leurs projets récents ou en cours figurent : des interventions pour le Lincoln Center à New York, dont l'extension de la Juilliard School of Music, école de musique (2009) ; la rénovation de l'Alice Tully Hall (2006–09) et le Hypar Restaurant (2010) ; la reconversion de la High Line à New York, section de voie ferroviaire suspendue de 2,4 km, en parc (2009) ; le Centre des arts de la création à l'université Brown (Creative Arts Center, Providence, Rhode Island, 2010) ; le Musée de l'image et du son (Rio de Janeiro, 2012) ; le Broad Museum (Los Angeles, 2013) ; l'Art Museum et Pacific Film Archive de l'université de Californie à Berkeley (2014) et la Bubble, espace gonflable pour événements (Washington, 2010–12, publié ici).

BUBBLE
Washington, D.C., USA, 2010–12

Address: National Mall, Washington, D.C., USA
Area: 1208 m². Client: Hirshhorn Museum and Sculpture Garden
Cost: not disclosed

The modernist form of the Hirshhorn Museum on the Mall in Washington, D.C., is the work of the noted architect Gordon Bunshaft (1974). Diller Scofidio + Renfro have designed an inflatable event space for the circular inner courtyard of the museum. "The **BUBBLE**," they write, "is an architecture of air: a pneumatic structure enclosed only by a thin translucent membrane that squeezes into the void of the building and oozes out the top and beneath its mass." The Bubble, accommodating between 500 and 800 people, would be put in place twice a year, in the spring and fall. A series of cable rings keep the Bubble from contact with the actual courtyard walls.

Die moderne Formensprache des Hirshhorn Museum an der Mall in Washington D.C. ist das Werk des renommierten Architekten Gordon Bunshaft (1974). Diller Scofidio + Renfro entwarfen einen aufblasbaren Veranstaltungsraum für den runden Innenhof des Museums. „**BUBBLE**", schreiben sie, „ist eine Architektur aus Luft: eine pneumatische Konstruktion, die lediglich von einer dünnen, transluzenten Membran umschlossen ist, die in die Aussparung des Gebäudes hineingepresst ist und über- und unterhalb der Gebäudemasse hervortritt." Bubble bietet Raum für 500 bis 800 Besucher und soll zweimal jährlich, im Frühjahr und im Herbst, installiert werden. Eine Reihe von Stahlkabelringen verhindert direkten Kontakt zwischen der Blase und den Mauern des Innenhofs.

De style très moderniste, le musée Hirshhorn près du Mall à Washington est l'œuvre du célèbre architecte Gordon Bunshaft (1974). Diller Scofidio + Renfro ont conçu un espace gonflable pour événements, destiné à la cour intérieure circulaire de ce bâtiment. « La **BUBBLE**, écrivent-ils, est une architecture de l'air : une structure pneumatique enfermée dans une fine membrane translucide qui se glisse dans le vide du bâtiment et tente de s'en extraire par le haut et le bas. » La bulle, qui peut recevoir de 500 à 800 visiteurs, devrait être mise en place deux fois par an, au printemps et à l'automne. Un système de câbles l'empêche de se plaquer contre les murs de la cour.

Although inflatable structures have frequently been used in a cultural context, here Diller Scofidio + Renfro make the added volume conform to the original building, allowing it to bubble out of its confines.

Im kulturellen Kontext sind aufblasbare Strukturen bereits häufig zum Einsatz gekommen, doch hier gelingt es Diller Scofidio + Renfro, die bauliche Erweiterung in den ursprünglichen Baukörper einzupassen: Sie quillt buchstäblich aus ihm heraus.

On utilise souvent des structures gonflables dans le contexte de manifestations culturelles. Diller Scofidio + Renfro a intégré le nouveau volume au bâtiment existant tout en lui laissant la possibilité de « fuir » hors de ses limites.

A rendering and a section drawing give an idea of how the bubble occupies the central space of the museum and even seems to extrude through a ground-floor opening.

Rendering und Querschnitt illustrieren, wie die Blase den Kern des Museums ausfüllt und aus einer Öffnung im Erdgeschoss herauszuquillen scheint.

Un rendu et une coupe précisent la façon dont la bulle occupe le volume central du musée et semble tenter de s'échapper par une ouverture laissée au rez-de-chaussée.

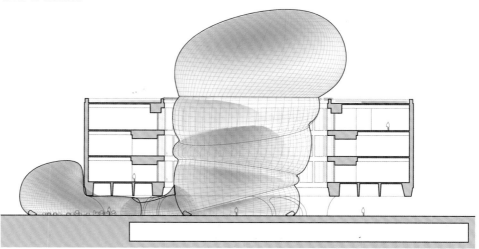

ECOSISTEMA URBANO

Ecosistema Urbano Arquitectos Ltd.
Estanislao Figueras 6
28008 Madrid
Spain

Tel/Fax: +34 91 559 16 01
E-mail: info@ecosistemaurbano.com
Web: www.ecosistemaurbano.com

Ecosistema Urbano was created in 2000 by **BELINDA TATO**, born in Madrid in 1971, who studied at the ETSA of Madrid (1999) and the Bartlett School of Architecture, London (1996), and **JOSE LUIS VALLEJO**, born in Bilbao in 1971, who also studied at the ETSAM (1999) and Bartlett School (1996). Since 2007 **MICHAEL MORADIELLOS**, born in Brussels in 1979, who studied at the Victor Horta School in Brussels, has been a partner of Ecosistema Urbano, and in 2008 a fourth partner, **DOMENICO DI SIENA** (born in Rome in 1979), who studied at La Villette in Paris and at the L. Quaroni school in Rome, joined the group. Currently the team is involved in research projects concerning the future of city design that they call "eco-techno-logical cities," financed by the Spanish Ministry of Industry. They are working on several urban proposals for different Spanish municipalities (see the Ecoboulevard of Vallecas in Madrid, Spain, 2006), and one of their projects—Air Tree, Madrid Pavilion Public Space (published here)—represented Madrid at Shanghai Expo 2010 in China. They have also worked on an Internet network (ecosistemaurbano.org, 2007–10).

Ecosistema Urbano wurde 2000 gegründet: von **BELINDA TATO**, 1971 in Madrid geboren, Studium an der ETSA Madrid (1999) und der Bartlett School of Architecture, London (1996), und **JOSE LUIS VALLEJO**, 1971 in Bilbao geboren, ebenfalls Studium an der ETSAM (1999) und der Bartlett School (1996). Seit 2007 ist auch **MICHAEL MORADIELLOS**, 1979 in Brüssel geboren, Studium am Institut Supérieur d'Architecture Victor Horta in Brüssel, Partner bei Ecosistema Urbano; 2008 schloss sich **DOMENICO DI SIENA** (1979 in Rom geboren), Studium La Villette, Paris, und Architekturfakultät L. Quaroni in Rom, als vierter Partner der Gruppe an. Zur Zeit arbeitet das Team an Forschungsprojekten zur Zukunft der Stadtplanung – etwas, das sie „öko-techno-logische Stadt" nennen –, finanziert vom spanischen Ministerium für Industrie. Sie arbeiten an einer Reihe von Stadtplanungsentwürfen für verschiedene spanische Gemeinden (siehe Ecoboulevard in Vallecas, Madrid, 2006). Ein Projekt des Büros – Air Tree, Pavillon und öffentlicher Bereich, Stadt Madrid (hier vorgestellt) – präsentierte die spanische Hauptstadt auf der Expo 2010 in Shanghai. Das Team hat außerdem an einem Internet-Netzwerk (ecosistemaurbano.org 2007–10) gearbeitet.

Ecosistema Urbano a été fondée en 2000 par **BELINDA TATO**. Née à Madrid en 1971, elle a étudié à l'ETSA de Madrid (1999) et à la Bartlett School de Londres (1996). **JOSÉ LUIS VALLEJO**, né à Bilbao en 1971, a également étudié à l'ETSA (1999) et à la Bartlett School (1996). Depuis 2007, **MICHAEL MORADIELLOS**, né à Bruxelles en 1979, qui a étudié à l'École Victor-Horta à Bruxelles, est devenu partenaire de l'agence, puis, en 2008, **DOMENICO DI SIENA**, né à Rome en 1979, a rejoint le groupe. Ce dernier a étudié à Institut Supérieur d'Architecture de Paris-La Villette et à l'École L. Quaroni à Rome. Actuellement, l'équipe se consacre à des projets de recherche sur le futur des villes qu'ils appellent les « cités éco-techno-logiques », financés par le ministère espagnol de l'Industrie. Ils travaillent sur plusieurs projets pour diverses villes espagnoles (voir l'Écoboulevard de Vallecas, Madrid, 2006), et l'une de leurs propositions (Air Tree, Espace public du pavillon de Madrid, publié ici) représentait la capitale espagnole à l'Expo 2010 de Shanghaï. Ils ont également travaillé au montage d'un réseau Internet (ecosistemaurbano.org, 2007–10).

AIR TREE

Madrid Pavilion Public Space, Expo 2010, Shanghai, China, 2010

Area: 1000 m². Client: Fundación Madrid Global
Cost: €470 000

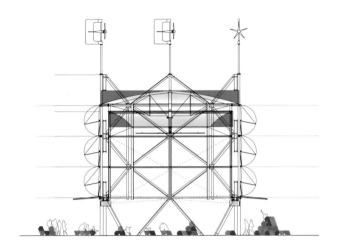

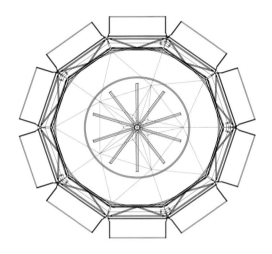

With its operable exterior shutters and high-flying red weather vanes, the pavilion has something of a martial appearance.

Mit seinen beweglichen Klappläden und den roten Wetterfahnen hoch oben auf dem Bau wirkt der Pavillon fast wie eine Burg.

Des volets extérieurs relevables et des girouettes haut perchées confèrent une allure quasi martiale à ce pavillon provisoire.

The **AIR TREE** is intended as a structure "capable of reactivating sites and creating the conditions to empower the use of the collective space. It is conceived as a technological urban furniture, a self-sufficient climatic comfort generator…" Textiles are used for changing video projections, while sensors alter the structure according to local climate conditions. A 7.3-meter-diameter fan is suspended 11.5 meters high inside the Air Tree using a tensegrity structure, but the height of the fan can be varied using a telescopic system according to the temperature inside and outside of the pavilion.

Der **AIR TREE** wurde als Konstruktion geplant, „die in der Lage ist, Grundstücke zu reaktivieren und ein Umfeld zu schaffen, das die Nutzung kollektiver Räume fördert. Konzipiert ist das Bauwerk als technologisches Stadtmöbel, als energieunabhängiger Generator angenehmer Klimabedingungen…" Textilmembrane dienen wechselnden Videoprojektionen, während Sensoren dafür sorgen, dass sich die Konstruktion den örtlichen klimatischen Bedingungen anpasst. Im Innern des Air Tree, auf einer Höhe von 11,5 m, wurde mithilfe eines Tensegrity-Tragwerks ein 7,3 m großer Ventilator installiert. Seine Höhe lässt sich mithilfe eines Teleskopsystems je nach Außen- und Innentemperatur im Pavillon justieren.

L'**AIR TREE** est une structure en tenségrité « capable de réactiver des sites et de créer les conditions d'une dynamisation de l'utilisation de l'espace collectif. C'est un mobilier urbain technologique dans lequel des capteurs modifient la structure en fonction des conditions climatiques. » Les parois textiles accueillent la projection de diverses vidéos tandis que les capteurs modifient la structure en fonction des conditions climatiques locales. Un ventilateur de 7,3 m de diamètre est suspendu à 11,5 m de hauteur à l'intérieur de l'Air Tree, hauteur qui varie en fonction de la température intérieure et extérieure grâce à un système télescopique.

With its changing video projections, the pavilion takes on a kaleidoscopic appearance that certainly enlivens exterior public space.

Wechselnde Videoprojektionen lassen den Pavillon wie ein Kaleidoskop erscheinen, das den öffentlichen Raum belebt.

Grâce à des projections vidéo sur sa façade, le pavillon prend à certains moments un aspect kaléidoscopique qui anime l'espace public.

The fact that the entire structure is also sensitive to climate, and with it the variable height of its fan mechanism, makes it even more attractive in moments of high summer heat.

Die gesamte Konstruktion ist klimasensibel; das höhenverstellbare Ventilatorensystem macht sie an heißen Sommertagen umso attraktiver.

Le pavillon tout entier réagit aux conditions climatiques grâce à la hauteur réglable du mécanisme de ventilation. Il en est d'autant plus apprécié du public.

OLAFUR ELIASSON

Olafur Eliasson
Studio Olafur Eliasson
Christinenstr. 18/19, Haus 2
10119 Berlin
Germany

E-mail: studio@olafureliasson.net
Web: www.olafureliasson.net

OLAFUR ELIASSON was born in 1967 in Copenhagen, Denmark, of Icelandic parents. He attended the Royal Academy of Fine Arts in Copenhagen (1989–95). Early in his career he moved to Germany, establishing Studio Olafur Eliasson as an experimental laboratory in Berlin. Eliasson lives and works in Copenhagen and Berlin. He has had solo exhibitions at the Musée d'Art Moderne de la Ville de Paris, the ZKM in Karlsruhe, and the 21st Century Museum of Contemporary Art in Kanazawa, and represented Denmark in the 2003 Venice Biennale. More recent solo exhibitions include "Take your time: Olafur Eliasson," which was organized by the San Francisco Museum of Modern Art (San Francisco, California, USA) and traveled to the Museum of Modern Art and PS1 Contemporary Art Center in New York (2007–08). His installations feature elements appropriated from nature—billowing steam evoking a water geyser, rainbows, or fog-filled rooms. By introducing "natural" phenomena, such as water, mist, or light, into an artificial setting, be it a city street or an art gallery, the artist encourages viewers to reflect on their perception of the physical world. This moment of perception, when viewers pause to consider what they are experiencing, has been described by Eliasson as "seeing yourself sensing." For the Icelandic National Concert and Conference Center in Reykjavik the artist has created the outer shell, based on his ongoing geometrical studies at Studio Olafur Eliasson in collaboration with Henning Larsen Architects. The installation *Mikroskop* (published here) was at the center of his 2010 solo exhibition at Martin-Gropius-Bau in Berlin, Germany.

OLAFUR ELIASSON wurde 1967 als Sohn isländischer Eltern in Kopenhagen geboren, wo er an der Königlich Dänischen Akademie für Bildende Künste studierte (1989–95). Bereits in den Anfängen seiner Laufbahn zog er nach Deutschland und gründete das Studio Olafur Eliasson als experimentelles Labor in Berlin. Heute lebt und arbeitet er in Kopenhagen und Berlin. Eliasson hatte Einzelausstellungen im Musée d'Art Moderne de la Ville de Paris, im ZKM in Karlsruhe, dem Museum für Kunst des 21. Jahrhunderts in Kanazawa und vertrat Dänemark auf der Biennale 2003 in Venedig. Jüngere Einzelausstellungen sind u.a *Take your time: Olafur Eliasson*, organisiert vom San Francisco Museum of Modern Art (San Francisco, Kalifornien). Die Schau reiste anschließend an das Museum of Modern Art und PS1 Contemporary Art Center in New York (2007–08). Für seine Installationen eignet er sich Naturerscheinungen an – wogenden Wasserdampf, der an Geysire erinnert, Regenbögen oder Räume voller Nebel. Durch das Versetzen „natürlicher" Phänomene – wie Wasser, Dunst oder Licht – in künstliche Umgebungen, sei es nun eine Straße oder eine Galerie, regt der Künstler die Betrachter an, über ihre Wahrnehmung der physischen Welt nachzudenken. Diesen Augenblick der Wahrnehmung, in dem Betrachter innehalten um nachzudenken, was sie gerade erleben, bezeichnete Eliasson als „sich selbst fühlen sehen". Für das Nationale Isländische Konzert- und Konferenzzentrum in Reykjavik gestaltete der Künstler die äußere Gebäudehülle und griff dabei auf fortdauernde Geometriestudien am Studio Olafur Eliasson in Zusammenarbeit mit Henning Larsen Architects zurück. Seine Installation *Mikroskop* (hier vorgestellt) war Herzstück seiner Einzelausstellung 2010 im Berliner Martin-Gropius-Bau.

OLAFUR ELIASSON est né en 1967 à Copenhague de parents islandais. Il a étudié à l'Académie royale des arts de Copenhague (1989–95). Très tôt dans sa carrière, il s'est installé en Allemagne où il a créé le Studio Olafur Eliasson à Berlin comme laboratoire expérimental. Eliasson vit et travaille à Copenhague et à Berlin. Il a fait l'objet d'expositions personnelles au Musée d'art moderne de la Ville de Paris, au ZKM de Karlsruhe, au Musée d'art contemporain du XXIᵉ siècle à Kanazawa, et a représenté le Danemark à la Biennale de Venise en 2003. Plus récemment, il a tenu une exposition personnelle intitulée « Take your Time : Olafur Eliasson » au Musée d'art moderne de San Francisco qui a également été présentée au PS1 et au Musée d'art moderne de New York (2007–08). Ses installations utilisent des éléments tirés de la nature : vapeur évoquant un geyser, arcs-en-ciel, salles remplies de brouillard, etc. En introduisant des phénomènes « naturels » comme l'eau, le brouillard ou la lumière dans un cadre artificiel, que ce soit une rue ou une galerie d'art, l'artiste incite les spectateurs à réfléchir sur leur perception du monde physique. Ce moment de perception, quand le spectateur s'arrête pour comprendre ce qu'il est en train d'expérimenter, est décrit par Eliasson dans sa formule « se voir ressentir ». Pour le Centre national islandais de concerts et de conférences de Reykjavik, il a créé une coque extérieure utilisant un parement issu de ses recherches permanentes sur la géométrie, menées en collaboration avec Henning Larsen Architects. L'installation *Mikroskop* (publiée ici) était la pièce centrale de son exposition personnelle au Martin-Gropius-Bau à Berlin (2010).

MIKROSKOP

Martin-Gropius-Bau, Berlin, Germany, 2010

Area: 17 x 18 x 27 meters. Client: not disclosed
Cost: not disclosed

This installation was at the center of the artist's 2010 solo exhibition "Innen Stadt Außen" (Inner City Out) at the Martin-Gropius-Bau in Berlin. This show included several interventions in public space. For **MIKROSKOP**, Eliasson installed walls of mirror foil up to the museum's central skylight, generating a kaleidoscopic space that infinitely reflects the metal framework of the skylight and the sky above. These mirror foil panels were attached to exposed scaffolding. Collapsing inner space and the outside, *Mikroskop* (Microscope) realized a central aspect of the exhibition which closely concerned itself with the relationship between the museum, the city, architecture, space, and perception.

Die Installation war zentrales Exponat der Einzelausstellung des Künstlers *Innen Stadt Außen*, die 2010 im Martin-Gropius-Bau in Berlin zu sehen war. Die Ausstellung umfasste darüber hinaus mehrere Interventionen im öffentlichen Raum. Für **MIKROSKOP** installierte Eliasson mit Spiegelfolie verblendete Wandsegmente bis hinauf zum zentralen Oberlicht des Museums, wodurch ein kaleidoskopartiger Raum entstand, der in unendlicher Folge das Tragwerk des Oberlichts und den Himmel darüber reflektierte. Die Segmente mit Spiegelfolie waren an einer frei liegenden Gerüstkonstruktion fixiert. In *Mikroskop* fielen Innen- und Außenraum zusammen. Die Arbeit verkörperte damit einen zentralen Aspekt der Ausstellung, die sich intensiv mit der Beziehung von Museum, Stadt, Architektur, Raum und Wahrnehmung befasste.

Cette installation occupait la place centrale de l'exposition consacrée à Eliasson au Martin-Gropius-Bau à Berlin en 2010, intitulée « Innen Stadt Außen » (la ville dedans-dehors). Cette exposition incluait diverses interventions dans l'espace public. Pour **MIKROSKOP**, Eliasson avait installé des murs en film-miroir montant jusqu'à la verrière centrale du musée pour créer un espace kaléidoscopique qui reflétait à l'infini l'ossature métallique de la verrière et le ciel. Ces panneaux réfléchissants étaient fixés à des échafaudages apparents. Fusionnant l'espace interne et l'extérieur, *Mikroskop* tenait un rôle central dans cette exposition consacrée aux relations entre le musée, la ville, l'architecture, l'espace et la perception.

Above, and left page, Mikroskop, 2010 (17 x 18 x 27 meters), installation views at the Martin-Gropius-Bau, Berlin. Below, a drawing of the work.

Oben und linke Seite, Mikroskop, 2010 (17 x 18 x 27 m), Installationsansichten aus dem Martin-Gropius-Bau, Berlin. Unten eine Zeichnung des Entwurfs.

Ci-dessus et page de gauche, Mikroskop (2010, 17 x 18 x 27 mètres), vue de l'installation au Martin-Gropius-Bau, Berlin. Ci-dessous, un dessin de l'œuvre.

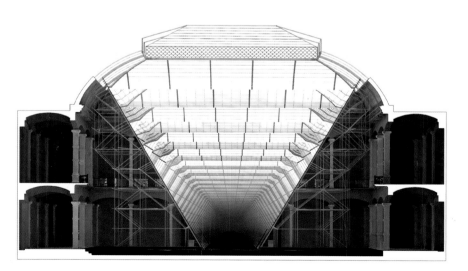

AMMAR ELOUEINI

AEDS Ammar Eloueini
5 Rue de l'Harmonie
75015 Paris
France

Tel/Fax: +33 1 48 42 49 44
E-mail: info@digit-all.net
Web: www.digit-all.net

AMMAR ELOUEINI was born in 1968 in Beirut, Lebanon. He received his degree as an architect from the École d'Architecture Paris-Villemin (DPLG, 1994) and an M.Sc in Advanced Architectural Design from Columbia University (New York, 1996). He created his present firm AEDS (Ammar Eloueini Digit-all Studio) in 1997. He is registered to work as an international architect with the AIA in New Orleans, where he is an Associate Professor at Tulane University, School of Architecture. His recent work includes the Orange Couch Coffee Shop (New Orleans, USA, 2008); PLEATS PLEASE Issey Miyake boutique (Toulouse, France, 2008); and an apartment remodeling (Paris, France, 2009). Current work includes the remodeling of another apartment in Paris (France, 2010–); Capsule, a performing art installation (San Francisco, USA, ongoing); the J House, a single-family house in New Orleans (Louisiana, USA, ongoing); and the remodeling of 52 SBD Landromats in Paris (France, ongoing). He has also worked on a number of exhibition designs, including "Le Tramway" (Pavillon de l'Arsenal, Paris, France, 2008, published here).

AMMAR ELOUEINI wurde 1968 in Beirut, Libanon, geboren. Er schloss sein Architekturstudium an der École d'Architecture Paris-Villemin ab (DPLG, 1994) und absolvierte einen M.Sc in Advanced Architectural Design an der Columbia University (New York, 1996). Sein heutiges Büro AEDS (Ammar Eloueini Digit-all Studio) gründete er 1997. Er ist als internationaler Architekt beim American Institute of Architects (AIA) in New Orleans eingetragen, wo er auch als Honorarprofessor an der Architekturfakultät der Tulane University lehrt. Zu seinen jüngeren Projekten zählen der Orange Couch Coffee Shop (New Orleans, USA, 2008), PLEATS PLEASE Issey Miyake Boutique (Toulouse, Frankreich, 2008) sowie der Umbau eines Apartments (Paris, 2009). Aktuelle Projekte sind u.a. der Umbau eines weiteren Apartments in Paris (2010–), Capsule, eine Bühneninstallation (San Francisco, USA, andauernd), das J House, ein Einfamilienhaus in New Orleans (Louisiana, USA, andauernd), sowie der Umbau der 52 SBD-Waschsalons in Paris (andauernd). Darüber hinaus entwarf er verschiedene Ausstellungsarchitekturen, darunter Le Tramway (Pavillon de l'Arsenal, Paris, 2008, hier vorgestellt).

Né en 1968 à Beyrouth, **AMMAR ELOUEINI** est diplômé de l'École d'architecture Paris-Villemin (DPLG, 1994) et a obtenu son M. Sc en conception architecturale avancée de l'université Columbia (New York, 1996). Il a créé son agence actuelle, AEDS (Ammar Eloueini Digit-all Studio), en 1997. Il est enregistré auprès de l'AIA de la Nouvelle-Orléans où il est professeur associé à l'École d'architecture de la Tulane University. Parmi ses réalisations récentes : le Orange Couch Coffee Shop (Nouvelle-Orléans, 2008) ; une boutique d'Issey Miyake PLEATS PLEASE (Toulouse, France, 2008) et la rénovation d'un appartement à Paris (2009). Actuellement, il travaille à la rénovation d'un autre appartement à Paris (2010–) ; au projet Capsule, installation d'art de performance (San Francisco, en cours) ; la J House, une maison individuelle de famille à la Nouvelle-Orléans (Louisiane, en cours), et à la rénovation de 52 laveries automatiques SBD à Paris (en cours). Il a également conçu plusieurs expositions dont « Le Tramway », au Pavillon de l'Arsenal (Paris, 2008, publié ici).

"LE TRAMWAY"

Pavillon de l'Arsenal, Paris, France, 2008

Area: 929 m². Client: Pavillon de l'Arsenal
Cost: not disclosed

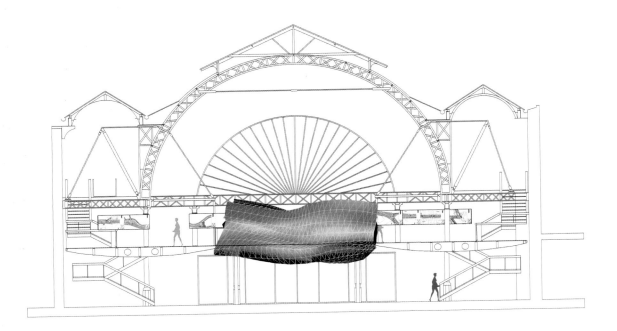

This exhibition design concerned the Pavillon de l'Arsenal, a space dedicated to the architecture and urban development of Paris. Under the title "**LE TRAMWAY**," the show dealt with the new Paris tramway lines that are intended to circle the city along the Boulevard des Maréchaux. Set up on the upper level of the Pavilion, which has a large open void with a bridge, the show made use of a polycarbonate "skin" suspended from the middle of this space. The architect states: "The exhibition design occupies the entire second floor and implements a strip 1 meter wide by 100 meters long where the trajectory of the tramway is unfolded, showing the different neighborhoods it crosses and connects." Ammar Eloueini points out that the polycarbonate skin acts as a light and sound barrier, with sound being amplified by reflections on its inner side.

Die Ausstellungsarchitektur wurde für den Pavillon de l'Arsenal entworfen, ein Forum, das der Architektur und Stadtentwicklung von Paris gewidmet ist. Die Ausstellung mit dem Titel „**LE TRAMWAY**" befasste sich mit der neuen Straßenbahnlinie, die die Stadt als Ringbahn entlang des Boulevard des Maréchaux umfahren wird. Die Schau wurde in der oberen Ebene des Pavillons gezeigt, zu der auch eine Brücke gehört, die einen offenen Raum überspannt. Im Zentrum dieses Raums wurde eine „Haut" aus Polycarbonat gespannt. Der Architekt erklärt: „Die Ausstellungsarchitektur besetzt die gesamte obere Etage und definiert einen 1 m breiten und 100 m langen Gang, an dem entlang sich der Verlauf der Straßenbahnlinie entfaltet. Hier werden die verschiedenen Stadtviertel, die sie durchquert und verbindet, präsentiert". Ammar Eloueini weist darauf hin, dass die Haut aus Polycarbonat als Licht- und Schallgrenze fungiert: Geräusche werden durch Reflexion an den Innenwänden verstärkt.

Cette exposition a été organisée pour le Pavillon de l'Arsenal, un lieu consacré à l'architecture et au développement urbain de Paris. Sous le titre « **LE TRAMWAY** », elle présentait la nouvelle ligne de tramway parisienne qui fera le tour de la capitale par les boulevards des Maréchaux. Installée en mezzanine autour d'un grand vide franchi par une passerelle, l'exposition faisait appel à une « peau » de polycarbonate suspendue à partir du centre du volume. « L'exposition occupe la totalité du second niveau du Pavillon et met en œuvre une bande de 1 m de large sur 100 m de long qui reprend le trajet du tramway et montre les différents quartiers qu'il traverse et relie », explique l'architecte. La « peau » de polycarbonate agit comme une barrière pour le son et la lumière, le son étant amplifié par sa réflexion sur sa face interne.

A general view of the installation in the Pavillon de l'Arsenal, not far from the Place de la Bastille in Paris, 2008.

Eine Gesamtansicht der Installation im Pavillon de l'Arsenal, unweit der Pariser Place de la Bastille, 2008.

Vue générale de l'installation du Pavillon de l'Arsenal, non loin de la place de la Bastille, Paris, 2008.

Drawings and images of the installation show the ways in which the architect formed and deformed the polycarbonate skin he used to create a pathway to lead visitors through the space.

Zeichnungen und Aufnahmen der Installation veranschaulichen, wie der Architekt die Haut aus Polycarbonat formte und verformte. Sie umfing einen Laufsteg, der die Besucher durch den Ausstellungsraum führte.

Les dessins et les images de l'installation montrent comment l'architecte a formé et déformé la peau en polycarbonate utilisée pour créer un cheminement guidant les visiteurs à travers l'exposition.

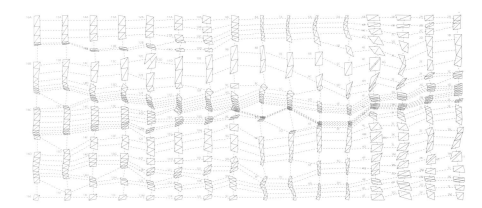

"Imperfetto

ESSENTIA

Essentia S.r.l.
Via D'Azeglio 21
40123 Bologna
Italy

Tel: +39 051 18 89 88 88
E-mail: info@essentiart.com
Web: www.essentiart.com

The principals of Essentia are **LEONARDO GUERRA SERÀGNOLI**, born in Rome in 1980, and **DARIA KHAN**, born in Moscow in 1987. Guerra Seràgnoli graduated from the Berklee College of Music in Film Scoring and is a founder and Managing Director of Essentia S.r.l. He works as a filmmaker. Daria Khan graduated from Lomonosov Moscow State University in the History of Art and worked at the Cazeau-La Beraudière Gallery in Paris, before becoming an independent curator. "Imperfetto" (Spazio Carbonesi, Bologna, 2010, published here) was their first project. Their next one will be "Svoboda" (Spazio Carbonesi, Bologna, 2011).

Essentia arbeitet unter Leitung von **LEONARDO GUERRA SERÀGNOLI**, geboren 1980 in Rom, und **DARIA KHAN**, geboren 1987 in Moskau. Guerra Seràgnoli schloss sein Studium der Filmmusik am Berklee College of Music ab und ist Gründer und Geschäftsführer von Essentia S.r.l. Er arbeitet als Filmemacher. Daria Khan schloss ihr Studium der Kunstgeschichte an der Staatlichen Lomonossov-Universität Moskau ab und arbeitete für die Galerie Cazeau-La Beraudière in Paris, bevor sie sich als freie Kuratorin selbstständig machte. *Imperfetto* (Spazio Carbonesi, Bologna, 2010, hier vorgestellt) war ihr erstes gemeinsames Projekt; geplant ist als nächstes Projekt *Svoboda* (Spazio Carbonesi, Bologna, 2011).

L'agence Essentia est animée par **LEONARDO GUERRA SERÀGNOLI**, né à Rome en 1980, et **DARIA KHAN**, née à Moscou en 1987. Guerra Seràgnoli, diplômé du Collège de musique Berklee en musique de films, est le fondateur et directeur gérant d'Essentia S.r.l. Il est réalisateur de films. Daria Khan, diplômée en histoire de l'art de l'Université d'État Lomonosov à Moscou, a travaillé à la galerie Cazeau-La Beraudière à Paris avant de devenir commissaire indépendante. Imperfetto (« Imparfait », Spazio Carbonesi, Bologne, 2010, publié ici) est leur premier projet commun. Le prochain sera « Svoboda » (Spazio Carbonesi, Bologne, 2011).

"IMPERFETTO"

Spazio Carbonesi, Bologna, Italy, 2010

Area: 604 m². Client: not disclosed
Cost: not disclosed

The exhibition "**IMPERFETTO**" took place during the 2010 Bologna Art Fair (Art First). The Spazio Carbonesi is located in Palazzo Zambeccari and was part of the Arte Fiera Off circuit, where it was viewed by about 2000 people. Daria Khan states: "*Imperfetto* means that we decided to use the unfinished elements of the space (imperfect space) together with the art installations to create a window for the audience in which they could walk on the edge between past and future, with the chance to participate in the completion of the show's emotional texture with their own visions and fantasies." In fact, the real substance of the intervention of Essentia was in the "path" they created within the space. "The whole concept," states Daria Khan, "was to let artists fill the space with their works with the unique chance to operate in a skeleton-like environment and then, on our side, to prepare around the works of art a path made of specific design interventions." The organizers have planned another show in the Spazio Carbonesi called "Svoboda" (January–February 2011).

Die Ausstellung **IMPERFETTO** fand während der Kunstmesse Art First 2010 in Bologna statt. Der Spazio Carbonesi befand sich im Palazzo Zambeccari und wurde im Rahmen des Arte-Fiera-Off-Rundgangs von rund 2000 Besuchern gesehen. Daria Khan erklärt: „*Imperfetto* bedeutet, dass wir uns entschieden hatten, die unfertigen Aspekte des Raums (den im-perfekten Raum) im Zusammenspiel mit den Kunstinstallationen zu nutzen, um ein Fenster für das Publikum zu schaffen, das ihnen ermöglichte, an der Grenze von Vergangenheit und Zukunft zu verharren. So hatten sie die Gelegenheit, das emotionale Geflecht der Ausstellung partizipativ zu ergänzen, und zwar durch ihre eigenen Visionen und Fantasien." Tatsächlich war die eigentliche Intervention von Essentia der „Pfad", den sie im Raum definierten. „Das ganze Konzept", so Daria Khan, „bestand darin, die Künstler den Raum mit ihren Arbeiten füllen zu lassen und ihnen die einzigartige Gelegenheit zu bieten, in einem fast skelettartigen Umfeld zu arbeiten; für uns bedeutete das, einen Pfad aus individuellen Design-Interventionen zu gestalten, der um die Kunstwerke herum verlief." Die Organisatoren planten eine weitere Ausstellung im Spazio Carbonesi unter dem Titel *Svoboda* (Januar–Februar 2011).

L'exposition « **IMPERFETTO** » s'est déroulée pendant la Foire de l'art 2010, Art First, à Bologne. Logé dans le palais Zambeccari, le Spazio Carbonesi, qui fait partie du circuit Arte Fiera Off, a été visité par 2000 personnes environ. « *Imperfetto* signifie que nous avons décidé d'utiliser les éléments non finis de l'espace (espace imparfait) parallèlement aux installations artistiques, pour créer une fenêtre à travers laquelle le public peut se déplacer à la limite du passé et du futur, et participer à l'enrichissement de la texture émotionnelle de l'exposition par ses propres visions et son imagination », explique Daria Khan. Concrètement, l'intervention d'Essentia repose sur un « cheminement » créé dans l'espace. « Le concept global, poursuit Daria Khan, était de laisser les artistes remplir l'espace de leurs œuvres en profitant de la chance unique d'opérer dans un environnement de type squelette, puis, de notre côté, de mettre en place autour des œuvres d'art un cheminement à l'aide d'interventions de design spécifiques. » Les organisateurs ont prévu une autre exposition intitulée « Svoboda » qui se déroulait également dans le Spazio Carbonesi (janvier–février 2011).

This page, a sketch showing the overall layout and the placement of the works of art. On the right page, an installation by Rostan Tavasiev, Antiquity.

Auf dieser Seite eine Skizze des Grundrisses im Überblick; eingezeichnet ist auch die Platzierung der Kunstwerke. Gegenüber Antiquity, eine Installation von Rostan Tavasiev.

Sur cette page, croquis du plan d'ensemble et du placement des œuvres d'art. Page de droite : installation de Rostan Tavasiev, Antiquity.

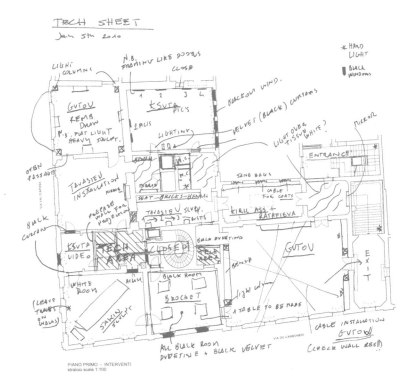

Above, an installation by the artist
Rostan Tavasiev called Naughtiness.
The designers and the artists played
on the rapport between contemporary
art and the older building.

Oben Naughtiness, eine Installation
von Rostan Tavasiev. Architekten und
Künstler spielten mit dem Spannungs-
feld zwischen zeitgenössischer Kunst
und historischer Architektur.

Ci-dessus, une installation de l'artiste
Rostan Tavasiev intitulée Naughtiness
(Mauvaise conduite). Les concepteurs
et l'artiste ont joué sur le rapport
entre l'art contemporain et le bâtiment ancien.

This page, right, and bottom left page, the work of Maxim Ksuta, called Behind the Mirror. *Below, floor plans with the names of the artists written in.*

Behind the Mirror, *eine Arbeit von Maxim Ksuta (rechts und linke Seite unten). Unten Grundrisse mit den Namen der Künstler.*

Sur cette page à droite et page de gauche, en bas : œuvre de Maxim Ksuta : Behind the Mirror *(De l'autre côté du miroir). Ci-dessous, plans au sol reprenant les noms des artistes exposés.*

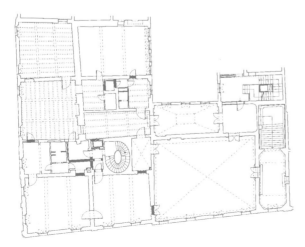

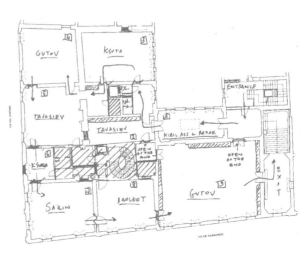

Left, a work by Dimitri Gutov called
Parallax and above, Roman Sakin's
Forest installation. Right, the location
of the exhibition.

Links Parallax, *eine Arbeit von Dimitri
Gutov, oben Roman Sakins Installation*
Forest. *Rechts der Ausstellungsort in
seinem Umfeld.*

À gauche, œuvre de Dimitri Gutov,
Parallax *(Parallaxe) et, ci-dessus,
l'installation* Forest *(Forêt) de Roman
Sakin. À droite, l'immeuble de
l'exposition.*

ESTABLISHED & SONS

Established & Sons
5–7 Wenlock Road
London N1 7SL
UK

Tel: +44 20 76 08 09 90
Fax: +44 20 76 08 01 10
E-mail: info@establishedandsons.com
Web: www.establishedandsons.com

ESTABLISHED & SONS, created in 2005, is a London-based producer of modern and contemporary furniture which is part of the Caparo Industries Group, a manufacturer and supplier of steel and engineering products for the automotive industry. The Chairman of the firm is Angad Paul, the Chief Executive of Caparo Group. The cofounder and former CEO of Established & Sons was Alasdhair Willis, the former Publishing Director of the Wallpaper* Group, before he left in 2008. The present CEO is Maurizio Mussati, the former Managing Director of Lighting at Moooi, who joined the firm in 2008. Sebastian Wrong, cofounder and Design Director, was born in 1971 and studied sculpture at Norwich School of Art, before forming his own manufacturing company. They have worked with such design stars as Zaha Hadid, Konstantin Grcic, the architects Caruso St. John, Jasper Morrison, and Amanda Levete—one of the founding partners of Future Systems, and presented their work at the international furniture fair in Milan, "Established & Sons / Milan 2009," La Pelota (Milan, Italy, 2009, published here).

ESTABLISHED & SONS, gegründet 2005, ist Hersteller moderner und zeitgenössischer Möbel mit Sitz in London. Das Unternehmen ist Teil der Caparo Industries Group, die Stahl- und Maschinenerzeugnisse für die Automobilindustrie produziert. Der Vorsitz der Firma liegt bei Angad Paul, Geschäftsführer der Caparo Group. Mitbegründer und ehemaliger Geschäftsführer von Established & Sons war Alasdhair Willis, zuvor Verlagsleiter der Wallpaper* Group. 2008 verließ er das Unternehmen. Geschäftsführer ist seitdem Maurizio Mussati, ehemals Geschäftsführer für den Bereich Leuchten bei Moooi. Sebastian Wrong, ebenfalls Mitbegründer und Design Director, geboren 1971, studierte Skulptur an der Norwich School of Art, ehe er seine eigene Produktionsfirma gründete. Die Firma kooperierte bereits mit Stardesignern wie Zaha Hadid, Konstantin Grcic, den Architekten Caruso St. John, Jasper Morrison und Amanda Levete, Mitbegründerin von Future Systems, und präsentierte ihr Programm auf der internationalen Möbelmesse in Mailand: *Established & Sons / Milan 2009*, La Pelota (Mailand, 2009, hier vorgestellt).

ESTABLISHED & SONS, créé en 2005, est une entreprise londonienne de production et d'édition de mobilier moderne et contemporain qui fait partie du Caparo Industries Group, fabricant et fournisseur de produits en acier et de solutions d'ingénierie pour l'industrie automobile, présidé par Angad Paul. Le cofondateur et ancien président-directeur général d'Established & Sons était Alasdhair Willis, ancien directeur de la publication du Wallpaper* Group, avant de le quitter en 2008. L'actuel président-directeur général est Maurizio Mussati, ex-directeur de département « éclairage » de Moooi, qui a rejoint l'entreprise en 2008. Sebastian Wrong, cofondateur et directeur du design, est né en 1971, a étudié la sculpture à l'École d'art de Norwich, avant de créer sa propre société de production. Ils ont collaboré avec des stars du design ou de l'architecture comme Zaha Hadid, Konstantin Grcic, Caruso St. John, Jasper Morrison et Amanda Levete, l'une des cofondatrices de Future Systems, et ont présenté leur production au Salon international du meuble de Milan : « Established & Sons / Milan 2009 », La Pelota (Milan, 2009, publié ici).

"ESTABLISHED & SONS / MILAN 2009"

La Pelota, Milan, Italy, 2009

Area: 1750 m². Client: Established & Sons
Cost: not disclosed

The designers created roughly formed enclosures with untreated wood, contrasting markedly with the sophisticated nature of their products.

Die Designer gestalteten grob gezimmerte „Räume" aus unbehandeltem Holz: Ein bewusster Kontrast zu den hochwertigen Produkten der Firma.

Les designers ont créé de petits enclos en bois non traité qui contrastent fortement avec la sophistication stylistique de leurs produits.

Another overview of the exhibition space in Milan in 2009, and, below, a detailed plan of the rectangular layout of the area.

Eine weitere Gesamtansicht des Mailänder Messestands 2009. Unten ein detaillierter Grundriss der rechteckigen Ausstellungsfläche.

Autre vue de l'exposition tenue à Milan en 2009 et, ci-dessous, plan détaillé de l'aménagement de l'espace.

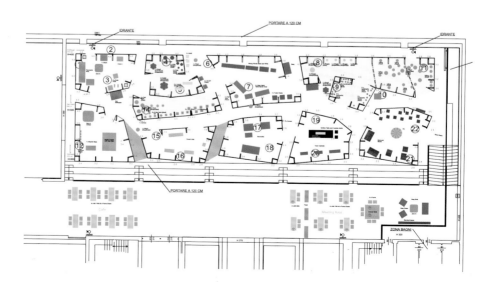

This temporary exhibition was open between April 22 and 26, 2009, during the Milan Salone Internazionale del Mobile. It was held in La Pelota, a former sports arena. Established & Sons launched a total of 16 new designs in Milan in 2009 and began work with Jason Bruges Studio, Mattali Crasset, Front Design, and Ronan and Erwan Bouroullec. The installation spanned the entire floor space of La Pelota with roughly stacked walls ranging from two to four meters in height, making use of 30 tons of untreated American tulipwood. "This year's installation is an intimate, entrenched settlement, an exposed timber flow, raw and basic, formal and frugal and ultimately recycled into product." stated Sebastian Wrong. 13 low-lit zones with "trenchlike corridors" were used to "create a sense of density and intensity of space."

Die temporäre Installation war vom 22. bis 26. April 2009 während der Internationalen Mailänder Möbelmesse in La Pelota zu sehen, einem ehemaligen Sportstadion. Established & Sons präsentierte 2009 insgesamt 16 neue Entwürfe in Mailand und kooperierte erstmals mit Jason Bruges Studio, Mattali Crasset, Front Design und Ronan und Erwan Bouroullec. Die Installation belegte mit ihren roh zusammengezimmerten Wänden, die zwischen zwei und vier Meter hoch waren und für die 30 t unbehandeltes amerikanisches Tulpenbaumholz verarbeitet wurden, die gesamte Nutzfläche von La Pelota. „Die diesjährige Installation ist eine intime, schützengrabenähnliche Siedlung, ein Fließen aus unverkleidetem Bauholz, rau und simpel, formell und frugal und letztendlich recycelt zu einem Produkt", erklärte Sebastian Wrong. 13 verhalten beleuchtete Zonen mit „schützengrabenähnlichen Korridoren" trugen dazu bei, dass „der Raum dichter und intensiver erlebt" wurde.

Cette exposition temporaire s'est tenue du 22 au 26 avril 2009 pendant le Salon international du meuble de Milan à La Pelota, une ancienne salle de sport. Established & Sons lançait à cette occasion 16 nouveaux produits et commençait à travailler avec le Jason Bruges Studio, Mattali Crasset, Front Design et les frères Ronan et Erwan Bouroullec. L'installation composée de cloisonnements de 2 à 4 m de haut faits d'empilements de pièces de bois (soit 30 tonnes de bois de tulipier américain brut) occupait la totalité du sol de la salle. « L'installation de cette année est un enracinement intime, un flux de bois, brut et basique, elle est formelle et modeste et finira recyclée dans les produits », précisait Sebastian Wrong. 13 zones faiblement éclairées, parcourues de « corridors-tranchées », créaient un « sentiment de densité et d'intensité de l'espace ».

Despite its apparently arbitrary nature, the stacking of the wood reveals a good deal of sophistication in these images, again, contrasting with the objects and furniture presented by Established & Sons.

Die vermeintlich willkürlich übereinander geschichteten Holzlatten sind, wie diese Bilder zeigen, tatsächlich eine ausgeklügelte Konstruktion und kontrastieren mit den Objekten und Möbelentwürfen von Established & Sons.

Malgré une implantation apparemment arbitraire, les cloisonnements de bois font preuve ici d'une certaine sophistication qui contraste avec les objets et meubles d'Established & Sons.

FANTASTIC NORWAY

Fantastic Norway
Storgata 37a
0182 Oslo
Norway

Tel: +47 40 84 84 00 / +47 95 18 82 15
E-mail: mail@fantasticnorway.no
Web: www.fantasticnorway.no

ERLEND BLAKSTAD HAFFNER was born in 1980. He attended the Bergen School of Architecture (B.A. in Architecture, Bergen, Norway, 2000–03), the Bartlett UCL (London, Diploma Affiliate in Architecture, 2005–06), and London Metropolitan University (M.Arch, 2006–07). He has been Chairman of Fantastic Norway since 2004. **HÅKON MATRE AASARØD** was born in 1979 and received his B.A. in Architecture from the Bergen School of Architecture (Bergen, Norway, 2000–03) and his M.Arch from the Oslo School of Architecture and Design (Oslo, Norway, 2006–07). He has been a partner of Fantastic Norway since 2005. They were hosts for a program on architecture on NRK television (2010). Their work includes temporary exhibition designs such as Cardboard Cloud (Oslo, Norway, 2009, published here) and "Walking Berlin," in the context of the 2009 International Design Festival DMY in the German capital. Other projects include a headquarters building for the firm bygg AS (Trøndelag, Norway, 2010–ongoing) and an analysis of the problems of Kolstad, the largest "satellite town" near Trondheim (Norway), using a caravan that they installed there in order to be in close contact with inhabitants.

ERLEND BLAKSTAD HAFFNER wurde 1980 geboren. Er besuchte die Architekturhochschule Bergen (B.A. in Architektur, Bergen, Norwegen, 2000–03), die Bartlett UCL (London, Diploma Affiliate in Architektur, 2005–06) sowie die London Metropolitan University (M.Arch, 2006–07). Seit 2004 ist er Direktor von Fantastic Norway. **HÅKON MATRE AASARØD** wurde 1979 geboren und absolvierte seinen B.A. in Architektur an der Architekturhochschule Bergen (Norwegen, 2000–03) sowie einen M.Arch an der Architektur- und Designhochschule Oslo (Norwegen, 2006–07). Seit 2005 ist er Partner bei Fantastic Norway. Das Team moderierte eine Architektursendung für den norwegischen Fernsehsender NRK (2010). Zu ihren Projekten zählen temporäre Ausstellungsarchitekturen wie Cardboard Cloud (Oslo, Norwegen, 2009, hier vorgestellt) oder Walking Berlin, im Rahmen des Internationalen Designfestivals DMY 2009 in der deutschen Hauptstadt. Weitere Projekte sind u.a. eine Firmenzentrale für bygg AS (Trøndelag, Norwegen, 2010–andauernd) sowie eine Problemanalyse der Stadt Kolstad, einer der größten Satellitenstädte in der Nähe von Trondheim (Norwegen), für die sie einen Wohnwagen einsetzten, um eng mit den Einwohnern kooperieren zu können.

ERLEND BLAKSTAD HAFFNER, né en 1980, a étudié à l'École d'architecture de Bergen (B. A. en architecture, Norvège, 2000–03), à la Bartlett UCL (Londres, diplôme affilié en architecture, 2005–06) et à la London Metropolitan University (M. Arch, 2006–07). Il est président de Fantastic Norway depuis 2004. **HÅKON MATRE AASARØD**, né en 1979, a obtenu son B. A. en architecture à l'École d'architecture de Bergen (Norvège, 2000–03) et son M. Arch à l'École de design et d'architecture d'Oslo (2006–07). Il est partenaire de Fantastic Norway depuis 2005. Ils ont tous deux animé un programme sur l'architecture pour la chaîne de télévision NRK (2010). Parmi leurs réalisations : des projets d'expositions temporaires comme le Cardboard Cloud (Nuage de carton, Oslo, 2009, publié ici) ou « Walking Berlin », dans le cadre du Festival international de design de Berlin, DMY (2009). Parmi leurs autres projets figurent le siège social de la firme bygg AS (Trøndelag, Norvège, 2010–en cours) et une analyse des problèmes de Kolstad, la plus grande ville-satellite de Trondheim, dans laquelle ils ont installé une caravane pour être au plus proche des habitants.

CARDBOARD CLOUD

Oslo, Norway, 2009

Area: 350 m². Client: Center for Design and Architecture (DogA)
Cost: €6000

CARDBOARD CLOUD was an exhibition design by Fantastic Norway for the main hall of the Center for Design and Architecture (DogA) in Oslo. The exhibition called "5X70m2" displayed work done by the best Norwegian design students. The architects state: "Since the exhibition was intended to present brand-new design objects, we decided to base the architectural concept on the thrill of unpacking. The installation consisted of over 3000 hanging cardboard boxes resembling a large pixilated cloud, hovering over the exhibited material. The construction created a large variety of spaces, from cavelike to lifted and open areas, inside the 350-square-meter exhibition hall. The objects and design concepts were exhibited both inside and outside the boxes." The architects proudly point out that after the event the cardboard boxes were recycled, leaving "only wires as leftovers."

CARDBOARD CLOUD (dt. Kartonwolke) wurde von Fantastic Norway als Ausstellungsarchitektur für die Hauptlobby im Zentrum für Design und Architektur (DogA), Oslo, gestaltet. Die Ausstellung *5X70m2* zeigte Arbeiten der besten Designstudenten Norwegens. Die Architekten erklären: „Da es bei dieser Ausstellung darum ging, brandneue Designobjekte zu präsentieren, entschieden wir uns, die Faszination des Auspackens als Aufhänger für das architektonische Grundkonzept zu wählen. Die Installation bestand aus über 3000 hängenden Pappkartons, die wie eine große Pixel-Wolke wirkten und über den Exponaten schwebten. Durch diese Konstruktion entstand eine Vielfalt von Räumen in der 350 m² großen Ausstellungshalle – von höhlenartigen Bereichen bis hin zu erhöhten, offenen Zonen. Die Objekte und Konzepte wurden sowohl in, als auch außerhalb der von den Kartons definierten Zonen präsentiert." Die Architekten weisen stolz darauf hin, dass die Pappkartons nach der Ausstellung recycelt wurden, sodass „lediglich die Drähte übrig blieben".

CARDBOARD CLOUD est une exposition conçue par Fantastic Norway pour le hall principal du Centre de design et d'architecture (DogA) d'Oslo. L'exposition intitulée « 5x70m2 » présentait les travaux des meilleurs étudiants en design norvégiens. « Comme l'idée de l'exposition était de présenter des objets entièrement nouveaux, nous avons décidé de faire reposer notre concept architectural sur l'excitation du moment du déballage. L'installation se composait de 3000 boîtes de carton faisant penser à un gros nuage pixellisé suspendu au-dessus des objets exposés. Cette construction générait une grande diversité d'espaces, zones caverneuses, ouvertes ou surélevées à l'intérieur du hall de 350 m². Les objets et les concepts de design étaient présentés aussi bien en dedans qu'en dehors des boîtes », expliquent les architectes. Ils font remarquer avec satisfaction qu'une fois l'exposition terminée, les boîtes ont été recyclées pour ne laisser que « quelques fils et déchets ».

An elevation of the installation and photos show how the architects installed suspended cardboard boxes. The overall result seen from above resembles an urban pattern.

Aufriss und Aufnahmen veranschaulichen die Installation der abgehängten Kartons. Von oben erinnert das Gesamtbild an eine urbane Struktur.

L'élévation et les photos montrent le principe de suspension des boîtes en carton. En vue plongeante, le résultat évoque un paysage urbain.

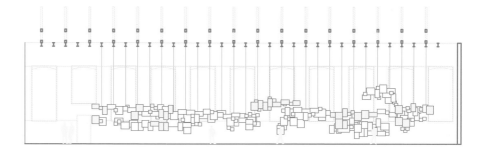

MARK FISHER

Stufish
The Mark Fisher Studio

Tel: +44 20 73 83 88 33
E-mail: studio@stufish.co.uk
Web: www.stufish.com

MARK FISHER, born in 1947, is a British architect and production designer of live shows and events. He graduated from the Architectural Association School of Architecture (AA) in London in 1971. He was a Unit Master at the AA from 1973 to 1977. In 1984 he set up the Fisher Park Partnership with Jonathan Park. The partnership was dissolved in 1994, when he established Stufish, the Mark Fisher Studio. Fisher has designed touring rock shows for many popular artists including Pink Floyd (*The Wall*, United States and Europe, 1980–81); The Rolling Stones (*Steel Wheels* world tour, 1989–90; *A Bigger Bang* world tour, 2005, published here); U2 (*ZooTV* world tour, 1992–93; *Popmart* world tour, 1997–98; *360°* world tour, 2009–11, also published here); Tina Turner; AC/DC; and Metallica. He has designed permanent installations including *Aquamatrix*, the lagoon show at Lisbon Expo '98; and *OVO*, the Millennium Show at the Dome in London (UK, 2000). His architectural projects include the Theater for *KÀ* at the MGM Grand in Las Vegas (USA, 2004) and the Golden Atrium at the Wynn resort in Macau (2007). He has also designed opening and closing ceremonies for the Olympic Games (Turin 2006, and Beijing 2008, also published here), and stage sets for theatrical shows including *We Will Rock You* and both *KÀ* and *Viva Elvis* by the Cirque du Soleil in Las Vegas.

MARK FISHER, geboren 1947, ist ein britischer Architekt und Setdesigner für Liveshows und -veranstaltungen. Sein Studium schloss er 1971 an der Architectural Association School of Architecture (AA) in London ab, wo er von 1973 bis 1977 Unit Master war. 1984 gründete er gemeinsam mit Jonathan Park die Firma Fisher Park Partnership. Als sich die Partner 1994 trennten, gründete Fisher sein Büro Stufish, kurz für Mark Fisher Studio. Fisher hat Tourneebühnen für zahlreiche bekannte Rockbands entworfen, darunter Pink Floyd (*The Wall*, USA- und Europatournee, 1980–81), die Rolling Stones (*Steel Wheels* Worldtour, 1989–90, *A Bigger Bang* Worldtour, 2005, hier vorgestellt), U2 (*ZooTV* Worldtour, 1992–93, *Popmart* Worldtour, 1997–98, *360°* Worldtour, 2009–11, ebenfalls hier vorgestellt) sowie für Tina Turner, AC/DC und Metallica. Fisher hat darüber hinaus dauerhafte Installationen entworfen, so etwa *Aquamatrix*, eine Licht- und Musikshow auf der Expo '98 in Lissabon oder *OVO*, die Millennium-Show im Millenium-Dome in London (2000). Zu seinen architektonischen Projekten zählen das Theater für *KÀ* im MGM Grand in Las Vegas (USA, 2004) sowie das Golden Atrium im Wynn Resort in Macau (2007). Außerdem gestaltete Fisher Eröffnungs- und Abschlussfeiern für die Olympischen Spiele (Turin 2006 und Peking 2008, ebenfalls hier vorgestellt) sowie die Szenografie für Bühnenshows wie *We Will Rock You* und *KÀ* sowie *Viva Elvis* vom Cirque du Soleil in Las Vegas.

MARK FISHER, né en 1947, est un architecte et concepteur britannique de spectacles et d'événements. Diplômé de l'école d'architecture de l'Architectural Association (AA) de Londres en 1971, il a été responsable d'unité à l'AA de 1973 à 1977. En 1984, il a créé le « Fisher Park Partnership » avec Jonathan Park, qui a été dissous en 1994, date à laquelle il a fondé Stufish, le Mark Fisher Studio. Fisher a conçu le dispositif scénique de tournées de nombreux groupes de rock célèbres, dont Pink Floyd (*The Wall*, États-Unis et Europe, 1980–81) ; les Rolling Stones (*Steel Wheels*, tournée mondiale, 1989–90 ; *A Bigger Bang*, tournée mondiale, 2005, publiée ici) ; U2 (*ZooTV*, tournée mondiale, 1992–93 ; *Popmart*, tournée mondiale, 1997–98 ; *360°*, tournée mondiale, 2009–11, publiée ici) ; Tina Turner ; AC/DC et Metallica. Il a conçu diverses installations permanentes, dont *Aquamatrix*, le show sur la lagune de l'Expo '98 de Lisbonne et *OVO*, le spectacle du dôme du Millenium à Londres en 2000. Parmi ses projets architecturaux figurent le théâtre pour *KÀ* au MGM Grand à Las Vegas (2004) et le Golden Atrium du Wynn Resort à Macau (2007). Il a également conçu les cérémonies d'ouverture et de clôture des Jeux olympiques de Turin 2006 et de Pékin 2008 (publiées ici), et les décors pour des spectacles comme *We Will Rock You* ainsi que *KÀ* et *Viva Elvis* du Cirque du Soleil à Las Vegas.

THE ROLLING STONES
A BIGGER BANG WORLD TOUR

2005

Area: 60 m (wide); 20 m (deep); 24 m (high). Client: The Rolling Stones. Cost: not disclosed.
Collaboration: Jeremy Lloyd (Technical Director)

The first sketches for the stage design "explored decadent, picturesque fantasies of grand 19th-century opera house décor." It was decided that part of the audience would be placed behind the band in boxes that brought opera to mind. As the design developed, the boxes became "sweeping expressionist balconies" forming a streamlined stage back wall. A large high-resolution LED video screen was set between the balconies. Low-resolution LED video panels set upstage from the balconies created a luminous backdrop to silhouette the audience. The primary structure, which took about 30 hours to erect, was mostly made from rented stock components. Two lines of masts and trusses supported a series of cantilever brackets that provided bearing for the audience balconies and lifting points for the panels. Three sets of the primary structures were used to keep up with the ongoing performances. One set only of the panels, video screens, performance stage, and other technical components traveled from show to show. They were installed during the final 24 hours before the show, and taken down and moved on to the next city immediately afterwards.

Die ersten Skizzen für das Bühnenbild waren „dekadente, malerische Vorstellungen von großartiger Opernhausopulenz des 19. Jahrhunderts". Die Überlegung war, einen Teil des Publikums hinter der Band in Logen unterzubringen, was an ein Opernhaus erinnern sollte. Im Zuge des Entwurfsprozesses wurden aus den Logen „ausgreifende expressionistische Balkone", die eine stromlinienförmige Rückwand hinter der Bühne bildeten. Zwischen den Balkonen befand sich eine hochauflösende LED-Videowand. Über den Balkonen waren LED-Videowände mit niedrigerer Auflösung montiert, die eine leuchtende Kulisse hinter den Schattenrissen der Gäste bildeten. Die Hauptkonstruktion, deren Aufbau 30 Stunden in Anspruch nahm, wurde überwiegend aus gemieteten Standard-Bühnenbauelementen realisiert. Zwei Reihen von Masten und Traversen stützten eine Anzahl auskragender Träger, die als Auflager für die Publikumsbalkone und Hebepunkte für die Frontpaneele dienten. Um dem Terminplan der Tournee gerecht zu werden, war die Basiskonstruktion in dreifacher Ausführung im Einsatz. Frontpaneele, Videoeinwände, die eigentliche Bühne und weitere technische Komponenten waren in einfacher Ausführung vorhanden und reisten von Konzert zu Konzert. Diese wurden in den letzten 24 Stunden vor der Show installiert, sofort nach dem Konzert demontiert und in die nächste Stadt transportiert.

Les premiers croquis du dispositif scénique « exploraient la fantaisie décadente et pittoresque des grands décors d'opéra du XIXᵉ siècle ». Une partie du public était placée derrière le groupe, dans des loges évoquant une salle d'opéra. Au fur et à mesure du développement du projet, ces loges devinrent des « balcons expressionnistes enveloppants », formant un fond de scène stylisé. Un vaste écran vidéo à DEL haute résolution fut installé entre les balcons. Des panneaux vidéo à DEL basse résolution suspendus des balcons au-dessus de la scène créaient un fond lumineux qui faisait paraître le public en silhouette. La structure principale, qui demandait environ 30 heures de montage, était principalement composée d'éléments standard loués. Deux rangs de mâts et de fermes soutenaient une série de consoles en porte-à-faux sur lesquelles reposaient les balcons et les points de levages des panneaux vidéo. Trois jeux de structures primaires furent utilisés pour respecter le calendrier des spectacles. Le reste – panneaux d'écrans vidéo, scène et autres composants techniques – était transporté de spectacle en spectacle, installé au cours des 24 heures précédant la représentation, puis démonté et transporté dans la ville suivante immédiatement après.

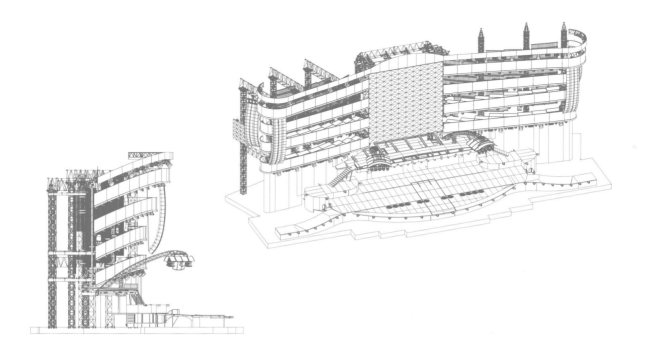

Drawings and photos give an idea of the architectural scale of the tour structures, seen above and below during concerts.

Zeichnungen und Aufnahmen geben eine Vorstellung von den Dimensionen der Tour-Aufbauten. Oben und unten die Bühne im Konzert.

Dessins et photos donnent une idée de l'échelle architecturale de ces décors de scène. En haut et en bas, vues pendant les concerts.

BEIJING OLYMPICS 2008 OPENING CEREMONY, "DREAM SPHERE"

Beijing, China, 2008

Area: 19 m (diameter); 24 m (high). Client: (BOCOG) Beijing Organizing Committee of the Olympic Games. Cost: not disclosed.
Collaboration: Yu Jianping (Director of Technology Group for Opening Ceremony)

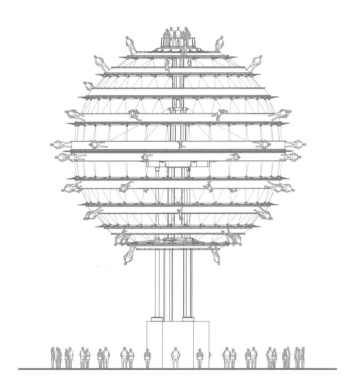

The sphere was made up of nine latitudinal rings, with a performance location for a group of singers at its north pole. The rings were structural trusses that functioned as running and rigging tracks for up to 60 performers who could run around them, always with their feet pointing inwards, toward the center of the globe. The rigging was arranged to allow the performers to run, to leap, to turn summersaults, and, at the lower latitudes, to fly around the sphere upside down. The rings were also designed so that they would pack down into a space only five meters high for storage in the lift chamber beneath the stadium. The sphere was lifted from its north pole by a telescoping mast 24 meters high.

Die Kugel bestand aus neun horizontalen Ringen; an ihrem „Nordpol" befand sich ein kleiner Bühnenbereich für eine Gruppe von Sängern. Die ringförmigen Stege waren zugleich lasttragende Traversen, die den bis zu 60 Schaustellern als Laufbahn dienten und mit einem Schienensystem zum Anseilen ausgestattet waren; sie konnten darauf laufen, springen, Saltos schlagen und – im unteren Bereich – kopfüber um die Kugel fliegen. Darüber hinaus waren die Ringe so konstruiert, dass sie sich auf eine Höhe von nur fünf Metern zusammenfahren und in einer Hubkammer unter dem Stadion verstauen ließen. Die Kugel wurde mithilfe eines 24 m hohen Telekopmasts hochgefahren, der an seinem „Nordpol" fixiert war.

Cette sphère était constituée de neuf anneaux horizontaux surmontés au nord d'une plate-forme réservée à un groupe de chanteurs. Les anneaux étaient en fait des poutres structurelles servant de pistes de course et de gréage à près de soixante exécutants qui s'y déplaçaient attachés par des câbles, couraient, sautaient, faisaient des culbutes, et, en partie inférieure, pouvaient même voler autour de la sphère. Ces anneaux se compressaient sur 5 m de haut seulement pour se ranger au pied de la cage de leur ascenseur, sous le stade. La sphère était soulevée par le haut par un mât télescopique de 24 m de hauteur.

The surprising spherical form of the structure, together with its lighting and the acrobatic performance of participants, gives an unreal or "fantastic" aspect to this work.

Mit ihrer erstaunlichen Kugelform und dank Lichtregie und Akrobatik der Schausteller wirkt die Konstruktion unwirklich und geradezu „fantastisch".

L'étonnante forme sphérique de la structure, ainsi que son éclairage et la performance acrobatique des artistes, donnent un aspect irréel fantastique à cette réalisation.

The sphere changes colors, and also its form, as the section drawing below shows: the round shape is flattened to allow the sphere to "grow" out of its supporting platform.

Die Kugel ändert nicht nur ihre Farbe, sondern auch ihre Form, wie der Aufriss zeigt: Flach zusammengefahren kann sie im Unterbau versenkt werden und von dort wieder „auftauchen".

La sphère change de couleurs mais aussi de forme, comme le montre la coupe : le support cylindrique rentre dans le sol pour lui permettre de se déployer de sa plate-forme.

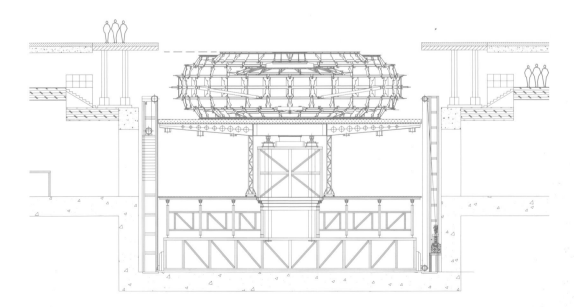

U2, *360°* WORLD TOUR

2009–11

Area: 64 m long x 48.5 m wide x 52 m high. Client: U2. Cost: not disclosed.
Collaboration: Willie Williams (Show Director), Chuck Hoberman (Transforming LED Screen Concept),
Jeremy Lloyd (Technical Director)

A 180-ton portable superstructure spans the full width of a typical football field, enclosing not only the performance stage and band, but also several thousand spectators. The superstructure is also intended to provide support for almost 200 tons of technical equipment rigged over the stage. The superstructure is typically erected during a three-day period preceding the show day. Three complete superstructures are used to meet the timetable of the tour. While one structure is being used for a performance, another is being erected in a different city, and the third is being dismantled and moved to another city. A single set of technical equipment is used for all the shows. On the show day, the superstructure is loaded with the technical equipment: a transformable LED screen (designed with Chuck Hoberman), lighting instruments, and loudspeakers. The performance stage, which houses all the band equipment, is built beneath the superstructure. The loading operation takes approximately 10 hours. After the show performance, the stage and technical equipment are demounted in approximately four hours. Thus the technical equipment is typically on site for less than 24 hours.

Die transportablen, 180 t schweren Aufbauten überspannen die gesamte Breite eines konventionellen Fußballfelds und rahmen nicht nur die Bühne und die Band, sondern mehrere Tausend Konzertbesucher ein. Darüber hinaus wurde die Konstruktion so konzipiert, dass sich fast 200 t Technik über der Bühne unterbringen lassen. In der Regel werden die Aufbauten in nur drei Tagen vor einem Konzert errichtet. Die Bühne wurde in dreifacher Ausfertigung realisiert, um dem Zeitplan der Tournee gerecht werden zu können. Während eine Bühne für das Konzert genutzt wird, wird die zweite bereits in einer anderen Stadt aufgebaut. Die dritte wird unterdessen abgebaut und an den darauffolgenden Spielort transportiert. Die Technik liegt in einfacher Ausführung vor und kommt an allen Orten gleichermaßen zum Einsatz. Am Konzerttag werden die Aufbauten mit der Bühnentechnik ausgestattet: einer wandlungsfähigen LED-Leinwand (entworfen mit Chuck Hoberman), Lichttechnik und Lautsprechern. Die eigentliche Bühne, in der das gesamte Equipment für die Band untergebracht ist, befindet sich unter den Aufbauten. Das Bestücken der Aufbauten mit der Technik dauert rund 10 Stunden. Nach dem Konzert werden Bühne und Technik in rund vier Stunden wieder abgebaut. Entsprechend befindet sich die Technik im Durchschnitt weniger als 24 Stunden an jedem Spielort.

Cette structure mobile de 180 tonnes, de la surface d'un stade de football, réunit non seulement la scène et le groupe, mais aussi plusieurs milliers de spectateurs. Érigée en trois jours avant chaque représentation, elle sert aussi de support à près de 200 tonnes d'équipements techniques suspendus au-dessus de la scène. Trois exemplaires en ont été construits pour respecter le calendrier de la tournée. Pendant que l'un est utilisé pour un spectacle, un autre est monté dans la ville suivante, tandis que le troisième est en cours de démontage et transporté dans une autre ville. Un seul jeu d'équipements techniques – écran à DEL transformable (conçu avec Chuck Hoberman), éclairages et haut-parleurs – est cependant utilisé pour tous les spectacles et mis en place le jour de la représentation. La scène, sur laquelle se trouvent tous les équipements sonores utilisés par les artistes, est logée sous la structure. L'opération de montage prend environ dix heures. Après le spectacle, la scène et les équipements techniques sont démontés en quatre heures environ et, de cette façon, toute la partie technique reste en place moins de 24 heures.

Borrowing a page from science fiction or video games, the 360° world tour stage has an arachnid appearance that allows it to support video screens and audio material.

Die Bühnenbauten für die 360° Worldtour erinnern an Sciencefiction-Filme oder Videospiele. Die spinnenartige Konstruktion trägt Videoleinwände und Soundsysteme.

Arachnéenne, la scène de la tournée mondiale 360° emprunte à la science-fiction ou aux jeux vidéo. Elle sert de support à des écrans vidéo et des baffles.

The unusual shape of the stage
mechanism allows the heavy amplification and light projection equipment
to be lifted above the performers,
who can be seen from all sides.

Dank der ungewöhnlich konstruierten
Aufbauten konnte die schwere Sound-
und Lichttechnik über der Bühne installiert werden, sodass die Band von
allen Seiten zu sehen ist.

La forme inhabituelle du mécanisme
scénique permet de placer le lourd
système d'amplification et de projection au-dessus des artistes qui sont
ainsi visibles de tous les côtés.

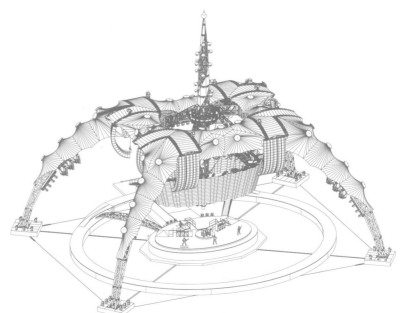

Set Design for Medea *and* Oedipus at Colo

MASSIMILIANO AND DORIANA FUKSAS

Massimiliano and Doriana Fuksas
Piazza del Monte di Pietà 30 / 00186 Rome / Italy
Tel: +39 06 68 80 78 71 / Fax: +39 06 68 80 78 72
E-mail: office@fuksas.it
Web: www.fuksas.it

MASSIMILIANO FUKSAS, born in 1944 in Rome, Italy, received his degree in Architecture at the "La Sapienza" University of Rome in 1969. He founded a studio in Rome in 1967 and opened an office in Paris in 1989. He won the 1999 Grand Prix d'Architecture in France and was the Director of the 7th Architecture Biennale in Venice (1998–2000). He has worked with **DORIANA MANDRELLI FUKSAS** since 1985. She attended the Faculty of Architecture at the "La Sapienza" University of Rome and has been responsible for design in the firm since 1997. In France, Fuksas completed the Mediatheque in Rézé (1987–91); the National Engineering School in Brest (ENIB ISAMOR, 1990–92); and the Maison des Arts at the Michel de Montaigne University in Bordeaux (1992–95). His Cor-ten steel entrance for the caves at Niaux (1988–93) shows, as did the Maison des Arts in Bordeaux, that Fuksas has a sustained interest in contemporary sculpture and art. More recently, Fuksas completed the Ferrari Research Center (Maranello, Italy, 2001–04); Fiera Milano (Rho-Pero, Milan, Italy, 2002–05); Zenith Strasbourg (Eckbolsheim, Strasbourg, France, 2003–07); the Armani Ginza Tower (Tokyo, Japan, 2005–07); a Church in Foligno (Italy, 2001–09); Emporio Armani Fifth Avenue (New York, New York, USA, 2009); MyZeil Shopping Mall (Frankfurt, Germany, 2009); Admirant Entrance Building (Eindhoven, Holland, 2003–10); 18 Septemberplein (Eindhoven, Holland, 2003–10); and Lyon Confluence (Lyon, France, 2005–10). Upcoming work includes the French National Archives (Paris, France, 2005–11); Lycée Hôtelier Marianne (Montpellier, France, 2006–11); Terminal 3 International Shenzhen Bao'an Airport (Shenzhen, China, 2008–12; House of Justice (Tbilisi, Georgia, 2010–); and the Rhike Park Music Theater and Exhibition Hall (Tbilisi, Georgia, 2010–).

MASSIMILIANO FUKSAS wurde 1944 in Rom geboren und schloss sein Architekturstudium 1969 an der Universität Rom „La Sapienza" ab. 1967 gründete er ein Studio in Rom und eröffnete 1989 ein Büro in Paris. 1999 wurde er in Frankreich mit dem Grand Prix d'Architecture ausgezeichnet und war Direktor der 7. Architekturbiennale von Venedig (1998–2000). Seit 1985 arbeitet er mit **DORIANA MANDRELLI FUKSAS** zusammen. Sie studierte an der Fakultät für Architektur der „La Sapienza" in Rom und ist seit 1997 verantwortlich für die Entwürfe des Büros. In Frankreich realisierte Fuksas die Mediathek in Rézé (1987–91) sowie die Nationale Hochschule für Bauingenieurwesen (ENIB ISAMOR, 1990–92) und das Maison des Arts an der Universität Michel de Montaigne in Bordeaux (1992–95), das ebenso wie der vom Büro aus Cor-ten-Stahl gestaltete Eingangsbereich zu den Höhlen von Niaux (1988–93) belegt, dass Fuksas ein anhaltendes Interesse für zeitgenössische Skulptur und Kunst hat. In jüngerer Zeit konnte Fuksas das Ferrari-Forschungszentrum (Maranello, Italien, 2001–04), die Fiera Milano (Rho-Pero, Mailand, 2002–05), das Zenith Strasbourg (Eckbolsheim, Frankreich, 2003–07), den Armani Ginza Tower (Tokio, 2005–07), eine Kirche in Foligno (Italien, 2001–09), Emporio Armani Fifth Avenue (New York, USA, 2009), das Einkaufszentrum MyZeil (Frankfurt am Main, 2009), das Admirant Entrance Building (Eindhoven, Holland, 2003–10), 18 Septemberplein (Eindhoven, Holland, 2003–10) sowie Lyon Confluence (Lyon, Frankreich, 2005–10) fertigstellen. Geplante Projekte sind u.a. das Französische Nationalarchiv (Paris, 2005–11), das Lycée Hôtelier Marianne (Montpellier, Frankreich, 2006–11), das Terminal 3 am Flughafen Shenzhen Bao'an (Shenzhen, China, 2008–12), ein Gerichtsgebäude (Tblisi, Georgien, 2010–) sowie Musiktheater und Messehallen im Rhike Park (Tblisi, Georgien, 2010–).

MASSIMILIANO FUKSAS, né en 1944 à Rome, est diplômé d'architecture de l'université romaine La Sapienza (1969). Il crée une agence à Rome en 1967 et ouvre un bureau à Paris en 1989. En 1999, il remporte en France le Grand Prix d'architecture. Il a été directeur de la VIIe Biennale d'architecture de Venise (1998–2000) et travaille avec **DORIANA MANDRELLI FUKSAS** depuis 1985. Ctte dernière, qui a également étudié à la faculté d'architecture de l'université romaine La Sapienza, est responsable du design à l'agence depuis 1997. La présence en France de Massimiliano Fuksas a été marquée par plusieurs réalisations comme la médiathèque de Rézé (1987–91) ; l'École nationale des ingénieurs de Brest (ENIB ISAMOR, 1990–92) ou la Maison des Arts à l'université Michel-de-Montaigne à Bordeaux (1992–95). Son entrée en acier Corten pour les grottes de Niaux (1988–93) montre, comme la Maison des Arts de Bordeaux, son intérêt soutenu pour l'art et la sculpture contemporains. Parmi ses réalisations plus récentes : le Centre de recherches Ferrari (Maranello, Italie, 2001–04) ; la Foire de Milan (Rho-Pero, Milan, 2002–05) ; le Zénith de Strasbourg (Eckbolsheim, Strasbourg, 2003–07) ; la tour Armani Ginza (Tokyo, 2005–07) ; une église à Foligno (Italie, 2001–09) ; l'Emporio Armani Fifth Avenue (New York, 2009) ; le centre commercial MyZeil (Francfort-sur-le-Main, 2009) ; l'entrée de l'immeuble Admirant (Eindhoven, Pays-Bas, 2003–10) ; le « 18 Septemberplein » (Eindhoven, Pays-Bas, 2003–10) et Lyon Confluence (France, 2005–10). L'agence travaille actuellement sur le projet des Archives nationales de France (Pierrefitte, près de Paris, 2005–11) ; le lycée hôtelier Marianne (Montpellier, France, 2006–11) ; le terminal 3 de l'aéroport international Bao'an de Shenzhen (Shenzhen, Chine, 2008–12) ; un palais de justice (Tbilisi, Georgie, 2010–) et le théâtre de Musique du parc Rhike et sa salle d'expositions (Tbilissi, Georgie, 2010).

SET DESIGN FOR
MEDEA AND *OEDIPUS AT COLONUS*

Syracuse, Italy, 2009

Area: not disclosed. Client: INDA Instituto Nazionale Dramma Antico. Cost: not disclosed.
Collaboration: Frauke Stenz (Project Leader)

The advantage of having a talented architect create a stage design is visible in the image below, where the simplicity of the set shows not only the stage but the outdoor setting to its best advantage.

Das Bild unten zeigt, welchen Vorteil es hat, das Bühnenbild von einem versierten Architekten gestalten zu lassen: Die Schlichtheit der Kulisse bringt nicht nur die Bühne, sondern auch die Umgebung zur Geltung.

L'avantage d'avoir recours à un architecte de talent pour la création d'une scène est illustré par la photo ci-dessous. La simplicité du décor met la scène, ainsi que le cadre extérieur, en valeur.

The architects conceived of the stage design as a "concave blade," as is visible in the photos and the sketches on this page.

Die Architekten entwickelten das Bühnenbild aus dem Motiv einer „konkaven Klinge", wie auf den Ansichten und Zeichnungen dieser Doppelseite zu sehen.

Les architectes ont conçu une scène en « lame concave », comme le montrent les photos et les croquis de cette page.

The architects designed these **SETS** for the Greek Theater in Syracuse for performances of **MEDEA** by Euripides and **OEDIPUS AT COLONUS** by Sophocles that occurred between May 9 and June 21, 2009. Massimiliano and Doriana Fuksas based their concept on the idea of the lost horizon of events depicted and the performances of these ancient plays in the past. "The idea of the horizon is very simple," says Fuksas. "It has to do with the concept of catharsis, and the landscape, place, actions, and conscience of spectators, not in the present, but in the past." Rather than any attempt to reconstitute such landscapes or scenery, the architects have chosen to represent the lost horizon with a "concave blade" that reflects the action and involves the public while inviting introspection. The very concept of architecture is reduced here to one of its purest and simplest forms.

Die Architekten gestalteten das **BÜHNENBILD** für Inszenierungen von **MEDEA** von Euripides und **ÖDIPUS AUF KOLONOS** von Sophokles, die vom 9. Mai bis 21. Juni 2009 im griechischen Amphitheater in Syrakus aufgeführt wurden. Konzeptueller Ausgangspunkt für Massimiliano und Doriana Fuksas war die Vorstellung von einem verlorenen Horizont sowie die alten Inszenierungen der antiken Theaterstücke. „Die Idee vom Horizont ist einfach", erläutert Fuksas. „Sie hat mit dem Begriff der Katharsis zu tun, mit der Landschaft, dem Ort, der Handlung und dem Gewissen der Zuschauer – nicht in der Gegenwart, sondern in früheren Zeiten." Doch statt solche Landschaften oder Szenerien nachzuempfinden, entschieden sich die Architekten, den verlorenen Horizont mithilfe einer „konkaven Klinge" zu symbolisieren, in der sich die Bühnenhandlung spiegelt und die zugleich das Publikum mit einbezieht und zur Introspektion einlädt. Hier wird das Grundkonzept der Architektur schlechthin auf eine ihrer reinsten und einfachsten Formen reduziert.

Les architectes ont conçu ces **DÉCORS** pour les représentations de la **MÉDÉE** d'Euripide et l'**ŒDIPE À COLONE** de Sophocle données du 9 mai au 21 juin 2009 à l'amphithéâtre grec de Syracuse. Le concept de Massimiliano et Doriana Fuksas repose sur l'idée de la perte de l'horizon des événements décrits par ces pièces datant de l'Antiquité. « L'idée de l'horizon est très simple, explique Fuksas, elle est liée au concept de catharsis, de paysage, de lieu, d'action et de conscience des spectateurs, non pas du présent mais du passé. » Plutôt que de tenter de reconstituer les paysages ou décors de l'Antiquité, les architectes ont choisi de représenter cet horizon perdu par une « lame concave » qui reflète l'action et implique le public, tout en invitant à l'introspection. Le concept même d'architecture est ici réduit à une de ses formes les plus pures et les plus simples.

Although the mirrored effect of the set generates complex reflections and amplifies the movement of the actors, the basic concept is extremely simple.

Der Spiegeleffekt erzeugt komplexe Reflexionen und verstärkt zugleich das Agieren der Darsteller auf der Bühne. Das Grundkonzept des Entwurfs ist dabei denkbar einfach.

Le concept de base est extrêmement simple. Les effets de miroirs sur le décor génèrent des reflets complexes et amplifient les mouvements des acteurs.

A photo (above) together with a model and a sketch demonstrate the close proximity of the actual realization to the concept of Massimiliano and Doriana Fuksas.

Die Aufnahme oben sowie Modell und Skizze (unten) belegen, wie eng die Umsetzung des Bühnenbilds dem Konzept von Massimiliano und Doriana Fuksas entspricht.

Photo, maquette et croquis montrent à quel point le projet de Massimiliano et Doriana Fuksas était proche de la réalisation finale.

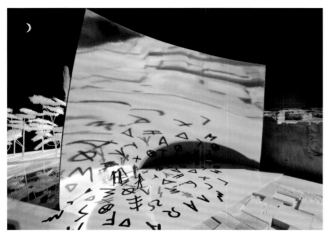

LAURENT GRASSO & PASCAL GRASSO

Laurent Grasso
19 Rue Decres
75014 Paris
France

Tel/Fax: +33 1 45 42 11 13
E-mail: laurentgrasso@gmail.com
Web: www.skny.com /
www.galeriechezvalentin.com

Pascal Grasso Architectures
41 Rue de la Mare
75020 Paris
France

Tel: +33 1 71 18 36 76
E-mail: contact@pascalgrasso.com
Web: www.pascalgrasso.com

LAURENT GRASSO was born in Mulhouse, France, in 1972. He studied at the École nationale des Beaux-Arts in Paris (1994–99), is a multimedia artist, and has worked with his brother Pascal on other projects, including a small screening room and a radio studio. **PASCAL GRASSO** was also born in Mulhouse, in 1976, and graduated from the Paris-Belleville school of architecture in 2002. From 2002 to 2004, he worked for Jean Nouvel, Métra et Associés, and Agnès B. Design. He created his own office, Pascal Grasso Architectures, in Paris in 2005. His work includes the design of the exhibition "Radio-Days," De Appel Art Center (Amsterdam, The Netherlands, 2006); design of the exhibition "Carte Blanche à Guillaume Houzé," Drouot Montaigne (Paris, 2008); an office for Callegari Berville Grey (Paris, 2008); Nomiya, Palais de Tokyo (Paris, 2009, published here); a showroom for Stella K, Champs-Elysées (Paris, 2010); and a private house in the south of France due for 2011 completion, all in France unless stated otherwise.

LAURENT GRASSO wurde 1972 in Mulhouse, Frankreich, geboren. Er studierte an der École nationale des Beaux-Arts in Paris (1994–99), ist Multimediakünstler und hat mit seinem Bruder Pascal bereits an anderen Projekten zusammengearbeitet, darunter ein kleiner Filmvorführraum und ein Radiostudio. **PASCAL GRASSO** wurde 1976 ebenfalls in Mulhouse geboren und schloss sein Studium 2002 an der Hochschule für Architektur in Paris-Belleville ab. Zwischen 2002 und 2004 arbeitete er für Jean Nouvel, Métra et Associés und Agnès B. Design. 2005 gründete er in Paris sein eigenes Büro, Pascal Grasso Architectures. Zu seinen Projekten zählen die Ausstellungsarchitektur für *Radio-Days*, De Appel Art Center (Amsterdam, Niederlande, 2006) und *Carte Blanche à Guillaume Houzé*, Drouot Montaigne (Paris, 2008), ein Büro für Callegari Berville Grey (Paris, 2008), das Restaurant Nomiya, Palais de Tokyo (Paris, 2009, hier vorgestellt), ein Showroom for Stella K, Champs-Elysées (Paris, 2010) sowie ein privater Wohnbau in Südfrankreich (voraussichtliche Fertigstellung 2011), alle in Frankreich, sofern nicht anders angegeben.

LAURENT GRASSO, né à Mulhouse en 1972, est diplômé de l'École nationale des beaux-arts de Paris (1994–99). Artiste multimédia, il a travaillé avec son frère sur d'autres projets, dont une petite salle de projection et un studio de radio. **PASCAL GRASSO**, né à Mulhouse en 1976, est diplômé de l'École d'architecture de Paris-Belleville (2002). De 2002 à 2004, il a travaillé pour Jean Nouvel, Métra et Associés et Agnès B. Design. Il a fondé son agence Pascal Grasso Architectures à Paris en 2005. Parmi ses réalisations : la conception d'une exposition « Radio-Days » au De Appel Art Center (Amsterdam, 2006) ; l'exposition « Carte Blanche à Guillaume Houzé » à Drouot Montaigne (Paris, 2008) ; des bureaux pour l'agence de publicité Callegari Berville Grey (Paris, 2008) ; le restaurant *Nomiya* au Palais de Tokyo (Paris, 2009, publié ici) ; un showroom pour Stella K (Champs-Elysées, Paris, 2010) et une résidence privée dans le sud de la France, prévue pour 2011.

NOMIYA

Palais de Tokyo, Paris, France, 2009

Area: 63 m². Client: Electrolux. Cost: not disclosed
Website: www.nomiya.org

This temporary, transportable restaurant with seating for 12 was set on the roof of the Palais de Tokyo in Paris between April and June 2009, offering guests a panoramic view of the Seine and the Eiffel Tower. The name **NOMIYA** is taken from a Japanese word signifying "very small restaurant." Built partially in the shipyards at Cherbourg, the 18-meter-long structure was brought to Paris in two pieces and assembled on the roof of the Palais de Tokyo. It is essentially a glass cabin with a perforated metal screen that covers the central cooking area. The interior of the restaurant, with its white Corian furniture and a gray wood floor, is described by the architect as "minimalist." LED lighting was placed between the metal skin of the structure and its glass core, with further LEDs suspended above the dining area.

Das temporäre, transportable Restaurant mit Sitzplätzen für 12 Gäste war zwischen April und Juni 2009 auf dem Dach des Palais de Tokyo installiert und bot den Gästen einen Panoramablick über die Seine und auf den Eiffelturm. Der Name **NOMIYA** bezieht sich auf das japanische Wort für „sehr kleines Restaurant". Die 18 m lange Konstruktion wurde teils in den Werften von Cherbourg gebaut, in zwei Teilen nach Paris transportiert und auf dem Dach des Palais de Tokyo montiert. Im Kern handelt es sich um einen Glaskasten mit einer Blende aus Lochblech, die den zentralen Kochbereich umfängt. Das Interieur des Restaurants mit seinen Einbauten aus weißem Corian und grauen Holzböden beschreibt der Architekt als „minimalistisch". Zwischen der Metallhaut und dem Glaskern der Konstruktion sind LED-Elemente integriert; über dem Essbereich hängen weitere LED-Leuchten.

Ce restaurant temporaire et transportable de douze couverts a été installé sur le toit-terrasse du Palais de Tokyo à Paris d'avril à juin 2009. Il offrait à ses clients une vue panoramique de la Seine et de la tour Eiffel. Le nom de **NOMIYA** signifie en japonais « très petit restaurant ». En partie construite dans les chantiers navals de Cherbourg, sa structure de 18 m de long a été amenée à Paris en deux parties et assemblée sur la toiture. Elle est essentiellement constituée d'une cabine vitrée dans laquelle un écran de métal perforé isole la partie centrale consacrée à la cuisine. L'intérieur décoré d'un sol en bois gris et de mobilier en Corian est présenté par l'architecte comme « minimaliste ». Un éclairage à base de DEL a été placé entre la peau métallique de la construction et le noyau de verre, d'autres luminaires à DEL étant suspendus au-dessus de l'aire des repas.

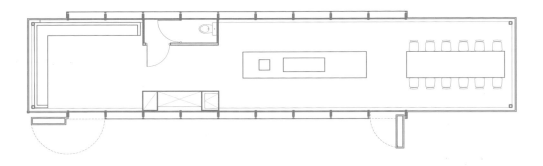

Traditionally a place for the display of modern art, the Palais de Tokyo is located above the Right Bank of the Seine with a commanding view of such monuments as the Eiffel Tower.

Der Palais de Tokyo, seit langem Ausstellungsort für zeitgenössische Kunst, liegt am rechten Seine-Ufer und bietet eindrucksvolle Sicht auf Sehenswürdigkeiten wie den Eiffelturm.

Lieu d'exposition d'art moderne à Paris, depuis sa création, le Palais de Tokyo domine la rive droite de la Seine et offre des vues sur divers monuments dont la tour Eiffel.

ZAHA HADID

Zaha Hadid Architects
Studio 9
10 Bowling Green Lane
London EC1R 0BQ
UK

Tel: +44 20 72 53 51 47
Fax: +44 20 72 51 83 22
E-mail: press@zaha-hadid.com
Web: www.zaha-hadid.com

ZAHA HADID studied architecture at the Architectural Association (AA) in London beginning in 1972 and was awarded the Diploma Prize in 1977. She then became a partner of Rem Koolhaas in OMA and taught at the AA. She has also taught at Harvard, the University of Chicago, in Hamburg, and at Columbia University in New York. In 2004, Zaha Hadid became the first woman to win the coveted Pritzker Prize. She completed the Vitra Fire Station (Weil am Rhein, Germany, 1990–94) and exhibition designs such as that for "The Great Utopia" (Solomon R. Guggenheim Museum, New York, USA, 1992). More recently, Zaha Hadid has entered a phase of active construction with such projects as the Lois & Richard Rosenthal Center for Contemporary Art (Cincinnati, Ohio, USA, 1999–2003); Phaeno Science Center (Wolfsburg, Germany, 2001–05); the Central Building of the new BMW Assembly Plant in Leipzig (Germany, 2005); Ordrupgaard Museum Extension (Copenhagen, Denmark, 2001–05); the Mobile Art, Chanel Contemporary Art Container (various locations, 2007–); and the MAXXI, the National Museum of 21st Century Arts (Rome, Italy, 1998–2009). Current projects include the Guangzhou Opera House (Guangzhou, China, 2006–10); the Sheik Zayed Bridge (Abu Dhabi, UAE, 2005–12); and the Aquatics Center for the London 2012 Olympic Games (UK).

ZAHA HADID studierte ab 1972 an der Architectural Association (AA) in London und erhielt 1977 den Diploma Prize. Anschließend wurde sie Partnerin von Rem Koolhaas bei OMA und unterrichtete an der AA. Darüber hinaus lehrte sie in Harvard, an der Universität von Chicago, in Hamburg sowie an der Columbia University in New York. 2004 wurde Zaha Hadid als erste Frau mit dem begehrten Pritzker-Preis ausgezeichnet. Sie realisierte u.a. eine Feuerwache für Vitra (Weil am Rhein, Deutschland, 1990–94) und Ausstellungsarchitekturen wie *The Great Utopia* (Solomon R. Guggenheim Museum, New York, 1992). In jüngerer Zeit begann eine Phase des aktiven Bauens für Hadid, etwa mit dem Lois & Richard Rosenthal Center for Contemporary Art (Cincinnati, Ohio, 1999–2003), dem Phaeno Wissenschaftszentrum (Wolfsburg, 2001–05), dem Zentralgebäude des neuen BMW-Werks in Leipzig (2005), dem Anbau für das Museum Ordrupgaard (Kopenhagen, 2001–05), dem Mobile Art, Chanel Contemporary Art Container (verschiedene Standorte, 2007–) sowie dem MAXXI Nationalmuseum für Kunst des 21. Jahrhunderts (Rom, 1998–2009). Aktuelle Projekte sind u.a. das Opernhaus in Guangzhou (Guangzhou, China, 2006–10) sowie die Scheich-Zajed-Brücke (Abu Dhabi, VAE, 2005–12) und das Aquatics Center für die Olympiade 2012 in London.

ZAHA HADID a étudié à l'Architectural Association (AA) de Londres de 1972 à 1977, date à laquelle elle a reçu le prix du Diplôme. Elle est ensuite devenue partenaire chez Rem Koolhaas à OMA et a enseigné à l'AA ainsi qu'à Harvard, à l'université de Chicago, à Hambourg et à l'université Columbia à New York. En 2004, elle a été la première femme à remporter le prix Pritzker. Parmi ses réalisations : un poste d'incendie pour Vitra (Weil am Rhein, Allemagne, 1990–94) et des expositions comme « La Grande Utopie » au Solomon R. Guggenheim Museum (New York, 1992). Plus récemment, elle est entrée dans une phase active de grands chantiers avec des réalisations comme le Centre Lois & Richard Rosenthal pour l'art contemporain (Cincinnati, Ohio, 1999–2003) ; le centre scientifique Phaeno (Wolfsburg, Allemagne, 2001–05) ; le bâtiment central de la nouvelle usine BMW de Leipzig (2005) ; l'extension du musée Ordrupgaard (Copenhague, 2001–05) ; le pavillon Mobile Art, Chanel Contemporary Art Container (divers lieux, 2007–) ; et le Musée national des arts du XXIe siècle (MAXXI, Rome, 1998–2009). Parmi ses projets récents figurent l'Opéra de Guangzhou (Chine, 2006–10) ; le pont Cheikh Zayed (Abou Dhabi, EAU, 2005–12) et l'Aquatics Center pour les Jeux olympiques de Londres 2012.

"EGYPT—MOTHER OF THE WORLD," EGYPTIAN PAVILION

Expo 2010, Shanghai, China, 2010

Area: 1000 m². Client: GOIEF/EECA, Egypt. Cost: not disclosed.
Collaboration: NUSSLI, Switzerland (Project Manager), Xian Dai Design Institute Shanghai
(Executive Architect/Contractor)

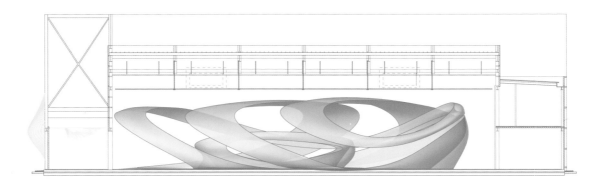

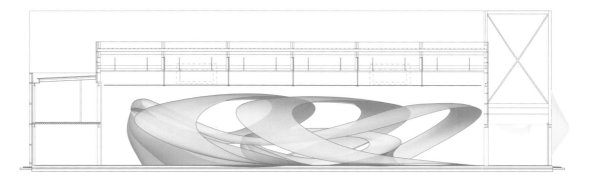

The architects state: "The design concept '**MOTHER OF THE WORLD**' derives from the column of Hathor, the Mother of the Gods, which is the centerpiece of the Egyptian exhibition at Shanghai World Expo 2010." The architectural part is related to a single, enveloping fabric ribbon that continues from the façade into the space and the exhibition. The ribbon "combines ceiling, floor, and walls in a spatial continuum to showcase the artifacts and becomes a projection surface for an astonishing moving-image installation—a film commissioned and designed especially for the fluid surfaces of the ribbon within the Egyptian Pavilion." The forms seen here are quite typical of other installations by Zaha Hadid, breaking down the usual distinctions between architectural elements to emphasize the continuity which, here, symbolically ties together the past and future of Egypt.

Die Architekten erklären: „Das gestalterische Konzept ‚**MUTTER DER WELT**' leitet sich von der Hathorsäule ab (benannt nach der Muttergöttin Hathor), die das Herzstück der ägyptischen Ausstellung auf der Expo 2010 in Shanghai ist". Die Architektur ähnelt einem kontinuierlichen, alles umschließenden Stoffband, das sich von der Fassade in den Innenraum und die Ausstellung hinein fortsetzt. Das Band „verbindet Decke, Boden und Wand zu einem räumlichen Kontinuum, in dem die Kunstwerke präsentiert werden, und wird zur Projektionsfläche für eine bemerkenswerte Installation aus bewegten Bildern – einem Film, der eigens für die fließenden Oberflächen des Bands im ägyptischen Pavillon in Auftrag gegeben und realisiert wurde". Die hier zu sehenden Formen sind insofern recht typisch für Hadids übrige Installationen, als sie die üblichen Grenzen zwischen unterschiedlichen architektonischen Elementen verwischen und stattdessen eine Kontinuität betonen, das in diesem Fall symbolisch Vergangenheit und Gegenwart Ägyptens in sich vereint.

Comme l'explique l'architecte : « Le concept de "**MÈRE DU MONDE**" est issu de la colonne de Hathor, mère des dieux, qui est l'élément central de la participation égyptienne à l'Exposition universelle de Shanghaï 2010. « Le parti architectural est celui d'un ruban de tissu enveloppant qui se déroule de la façade à l'intérieur du volume et de l'exposition. Ce ruban « relie le plafond, le sol et les murs dans un *continuum* spatial qui met en avant les artefacts exposés, et se transforme en surface de projection pour une étonnante installation vidéo – un film spécialement commandé et conçu pour la surface fluide du ruban ». Assez caractéristiques des autres installations de Zaha Hadid, les formes bousculent les distinctions habituelles entre les composants architecturaux et développent une continuité qui, dans ce cas précis, relie symboliquement le passé et le futur de l'Égypte.

The looping, enveloping forms
imagined by Hadid within the largely
rectilinear pavilion are typical of her
design work, here generating new
surfaces within more traditional walls
and ceilings.

Die verschlungenen, ausgreifenden
Formen, die Hadid im Innenraum des
rechtwinkligen Pavillons gestaltete,
sind typisch für ihr Werk. Zwischen
den eher konventionellen Wänden und
Decken entstehen vollkommen neuartige Oberflächen.

Les formes enveloppantes en boucle
imaginées par Hadid à l'intérieur d'un
pavillon essentiellement orthogonal
sont typiques de son travail. L'architecte crée ainsi de nouveaux plans
dans le cadre de murs, de sols et de
plafonds traditionnels.

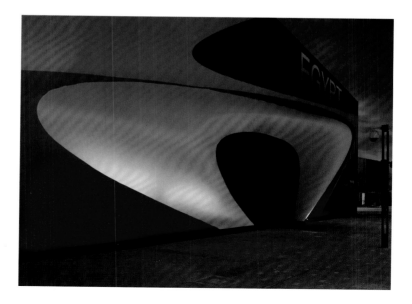

HEATHERWICK STUDIO

Heatherwick Studio
356–364 Gray's Inn Road
London WC1X 8BH
UK

Tel: +44 20 78 33 88 00
Fax: +44 20 78 33 84 00
E-mail: studio@heatherwick.com
Web: www.heatherwick.com

THOMAS HEATHERWICK founded Heatherwick Studio in 1994. The firm deals in architecture, sculpture, urban infrastructure, product design, exhibition design, and "strategic thinking." Its 25-member team is led by the Director Thomas Heatherwick. Born in London in 1970, Heatherwick studied three-dimensional design at Manchester Metropolitan University and completed his studies at the Royal College of Art in London. Heatherwick Studio has three Associate Directors: Fred Manson, architect and former Director of Environment for the London Borough of Southwark; Ron Packman, principal, Packman Lucas; and Maisie Rowe, a landscape architect. The studio's work includes the Rolling Bridge (Paddington Basin, London, 2005); La Maison Unique (New York, New York, USA, 2006); East Beach Café (Littlehampton, 2005–07); Paperhouse (London, 2009); 16 Creative Units for the Aberystwyth Arts Center at the University of Wales in Aberystwyth (Wales, 2009); and the UK Pavilion at Expo 2010 in Shanghai (China, 2010, published here). Current projects include a monastic building in Sussex (UK); the Pacific Place Shopping Center (Hong Kong, China, ongoing); and a power station in Teesside (UK), all in the UK unless stated otherwise. The studio is also involved in designing the new Routemaster bus in London.

THOMAS HEATHERWICK gründete Heatherwick Studio 1994. Das Büro beschäftigt sich mit Architektur, Skulptur, städtischer Infrastruktur, Produktdesign, Ausstellungsdesign und „strategischem Denken". Das 25-köpfige Team arbeitet unter der Leitung von Thomas Heatherwick. Heatherwick wurde 1970 in London geboren, studierte 3D-Design an der Manchester Metropolitan University und schloss sein Studium am Royal College of Art in London ab. Heatherwick Studio hat drei außerordentliche Direktoren: Fred Manson, Architekt und ehemaliger Umweltbeauftragter für den Londoner Bezirk Southwark, Ron Packman, Direktor von Packman Lucas, und Maisie Rowe, Landschaftsarchitektin. Zu den Projekten des Teams zählen die Rolling Bridge (Paddington Basin, London, 2005), La Maison Unique (New York, 2006), East Beach Café (Littlehampton, 2005–07), Paperhouse (London, 2009), 16 Ateliers für das Aberystwyth Arts Center an der Universität Wales in Aberystwyth (Wales, 2009) sowie der Britische Pavillon für die Expo 2010 in Shanghai (China, 2010, hier vorgestellt). Aktuelle Projekte sind u.a. ein Klostergebäude in Sussex, das Pacific Place Shoppingcenter (Hongkong, China, in Arbeit), und ein Kraftwerk in Teesside, alle in Großbritannien, sofern nicht anders angegeben. Das Studio ist außerdem am Entwurf für die neuen Routemaster-Busse in London beteiligt.

THOMAS HEATHERWICK a fondé Heatherwick Studio en 1994. L'agence se consacre à l'architecture, à la sculpture, aux infrastructures urbaines, au design produit, à la conception d'expositions et à la recherche stratégique. Son équipe de 25 collaborateurs est dirigée par Thomas Heatherwick. Né à Londres en 1970, celui-ci a étudié le design tridimensionnel à la Manchester Metropolitan University, puis au Royal College of Art de Londres. Heatherwick Studio est animé par ses trois directeurs-associés : Fred Manson, architecte et ancien directeur de l'environnement du *borough* londonien de Southwark ; Ron Packman, directeur de l'agence d'ingénierie Packman Lucas, et Maisie Rowe, architecte-paysagiste. Parmi leurs réalisations : le Rolling Bridge (Pont roulant, Paddington Basin, Londres, 2005) ; la Maison unique (New York, 2006) ; l'East Beach Café (Littlehampton, 2005–07) ; la Paperhouse (maison de papier, Londres, 2009) ; 16 postes de travail pour l'Aberystwyth Arts Center de l'université du Pays de Galles à Aberystwyth (2009) et le Pavillon britannique pour Expo 2010 à Shanghaï (2010, publié ici). Actuellement, l'agence travaille sur un projet de bâtiment monastique dans le Sussex (GB) ; le centre commercial Pacific Place (Hong Kong, en cours) ; une centrale électrique à Teesside (GB) ; ainsi qu'au design d'un nouveau modèle de bus Routemaster pour les transports publics londoniens.

UK PAVILION

Expo 2010, Shanghai, China, 2010

Area: 105 m² (Seed Cathedral); 4490 m² (landscape area). Client: UK Foreign and Commonwealth Office
Cost: not disclosed. Collaboration: Adams Kara Taylor (Structural Engineers), Atelier Ten (Environmental Engineering),
Safe Consulting (Fire and Risk Engineering)

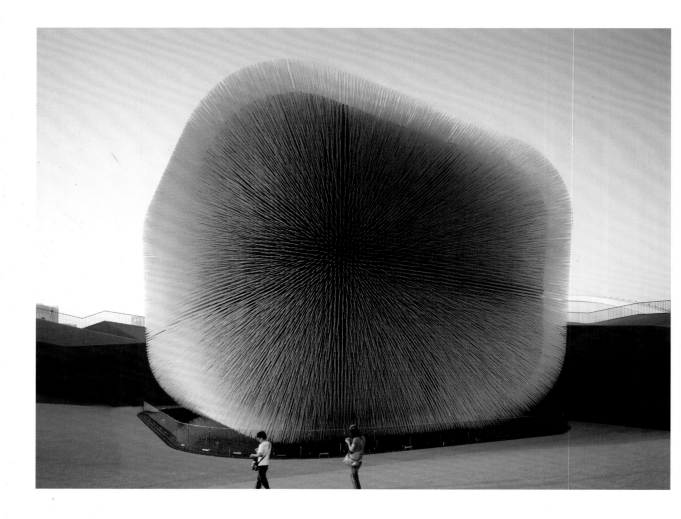

The irregular, hirsute image of the UK Pavilion as seen from the exterior immediately places it a category apart in contemporary architecture.

Der britische Pavillon wirkt von außen unregelmäßig und behaart und behauptet ein ganz eigenes Terrain in der zeitgenössischen Architektur.

L'image hérissée du Pavillon britannique vue de l'extérieur le range dans une catégorie à part de l'architecture contemporaine.

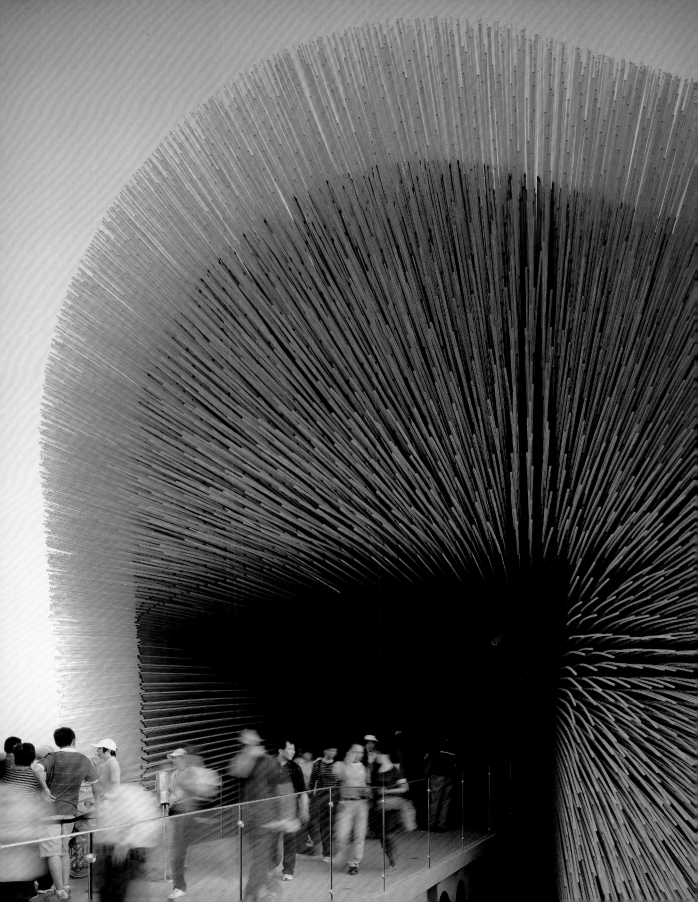

The idea at the center of the **UK PAVILION** was to involve Kew Gardens' Millennium Seed Bank in the project. The Seed Bank is meant to collect the seeds of 25% of the world's plant species by 2020. Using an array of no less than 60 000 slender transparent fiber optic rods, each 7.5 meters in length and each encasing one or more seeds at its tip, the designer has created what he calls the Seed Cathedral. Made of a steel and timber composite structure that holds the fiber optic rods, the finished pavilion is really defined most clearly by its hirsute appearance. As the designer describes the rods: "During the day, they draw daylight inwards to illuminate the interior. At night, light sources inside each rod allow the whole structure to glow. As the wind moves past the building, its optic 'hairs' gently move to create a dynamic effect." A public space with artificial grass provides a rest area for visitors, while a circulation zone on three edges of the site houses three environmental installations designed by the London design studio Troika.

Zentrale Idee des **BRITISCHEN PAVILLONS** war die Einbindung der Millennium Seedbank (Saatgutarchiv) in Kew Gardens in das Projekt. Die Seedbank plant, bis 2020 das Saatgut von 25 % aller Pflanzenarten weltweit zusammenzutragen. Mithilfe von nicht weniger als 60 000 schlanken transparenten Glasfaserstäben mit einer Länge von je 7,5 m, in deren Spitzen sich je einer oder mehrere Samen befinden, gestaltete der Designer die sogenannte Seed Cathedral (Saatgut-Kathedrale). Der Pavillon, dessen Glasfaserstäbe von einer Kompositkonstruktion aus Stahl und Holz getragen werden, zeichnet sich besonders durch sein haariges Erscheinungsbild aus. Der Designer beschreibt die Stäbe wie folgt: „Tagsüber leiten sie Tageslicht nach innen und belichten den Innenraum. Nachts leuchtet der gesamte Bau durch Lichtquellen, die in die Stäbe integriert sind. Streicht der Wind über das Gebäude, bewegen sich die optischen ‚Haare' sanft und sorgen für dynamische Effekte." Ein öffentlicher Bereich mit künstlicher Rasenfläche steht den Besuchern als Ruhezone zur Verfügung. Auf den Verkehrsflächen an drei Ecken des Grundstücks befinden sich drei Umweltinstallationen, entworfen vom Londoner Designstudio Troika.

L'idée centrale du **PAVILLON BRITANNIQUE** est issue d'un partenariat avec la Millennium Seed Bank des Kew Gardens. Cette banque de semences devrait collecter 25 % des espèces végétales du monde d'ici à 2020. L'architecte-designer a créé ce qu'il appelle une « Cathédrale des semences » grâce à pas moins de 60 000 fines tiges de fibre optique de 7,5 m de long chacune, présentant à leur extrémité une ou plusieurs semences. Comme l'explique Heatherwick : « Pendant le jour, ces fibres attirent la lumière naturelle qui illumine l'intérieur. La nuit, des sources lumineuses intégrées à chaque tige font irradier la structure tout entière. Quand le vent balaye le pavillon, ces "poils" optiques se balancent doucement en créant un effet dynamique. » Un espace au sol en gazon artificiel sert de lieu de repos pour les visiteurs. Une zone de circulation aménagée sur trois côtés longe trois installations environnementales conçues par le studio de design londonien Troika.

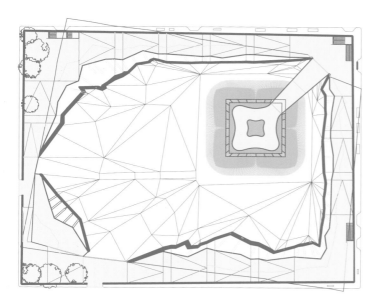

A site plan, section, and photo give a clear idea of the overall form and appearance of the UK Pavilion in Shanghai.

Lageplan, Querschnitt und Aufnahme vermitteln anschaulich Eindrücke von der formalen Gesamtstruktur und dem Erscheinungsbild des britischen Pavillons in Shanghai.

Le plan du terrain, une coupe et la photo de droite donnent une idée précise de la forme d'ensemble et de l'aspect inhabituel du Pavillon britannique à Shanghaï.

ICD/ITKE

Institute for Computational Design /
Institute of Building Structures and Structural Design
Universität Stuttgart
Keplerstr. 11 / 70174 Stuttgart / Germany

Tel: +49 711 68 58 19 20 / Fax: +49 711 68 58 19 30
E-mail: mail@icd.uni-stuttgart.de / info@itke.uni-stuttgart.de
Web: www.icd.uni-stuttgart.de / www.itke.uni-stuttgart.de

The **INSTITUTE FOR COMPUTATIONAL DESIGN** (ICD) and the **INSTITUTE OF BUILDING STRUCTURES AND STRUCTURAL DESIGN** (ITKE) are part of the Faculty of Architecture and Urban Planning at the University of Stuttgart. Through teaching, the ICD establishes a practical foundation in the fundamentals of parametric and algorithmic design strategies. Professor Achim Menges is an architect and Director of the ICD. He is also currently a Visiting Professor of Architecture at Harvard University's Graduate School of Design and Visiting Professor for the Emergent Technologies and Design Graduate Program at the Architectural Association in London. Born in Dusseldorf in 1962, Jan Knippers received his Ph.D. in Structural Engineering from the Technical University Berlin (1983–92). Since 2000, he has been a Professor and Head of the ITKE. ITKE works in the teaching and research of highly efficient building structures and new materials, such as foils, textiles, and biopolymers, as well as realizing prototypes for industry. The ICD's and ITKE's goal is to prepare students for the continuing advancement of computational processes in architecture, as they merge the fields of design, engineering, planning, and construction. The interrelation of such topics is exposed as both a technical and intellectual venture of formal, spatial, constructional, and ecological potentials. Together they realized the ICD/ITKE Research Pavilion (Stuttgart, Germany, 2010) published here.

Das **INSTITUT FÜR COMPUTERBASIERTES ENTWERFEN** (ICD) und das **INSTITUT FÜR TRAGKONSTRUKTION UND KONSTRUKTIVES ENTWERFEN** (ITKE) sind Teil der Fakultät für Architektur und Stadtplanung der Universität Stuttgart. Durch sein Lehrangebot schafft das ICD praktische Grundlagen für parametrische und algorithmische Entwurfsstrategien. Professor Achim Menges ist Architekt und Direktor des ICD. Darüber hinaus ist er Gastprofessor für Architektur an der Graduate School of Design in Harvard sowie Gastprofessor für den Aufbaustudiengang Emergent Technologies and Design an der Architectural Association in London. Jan Knippers, 1962 in Düsseldorf geboren, studierte Bauingenieurwesen an der TU Berlin, wo er auch promovierte (1983–92). Seit 2000 ist er Professor und Leiter am ITKE. In Lehre und Forschung widmet sich das ITKE hocheffizienten Tragwerken und neuartigen Baumaterialien wie Folien, Textilien oder Biopolymeren und entwickelt Prototypen für die Industrie. Gemeinsames Ziel von ICD und ITKE ist es, die Studierenden auf den Umgang mit sich ständig wandelnden computerbasierten Prozessen in der Architektur vorzubereiten; hierbei verschwimmen die Grenzen zwischen Entwerfen, Bautechnik, Planung und Konstruktion. Diese Wechselbeziehungen sind eine technische und intellektuelle Herausforderung, ein Unterfangen mit hohem gestalterischen, räumlichen, konstruktiven und ökologischen Potenzial. Gemeinsam realisierten die Institute den hier vorgestellten ICD/ITKE-Forschungspavillon (Stuttgart, 2010).

L'**INSTITUT DE DESIGN INFORMATIQUE** (ICD) et l'**INSTITUT DE CONSTRUCTION ET DE DESIGN DE STRUCTURES** (ITKE) font tous deux partie de la faculté d'architecture et d'urbanisme de l'université de Stuttgart. Par son enseignement, l'ICD offre une formation pratique aux fondamentaux des stratégies de conception paramétrique et algorithmique. Le professeur Achim Menges est architecte et directeur de l'ICD, professeur d'architecture invité à l'École supérieure de design de l'université de Harvard et professeur invité pour le programme d'études supérieures de conception et de technologies émergentes à l'Architectural Association de Londres. Né à Düsseldorf en 1962, Jan Knippers est Ph. D. en ingénierie structurelle de l'université technique de Berlin (1983–92). Depuis 2000, il est professeur et directeur de l'ITKE. L'ITKE travaille pour l'enseignement et la recherche de formes de construction hautement sophistiquées et sur de nouveaux matériaux, tels que membranes, textiles ou biopolymères, tout comme il réalise des prototypes pour l'industrie. L'objectif de l'ICD et ITKE est de préparer ses étudiants aux avancées permanentes des processus informatiques en architecture dans une fusion des domaines de la conception, de l'ingénierie, de la planification et de la construction. La relation entre ces domaines passe par une recherche à la fois technique et intellectuelle sur les potentiels formels, spatiaux, constructifs et écologiques. Ensemble, ils ont réalisé le pavillon de recherche ICD/ITKE (Stuttgart, 2010), publié ici.

ICD/ITKE RESEARCH PAVILION

Stuttgart, Germany, 2010

Address: Keplerstr. 17, University of Stuttgart, Stuttgart, Germany
Area: 85 m². Client: ICD/ITKE. Cost: not disclosed. Collaboration: Andreas Eisenhardt,
Manuel Vollrath, Kristine Wächter

This is the result of a collaboration between two University of Stuttgart entities, the Institute for Computational Design headed by Achim Menges and the Institute of Building Structures and Structural Design headed by Jan Knippers. Designed between October 19, 2009 and June 24, 2010, this pavilion was built between June 24 and July 23, 2010. The structure of the pavilion is based on bent birch plywood strips. According to the ICD: "The strips are robotically manufactured as planar elements, and subsequently connected, so that elastically bent and tensioned regions alternate along their length. The force that is locally stored in each bent region of the strip, and maintained by the corresponding tensioned region of the neighboring strip, greatly increases the structural capacity of the system." The entire structure, with a diameter of more than 10 meters, was built using only 6.5-millimeter-thick birch plywood sheets. The 500 unique pieces necessary were manufactured in the University's robotics plant.

Der Bau entstand als kollaboratives Projekt zweier Institute der Universität Stuttgart, des Instituts für Computerbasiertes Entwerfen (ICD), geleitet von Achim Menges, sowie des Instituts für Tragkonstruktionen und Konstruktives Entwerfen (ITKE) unter Leitung von Jan Knippers. Der zwischen dem 19. Oktober 2009 und 24. Juni 2010 entworfene Pavillon wurden zwischen 24. Juni 2010 und 23. Juli 2010 realisiert. Die Konstruktion des Pavillons besteht aus gebogenen Birkensperrholzstreifen. Das ICD erklärt: „Die Streifen werden robotisch als plane Elemente gefertigt und schließlich miteinander verkoppelt, sodass sich der Länge nach abwechselnd elastisch gebogene und unter Eigenspannung versetzte Abschnitte ergeben. Die Kraft, die sich in den gebogenen Zonen der Streifen aufbaut und von der entsprechenden unter Eigenspannung gesetzten Region benachbarter Streifen aufgefangen wird, steigert die Tragfähigkeit des Systems erheblich." Die gesamte Konstruktion hat einen Durchmesser von über 10 m und wurde aus nur 6,5 mm starken Birkensperrholzstreifen gebaut. Die 500 individuell geformten Einzelteile wurden in der universitätseigenen robotischen Fertigungsanlage gefräst.

Ce pavillon est l'aboutissement d'une collaboration entre deux instituts de l'université de Stuttgart, l'Institut de design informatique dirigé par Achim Menges et l'Institut de construction et de design de structures dirigé par Jan Knippers. Conçu du 19 octobre 2009 au 24 juin 2010, ce petit bâtiment a été édifié entre le 24 juin et le 23 juillet 2010. De plus de 10 m de diamètre, la structure toute entière est composée de bandes de contreplaqué de bouleau de 6,5 mm d'épaisseur. Selon la présentation de l'ICD : « Ces bandes sont fabriquées par des robots sous forme d'éléments planaires, réunis ensuite entre eux de telle façon que sur toute leur longueur alternent des zones cintrées et en tension. La force qui se concentre localement dans chaque zone cintrée de la bande est maintenue par la zone en tension correspondante de la bande voisine, ce qui accroît de façon importante la capacité structurelle du système. » Les 500 pièces de bois uniques nécessaires ont été fabriquées dans les ateliers robotisés de l'université.

The use of computerized design and manufacturing to create the bent plywood strips that form the pavilion gives it an unexpected appearance, halfway between mathematics and nature.

Mithilfe computerbasierter Entwurfs- und Fertigungsprozesse entstand ein ungewöhnlicher Pavillon aus gebogenen Sperrholzstreifen, der scheinbar zwischen Mathematik und Natur zu verharren scheint.

Le recours à des techniques de conception et de fabrication informatisées a permis de créer ces bandeaux de contreplaqué cintré qui donnent au pavillon un aspect surprenant, quelque part entre mathématiques et nature.

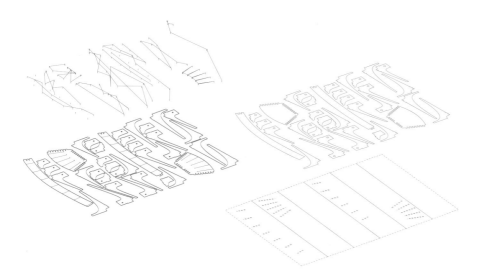

Night photos and an exploded axonometric drawing show the protecting
curve of the roof that rises up on one
side to admit visitors.

*Nächtliche Ansichten und eine Explo-
sionszeichnung veranschaulichen
die Form des schützend gebogenen
Dachs, das an einer Seite als Eingang
für Besucher hochgezogen ist.*

Ces images nocturnes et la décompo-
sition axonométrique montrent comment la courbe de la couverture se
soulève d'un côté pour laisser entrer
les visiteurs.

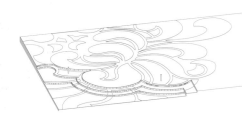

TOYO ITO

Toyo Ito & Associates, Architects
1–19–4 Shibuya
Shibuya-ku
Tokyo 150–0002
Japan

Tel: +81 33 409 5822
Fax: +81 33 409 5969

Born in 1941 in Seoul, South Korea, **TOYO ITO** graduated from the University of Tokyo in 1965 and worked in the office of Kiyonori Kikutake until 1969. He created his own office, Urban Robot (URBOT), in Tokyo in 1971, assuming the name of Toyo Ito & Associates, Architects in 1979. He was awarded the Golden Lion for Lifetime Achievement from the 8th International Venice Architecture Biennale in 2002 and the RIBA Gold Medal in 2006. His completed work includes the Silver Hut (Nakano, Tokyo, 1982–84); Tower of the Winds (Yokohama, Kanagawa, 1986); Yatsushiro Municipal Museum (Yatsushiro, Kumamoto, 1988–91); and the Elderly People's Home (1992–94) and Fire Station (1992–95) both located in the same city of Kyushu. Other projects include his Nagaoka Lyric Hall (Nagaoka, Niigata, 1993–96) and Odate Jukai Dome Park (Odate, Akita, 1993–97). One of his most successful and widely published projects, the Sendai Mediatheque, was completed in 2001, while in 2002 he designed a temporary Pavilion for the Serpentine Gallery in London (UK). More recently, he has completed TOD'S Omotesando Building (Shibuya-ku, Tokyo, 2003–04); the Island City Central Park Grin Grin (Fukuoka, Fukuoka, 2004–05); the Tama Art University Library (Hachioji City, Tokyo, 2005–07); the ZA-KOENJI Public Theater (Tokyo, 2006–08); and the Main Stadium for the World Games 2009 (Kaohsiung, Taiwan, 2006–09), all in Japan unless stated otherwise.

TOYO ITO wurde 1941 in Seoul, Südkorea, geboren und schloss sein Studium 1965 an der Universität Tokio ab. Bis 1969 arbeitete er im Büro von Kiyonori Kikutake. Sein eigenes Büro Urban Robot (URBOT) gründete er 1971 in Tokio, seit 1979 firmiert er unter dem Namen Toyo Ito & Associates, Architects. 2002 wurde er auf der 8. Architekturbiennale in Venedig mit dem Goldenen Löwen für sein Lebenswerk ausgezeichnet, 2006 mit der RIBA-Goldmedaille. Zu seinen realisierten Bauten zählen Silver Hut (Nakano, Tokio, 1982–84), Tower of the Winds (Yokohama, Kanagawa, 1986), das Stadtmuseum Yatsushiro (Yatsushiro, Kumamoto, 1988–91) sowie ein Altenheim (1992–94) und eine Feuerwache (1992–95), beide in derselben Stadt Kyushu. Weitere Projekte sind die Nagaoka Lyric Hall (Nagaoka, Niigata, 1993–96) und sein Odate Jukai Dome Park (Odate, Akita, 1993–97). Eines seiner bekanntesten und meistpublizierten Projekte, die Mediathek in Sendai, konnte 2001 fertiggestellt werden. 2002 entwarf er einen temporären Pavillon für die Serpentine Gallery in London. In jüngster Zeit realisierte er das Omotesando Building für TOD'S (Shibuya-ku, Tokio, 2003–04), den Island City Hauptpark Grin Grin (Fukuoka, Fukuoka, 2004–05), die Universitätsbibliothek der Tama Art University (Hachioji City, Tokio, 2005–07), das ZA-KOENJI Theater (Tokio, 2006–08) sowie die Sportarena für die World Games 2009 (Kaohsiung, Taiwan, 2006–09), alle in Japan, sofern nicht anders angegeben.

Né en 1941 à Séoul (Corée du Sud), **TOYO ITO**, diplômé d'architecture de l'université de Tokyo en 1965, a travaillé pour l'agence de Kiyonori Kikutake jusqu'en 1969. Il a créé sa propre agence, Urban Robot (URBOT) à Tokyo en 1971, qui a pris le nom de Toyo Ito & Associates, Architects en 1979. Il a reçu le Lion d'or pour l'ensemble de sa carrière lors de la VIIIe Biennale internationale d'architecture de Venise en 2002 et la médaille d'or du RIBA en 2006. Parmi ses réalisations figurent : la résidence Silver Hut (Nakano, Tokyo, 1982–84) ; la Tour des vents (Yokohama, Kanagawa, 1986) ; le Musée municipal de Yatsushiro (Kumamoto, 1989–91) ; une maison de retraite (1992–94) et une caserne de pompiers (1992–95) dans la ville de Kyushu. Parmi les autres projets : le Nagaoka Lyric Hall (Nagaoka, Niigata, 1993–96) et le stade Odate Jukai Dome Park (Odate, Akita, 1993–97). L'une de ses réalisations les plus remarquables et les plus médiatisées a été la médiathèque de Sendaï (2001). Il a conçu un pavillon temporaire pour la Serpentine Gallery à Londres en 2002. Plus récemment, il a achevé l'immeuble TOD'S d'Omotesando (Shibuya-ku, Tokyo, 2003–04) ; le parc central Grin Grin d'Island City (Fukuoka, 2003–05) ; la nouvelle bibliothèque de l'Université d'art Tama (Hachiogi City, Tokyo, 2005–07) ; le théâtre ZAKOENJI (Tokyo, 2006–08) et le stade principal des Jeux mondiaux 2009 (Kaoshiung, Taïwan, 2006–09).

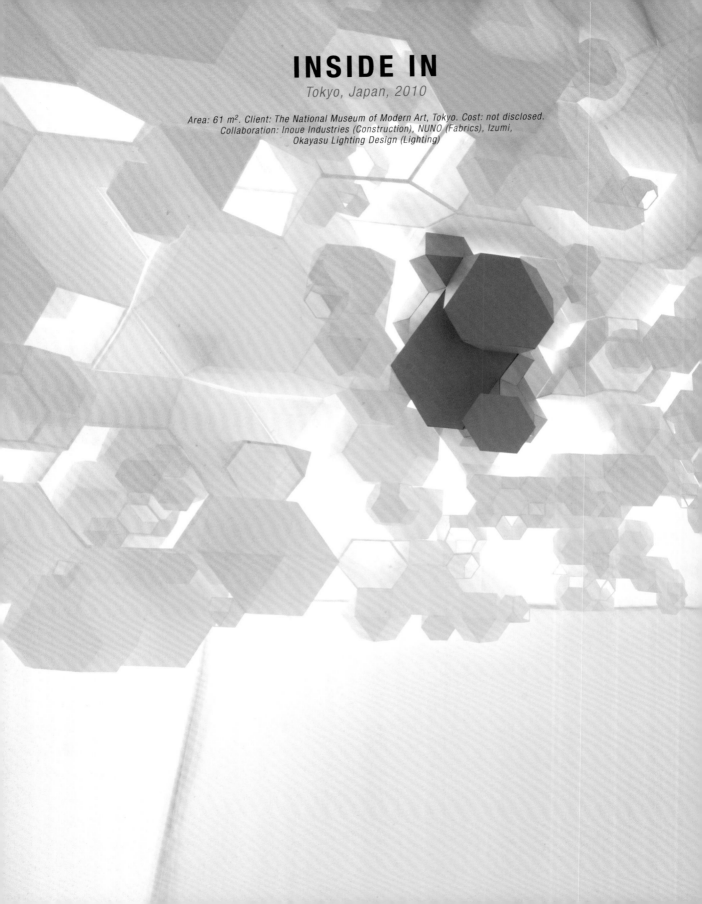

INSIDE IN
Tokyo, Japan, 2010

Area: 61 m². Client: The National Museum of Modern Art, Tokyo. Cost: not disclosed.
Collaboration: Inoue Industries (Construction), NUNO (Fabrics), Izumi,
Okayasu Lighting Design (Lighting)

This museum installation **INSIDE IN** constructed in April 2010, was made with fabric, steel pipes, acrylic opal panels, aluminum mesh, and sheet polypropylene and is related in its polyhedron structure to the Imabari Toyo Ito Architecture Museum currently being designed by the architect in Omishima, Ehime, Japan. Seeking to create a "soft and topologically distorted space," Toyo Ito employed polyhedrons half the size of the ones to be used in Imabari. He states: "We were eager to create new spatial experiences that are beyond our imagination with the polyhedrons, and through this exhibition we have the opportunity to experiment with the modules to create exciting internal spaces." Ito's polyhedrons were set in the midst of a larger (196 m²) gallery in the museum for this temporary exhibition.

Die im April 2010 errichtete Museumsinstallation **INSIDE IN** bestand aus Textil, Stahlrohren, Milchglassegmenten aus Acrylglas, Aluminiummaschendraht und Polypropylenfolie und ähnelt der Polyeder-Konstruktion, die der Architekt derzeit für das Toyo Ito Architekturmuseum in Imabari auf Omishima, Präfektur Ehime, Japan, entwickelt. Toyo Ito, dem es darum ging, einen „weichen und topologisch verzerrten Raum" zu schaffen, arbeitete mit Polyedern, die halb so groß sind wie die Polyeder in Imabari. Er führt aus: „Wir wollten mit den Polyedern unbedingt neue räumliche Erfahrungen schaffen. Mit dieser Ausstellung haben wir die Gelegenheit, mit den Modulen zu experimentieren und faszinierende Innenräume zu gestalten." Itos Polyeder befanden sich im Zentrum eines großen (196 m² großen) Ausstellungsraums im Museum, der dieser Sonderschau gewidmet war.

L'installation **INSIDE IN**, montée dans une galerie de 196 m² d'un musée en avril 2010, a été réalisée en tissu, tubes d'acier, panneaux d'acrylique opalin, maillage d'aluminium et feuilles de polypropylène. Sa structure polyédrique rappelle le projet du Musée d'architecture Toyo Ito Imabari que conçoit actuellement l'architecte pour Omishima, dans la préfecture d'Ehime au Japon. Cherchant à créer un « espace doux et topologiquement déformé », Toyo Ito a utilisé des polyèdres de la moitié de la taille de ceux retenus pour Imabari. « À travers ces polyèdres, nous avons voulu créer de nouvelles expériences spatiales qui aillent au-delà de notre imagination et cette exposition nous a donné l'opportunité d'expérimenter ces modules pour créer des espaces étonnants et stimulants. »

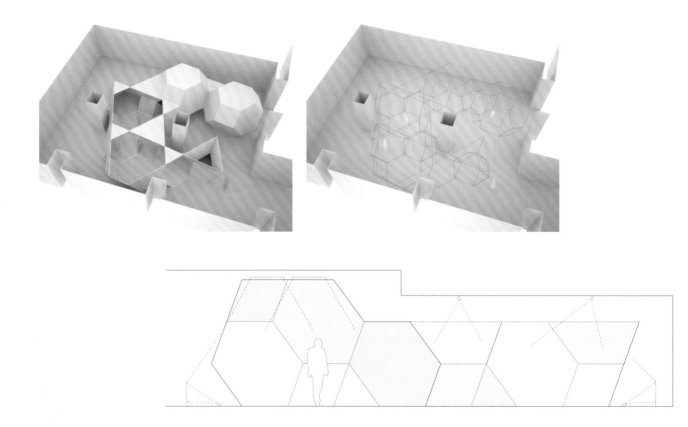

Using basic geometric forms and such materials as acrylic opal panels, Toyo Ito succeeds in altering the visitor's perception of space.

Mit einfachen geometrischen Formen und Materialien wie Milchglassegmenten aus Acrylglas gelingt es Toyo Ito, die Raumwahrnehmung der Besucher zu beeinflussen.

À partir de formes géométriques basiques et de matériaux comme les panneaux d'acrylique opalin, Toyo Ito réussit à modifier la perception de l'espace.

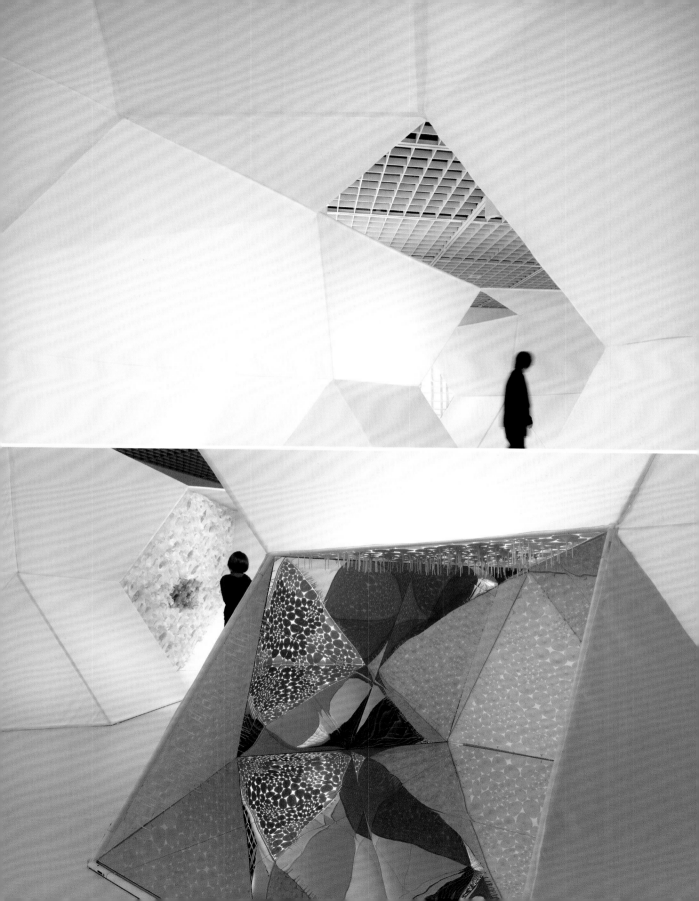

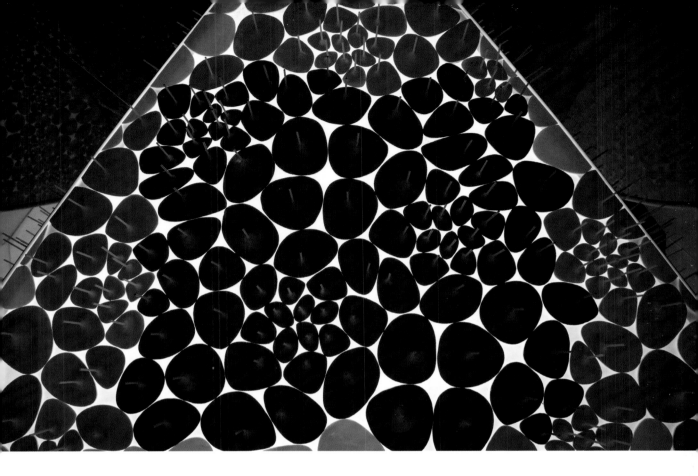

Toyo Ito has always shown an interest in forms that create a series of sensory dislocations—much in the same way that his younger colleagues of SANAA have done in recent years.

Toyo Ito interessiert sich schon immer für Formen, mit denen sich räumliche Desorientierung erzeugen lässt – ähnlich wie seine jüngeren Kollegen von SANAA in den letzten Jahren.

Toyo Ito a toujours fait preuve d'un grand intérêt pour les formes qui provoquent une dislocation sensorielle, attitude assez proche de ce que ses jeunes confrères de SANAA ont tenté ces dernières années.

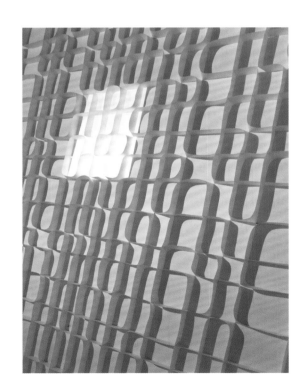

JIAKUN ARCHITECTS

Jiakun Architects
2–7F, Block 11, 3# Yulin Nanlu
610041 Chendu
Sichuan
China

Tel: +86 28 8556 8899
Fax: +86 28 8558 9491
E-mail: jkads@263.net
Web: www.jiakun.com

LIU JIAKUN graduated from the Department of Architecture of the Chongqing Institute of Architecture and Engineering. After working in Tibet and Sinkiang, he established Jiakun Architects in 1999. Among Liu Jiakun's works are the Luyeyuan Stone Sculpture Art Museum (Chengdu, Sichuan, 2002); the Sculpture Department of the Sichuan Fine Arts Institute (Chongqing, 2004); Qingpu Construction Exhibition Center (Shanghai, 2006); the Guangzhou Times Rose Garden (Guangzhou, 2006); the Museum of Clocks of the Cultural Revolution (Anren Town, Sichuan, 2007); Shanghai Xiang-dong Buddha Statue Museum (Shanghai, 2008); and *With the Wind 2009*—Civic Center (Shenzhen, 2009, published here), all in China. Liu Jiakun states that "a good design equals using limited resources in a creative way."

LIU JIAKUN schloss sein Studium an der Fakultät für Architektur am Chongqing Institut für Architektur und Bauingenieurwesen ab. Er gründete sein Büro Jiakun Architects 1999, nachdem er in Tibet und Sinkiang gearbeitet hatte. Zu Liu Jiakuns Projekten zählen das Luyeyuan-Museum für Steinbildhauerei (Chengdu, Sichuan, 2002), die Fakultät für Bildhauerei am Institut für Bildende Künste von Sichuan (Chongqing, 2004), das Qingpu Construction Exhibition Center (Shanghai, 2006), der Times-Rosengarten in Guangzhou (Guangzhou, 2006), das Museum der Uhren der Kulturrevolution (Stadt Anren, Sichuan, 2007), das Buddha-Museum in Shanghai Xiang-dong (Shanghai, 2008) sowie das Bürgerzentrum With the Wind 2009 (Shenzhen, 2009, hier vorgestellt), alle in China. Liu Jiakun erklärt: „Ein guter Entwurf ist der kreative Umgang mit begrenzten Ressourcen."

LIU JIAKUN est diplômé du département d'architecture de l'Institut d'architecture et d'ingénierie de Chongqing. Après avoir travaillé au Tibet et dans le Sinkiang, il crée son agence Jiakun Architects en 1999. Parmi ses références : le Musée de la sculpture de pierre de Luyeyuan (Chengdu, Sichuan, 2002) ; le département de sculpture de l'Institut des beaux-arts du Sichuan (Chongqing, 2004) ; le Centre d'expositions sur le bâtiment de Qinqpu (Shanghaï, 2006) ; la roseraie de Guangzhou (Guangzhou, 2006) ; le Musée des horloges de la Révolution culturelle (Anren, Sichuan, 2007) ; le Musée de la statue du bouddha de Xiang-dong (Shanghaï, 2008) et *With the Wind 2009* – Centre municipal (Shenzhen, 2009, publié ici). Pour Liu Jiakun : « Faire un bon projet signifie utiliser des ressources limitées de façon créative. »

WITH THE WIND 2009—CIVIC CENTER

Shenzhen, China, 2009

*Area: 320 m². Client: Shenzhen Architecture Urbanism Biennale
Cost: not disclosed*

This installation was set up on the plaza of the Shenzhen Civic Center on the occasion of the 2009 Biennale. "This temporary structure," says the architect, "imitates the undulated profile of the roof on the Civic Center; it provides the Biennale and urban public with a public gathering space and demonstrates the character of participation from the general public. The colored balloons not only act as structural mechanism for the temporary structure, but also create a happy ambiance out of Chinese tradition for the Biennale." The main material used was a 32 x 10-meter stretch of sun-shading net supported by nylon string and 14 three-meter-diameter balloons. Twenty-eight used tires were used to anchor the installation that rose six to nine meters off the ground. Liu Jiakun had previously installed a similar 18 x 6-meter work in Chengdu (*Flowing with the Wind*, 2002).

Die Installation war anlässlich der Biennale 2009 auf dem Vorplatz der Stadthalle von Shenzhen zu sehen. „Die temporäre Konstruktion", erklärt der Architekt, „ist dem geschwungenen Dach der Stadthalle nachempfunden und bietet der Biennale und den Bürgern der Stadt einen öffentlichen Treffpunkt. Zugleich belegt sie die Beteiligung der breiten Öffentlichkeit. Die farbigen Ballons dienen nicht nur als Tragwerk für die temporäre Konstruktion, sondern schaffen auch ein fröhliches Ambiente für die Biennale, das chinesische Traditionen aufgreift." Primäres Material war ein 32 x 10 m großes Sonnenschutznetz, das an Nylonschnüren von 14 Ballons mit einem Durchmesser von je 3 m abgehängt war. Verankert war die sechs bis neun Meter über dem Boden schwebende Installation mit 28 alten Autoreifen. Liu Jiakun hatte bereits in Chengdu eine ähnliche, 18 x 6 m große Installation realisiert (*Flowing with the Wind*, 2002).

Cette installation a été spécifiquement créée pour la place qui s'étend devant le Centre municipal de Shenzhen à l'occasion de la Biennale de 2009. « Cette structure temporaire, explique l'architecte, imite le profil ondulé du toit du Centre municipal ; elle offre au public de la ville et de la Biennale un espace de rencontre et s'appuie sur la capacité du grand public à participer. Les ballons de couleur non seulement fonctionnent et sont un mécanisme structurel, mais aussi créent une ambiance joyeuse inspirée de la tradition chinoise. » Le matériau principal mis en œuvre était un filet d'ombrage élastique de 32 x 10 m soutenu par des cordes de nylon et 14 ballons de 3 m de diamètre. L'installation qui mesurait de 6 à 9 m de haut était ancrée au sol par 28 pneus usagés. Liu Jiakun avait déjà installé une œuvre similaire de 18 x 6 m à Chengdu (*Flowing in the Wind*, 2002).

Using helium-filled balloons, the architect imagines a floating roof, tethered to the ground over a seating and performance area.

Mit heliumgefüllten Ballons realisierte der Architekt ein schwebendes Dach, das über einem Bühnen- und Sitzbereich am Boden vertäut ist.

L'architecte a imaginé une toiture suspendue à des ballons d'hélium, qui protège la zone où sont donnés des spectacles.

ADAM KALKIN

Adam Kalkin
Quik Build LLC
59–65 Mine Brook Road
Bernardsville, NJ 07924
USA

E-mail: sonofderrida@aol.com
Web: www.architectureandhygiene.com

ADAM KALKIN was born in 1965 and attended Vassar College (class of 1984), the Washington University School of Architecture (1990), and the Architectural Association in London (1992). He was a winner of the Progressive Architecture Young Architects Award (1990). He has written a number of books about temporary architecture, such as *Quik Build, Adam Kalkin's ABC of Container Architecture* (Bibliotheque McLean, London, 2008). He is one of the more active architects in the area of container-based structures, having used them to design luxury homes, refugee housing, and a museum extension. In fact, Kalkin has frequently said that he does not consider himself an architect. He devised the Quik House, a prefabricated residence (2004–ongoing, one example from 2008 published here) made from five shipping containers that can be completed in three months. Kalkin has also worked in such unusual circumstances as collaboration with the fashion model Natalia Vodianova and the Naked Heart Foundation to build 200 playhouses for poor children across Russia, or with the US Army in Kabul. Although he most frequently reuses shipping containers, he has found a broad variety of potential uses for these, such as the illy Push Button House (2007, also published here).

ADAM KALKIN wurde 1965 geboren und besuchte das Vassar College (Abschlussklasse 1984), die Fakultät für Architektur der Washington University (1990) und die Architectural Association in London (1992). 1990 wurde er mit dem Progressive Architecture Young Architects Award ausgezeichnet. Er schrieb mehrere Bücher über zeitgenössische Architektur, darunter *Quik Build, Adam Kalkin's ABC of Container Architecture* (Bibliotheque McLean, London, 2008). Er zählt zu den aktiveren Architekten im Bereich Bauen mit Containern und nutzte sie bereits für Entwürfe von Luxushäusern, Flüchtlingsunterkünften und die Erweiterung eines Museums. Tatsächlich äußerte Kalkin des öfteren, er verstehe sich nicht als Architekt. Er konzipierte das Quik House, ein Fertighaus aus fünf Containern (2004–andauernd, ein Beispiel von 2008 ist hier vorgestellt), das in nur drei Monaten fertiggestellt werden kann. Kalkin hat darüber hinaus unter ungewöhnlichen Umständen gearbeitet, etwa bei der Realisierung von 200 Spielhäusern für Kinder in Armut in Russland, eine Kollaboration mit dem Model Natalia Vodianova und der Naked Heart Foundation, oder mit der US Army in Kabul. Obwohl er zumeist mit gebrauchten Frachtcontainern arbeitet, hat er eine große Bandbreite potenzieller Nutzungsformen gefunden, etwa mit seinem illy Push Button House (2007, ebenfalls hier vorgestellt).

ADAM KALKIN, né en 1965, a étudié à Vassar College à partir de 1984, à l'École d'architecture de Washington University (1990) et à l'Architectural Association de Londres (1992). Il a remporté le prix des jeunes architectes de Progressive Architecture (1990) et a écrit un certain nombre d'ouvrages sur l'architecture temporaire comme *Quik Build, Adam Kalkin's ABC of Container Architecture* (Bibliothèque McLean, Londres, 2008). C'est un des architectes les plus actifs dans le secteur de la construction à base de conteneurs qu'il utilise pour réaliser des logements de luxe, des logements pour réfugiés ou l'extension d'un musée. En fait, Kalkin a fréquemment affirmé qu'il ne se considérait pas comme un architecte. Il a conçu la Quik House, résidence préfabriquée (à partir de 2004, projet en cours, dont un exemple datant de 2008 est publié ici) composée de cinq conteneurs et réalisable en trois mois. Il a également travaillé dans des circonstances inhabituelles comme, par exemple, lors de sa collaboration avec le top-modèle Natalia Vodianova et la Naked Heart Foundation pour construire 200 maisons de récréation destinées aux enfants pauvres de Russie, ou avec l'armée américaine à Kaboul. Il a imaginé une multiplicité d'utilisations potentielles des conteneurs, comme dans sa illy Push Button House (2007, publiée ici).

QUIK HOUSE

Tewksbury, New Jersey, USA, 2008

Area: 186 m². Client: T. Gabashvili. Cost: variable

The **QUIK HOUSE** is a prefabricated kit house designed by Adam Kalkin from recycled shipping containers. It has three bedrooms and two and one-half bathrooms. The architect states: "The shell assembles within one day at your site; you will have a fully enclosed building. From start to finish, it should take no longer than three months to complete your house." Four, five, or more stacked steel shipping containers available either in orange or in a more natural "rust" finish can be installed within about five months from the original order, at a cost ranging upwards from $76 000, plus shipping costs. The idea of this stacking came to Kalkin from the piles of containers he saw near New York ports.

Das **QUIK HOUSE** ist ein Fertighaus-Bausatz aus recycelten Frachtcontainern, entworfen von Adam Kalkin. Das Haus hat drei Schlafzimmer und zweieinhalb Bäder. Der Architekt führt aus: „Der Rohbau lässt sich innerhalb eines Tages auf einem Grundstück errichten, danach steht eine vollständig umbaute Gebäudehülle. Vom ersten bis zum letzten Tag dürfte es nicht länger als drei Monate dauern, das Haus fertigzustellen." Vier, fünf oder mehr übereinandergestapelte Frachtcontainer, erhältlich in orange oder natürlicherer „Rost"-Optik lassen sich in rund fünf Monaten nach Auftragsvergabe installieren. Das Budget beläuft sich ab 76 000 Dollar aufwärts zuzüglich Transportkosten. Der Gedanke, die Container zu stapeln, kam Kalkin als er gestapelte Container in der Nähe der New Yorker Häfen sah.

La **QUIK HOUSE** est une résidence préfabriquée livrée en kit, conçue par Adam Kalkin à partir de conteneurs d'expédition recyclés. Elle possède trois chambres, deux salles de bains et une salle d'eau. Pour l'architecte : « La coque s'assemble sur votre terrain en une journée ; vous disposez alors d'une construction hors d'eau. Du début à la fin du chantier, trois mois devraient suffire pour terminer cette maison. » Quatre, cinq conteneurs d'acier empilés, voire plus, de couleur orange ou de tonalité rouille plus naturelle, peuvent être installés sur place dans les cinq mois qui suivent la commande pour un coût allant à partir de 76 000 dollars, plus les frais d'expédition. L'idée d'empilement est venue à Kalkin en observant des piles de conteneurs dans les ports de New York.

Containers assembled in a warehouse give an idea of how the architect takes these ordinary industrial objects and makes them into an unusual residence.

Die Containerinstallation in einem Lagerhaus lässt ahnen, wie der Architekt aus alltäglichen Industrieobjekten ungewöhnliche Wohnbauten schafft.

Cet assemblage de conteneurs dans un entrepôt donne une idée de la façon dont l'architecte s'empare d'objets industriels pour les transformer en logements.

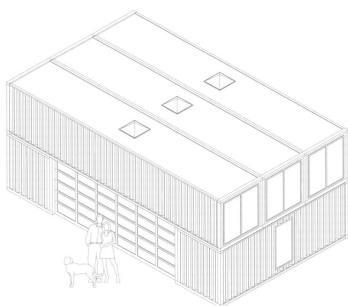

The Quik House, photographed above, is made up of stacked units like the ones shown in the axonometric drawing to the left.

Das Quik House (oben) besteht aus übereinander gestapelten Einheiten, ähnlich wie der Bau auf der Axonometrie links.

La Quik House, photographiée ci-dessus, est composée de conteneurs empilés, comme le montre la vue axonométrique de gauche.

The rather luxurious appearance of the inside of the house belies its industrial origins, though the architect does nothing to hide the origins of the forms.

Das gehobene Wohnambiente der Räume lässt die industriellen Ursprünge des Hauses nicht ahnen, obwohl der Architekt diese Herkunft keineswegs kaschiert.

L'aspect assez luxueux de l'intérieur de la maison dissimule ses origines industrielles, même si l'architecte n'a pas tenté de masquer à l'extérieur l'origine de ses formes.

An outdoor patio with another stacked container house in the background. Large sliding windows are cut into the original container frames.

Ein Blick auf die Terrasse mit den gestapelten Containereinheiten eines anderen Wohnbaus im Hintergrund. In die ursprüngliche Rahmenkonstruktion der Container wurden Öffnungen für großflächige Schiebefenster geschnitten.

Un patio extérieur fait le lien avec une autre maison-conteneur. Les grandes baies coulissantes sont découpées dans la structure même des conteneurs.

ILLY PUSH BUTTON HOUSE

Venice, Italy, and other locations, 2007

Area: 44.6 m². Client: illy. Cost: not disclosed.
Collaboration: Quik Build

With careful study of space within the framework of the industrial container, Adam Kalkin creates an entire "home" that pops out of this foldable structure.

In Adam Kalkins durchdachter Raumstudie entfaltet sich aus dem Gerüst eines Frachtcontainers ein komplettes „Eigenheim", das mithilfe eines Klappmechanismus ausgefahren wird.

Grâce à une étude approfondie du volume intérieur d'un conteneur industriel, Adam Kalkin a créé une « maison » qui naît du déploiement de sa structure.

The Italian coffee firm illy collaborated with Adam Kalkin to create "a dramatic work of living art—the **ILLY PUSH BUTTON HOUSE**, a 'five-room home' with a kitchen, dining room, bedroom, living room, and library constructed within a standard industrial shipping container." The structure transforms using a hydraulic system at the push of a button from what appears to be a perfectly normal container into a very open and schematic representation of a home, which could coincidentally be used to serve coffee. The Push Button House was first shown at the Venice Biennale in June 2007. In December 2007, it was exhibited in New York City at the Time Warner Center. As part of the New York Wine & Food Festival, in October 2008, the Push Button House was again seen in Manhattan's Meatpacking District.

Im Zuge einer Kollaboration des italienischen Kaffeeherstellers illy mit Adam Kalkin entstand „ein dramatisches, lebendes Kunstwerk – das **ILLY PUSH BUTTON HOUSE**, eine ‚5-Zimmer-Wohnung' mit Küche, Esszimmer, Schlafzimmer, Wohnzimmer und Bibliothek, gebaut aus einem Standard-Frachtcontainer". Die Konstruktion verwandelt sich dank eines Hydrauliksystems per Knopfdruck: Aus einem normalen Container wird ein offenes, schematisiertes Haus, das sich zufälligerweise auch für den Ausschank von Kaffee eignet. Erstmals präsentiert wurde das Push Button House auf der Biennale von Venedig im Juni 2007. Im Dezember 2007 wurde es im Time Warner Center in New York ausgestellt. Im Oktober 2008 war das Push Button House ein weiteres Mal im Rahmen des New York Wine & Food Festivals im Meatpacking District zu sehen.

La marque de café italienne illy a collaboré avec Adam Kalkin pour créer « une œuvre d'art vivant spectaculaire, la **ILLY PUSH BUTTON HOUSE**, une résidence de cinq pièces avec cuisine, salle à manger, chambre, séjour et bibliothèque construite à partir de conteneurs d'expédition industriels standard ». Grâce à un système hydraulique commandé par un bouton, la structure passe de l'état de conteneur normal à celui d'une maison schématique ouverte, qui peut également servir de cafétéria. Elle a été présentée pour la première fois à la Biennale de Venise en juin 2007. En décembre 2007, elle a été exposée au Time Warner Center à New York, puis dans le quartier du Meatpacking dans le cadre du festival « Wine & Food » de New York en octobre 2008.

The illy Push Button House in its fully closed configuration—with only the "illy" sign to give away the unusual nature of the contents.

Das illy Push Button House in geschlossenem Zustand – nur das „illy"-Schild lässt den ungewöhnlichen Inhalt des Containers ahnen.

Ci-dessus, la maison en configuration fermée. Seule l'enseigne « illy » fait s'interroger sur la nature de son contenu.

Above, the house in the process of being unfolded. Right, the "living and dining" area of this very open structure, meant more as a demonstration than an actual living space.

Oben das Haus während des Klapp-vorgangs. Rechts der „Ess- und Wohnbereich" der extrem offenen Konstruktion, die eher zu Demonstrationszwecken dient und weniger als Wohnraum genutzt wird.

Ci-dessus, la maison en cours de déploiement. À droite, la zone de « repas et de vie » de cette construction totalement ouverte qui est davantage un exercice qu'un véritable espace à vivre.

IRA KOERS, ROELOF MULDER

Bureau Ira Koers
Oostelijke Handelskade 12 E
1019 BM Amsterdam
The Netherlands

Tel: +31 20 419 75 54
Fax: +31 20 419 75 53
E-mail: info@irakoers.nl
Web: www.irakoers.nl

Studio Roelof Mulder
Oostelijke Handelskade 12 E
1019 BM Amsterdam
The Netherlands

Tel: +31 20 419 06 66
Fax: +31 20 419 06 68
E-mail: info@roelofmulder.com
Web: www.roelofmulder.com

IRA KOERS was born in 1970 and studied architecture at the Gerrit Rietveld Academie in Amsterdam. She has worked as an independent designer and architect since 1996, creating her own firm, Bureau Ira Koers, in Amsterdam in 2003. Her projects include Up-Stairs (three public stairways in OMA's City Center, Almere, 2006); Yburg residential building (Amsterdam, 2006); and MySpace, five residences in Haarlem (2009), all in the Netherlands. **ROELOF MULDER** was born in 1962 and studied fine arts at the Academy in Arnhem and design at the Jan van Eyck Academy in Maastricht. His firm, Studio Roelof Mulder, works in graphic design, font design, and exhibition and interior design. His recent work includes "Me and My Character," Platform 21 (Amsterdam, exhibition design, 2006); *A-Maze, People of the Labyrinths* (Arnhem, book design, 2007); Art Director in Amsterdam for *Frame* Magazine (2009–10); and Saved By Droog (Droog, Milan, product design, 2010). Together they realized the Library of the University of Amsterdam (Amsterdam, The Netherlands, 2009) published here.

IRA KOERS wurde 1970 geboren und studierte Architektur an der Gerrit Rietveld Academie in Amsterdam. Sie arbeitet seit 1996 als freie Designerin und Architektin und gründete ihr eigenes Büro, Bureau Ira Koers, 2003 in Amsterdam. Zu ihren Projekten zählen Up-Stairs (drei öffentliche Treppenanlagen im von OMA geplanten Stadtzentrum von Almere, 2006), Wohnbau in Ijburg (Amsterdam, 2006) sowie MySpace, fünf Häuser in Haarlem (2009), alle in den Niederlanden. **ROELOF MULDER** wurde 1962 geboren und studierte Kunst an der Akademie Arnhem und Design an der Jan van Eyck Akademie in Maastricht. Sein Büro Studio Roelof Mulder arbeitet in den Bereichen Grafikdesign, Typografie, Ausstellungs- und Innenarchitektur. Zu seinen aktuellen Projekten und Tätigkeiten zählen *Me and My Character*, Platform 21 (Amsterdam, Ausstellungsarchitektur, 2006), *A-Maze, People of the Labyrinths* (Arnhem, Buchgestaltung, 2007), Artdirection in Amsterdam für die Zeitschrift *Frame* (2009–10) und Saved By Droog (Droog, Mailand, Produktdesign, 2010). Gemeinsam realisierten die beiden die Universitätsbibliothek in Amsterdam (Amsterdam, Niederlande, 2009, hier vorgestellt).

IRA KOERS, née en 1970, a étudié l'architecture à l'Académie Gerrit Rietveld d'Amsterdam. Elle a commencé par travailler comme designer et architecte freelance en 1996, puis a fondé son agence, Bureau Ira Koers, à Amsterdam en 2003. Parmi ses projets figurent les Up-Stairs (trois escaliers publics dans le centre-ville d'Almere dus à OMA, 2006) ; l'immeuble résidentiel Yburg (Amsterdam, 2006) et MySpace, cinq résidences à Haarlem (2009). **ROELOF MULDER**, né en 1962, a étudié les beaux-arts à l'Académie d'Arnhem et le design à l'Académie Jan van Eyck à Maastricht. Son agence, Studio Roelof Mulder, intervient dans les domaines du design graphique, du design typographique et de la conception d'expositions et d'aménagements intérieurs. Parmi ses travaux récents : « Me and My Character », Platform 21 (conception d'exposition, Amsterdam, 2006) ; *A-Maze, People of the Labyrinths* (design graphique, Arnhem, 2007) ; la direction artistique du magazine *Frame* (Amsterdam, 2009–10) et le projet expérimental Saved By Droog (« Sauvé par Droog », Milan, design de produit, 2010). Ils ont réalisé ensemble la bibliothèque de l'université d'Amsterdam publiée ici (2009).

LIBRARY OF THE UNIVERSITY OF AMSTERDAM

Amsterdam, The Netherlands, 2009

Area: 2300 m². Client: University of Amsterdam. Cost: not disclosed

The accumulation of red crates in this temporary facility gives it a strong interior personality—and obviously serves its functional purposes.

Die Menge roter Kästen gibt der temporären Einrichtung ein markantes Profil; ganz offensichtlich wird sie ihrer Funktion vollauf gerecht.

L'accumulation de caissons rouges de cette installation temporaire lui donne un style très actuel mais répond à des besoins fonctionnels précis.

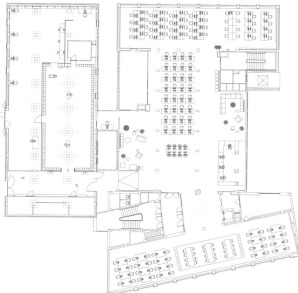

Although the university had plans to build a new library, they asked Koers and Mulder to create a temporary interior design, including study rooms, 235 work posts, a cafeteria, an information center, and an automated lending facility. They designed this last area with 1105 red crates containing red cases. They explain: "To offer students a good second home, we wanted to achieve two important things: a space like the white page of a book where the students themselves would play the main role in determining how it is filled in, and in certain areas a domestic atmosphere where the students could also study informally." The jury that granted this project the Great Indoors Award (2009) stated: "The modest budgets and the temporary nature, in combination with the abstract design quality, make this project a clear winner. In recent years, contemporary interiors have frequently been framed around themes, certainly where temporality has been in play. The jury unanimously appreciated the fact that this interior was defined by an abstract functionality, offering broad latitude for reflection."

Obwohl die Universität bereits eine neue Bibliothek plante, beauftragte man Koers und Mulder mit einer temporären Lösung für die Gestaltung der Innenräume. Sie umfasste Arbeitsräume, 235 Lernplätze, eine Caféteria, ein Informationszentrum und eine automatisierte Leihstelle. Letztere gestaltete das Team mit 1105 roten Wannen, die mit roten Boxen bestückt sind. Sie erklären: „Um den Studierenden ein ansprechendes zweites Zuhause zu bieten, wollten wir zwei entscheidende Dinge erreichen: einen Raum, der wie die weiße Seite eines Buchs funktioniert, bei dem die Studenten also selbst in zentraler Rolle entscheiden können, wie sie ihn füllen; in bestimmten Bereichen wiederum eine wohnliche Atmosphäre, wo die Studenten entspannt lernen können." Die Jury, die diesem Projekt den Great Indoors Award (2009) zuerkannte, erklärte: „Das bescheidene Budget und der temporäre Charakter – in Kombination mit der abstrakten Qualität des Designs – machten dieses Projekt zum klaren Sieger. In den letzten Jahren orientierten sich zeitgenössische Interieurs häufig an Themen, jedenfalls dort, wo es um temporäre Lösungen ging. Die Jury würdigte einhellig die Tatsache, dass dieses Interieur von abstrakter Funktionalität geprägt ist und großen Spielraum für Deutungen lässt."

Bien que l'université ait en projet la construction d'une nouvelle bibliothèque, elle a demandé à Koers et Mulder de lui créer des aménagements intérieurs temporaires, comprenant des salles de lecture, 235 postes de travail, un centre d'informations, une installation de prêts automatisée et une caféteria. La section des prêts se présente sous la forme de 1105 cadres rouges contenant des casiers de la même couleur. « Pour apporter aux étudiants une sorte de second foyer, nous avions deux buts importants : un espace vierge comme la page blanche d'un livre dans lequel les étudiants joueraient le rôle principal en déterminant eux-mêmes comment le remplir et, dans certaines zones, une atmosphère domestique dans laquelle ils pourraient également étudier, mais de façon plus informelle », expliquent les architectes. Le jury, qui a accordé à ce projet le prix Great Indoors (2009), a déclaré : « La modestie du budget et la nature temporaire des installations combinées à la qualité abstraite du projet, en font un vainqueur évident. Au cours des dernières années, les intérieurs contemporains se sont fréquemment concentrés sur des thématiques dans lesquelles le temps était mis en jeu. Le jury a apprécié à l'unanimité que cet intérieur se définisse par sa fonctionnalité abstraite, tout en offrant une vaste latitude à la réflexion. »

With their clean sense of design and taste for bright colors, the architects make a highly attractive environment out of what might have been considered space that was not worth such efforts, given the temporary nature of the library.

Mit ihrem ausgeprägten Gespür für Design und einer Vorliebe für kräftige Farben gestalteten die Architekten ein höchst attraktives Umfeld – obwohl die Bibliothek lediglich als temporäre Lösung gedacht war und manchen vielleicht nicht der Mühe wert erschienen wäre.

Par leur sens du design et leur goût des couleurs vives, les architectes ont réalisé un environnement très séduisant pour un projet qui aurait pu sembler peu intéressant étant donnée sa nature temporaire.

Where red and yellow dominate other spaces, here the architects have chosen to emphasize gray, white, and black, again in a carefully orchestrated spatial study.

Waren die übrigen Räume primär in Rot und Gelb gehalten, entschieden sich die Architekten hier für eine Palette aus Grau, Weiß und Schwarz. Auch dieser Raum ist bis ins Detail durchgestaltet.

Alors que le rouge et le jaune dominent les autres salles, les architectes ont choisi de mettre ici l'accent sur le gris, le noir et le blanc qui participent à l'orchestration soignée de l'espace.

ADOLF KRISCHANITZ

Architekt Krischanitz ZT GmbH
Getreidemarkt 1
1060 Vienna
Austria

Tel: +43 1 586 14 06 10
Fax: +43 1 586 14 06 22
E-mail: office@krischanitz.at
Web: www.krischanitz.at

ADOLF KRISCHANITZ was born in 1946 in Schwarzach/Pongau, Austria. During his studies of architecture at the Technical University of Vienna, he cofounded Missing Link with Angela Hareither and Otto Kapfinger. From 1991 to 1995 Adolf Krischanitz was the President of the Secession in Vienna. He has acted as a Visiting Professor and teacher in Vienna, Munich, Karlsruhe, and Berlin, and since 1992 he has been a Professor of Design and Urban Renewal at Berlin University of the Arts. Since 2002, Adolf Krischanitz has worked in cooperation with Alfred Grazioli on the expansion of the Museum Rietberg (Zurich, Switzerland, 2002–07). With Birgit Frank, he designed a Research Laboratory for the Novartis Campus (Basel, Switzerland, 2003–08). Other work includes a Housing and Business development on Lindengasse (Vienna, Austria, 2004–08) and the Temporary Kunsthalle Berlin (Berlin, Germany, 2008, published here). Since 2007, he has been working on the renewal and extension of 20er-Haus in Vienna, a former world exhibition pavilion (Brussels, Belgium, 1958), and a modernization and extension of the Kunstuniversität Linz, University for Art and Industrial Design (Linz, Austria).

ADOLF KRISCHANITZ wurde 1946 in Schwarzach/Pongau, Österreich, geboren. Während seines Architekturstudiums an der TU Wien gründete er Missing Link mit Angela Hareither und Otto Kapfinger. Von 1991 bis 1995 war Adolf Krischanitz Präsident der Wiener Secession. Er war Gastprofessor und Dozent in Wien, München, Karlsruhe und Berlin und ist seit 1992 Professor für Entwerfen und Stadterneuerung an der Universität der Künste Berlin. Seit 2002 hat Adolf Krischanitz in Kooperation mit Alfred Grazioli an der Erweiterung des Rietbergmuseums (Zürich, Schweiz, 2002–07) gearbeitet. Mit Birgit Frank entwarf er ein Forschungslabor für den Novartis Campus (Basel, Schweiz, 2003–08). Andere Projekte sind u.a. das Wohn- und Geschäftshaus Lindengasse (Wien, Österreich, 2004–08) sowie die Temporäre Kunsthalle Berlin (Berlin, 2008, hier vorgestellt). Seit 2007 arbeitet er an Umbau und Erweiterung des 20er-Hauses in Wien, ursprünglich als Ausstellungspavillon für die Expo 58 erbaut (Brüssel, Belgien, 1958), und an einer Modernisierung und Erweiterung der Kunstuniversität Linz, Universität für künstlerische und industrielle Gestaltung (Linz, Österreich).

ADOLF KRISCHANITZ est né en 1946 à Schwarzach/Pongau, en Autriche. Au cours de ses études d'architecture à l'université technique de Vienne, il fonde Missing Link avec Angela Hareither et Otto Kapfinger. De 1991 à 1995, il préside la Secession à Vienne. Après avoir été professeur invité et enseignant à Vienne, Munich, Karlsruhe et Berlin, il est, depuis 1992, professeur de conception et de rénovation urbaine à l'Université des arts de Berlin. Depuis 2002, il a travaillé en collaboration avec Alfred Grazioli sur l'extension du Musée Rietberg (Zurich, 2002–07). Avec Birgit Frank, il a conçu le Laboratoire de recherches du campus Novartis à Bâle (2003–08). Parmi ses autres réalisations : un ensemble de logements et de bureaux sur Lindengasse à Vienne (2004–08) et la Kunsthalle temporaire (Berlin, 2008, publiée ici). Depuis 2007, il travaille sur la rénovation et l'extension d'une maison des années 1920 à Vienne, un ancien pavillon de l'Exposition universelle de Bruxelles (1958), ainsi que sur la modernisation et l'extension de la Kunstuniversität Linz, Université d'art et de design industriel (Linz, Autriche).

TEMPORARY KUNSTHALLE BERLIN

Berlin, Germany, 2008

*Address: Schlossfreiheit 1, Schlossplatz, 10178 Berlin, Germany
Area: 1406 m². Client: Cube Kunsthalle Berlin gGmbH i.L. Cost: €1.5 million.
Collaboration: Anke Hafner (Project Leader), Sebastian Murr, Filip Steins*

With its bright blue-and-white color scheme the Temporary Kunsthalle makes no effort to blend into its surroundings—quite the contrary actually.

Mit ihrer leuchtend blau-weißen Farbgebung legte es die Temporäre Kunsthalle nicht darauf an, mit ihrem Umfeld zu verschmelzen – eher im Gegenteil.

Par ses couleurs – bleu vif et blanc – la Temporäre Kunsthalle ne fait aucun effort pour se fondre dans son environnement, bien au contraire.

This temporary contemporary art exhibition facility was erected on the Schlossplatz in Berlin. With a footprint measuring 20 x 56.25 meters, the structure is 11 meters tall. The very large façade of the building, located in one of Berlin's most prominent squares, was used to feature different artists' works. The design is described by the institution as "functional and clear." An entrance foyer contains the ticket desk, a bookshop, and some smaller spaces, with a café on the southern end. The main exhibition space, adjoining the foyer, is 30 meters long by 20 meters wide and has a 10.5-meter ceiling height. The structure is made of wood anchored in strip foundations. The exterior skin and the inner walls of the three main areas are made of fiber-cement panels. After a period of two years Temporary **TEMPORARY KUNSTHALLE BERLIN** was closed as planned in August 2010.

Die temporäre Ausstellungshalle für zeitgenössische Kunst wurde auf dem Berliner Schlossplatz errichtet. Der Bau mit einer Grundfläche von 20 x 56,25 m war 11 m hoch. Auf der besonders großflächigen Fassade des Gebäudes, das auf einem der zentralsten Plätze Berlins lag, wurden Arbeiten verschiedener Künstler präsentiert. Der Träger bezeichnete das Design als „funktional und klar". Im Foyer der Halle befanden sich eine Kasse, eine Buchhandlung und verschiedene kleinere Räume; im südlichen Ende des Baus lag ein Café. Der an das Foyer angrenzende Hauptausstellungsraum war 30 m lang und 20 m breit, mit einer Deckenhöhe von 10,5 m. Die Konstruktion selbst bestand aus Holz auf einem Betonstreifenfundament. Außenhaut und Innenwände der drei Haupträume waren mit Faserzementplatten verschalt. Im August 2010 wurde die **TEMPORÄRE KUNSTHALLE BERLIN** wie geplant nach einer Laufzeit von zwei Jahren geschlossen.

Cette construction temporaire destinée à des expositions d'art contemporain a été érigée sur la Schlossplatz à Berlin, une des grandes places de la capitale allemande. Elle mesure 20 x 56,5 m, pour 11 m de haut. Sa très grande façade est utilisable pour la présentation des œuvres. Le projet est décrit par l'institution comme « fonctionnel et clair ». Un hall d'entrée regroupe la banque d'accueil, une librairie et quelques services moins importants, ainsi qu'un café au sud. La salle d'exposition principale, contigüe au hall d'accueil mesure 30 x 20 m pour une hauteur de plafond de 10,5 m. La structure en bois repose sur des fondations à semelle filante. La façade extérieure et les murs intérieurs des trois zones principales sont en panneaux de fibrociment. Après une période de deux années, la **TEMPORÄRE KUNSTHALLE DE BERLIN** a été fermée comme prévu en août 2010.

An elevation and the photo below make it clear that the design of the structure is entirely rectilinear and straightforward.

Élévation et photo montrant la simplicité orthogonale du volume.

Aufriss und Aufnahme unten machen deutlich, wie streng rechtwinklig und gänzlich schnörkellos der Entwurf des Gebäudes ist.

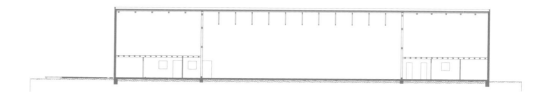

Above, a generous "white cube" exhibition space inside the gallery. Below, a plan showing this area in the center of the rectangle.

Oben ein Ausstellungsraum der Kunsthalle nach dem „white cube"-Prinzip. Unten ein Grundriss; der Ausstellungsraum liegt im Herzen des rechteckigen Baukörpers.

Ci-dessus, le généreux espace d'exposition est une simple « boîte blanche ». Ci-dessous, plan de cette même zone, au centre du bâtiment.

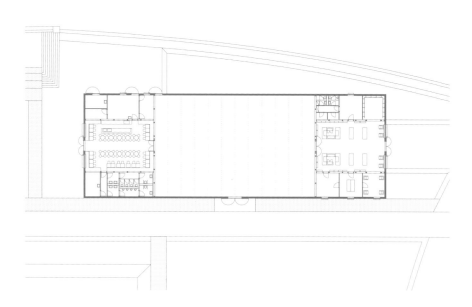

To the right, the café space, where
bright red recalls the use of saturated
color on the outside of the structure.
Below, a video installation in a dark-
ened gallery.

Rechts der Cafébereich, dessen in-
tensives Rot an die kräftigen Fassa-
denfarben denken lässt. Unten eine
Videoinstallation in den abgedunkel-
ten Ausstellungsräumen.

À droite, le café, dont le rouge vif
rappelle la couleur saturée de l'extérieur. Ci-dessous, une installation
vidéo.

LOT-EK

LOT-EK
55 Little West 12th Street
New York, NY 10014
USA

Tel: +1 212 255 9326
Fax: +1 212 255 2988
E-mail: info@lot-ek.com
Web: www.lot-ek.com

ADA TOLLA was born in 1964 in Potenza, Italy. She received her M.Arch from the Architecture Faculty of the "Federico II" University (Naples, 1982–89) and did postgraduate studies at Columbia University (New York, 1990–91). She is one of the two founding partners of LOT-EK, created in New York in 1993. She is currently an Associate Professor at Columbia University in the Graduate School of Architecture, Planning and Preservation. **GIUSEPPE LIGNANO** was born in Naples in 1963. He also received his M.Arch degree from the "Federico II" University (1982–89) and did postgraduate studies at Columbia at the same time as Ada Tolla. He is the other founding partner of LOT-EK and is currently an Associate Professor at Columbia University in the Graduate School of Architecture, Planning and Preservation. Their temporary work includes the Theater for One (Princeton University, Princeton, New Jersey, 2007); "X-Static Process" (Deitch Projects, New York, 2003, published here); Uniqlo Container Stores (New York, 2006, also published here); PUMACity (Alicante, Spain, and Boston, Massachusetts, 2008, also published here); and PUMA DDSM (South Street Seaport, New York, 2010), all in the USA unless stated otherwise.

ADA TOLLA wurde 1964 in Potenza, Italien, geboren. Sie absolvierte ihren M.Arch an der Fakultät für Architektur der Universität „Federico II" (Neapel, 1982–89) sowie ein Aufbaustudium an der Columbia University (New York, 1990–91). Sie ist eine der zwei Gründungspartner von LOT-EK, gegründet 1993 in New York. Aktuell lehrt Ada Tolla als außerordentliche Professorin am Graduiertenprogramm für Architektur, Stadtplanung und Denkmalschutz der Columbia University. **GIUSEPPE LIGNANO** wurde 1963 in Neapel geboren. Auch er absolvierte seinen M.Arch an der Universität „Federico II" (1982–89) sowie ein Aufbaustudium an der Columbia zeitgleich mit Ada Tolla. Er ist der zweite Gründungspartner von LOT-EK und derzeit außerordentlicher Professor am Graduiertenprogramm für Architektur, Stadtplanung und Denkmalschutz der Columbia University. Zu den temporären Projekten des Teams zählen das Theater for One (Princeton University, Princeton, New Jersey, 2007), *X-Static Process* (Deitch Projects, New York, 2003, hier vorgestellt), Uniqlo Container Stores (New York, 2006, ebenfalls hier vorgestellt), PUMACity (Alicante, Spanien, und Boston, Massachusetts, 2008, ebenfalls hier vorgestellt) sowie PUMA DDSM (South Street Seaport, New York, 2010), alle in den USA, sofern nicht anders angegeben.

ADA TOLLA, née en 1964 à Potenza (Italie), a obtenu son M. Arch à la faculté d'architecture de l'université Federico II de Naples (1982–89) et a effectué des études supérieures à l'université Columbia (New York, 1990–91). Elle est l'une des deux associés fondateurs de l'agence LOT-EK, créée à New York en 1993. Elle est actuellement professeure associée à l'université Columbia (École supérieure d'architecture, d'urbanisme et de conservation). **GIUSEPPE LIGNANO**, né à Naples en 1963, a également obtenu son M. Arch à l'université Federico II (1982–89) et a étudié à Columbia au même moment qu'Ada Tolla, avec laquelle il a fondé LOT-EK. Il est lui aussi professeur associé de l'université Columbia (École supérieure d'architecture, d'urbanisme et de conservation). Parmi leurs réalisations d'architecture temporaire : le Theater for One (université Princeton, Princeton, New Jersey, 2007) ; le « X-Static Process » (Deitch Projects, New York, 2003, publié ici) ; les magasins Uniqlo (New York, 2006, également publiés ici) ; PUMACity (Alicante, Espagne, et Boston, Massachusetts, 2008, également publié ici) et PUMA DDSM (South Street Seaport, New York, 2010).

"X-STATIC PROCESS"

New York, New York, USA, 2003; Tokyo, Japan, 2006;
Moscow, Russia, 2006; Seoul, South Korea, 2007

Area: 650 m². Client: Steven Klein and Madonna. Cost: not disclosed.
Collaboration: Maggie Peng, Koki Hashimoto

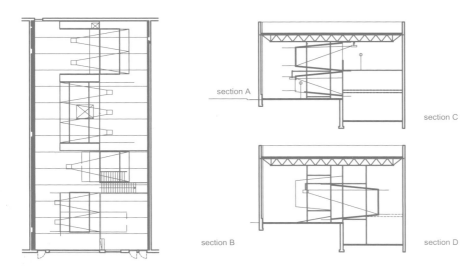

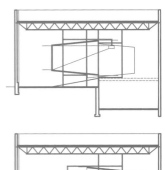

Section drawings show the basic simplicity of the installation with the projectors for the images clearly indicated.

Querschnitte verdeutlichen das einfache Grundprinzip der Installation. Die Platzierung der Projektoren ist klar zu erkennen.

Les dessins de coupe ci-dessus montrent la simplicité extrême de l'installation et les systèmes de projection.

This installation was intended for the animated photos of Madonna by Steven Klein. The architects state: "While conceptualizing the design for this exhibition, we have viewed Steven Klein's photos of Madonna like 'contemporary Caravaggio' paintings suspended on the edge between still and moving image and animated by sound." LOT-EK also compares the experience of visiting the show to "wandering through an Italian Baroque church, where one is captivated by the large, magically lit paintings that fill the walls of the side chapels." Held on pipe scaffolding, volumes that served as speakers appeared to float in space, while slanted floors and ceilings made some distances appear greater than they were, drawing spectators toward the images. It would seem that Madonna fully lived up to her name with this homage, and in any case that the architects took their task to heart.

Die Installation war für die Präsentation von animierten Fotografien gedacht, die Steven Klein von Madonna gemacht hatte. Die Architekten erklären: „Als wir das Konzept für die Ausstellungsarchitektur entwarfen, betrachteten wir Steven Kleins Fotos von Madonna wie ‚zeitgenössische Caravaggios', die an der Grenze zwischen statischem und bewegtem Bild verharren und durch den Ton lebendig werden". Außerdem vergleicht das Team von LOT-EK den Ausstellungsbesuch mit einem „Streifzug durch eine italienische Barockkirche, fasziniert von den großformatigen, magisch angestrahlten Gemälden an den Wänden der Seitenkapellen". Von einem Rohrgerüst abgehängte Volumina dienten als Lautsprecherboxen und schienen frei im Raum zu schweben. Geneigte Böden und Decken ließen räumliche Distanzen größer wirken, als sie waren, und zogen die Betrachter in die Bilder hinein. Fast scheint es, als wäre Madonna ihrem Namen mit dieser Hommage endlich gerecht geworden; zweifellos nahmen die Architekten ihre Aufgabe sehr ernst.

Cette installation a été réalisée pour exposer des photographies animées de la chanteuse Madonna prises par Steven Klein. Comme l'explique l'architecte : « En conceptualisant le projet de cette exposition, nous avons considéré les photos de Madonna par Steven Klein comme des "Caravage contemporains", quelque part entre images fixes et images de film, animées par le son. » LOT-EK compare également l'expérience du visiteur à « une promenade dans une église baroque italienne, où l'on est captivé par les grands tableaux magiquement éclairés qui décorent les murs des chapelles latérales ». Maintenus par des tubes d'échafaudage, les haut-parleurs semblaient flotter dans l'espace. Les inclinaisons des sols et des plafonds faisaient paraître les distances plus grandes qu'elles n'étaient en réalité et attiraient le spectateur vers les photographies. Il semble que Madonna a été finalement confirmée dans son image de star de la scène par cet hommage rendu, et que les architectes ont pris à cœur de le réaliser.

Within the exhibition area, the use of
pipe scaffolding is evident but takes
a secondary role as opposed to the
works themselves.

Die Verwendung von Gerüststangen
im Ausstellungsbereich ist auffällig,
spielt jedoch eine untergeordnete
Rolle gegenüber den künstlerischen
Arbeiten.

Si la présence des tubes d'échafaudage est très visible à l'intérieur, elle
ne joue qu'un rôle secondaire par
rapport à celle des œuvres.

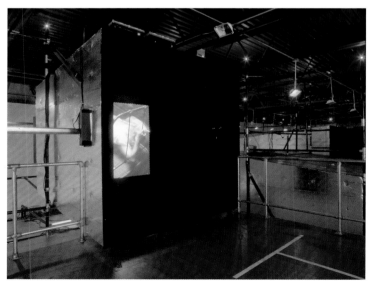

UNIQLO CONTAINER STORES

New York, New York, USA, 2006

Area: 15 m². Client: Uniqlo USA, Inc. Cost: $42 000.
Collaboration: Keisuke Nibe, Haruka Saito

Two 20 ft containers were used to tour New York, introducing the Uniqlo brand to the United States in 2006. The containers were outfitted as fully equipped "pop-up" stores including shelving, sales, and custom-designed fitting-room space. Mirrors at both ends of the containers created an illusion of greater space, while vertical windows were aligned with the shelving. Band lighting along the floors and ceiling provided the artificial light necessary. These brightly colored yellow or blue containers were just what was required to introduce the Japanese fashion chain to America.

2006 tourten zwei 20-Fuß-Container durch New York, um die Marke Uniqlo in den USA zu präsentieren. Die Container waren als „Pop-Up-Stores" ausgestattet, samt Regalen, Kasse und speziell angefertigten Umkleidekabinen. Spiegel an beiden Stirnwänden des Containers ließen den Raum größer wirken; vertikale Fensteröffnungen fügten sich in das Raster der Regale. Lichtbänder an Decke und im Boden sorgten bei Bedarf für künstliche Beleuchtung. Diese leuchtend bunten, gelben und blauen Container waren alles, was nötig war, um die japanische Modekette in Amerika einzuführen.

Pour lancer la marque Uniqlo aux États-Unis en 2006, deux conteneurs de 20 pieds de long ont été installés dans divers lieux à New York. Ils étaient équipés en boutiques temporaires : rayonnages, caisse, cabines d'essayage. Aux deux extrémités du conteneur, des miroirs agrandissaient l'espace. Les fenêtres verticales étaient alignées sur les rayonnages. Des bandeaux lumineux en limite du sol et du plafond fournissaient l'éclairage nécessaire. Ces conteneurs de couleurs vives – jaune ou bleu – étaient bien dans l'esprit du lancement de la chaîne japonaise en Amérique.

The idea of installing "pop-up" container stores in New York on a temporary basis, surely not easy on a regulatory basis, is both original and striking.

Das Konzept, Container als temporäre „Pop-Up-Stores" in New York zu platzieren, ist zweifellos ungewöhnlich und auffällig, dürfte angesichts der dortigen Bauvorschriften jedoch nicht leicht gewesen sein.

L'idée d'installer des magasins-conteneurs temporaires à New York – sans doute non envisageable sur une longue durée – est à la fois originale et surprenante.

Easily transportable by definition, the Uniqlo Container Stores succeeded in giving the brand a new image vis-à-vis their competition, an intention highlighted in the interior and exterior views on this page.

Die leicht transportierbaren Container Stores für Uniqlo verhalfen der Marke zu einem neuen Image und hoben sie von Wettbewerbern ab: Eine Zielsetzung, die auch an den Innen- und Außenansichten auf dieser Seite deutlich wird.

Facilement transportables par définition, les Uniqlo Container Stores donnent à la marque une image neuve par rapport à ses concurrents, intention soulignée par ces images.

PUMACITY

Alicante, Spain, and Boston, Massachusetts, USA, 2008

Area: 1022 m². Client: PUMA NA. Cost: not disclosed.
Collaboration: Keisuke Nibe, Koki Hashimoto

Containers are indeed meant to move, but they are just as readily interpreted as stacked, static objects. The architects have given the PUMACity store a sense of dynamism that suits both their fundamental nature and the image of the brand.

Container sind per se auf Mobilität angelegt, lassen sich aber auch problemlos übereinander stapeln und als statische Objekte einsetzen. Die Architekten verliehen dem PUMACity Store eine Dynamik, die nicht nur dem Charakter der Container gerecht wird, sondern ebenso dem Markenimage.

Si les conteneurs sont transportables, ils peuvent aussi être considérés comme des objets statiques. Les architectes ont donné à ce magasin PUMACity un dynamisme qui correspond à l'image de la marque et à la nature de son matériau.

PUMACITY was a transportable retail and event building made of 24 40 ft shipping containers. The structure was intended to follow the Puma sail boat in a cargo ship during the 2008 Volvo Ocean Race. The three-level stacked structure provided for large overhangs and terraces. A large reproduction of the white Puma logo marked the red exterior of the temporary building. Aside from two retail spaces, PUMACity contained offices, a press area, storage, a bar, and an event space. Before its use, the architects stated: "PUMACity is a truly experimental building that takes full advantage of the global shipping network already in place. At approximately 929 square meters of space, it will be the first container building of its scale to be truly mobile, designed to respond to all of the architectural challenges of a building of its kind, including international building codes, dramatic climate changes, and ease of assembly and operations."

PUMACITY war ein transportabler Verkaufsraum und Veranstaltungsort, gebaut aus 24 40-Fuß-Containern. Das Gebäude war entwickelt worden, um das Segelboot des Puma-Teams beim Volvo Ocean Race 2008 in einem Frachtschiff begleiten zu können. Die dreistöckige Stapelkonstruktion hatte mehrere große Auskragungen und Terrassen. Ein großformatiges weißes Puma-Logo zog sich über die rote Fassade des temporären Bauwerks. Neben zwei Verkaufsräumen waren in der PUMACity Büros, ein Pressebereich, Lagerräume, eine Bar und ein Eventbereich untergebracht. Noch vor der Einweihung erklärten die Architekten: „PUMACity ist ein absolut experimenteller Bau, der das bestehende globale Schifffahrtsnetz optimal nutzt. Mit seinen rund 929 m² Fläche wird es das erste Containergebäude dieser Größenordnung sein, das wirklich mobil ist. Dabei wird es sämtlichen architektonischen Herausforderungen eines Bauwerks dieser Art gerecht, etwa internationalen Bauvorschriften, dramatischen klimatischen Veränderungen sowie einfacher Montage und Bedienbarkeit."

PUMACITY était un ensemble transportable composé de 24 conteneurs d'expédition de 40 pieds de long, destinés à la vente au détail et à la tenue d'événements. Chargée dans un cargo, elle a suivi le voilier Puma pendant la Volvo Ocean Race de 2008. L'empilement des conteneurs sur trois niveaux avait permis de créer des terrasses et d'importants porte-à-faux. Un grand logo Puma peint en blanc sur le fond rouge des conteneurs signalait la présence de l'installation. En dehors de deux boutiques de vente, PUMACity contenait également des bureaux, un salon de presse, un bar, un espace pour événements et des stockages. « PUMACity est un bâtiment authentiquement expérimental qui profite pleinement du réseau des transports maritimes existants. Avec ses 929 m², ce sera le premier bâtiment en conteneur de cette échelle à être réellement mobile, conçu pour répondre à tous les défis architecturaux d'une construction de ce type, incluant les diverses réglementations de la construction internationale, les changements climatiques importants, et les facilités d'assemblage et de fonctionnement demandées. »

By shifting the container volumes, the architects create a cantilever-effect in the open position seen in the image above. The firm logo is deformed but still legible.

Durch das Verschieben der einzelnen Volumina gegeneinander entstehen in der geöffneten Position des Baukörpers Auskragungen. Das Firmenlogo wird verzerrt, bleibt aber erkennbar.

En faisant coulisser les conteneurs, les architectes ont créé un porte-à-faux (ci-dessus). Le logo de la marque est déformé mais reste lisible.

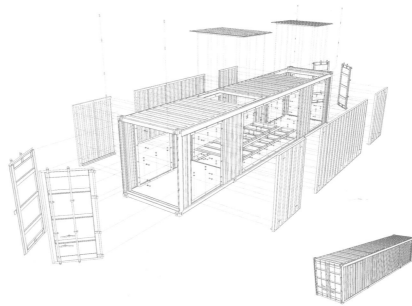

Both the cantilevering of the volumes and the use of a roof as a terrace confirm the playful nature of the project, while the drawing to the right gives a strong sense of organization and purpose to the design.

Sowohl die auskragenden Volumina als auch die Nutzung eines Dachs als Terrasse geben dem Projekt etwas Spielerisches. Die Zeichnung rechts veranschaulicht die Organisation und Zweckorientiertheit des Entwurfs.

La mise en porte-à-faux des volumes et la création d'une terrasse confirment la nature ludique du projet. À droite, dessin traduisant le fonctionnalisme et le sens de l'organisation du projet.

Using the original container surfaces,
but also cutting into them and opening the volumes, and finally by stacking the containers, LOT-EK makes
industrial objects exciting.

LOT-EK belässt die Oberflächen der
Container in ihrem ursprünglichen
Zustand, arbeitet mit Einschnitten,
öffnet die Volumina und stapelt sie
schließlich übereinander: So gewin-
nen alltägliche Industrieobjekte einen
ganz eigenen Reiz.

Reprenant les surfaces des conteneurs d'origine tout en découpant,
ouvrant et empilant les volumes,
LOT-EK a su donner un sens nouveau
à des objets purement industriels.

Seen from below at night, the store takes on the image of decidedly contemporary architecture. Right, drawings show the stacking and shifting of the containers.

In einer nächtlichen Untersicht präsentiert sich der Store dezidiert als zeitgenössische Architektur. Zeichnungen (rechts) illustrieren das Stapelprinzip und die Verschiebungen der Container gegeneinander.

Vu en contreplongée nocturne, le magasin prend une allure d'architecture très contemporaine. À droite, dessins sur la mise en place des conteneurs.

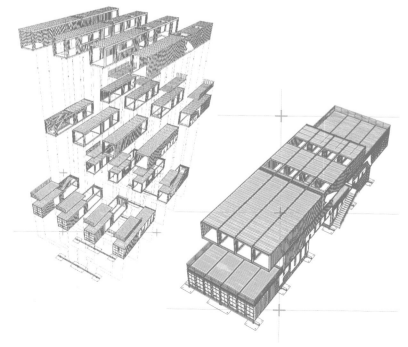

MAPT

MAPT—Mediating Architecture Process and Technology
Ryesgade 19C 1.tv
2200 Copenhagen
Denmark

Tel: +45 61 28 00 11/12
E-mail: lendager@mapt.dk / moller@mapt.dk
Web: www.mapt.dk

ANDERS LENDAGER, one of the founding principals of MAPT—Mediating Architecture Process and Technology, was born in Copenhagen, Denmark, in 1977 and received his degree from the University of Århus (1999–2005). He also attended SCI-Arc (2004). The other principal, **MODS MØLLER**, was born in Holstebro, Denmark, in 1978 and also obtained his degree from the University of Arhus (1999–2005), attending SCI-Arc in 2004. Their work includes the COP 15 Pavilion (Nordhavn, Copenhagen, 2009–10, published here); Won Hundred Showroom (Copenhagen, 2009–10); Bølgen Restaurant (Oslo, Norway, under construction); Galleriparken Public Garden (Vanløse, under construction); and the Herlev Shopping Mall (Herlev, also under construction), all in Denmark unless stated otherwise.

ANDERS LENDAGER, einer der Gründungspartner von MAPT – Mediating Architecture Process and Technology, wurde 1977 in Kopenhagen geboren und schloss sein Studium an der Universität Århus ab (1999–2005). Außerdem studierte er am Southern California Institute of Architecture (SCI-Arc, 2004). **MODS MØLLER**, zweiter Partner bei MAPT, wurde 1978 in Holstebro, Dänemark, geboren. Auch er schloss sein Studium an der Universität Århus ab (1999–2005) und besuchte das SCI-Arc 2004. Zu ihren Projekten zählen der COP 15 Pavillon (Nordhavn, Kopenhagen, 2009–10, hier vorgestellt), der Won Hundred Showroom (Kopenhagen, 2009–10), das Restaurant Bølgen (Oslo, Norwegen, im Bau), der öffentliche Garten Galleriparken (Vanløse, im Bau) sowie das Einkaufszentrum Herlev (Herlev, ebenfalls im Bau), alle in Dänemark, sofern nicht anders angegeben.

ANDERS LENDAGER, l'un des associés fondateurs de MAPT – Mediating Architecture Process and Technology, né à Copenhague en 1977, est diplômé de l'université d'Århus (1999–2005). Il a également étudié au Southern California Institute of Architecture (SCI-Arc, 2004). L'autre dirigeant de l'agence, **MODS MØLLER**, est né à Holstebro (Danemark) en 1978. Il est également diplômé de l'université d'Århus (1999–2005) et a étudié au SCI-Arc en 2004. Parmi leurs réalisations, toutes au Danemark, sauf mention contraire : le pavillon COP 15 (Nordhavn, Copenhague, 2009–10, publié ici) ; le showroom Won Hundred (Copenhague, 2009–10) ; le restaurant Bølgen (Oslo, en construction) ; le jardin public Galleriparken (Vanløse, en construction) et le centre commercial d'Herlev (Herlev, en construction).

COP 15 PAVILION

Nordhavn, Copenhagen, Denmark, 2009–10

Area: 150 m². Client: City of Copenhagen
Cost: not disclosed

The North Harbor Exhibition is part of the city of Copenhagen's effort to encourage sustainable urban development. In the case of the **COP 15 PAVILION** in the North Harbor, the architects state: "The idea is simple: take a surplus product like an old, empty shipping container and give it some value again. In this way you have a supremely sustainable solution which can quickly be made exclusive in spite of the materials' original use." Surplus materials from the wood and wind turbine industries were used inside the pavilion. After the exhibition, the city will use two of the containers for cultural events or as venues for local meetings. The architects point out that any number of other uses can be made of shipping containers that are sometimes judged too cheap to send back to their point of origin empty.

Die Nordhafen-Ausstellung ist Teil des Förderprogramms der Stadt Kopenhagen für nachhaltige Stadtentwicklung. Im Hinblick auf den **COP 15 PAVILLON** im Nordhafen erklären die Architekten: „Die Idee ist einfach: man nehme ein überschüssiges Produkt, etwa einen alten, leeren Frachtcontainer und werte ihn auf. Auf diese Weise findet sich eine außerordentlich nachhaltige Lösung, die sich trotz des ursprünglichen Nutzungszwecks des Baumaterials rasch zu etwas Exklusivem machen lässt." Im Innern des Pavillons kam Materialüberschuss aus der Holz- oder Windturbinenindustrie zum Einsatz. Nach Ende der Ausstellung wird die Stadt zwei der Container für kulturelle Veranstaltungen oder regionale Konferenzen nutzen. Die Architekten weisen darauf hin, dass sich Frachtcontainer, die oft als zu billig gelten, als sie leer an ihren Ursprungsort zurückzuverschiffen, für die unterschiedlichsten Zwecke nutzen lassen.

L'Exposition du port Nord s'est déroulée dans le cadre de la politique d'encouragement de la ville de Copenhague en faveur du développement durable urbain. Les architectes présentent ainsi l'idée du **PAVILLON COP 15** : « L'idée est simple : prendre un produit de récupération comme un vieux conteneur d'expédition vide et lui redonner une certaine valeur. Vous disposez ainsi d'une solution extrêmement durable, qui peut être rapidement personnalisée malgré l'origine de ces conteneurs. » Des matériaux de récupération issus des industries du bois et des éoliennes ont été utilisés pour l'intérieur du pavillon. Après l'exposition, la ville utilisera deux de ces conteneurs pour des événements ou des rencontres. L'architecte fait remarquer que l'on peut trouver de multiples utilisations pour ces conteneurs jugés parfois trop peu chers pour être réexpédiés à leur point de départ.

New ways of thinking and flexibility

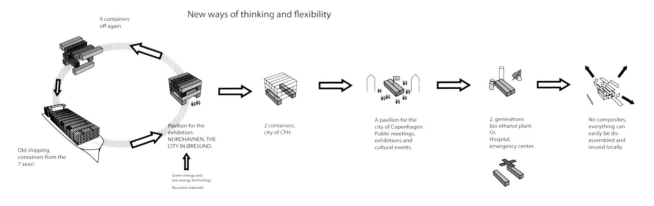

9 containers
off again

Old shipping
containers from the
7 seas!

Pavilion for the
exhibition:
NORDHAVNEN, THE
CITY IN ØRESUND.

Green energy and
low energy technology.

Recycled materials.

2 containers,
city of CPH.

A pavilion for the
city of Copenhagen.
Public meetings,
exhibitions and
cultural events.

2. generations
bio ethanol plant.
Or,
Hospital,
emergency center.

No composites,
everything can
easily be dis-
assembled and
reused locally.

Interior and exterior views of the
COP 15 Pavilion show how shipping
containers are assimilated into a
visibly contemporary form. Above, a
drawing of the "life cycle" of the
structure through the disassembly
and reuse of the containers.

Innen- und Außenansichten des COP
15 Pavillons: Hier werden Frachtcontainer zu einer sichtlich zeitgenössischen Architekturform. Oben eine
Zeichnung, die den Lebenszyklus des
Bauwerks illustriert, einschließlich De-
montage und möglicher Umnutzung.

Vues de l'intérieur et de l'extérieur du
pavillon COP 15 montrant comment les
conteneurs d'expédition créent une
forme réellement contemporaine.
Ci-dessus, dessin du cycle de vie du
projet et de ses différents stades de
démontage et de réutilisation.

KEN SUNGJIN MIN

SKM Architects
SKM Building
60–15 Samseong-dong, Gangnam-gu
Seoul 135–870
South Korea

Tel: +82 2 543 2027
Fax: +82 2 548 2027
E-mail: skm@skmarchitects.com
Web: www.skmarchitects.com

KEN SUNGJIN MIN received his B.Arch degree from the University of Southern California, School of Architecture (1989), and his M.Arch in Urban Design (MAUD) from the Harvard GSD (1993). He created SKM Architects in 1996. The recent work of the firm includes the GS Xi Gallery (Seoul, South Korea, 2007, published here); the Kumgang Ananti Golf & Spa Resort (Gangwon-do, North Korea, 2008); Lake Hills Suncheon Country Club (Suncheon, JeollaNam-do, South Korea, 2008); Asiana Airlines Weihai Point Golf & Resort (Weihai, China, 2009); Asiana Airlines Laolaobay Golf & Spa Resort (Saipan, Marianas, USA, 2009); Arumdaun Golf & Spa Resort (Chungcheong-nam-do, South Korea, 2009); Cheong Pyeong Village, 70 prestigious single-family houses (Gyeonggi-do, South Korea, in preliminary design); and the Anmyeun Island Newtown Master Plan (Chungcheongnam-do, South Korea, design phase).

KEN SUNGJIN MIN absolvierte seinen B.Arch an der Architekturfakultät der University of Southern California (1989) und seinen M.Arch in Urban Design (MAUD) an der Harvard GSD (1993). 1996 gründete er SKM. Zu den jüngeren Projekten des Büros zählen die GS Xi Gallery (Seoul, Südkorea, 2007, hier vorgestellt), der Kumgang Ananti Golf & Spa Resort (Gangwon-do, Nordkorea, 2008), der Lake Hills Suncheon Country Club (Suncheon, JeollaNam-do, Südkorea, 2008), der Asiana Airlines Weihai Point Golf & Resort (Weihai, China, 2009), der Asiana Airlines Laolaobay Golf & Spa Resort (Saipan, Marianas, USA, 2009), der Arumdaun Golf & Spa Resort (Chungche-ongnam-do, Südkorea, 2009), das Cheong Pyeong Village, 70 gehobene Einfamilienhäuser (Gyeonggi-do, Südkorea, in der Vorplanung) sowie der Masterplan für Anmyeun Island Newtown Master Plan (Chungcheongnam-do, South Korea, im Entwurf).

KEN SUNGJIN MIN a obtenu son B. Arch à l'École d'architecture de l'université de Californie du Sud (1989) et son M. Arch en urbanisme (MAUD) à l'Harvard GSD (1993). Il a créé SKM en 1996. Parmi les récentes réalisations de l'agence figurent la galerie GS Xi (Séoul, Corée du Sud, 2007, publiée ici) ; le golf et spa de Kumgang Ananti (Gangwon-do, Corée du Nord, 2008) ; le country club des collines de Suncheon (Suncheon, JeollaNam-do, Corée du Sud, 2008) ; le golf et hôtel de séjour de Weihai Point de la compagnie Asiana Airlines (Weihai, Chine, 2009) et le golf et spa Laolaobay de la même compagnie (Saipan, Marianas, États-Unis, 2009) ; le golf et spa d'Arumdaun (Chungcheongnam-do, Corée du Sud, 2009) ; le Cheong Pyeong Village, 70 résidences privées de luxe (Gyeonggi-do, Corée du Sud, en phase prélimi-naire de conception), et le plan directeur de la ville nouvelle de l'île d'Anmyeun (Chungcheongnam-do, Corée du Sud, en cours de conception).

GS XI GALLERY

Seoul, South Korea, 2007

Area: 5346 m². Client: GS E&C. Cost: $15 million.
Collaboration: Han Hyunsoo, Cho Seonggon, Moon Kyungmin

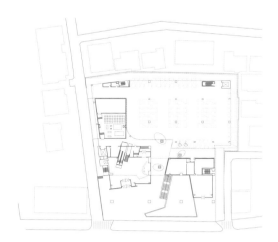

Plans show the divisions of the interior space which are intended to allow for the placement of model residences.

Grundrisse zeigen den untergliederten Innenraum, in den die geplanten Modellwohnungen integriert werden.

Plans de la division du volume intérieur et de l'implantation des maisons modèles.

The **GS XI GALLERY** is a temporary facility used by developers to sell apartments that they have conceived. Called model houses or sample houses, these are made out of reusable steel and economical modular panels and are normally destroyed after three to five years of use. The facility has temporary building permits that cover this period of occupation. The Xi Gallery is located near the Hapjeong Subway Station along the Yangwha Expressway, one of the major roads connecting the Seoul-Incheon Express with Seoul's Wall Street to the south, and Seoul's Metropolitan area to the north. It is also located near Hongik, Sogang, Yonsei, and Ewha Womans universities, which encourages younger visitors to come and look. The architects describe the project as a "housing cultural center." Auditoriums and educational rooms are located on the ground and first upper floor, while the model apartments are on the third and fourth floors. A warehouse space is used by developers to exhibit sample units. A single project (containing about five types of units) is usually on exhibit for three to five months. Within a year at least four projects are shown, resulting in the display and sale of about 20 types of units.

Die **GS XI GALLERY** ist eine temporäre Einrichtung, die Bauunternehmern den Verkauf von Wohnungen ermöglicht, die sie entwickelt haben. Die sogenannten Modell- oder Musterhäuser sind aus recyclingfähigem Stahl und ökonomischen Modulpaneelen konstruiert und werden in der Regel nach einer Nutzungsdauer von drei bis fünf Jahren wieder demontiert. Die Einrichtung verfügt über befristete Baugenehmigungen, die diese Wohndauer erlauben. Die Xi Gallery liegt unweit der U-Bahnstation Hapjeong am Yangwha Expressway, eine der Hauptstraßen, die den Seoul-Incheon Express nach Süden mit der Wall Street von Seoul und nach Norden mit dem Metropolitan-Viertel verbindet. Außerdem liegt sie in der Nähe der Universitäten Hongik, Sogang und Yonsei sowie der Ewha Womans University, wodurch auch ein jüngeres Publikum zu Besichtigungen kommt. Die Architekten beschreiben ihr Projekt als „Kultur-Wohnzentrum". Im Erdgeschoss und der ersten Etage befinden sich Auditorien und Lehrräume, während die Musterwohnungen im zweiten und dritten Geschoss untergebracht sind. Ein Lagerraum dient dem Bauträger zur Ausstellung der Musterwohneinheiten. Die Schauphase eines Projekts (mit je etwa fünf verschiedenen Wohnungstypen) beläuft sich in der Regel auf drei bis fünf Monate. Im Laufe eines Jahres werden mindestens vier Projekte gezeigt, sodass insgesamt rund 20 Mustertypen zu sehen sind.

La **GALERIE GS XI** est une installation temporaire utilisée par des promoteurs pour vendre leurs appartements. Ces appartements modèles sont fabriqués en acier recyclable et panneaux modulaires bon marché, puis sont normalement détruits après une durée d'utilisation de trois à cinq ans. Un permis de construire temporaire couvre cette période d'occupation. La galerie Xi est située près de la station de métro d'Hapjeong, le long de la voie express de Yangwha, l'une des principales artères reliant la Séoul-Incheon Express à Wall Street au sud et la zone métropolitaine de Séoul au nord ; elle se situe également à proximité des universités Hongik, Sogang, Yonsei et Ewha, ce qui permet à de jeunes visiteurs de venir. Les architectes présentent ce projet comme « un centre culturel consacré au logement ». Des auditoriums et des salles de formations sont installés au rez-de-chaussée et au premier étage, tandis que les appartements modèles sont implantés au deuxième et troisième étage. Un espace d'entreposage sert aux promoteurs à présenter les appartements. Un projet (environ cinq types d'appartements) est présenté pendant une durée de trois à cinq mois. En un an, au moins quatre projets sont ainsi exposés pour commercialiser une vingtaine de types d'appartements.

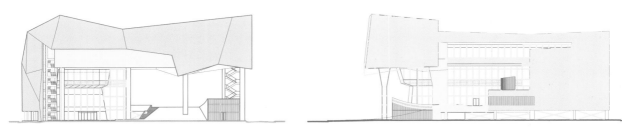

The building, as seen both in photos and in elevation drawings, serves as a kind of large shed whose interior space can be reordered according to present needs.

Der Komplex auf einer Ansicht (oben) und Aufrissen (unten) ist als großräumige Gebäudehülle angelegt, dessen Innenraum sich auf Wunsch konfigurieren lässt.

Le bâtiment, vu en photo et en élévations, est une vaste entrepôt dont le volume intérieur peut se reconfigurer en fonction des besoins.

Generous spaces at the heart of the building are atypical of such facilities and give a feeling of well-being that may well translate into sales of the housing models exposed inside.

Großzügige Freiflächen im Herzen des Gebäudekomplexes sind eher untypisch für Komplexe dieser Art und signalisieren Lebensqualität, was sich auf den Verkauf der angebotenen Wohnungen niederschlagen dürfte.

Les généreux volumes aménagés au cœur du bâtiment sont atypiques des équipements de ce genre. Ils créent un sentiment de bien-être favorable à la vente des maisons modèles exposées.

Let the green, internal spaces of the complex show the intelligent, varied treatment of the architectural surfaces and the combination with a garden atmosphere.

Ein Blick in den grünen Innenhofbereich des Komplexes (links) zeigt die durchdachte abwechslungsreiche sGestaltung der architektonischen Oberflächen und vermittelt zugleich die Atmosphäre eines Gartens.

L'aménagement des espaces verts intérieurs met en valeur la variété de traitement des surfaces architecturales et la création d'une atmosphère de jardin.

MIRALLES TAGLIABUE EMBT

Miralles Tagliabue Arquitectes Associats EMBT
Passatge de la Pau, 10 Bis. Pral.
08002 Barcelona
Spain

Tel: +34 934 12 53 42
Fax: +34 934 12 37 18
E-mail: info@mirallestagliabue.com
Web: www.mirallestagliabue.com

Born in Barcelona in 1955, **ENRIC MIRALLES** received his degree from the ETSA in that city in 1978. He died in 2000. He formed a partnership with Carme Pinós in 1983 and won a competition for the Igualada Cemetery Park on the outskirts of Barcelona in 1985 (completed in 1992). His work includes the Olympic Archery Ranges (Barcelona, 1989–91); the La Mina Civic Center (Barcelona, 1987–92); the Morella Boarding School (Castelló, 1986–94); and the Huesca Sports Hall (1988–94), all in Spain. The most visible recent project of the firm was the Scottish Parliament (Edinburgh, UK, 1998–2004). **BENEDETTA TAGLIABUE** was born in Milan, Italy, and graduated from the IUAV in Venice in 1989. She studied and worked in New York (with Agrest & Gandelsonas) from 1987 to 1989. She worked for Enric Miralles, beginning in 1992, first becoming a partner, then leading the studio after his death. Miralles Tagliabue EMBT completed the Rehabilitation of the Santa Caterina Market (Barcelona, 1997–2005); the Principal Building for the University Campus (Vigo, 2006); headquarters for Gas Natural (Barcelona, 2007); and the Public Library (Palafolls, 1997–2007), all in Spain; and the Spanish Pavilion for the Shanghai 2010 Expo (China, published here).

ENRIC MIRALLES wurde 1955 in Barcelona geboren und schloss sein Studium 1978 an der ETSA Barcelona ab. Er starb 2000. Miralles hatte 1983 gemeinsam mit Carme Pinós ein Büro gegründet, mit dem sie 1985 den Wettbewerb für die Friedhofsanlage in Igualada am Stadtrand von Barcelona gewannen (fertiggestellt 1992). Zu seinen Projekten zählen die Olympische Bogenschießanlage (Barcelona, 1989–91), das Stadtteilzentrum in La Mina (Barcelona, 1987–92), ein Internat in Morella (Castelló, 1986–94) sowie das Sportzentrum in Huesca (Huesca, 1988–94), alle in Spanien. Bekanntestes Projekt von Miralles Tagliabue in jüngerer Zeit ist das Schottische Parlament (Edinburgh, 1998–2004). **BENEDETTA TAGLIABUE** wurde in Mailand geboren und schloss ihr Studium 1989 am IUAV in Venedig ab. Von 1987 bis 1989 studierte und arbeitete sie in New York (bei Agrest & Gandelsonas). Ab 1992 kooperierte sie mit Enric Miralles, wurde erst Partnerin und leitet das Büro seit dem Tod von Miralles. Miralles Tagliabue EMBT betreute den Umbau der Markthalle Santa Caterina (Barcelona, 1997–2005), das Hauptgebäude auf dem Universitätscampus von Vigo (2006), die Zentrale von Gas Natural (Barcelona, 2007) und die Bibliothek in Palafolls (1997–2007), alle in Spanien, sowie den Spanischen Pavillon auf der Expo 2010 in Shanghai (China, hier vorgestellt).

Né à Barcelone en 1955, **ENRIC MIRALLES,** diplômé de l'ETSA en 1978, a disparu en 2000. Associé à Carme Pinós en 1983, il remporta le concours pour le cimetière du parc d'Igualada dans la banlieue de Barcelone en 1985 (achevé en 1992). Parmi ses réalisations : le stand de tir à l'arc olympique (Barcelone, 1989–91) ; le Centre municipal de La Mina (Barcelone, 1987–92) ; l'internat Morella (Castelló, 1986–94) ; et la salle de sports de Huesca Hall (1988–94). Le plus fameux projet réalisé par l'agence a été le Parlement écossais (Édimbourg, GB, 1998–2004). **BENEDETTA TAGLIABUE**, née à Milan, est diplômée de l'IUAV de Venise (1989). Elle a étudié et travaillé à New York avec Agrest & Gandelsonas de 1987 à 1989, puis avec Enric Miralles, à partir de 1992, devenant sa partenaire et prenant la tête de l'agence après la mort de celui-ci. Miralles Tagliabue EMBT a réalisé la réhabilitation du marché de Santa Caterina (Barcelone, 1997–2005) ; le bâtiment principal du campus universitaire de Vigo (2006) ; le siège de Gas Natural (Barcelone, 2007) ; une bibliothèque publique (Palafolls, 1997–2007) ainsi que le Pavillon espagnol de l'Exposition universelle de Shanghaï en 2010 (publié ici).

SPANISH PAVILION

Expo 2010, Shanghai, China, 2010

Area: 4716 m². Client: SEEI State Enterprise for International Exhibitions. Cost: not disclosed.
Collaboration: Makoto Fukuda, Salvador Gilabert, Igor Peraza (Project Directors)

This four-story steel structure, built on a 6000-square-meter site, is clad in glass and wicker. Interior materials are wicker, wood, and sheetrock. Aside from the exhibition area, the pavilion includes reception areas, a 150-seat auditorium, conference room, and press space. The **SPANISH PAVILION** was located near those of Switzerland, Poland, Belgium, and France. The architects state: "The Spanish Pavilion for the 2010 World Expo of Shanghai seeks to reflect upon the Spanish climate, as well as to recover the extraordinary craft of wickerwork in order to bring it back to life and to reinvent it as a new construction technique." The free-form structure makes use of a complex three-dimensional grid of tubular elements created with computer technologies. Wicker panels made in northeast China (Shangdong) were applied to the curving supports. The wicker is arranged in such a way that it forms a number of Chinese characters related to the concept of Chinese-Spanish friendship or cultural exchange.

Der auf einem 6000 m² großen Grundstück errichtete vierstöckige Bau wurde mit Glas und Korbgeflecht verblendet. Die im Innern verwendeten Materialien sind Korbgeflecht, Holz und Rigipsplatten. Neben der Ausstellungsfläche umfasst der Pavillon Empfangsbereiche, ein Auditorium mit 150 Plätzen, einen Konferenzsaal und einen Pressebereich. Der **SPANISCHE PAVILLON** lag unweit der Pavillons der Schweiz, Polens, Belgiens und Frankreichs. Die Architekten führen aus: „Der spanische Pavillon für die Expo 2010 in Shanghai soll das spanische Klima widerspiegeln, jedoch auch die außergewöhnliche Handwerkskunst des Korbflechtens wiederentdecken, um sie einerseits neu zu beleben und andererseits als neuartige Bautechnik zu entdecken." Die formal frei gestaltete Konstruktion basiert auf einem komplexen dreidimensionalen Raster aus Rohrelementen, das mithilfe von Computertechnologie entworfen wurde. Auf die geschwungenen Stützgerüste wurden Korbpaneele montiert, die in der nordostchinesischen Provinz Shandong gefertigt wurden. Die Korbelemente waren so angeordnet, dass sie die chinesischen Schriftzeichen für spanisch-chinesische Freundschaft oder Kulturaustausch nachempfanden.

Ce bâtiment de quatre niveaux, construit sur un terrain de 6000 m² était revêtu à l'extérieur de verre et d'osier, à l'intérieur d'osier, de bois et de carton-plâtre. Outre la partie consacrée aux expositions, il comprenait des aires de réception, un auditorium de 150 places, une salle de conférences et une salle de presse. Il était situé à côté des pavillons de la Suisse, de la Pologne, de la Belgique et de la France. Selon les architectes : « Le **PAVILLON ESPAGNOL** est une réflexion sur le climat espagnol qui cherche à s'appuyer sur l'extraordinaire artisanat de la vannerie pour le faire revivre et le réinventer par le biais d'une nouvelle technique de construction. » La structure de forme libre faisait appel à une trame tridimensionnelle complexe composée d'éléments tubulaires, dessinée par ordinateur. Des panneaux d'osier tressé fabriqués en Chine ont été appliqués sur ces supports incurvés. L'osier reproduisait un certain nombre de caractères chinois exprimant l'amitié sino-espagnole et les échanges culturels.

The unusual use of wicker panels for the exterior of the structure gives the pavilion an irregular, shifting appearance. Drawings show the relation of traditional wicker baskets to the architectural form.

Die ungewöhnlichen Paneele aus Korbgeflecht an der Fassade lassen den Pavillon unregelmäßig und geradezu bewegt erscheinen. Zeichnungen verdeutlichen das konzeptionelle Anknüpfen der architektonischen Form an traditionelle Korbwaren.

L'utilisation surprenante de panneaux d'osier pour l'extérieur du pavillon crée un aspect irrégulier, évolutif. Les dessins montrent le lien entre les traditionnels paniers d'osier et la forme architecturale.

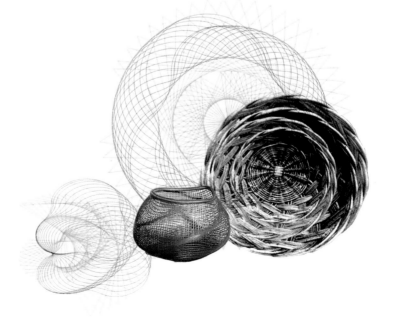

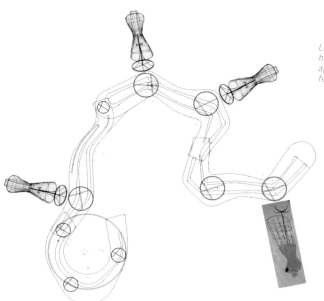

Layered and curving, the pavilion has an organic and almost "animal" appearance. A drawing outlines the forms of the interior reception desk.

Durch seine Schichtstruktur und die geschwungene Form wirkt der Pavillon organisch, fast wie ein Lebewesen. Die Zeichnung zeigt die Konturen des Empfangstresens im Innern des Baus.

Stratifié et curviligne, le pavillon présente un aspect organique, presque « animal ». Dessin du comptoir de réception intérieur.

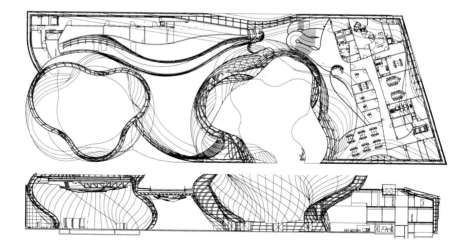

The interior allows the exterior wicker panels to be present while also permitting the creation of surprising, contemporary spaces. Above, a plan and a section show the bulbous flowing shape of the pavilion.

Auch im Innern des Baus sind die Korbpaneele der Außenfassade sichtbar; zugleich finden sich hier überraschend zeitgenössische Räume. Oben ein Grundriss sowie ein Querschnitt der bauchig-fließenden Formen des Pavillons.

De l'intérieur on perçoit la présence des panneaux d'osier qui ont permis de créer de surprenants volumes d'allure contemporaine. Ci-dessus, un plan et une coupe de la forme bulbeuse et fluide du pavillon.

MOS

MOS
92 William Street
New Haven, CT 06511
USA

Tel: +1 646 797 3046
Fax: +1 866 431 3928
E-mail: info@mos-office.net
Web: www.mos-office.net

MICHAEL MEREDITH was born in New York in 1971. He received his B.Arch degree from Syracuse University (1989–94) and his M.Arch from the Harvard GSD (1998–2000). He completed a residency at the Chinati Foundation (Marfa, Texas) in 2000. He is presently an Associate Professor of Architecture at the Harvard GSD. **HILARY SAMPLE** was born in Pennsylvania in 1971 and also attended Syracuse University (B.Arch), receiving her M.Arch from Princeton (2003). She completed a residency at the MacDowell Colony (Petersborough, New Hampshire) in 2006. She is an Assistant Professor at the Yale University School of Architecture. Michael Meredith and Hilary Sample created their present firm MOS in 2003. Their projects include the Hill House (Rochester, New York, USA, 2003); the Huyghe + Le Corbusier Puppet Theater, Harvard University Art Museums (Cambridge, Massachusetts, USA, 2004); the Floating House (Ontario, Canada, 2004–07); the Winters Studio (Ancram, New York, USA, 2006–07); Afterparty, PS1 Courtyard (Long Island City, New York, USA, 2009, published here); and the Creators Project Pavilion (New York, London, São Paulo, Seoul, Beijing, 2010, also published here). Current work includes an Inflatable Factory (Grand Bank, Newfoundland, Canada, 2011); Element House (Las Vegas, New Mexico, USA, 2011); Buddhist Child Home (Kathmandu, Nepal, 2012); and the Solo House (Spain, 2013).

MICHAEL MEREDITH wurde 1971 in New York geboren. Er absolvierte seinen B.Arch an der Syracuse University (1989–94) und seinen M.Arch an der Harvard GSD (1998–2000). 2000 hatte er einen Aufenthaltsstipendium an der Chinati Foundation (Marfa, Texas). Derzeit ist er Gastprofessor für Architektur am Harvard GSD. **HILARY SAMPLE** wurde 1971 in Pennsylvania geboren und besuchte ebenfalls die Syracuse University (B.Arch). Ihren M.Arch absolvierte sie an der Universität Princeton (2003). 2006 war sie Stipendiatin der MacDowell Colony (Petersborough, New Hampshire). Sie ist Assistenzprofessorin an Architekturfakultät der Universität Yale. Michael Meredith und Hilary Sample gründeten ihr derzeitiges Büro MOS 2003. Zu ihren Projekten zählen das Hill House (Rochester, New York, USA, 2003), das Huyghe + Le Corbusier Puppentheater, Harvard University Art Museums (Cambridge, Massachusetts, USA, 2004), das Floating House (Ontario, Kanada, 2004–07), das Winters Studio (Ancram, New York, USA, 2006–07), Afterparty, Hofinstallation am PS1 (Long Island City, New York, USA, 2009, hier vorgestellt) sowie der Pavillon für das Creators Project (New York, London, São Paulo, Seoul, Beijing, 2010, ebenfalls hier vorgestellt). Aktuelle Projekte sind u.a. die Inflatable Factory (Grand Bank, Neufundland, Kanada, 2011), das Element House (Las Vegas, New Mexico, USA, 2011), ein buddhistisches Kinderheim (Kathmandu, Nepal, 2012) und das Solo House (Spanien, 2013).

MICHAEL MEREDITH, né à New York en 1971, a obtenu son B. Arch à l'université de Syracuse (1989–94) et son M. Arch à l'Harvard GSD (1998–2000). Il a été invité en résidence à la Chinati Foundation (Marfa, Texas) en 2000. Il est actuellement professeur associé d'architecture à l'Harvard GSD. **HILARY SAMPLE**, née en Pennsylvanie en 1971, a également étudié à l'université de Syracuse (B. Arch), et a passé son M. Arch à Princeton (2003). Elle a été en résidence en 2006 à la MacDowell Colony (Petersborough, New Hampshire). Elle est professeure assistante à l'École d'architecture de l'université Yale. Michael Meredith et Hilary Sample ont créé leur agence MOS en 2003. Parmi leurs projets : la Hill House (« maison de la colline », Rochester, New York, 2003) ; le théâtre de marionnettes Huyghe + Le Corbusier, les musées d'art de l'université de Harvard (Cambridge, Massachusetts, 2004) ; la Floating House (« maison flottante », Ontario, Canada, 2004–07) ; le studio Winters (Ancram, New York, 2006–07) ; Afterparty, dans la cour de PS1 (Long Island City, New York, 2009, publié ici), et le pavillon du Creators Project (New York, Londres, São Paulo, Séoul, Pékin, 2010, également publié ici). Actuellement, ils travaillent sur un projet d'usine gonflable (Grand Bank, Newfoundland, Canada, 2011) ; l'Element House (« maison élément », Las Vegas, Nouveau-Mexique, États-Unis, 2011) ; un foyer bouddhiste pour enfants (Katmandou, Népal, 2012) et la maison Solo (Espagne, 2013).

AFTERPARTY, PS1 COURTYARD

Long Island City, New York, USA, 2009

Area: 929 m². Client: MoMA / PS1
Cost: not disclosed

Based on the idea of a gathering that occurs after a party, usually with the goal of relaxing, "this particular **AFTERPARTY** is a temporary urban shelter and passive cooling station for PS1 and its Warm Up events, an escape from the heat in a cooled-down PS1 courtyard," state the architects. They compare the dark thatched skin of this shelter to a Bedouin tent, seeking a certain return to "the primitive essentials of space, structure, and environment; a network of large, medium, and small cellular spaces allow for intimacy and social formations to thrive." Water reservoirs inside the spaces are used for their thermal mass to encourage airflow through the structures. The form of the "towers" also encourages cooling.

Angelehnt an das Prinzip, sich nach einer Party zu treffen, normalerweise um zu entspannen, war „diese spezielle **AFTERPARTY** ein temporärer urbaner Treffpunkt und zugleich eine passive Kühlstation für das PS1 und seine Warm-Up-Events, ein Zufluchtsort vor der Hitze in einem auf diese Weise abgekühlten PS1-Innenhof", erklären die Architekten. Sie vergleichen das dunkle Schilfdach des Unterstands mit einem Beduinenzelt, in gewisser Weise eine Rückkehr zu „den primitiven Ursprüngen von Raum, Baukonstruktion und Umwelt; ein Netzwerk großer, mittlerer und kleiner Zellen, die Intimität und soziale Begegnungen fördern". Wasserbecken in den einzelnen Raumzonen unterstützen dank ihrer thermalen Masse die Durchlüftung der Konstruktionen. Auch die Form der „Türme" trägt zum Kühleffekt bei.

S'inspirant de l'idée d'une réunion succédant à une réception, généralement dans l'objectif de se détendre, « cette **AFTERPARTY** particulière est un abri urbain temporaire et un lieu de détente passive conçu pour PS1, à l'occasion de ses manifestations intitulées Warm-Up-Events, une possibilité d'échapper à la chaleur en rejoignant la cour plus fraîche de PS1 », expliquent les architectes. Ils comparent le revêtement sombre en chaume de cet abri à une tente de Bédouins, et cherchent un certain retour « aux fondamentaux primitifs de l'espace, de la structure et de l'environnement ; un réseau d'espaces cellulaires grands, moyens et petits permet d'installer une certaine intimité et offre des possibilités de réunions de groupes sociaux ». Des réservoirs d'eau installés dans ces espaces servent de masse thermique régulatrice qui facilite la circulation de l'air à travers les structures. La forme en « tours » aide également au rafraîchissement de l'air.

A dark "thatched skin" related to desert tents arches through the courtyard of PS1 in Long Island City.

Eine dunkle „Schilfdachhaut", die Assoziationen an Wüstenzelte weckt, zieht sich durch den Innenhof des PS1 in Long Island City.

Une « peau de chaume » qui évoque la forme des tentes du désert développe ses arches dans la cour de PS1 à Long Island City.

A plan (below), which might recall a village layout, shows the form of the structure as it was erected in the courtyard of PS1.

Ein Grundriss (unten), der an ein Dorf erinnert, veranschaulicht die Gesamtanlage der Konstruktion im Hof des PS1.

Le plan ci-dessous, qui peut rappeler celui d'un village, montre la forme de la structure érigée dans la cour de PS1.

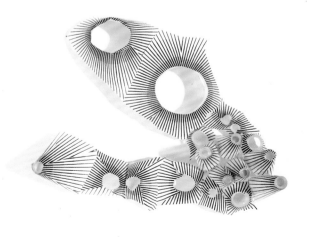

THE CREATORS PROJECT PAVILION

New York, London, São Paulo, Seoul, Beijing, 2010

Area: 56 m². Client: MoMA/PS1. Cost: not disclosed

Although the architects compare the form of this project to a kind of "vomit," it is apparent that they are creating an irregular form out of an accumulation of cubic elements.

Auch wenn die Architekten die formale Struktur des Projekts drastisch mit „Erbrochenem" vergleichen, beschreiben sie nichts anderes als die Bildung einer unregelmäßigen Form aus einer Ballung von Würfelelementen.

Même si les architectes comparent la forme de ce projet à une sorte de « vomi », il est clair qu'ils l'on créée à partir d'une accumulation de composants cubiques.

"This is not architecture," state the architects. "It's an experiment. We work on experiments that lead us into uncomfortable situations in parallel with architecture, in order to force ourselves to rethink things... In a way we are interested in an architecture vomited out, from an overindulgence in other architectures: a recognizable other of half-digested parts and pieces..." Using video game "physics engines" and cubes of glitter, MOS produced a semi-vaulted structure that appears "frozen for a moment." The installation makes use of interactive lights, and projections on the form "further undermine the stability of the object."

„Dies ist keine Architektur", erklären die Architekten. „Es ist ein Experiment. Parallel zur Architektur arbeiten wir mit Experimenten, die uns in unangenehme Situationen bringen, um uns zu zwingen, Dinge neu zu überdenken... In gewisser Weise interessieren wie uns für Architektur, die nach einem Überkonsum anderer Architekturen erbrochen wird: ein wiedererkennbares Anderes aus halbverdauten Einzelteilen..." Mithilfe von „Physik-Engines" aus der Videospieltechnik und glitzerüberzogenen Würfeln realisierte MOS eine Konstruktion, die ansatzweise ein Gewölbe bildet und wie eine „eingefrorene Momentaufnahme" wirkt. Die Installation arbeitet mit interaktiven Lichteffekten und Projektionen, die die „Stabilität des Objekts zusätzlich untergraben".

« Ce n'est pas de l'architecture », précisent les architectes. « C'est une expérience. Nous travaillons sur des expériences qui nous conduisent parfois à des situations inconfortables en parallèle avec l'architecture, afin de nous forcer à repenser les choses... D'une certaine façon, nous nous intéressons à une architecture vomie, à partir d'une surconsommation d'autres architectures : des parties et des morceaux reconnaissables ou à moitié digérés... » La construction est faite de cubes de matériau brillant. Des logiciels de simulation de jeux vidéo ont servi à rechercher des formes et à déterminer la détection des collisions entre les blocs qui viennent s'empiler, pour produire une sorte de sculpture en demi-arc « qui se fige un instant, avant de se stabiliser complètement ». Des éclairages et des projections interactifs s'inscrivent sur la forme obtenue pour « saper encore davantage la stabilité de l'objet ».

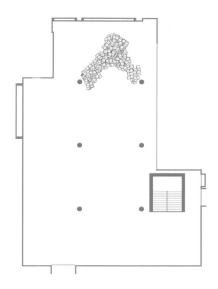

The assembled work (with a floor plan, above), as seen with and without the effects of the interactive lighting system.

Die realisierte Installation mit und ohne Einsatz des interaktiven Licht-systems. Oben das in den Grundriss eingezeichnete Werk.

L'œuvre assemblée (et le plan de la galerie, ci-dessus), avec et sans les effets d'éclairage interactif.

ERIC OWEN MOSS

Eric Owen Moss Architects
8557 Higuera Street
Culver City, CA 90232
USA

Tel: +1 310 839 1199
Fax: +1 310 839 7922
E-mail: mail@ericowenmoss.com
Web: www.ericowenmoss.com

Born in Los Angeles, California, in 1943, **ERIC OWEN MOSS** received his B.A. degree from UCLA in 1965 and his M.Arch from UC Berkeley in 1968. He also received an M.Arch degree at Harvard in 1972. He has been a Professor of Design at the Southern California Institute of Architecture since 1974 and has served as Director for the past eight years. He opened his own firm in Culver City in 1973. His built work includes the Central Housing Office, University of California at Irvine (Irvine, 1986–89); Lindblade Tower (Culver City, 1987–89); Paramount Laundry (Culver City, 1987–89); I.R.S. Building (Culver City, 1993–94); and Samitaur (Culver City, 1994–96), all in California. Other more recent work includes projects for the Queens Museum of Art (Queens, New York, 2001); the Beehive (Culver City, 2002); Stealth (Culver City, 2002); the Mariinsky and New Holland Cultural Center (Saint Petersburg, Russia, 2001–03); 3555 Hayden (Culver City, 2007); and the Samitaur Tower (Culver City, 2007–10). Ongoing projects are the Glass Tower, a high-rise office building (Los Angeles, California, 1998–); Sunset Doheny Hotel (West Hollywood, California, 2007–); 3585 Hayden (Culver City, 2008–); and a master plan for the Vienna University of Economics and Business (Vienna, Austria), all in the USA unless stated otherwise. Moss was Commissioner for the Austrian Pavilion at the 2010 Architecture Biennale (Venice, Italy).

ERIC OWEN MOSS wurde 1943 in Los Angeles geboren und absolvierte seinen B.A. 1965 an der UCLA, sowie 1968 einen M.Arch an der UC Berkeley. 1972 erwarb er zudem einen M.Arch in Harvard. Seit 1974 ist er Professor für Entwerfen am Southern California Institute of Architecture und seit acht Jahren auch Direktor des Instituts. Sein eigenes Büro eröffnete er 1973 in Culver City. Zu seinen realisierten Bauten zählen das Central Housing Office auf dem Campus der University of California in Irvine (1986–89), der Lindblade Tower (Culver City, 1987–89), der Paramount Waschsalon (Culver City, 1987–89), das I.R.S. Building (Culver City, 1993–94) sowie Samitaur (Culver City, 1994–96), alle in Kalifornien. Jüngere Arbeiten sind u.a. Projekte für das Queens Museum of Art (New York, 2001), der Beehive (Culver City, 2002), Stealth (Culver City, 2002), die Erweiterung des Mariinskij-Theaters (St. Petersburg, Russland, 2001–03), 3555 Hayden (Culver City, 2007) und der Samitaur Tower (Culver City, 2007–10). Aktuelle Projekte sind der Glass Tower, ein Bürohochhaus (Los Angeles, 1998–), das Sunset Doheny Hotel (West Hollywood, 2007–) und 3585 Hayden (Culver City, 2008–) sowie ein Masterplan für die Wirtschaftsuniversität Wien (Wien, Österreich), alle in den USA, sofern nicht anders angegeben. Moss war Kommissär des österreichischen Pavillons auf der Architekturbiennale 2010 in Venedig (Venedig, Italien).

Né à Los Angeles en 1943, **ERIC OWEN MOSS** a obtenu son B. A. à l'UCLA (1965) et son M. Arch à l'"UC Berkeley (1968). Il a également un M. Arch d'Harvard (1972). Il a ouvert son agence à Culver City en 1973, enseigne la conception architecturale au Southern California Institute of Architecture depuis 1974, et y a occupé les fonctions de directeur pendant les huit dernières années. Parmi ses réalisations, toutes en Californie : le Bureau central du logement de l'université de Californie à Irvine (Irvine, 1986–89) ; la tour Lindblade (Culver City, 1987–89) ; la blanchisserie Paramount (Culver City, 1987–89) ; les immeubles de l'I.R.S. (Culver City, 1993–94) et de Samitaur (Culver City, 1994–96). Plus récemment, il a réalisé des projets pour le Musée d'art de Queens (Queens, New York, 2001) ; la Beehive (« La ruche ») et Stealth (« Furtif »), tous deux à Culver City (2002) ; le théâtre Mariinsky et le centre culturel du quartier de la Nouvelle-Hollande (Saint-Pétersbourg, Russie, 2001–03) ; l'immeuble 3555 Hayden (Culver City, 2007) et la tour Samitaur (Culver City, 2007–10). Ses projets en cours sont la Glass Tower, un immeuble de bureaux de grande hauteur (« Tour de glace », Los Angeles, 1998–) ; le Sunset Doheny Hotel (Hollywood-Ouest, 2007–) ; l'immeuble 3585 Hayden (Culver City, 2008–) et le plan directeur de l'Université d'économie et de gestion de Vienne (Autriche). Moss a été commissaire du Pavillon autrichien pour la Biennale d'architecture de Venise 2010.

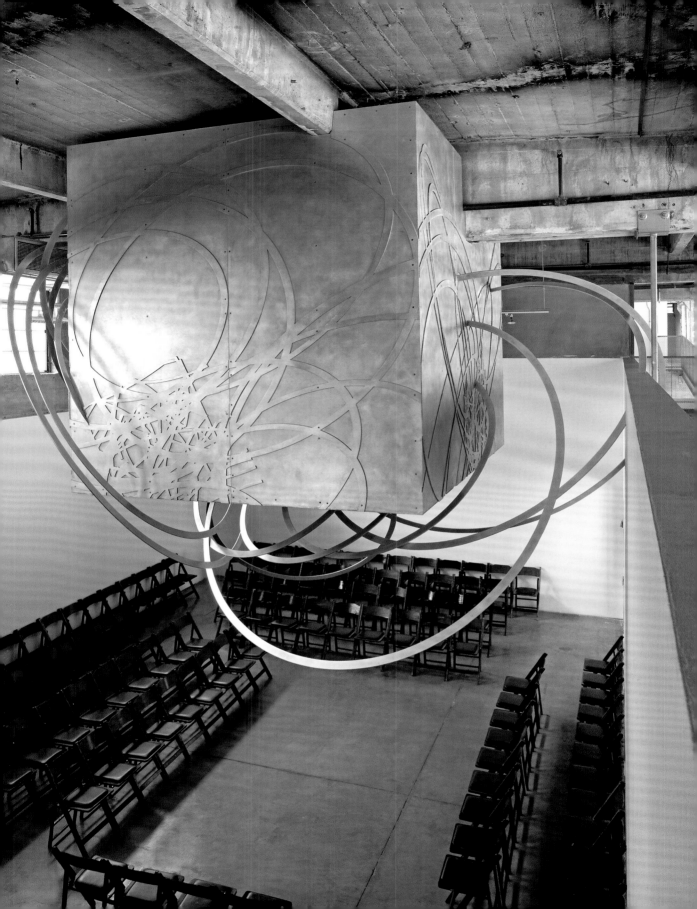

IF NOT NOW, WHEN?

Los Angeles, California, USA, and Vienna, Austria, 2009

Area: not applicable. Client: Southern California Institute of Architecture (SCI-Arc) and MAK. Cost: not disclosed.
Collaboration: Eric McNevin, Jose Herrasti, Maria Fernanda Oppermann Bento; Tom Farrage (Fabrication)

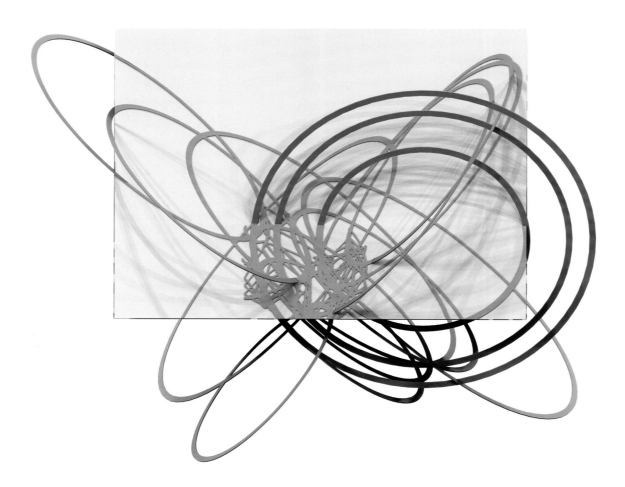

Making reference to his own earlier and upcoming work, Eric Owen Moss conceived this work as a point of discussion for SCI-Arc and other venues. An aluminum box representing the grid so familiar in modern architecture is circled by curves that escape its ordering volume. Moss explains: "Again, the ubiquitous grid of the surrounding concrete gallery space, and, by implication, the enduring grid pro forma that continues to inhabit the planning and architecture discourse is contested by the curvilinear spatial nemesis. It's past time to defoliate that grid. But if I do that, the opposition between orthogonal and curvilinear is gone. Architecture needs an enemy."

Anknüpfend an frühere Arbeiten und geplante Projekte konzipierte Eric Owen Moss diesen Entwurf als Diskussionsbeitrag für das SCI-Arc und weitere Standorte. Eine Aluminiumbox symbolisiert das aus der modernen Architektur so vertraute Raster; sie wird umfangen von Kreissegmenten, die dem ordnenden Körper scheinbar entweichen wollen. Moss erklärt: „Auch hier wird das allgegenwärtige Raster des Ausstellungsraums aus Beton – implizit auch das beharrliche formgebende Raster, das den Diskurs von Planung und Architektur nach wie vor prägt – von einer kurvenreichen räumlichen Nemesis in Frage gestellt. Es ist höchste Zeit, dieses Raster zu entblößen. Sobald ich dies jedoch tue, verlieren wir das Gegensatzpaar Orthogonal und Geschwungen. Architektur braucht ein Feindbild."

Faisant référence à ses œuvres antérieures et en cours, Eric Owen Moss a conçu cette intervention comme un lieu de discussion destiné au SCI-Arc ou à diverses manifestations. Une boîte en aluminium qui symbolise la trame familière de l'architecture moderne est encerclée de courbes qui tentent d'échapper à ce volume ordonné. « Là encore, la trame omniprésente de la galerie en béton qui l'entoure, et, par implication, la trame persistante *pro forma* qui continue à occuper le discours sur l'architecture et l'urbanisme est contestée par cette némésis spatiale curviligne. Le temps est vraiment venu de défolier cette trame. Mais si je le fais, l'opposition entre l'orthogonal et le curviligne disparaît. L'architecture a besoin d'un ennemi », explique Moss.

As seen in the drawings (left page and in plan below), the work of Eric Owen Moss takes the most basic architectural form, the cube, and breaks its regularity with a series of circular extrusions.

Wie auf den Zeichnungen (linke Seite und Grundriss unten) zu sehen, greift Eric Owen Moss für diese Arbeit auf das grundlegendste architektonische Element, den Kubus, zurück und bricht dessen Regelmäßigkeit mit kreisförmigen Extrusionen auf.

Comme le montrent les dessins (page de gauche et ci-dessous en plan), Eric Owen Moss s'est emparé de la forme architecturale la plus basique – le cube – dont il rompt l'aspect régulier par une série de projections circulaires.

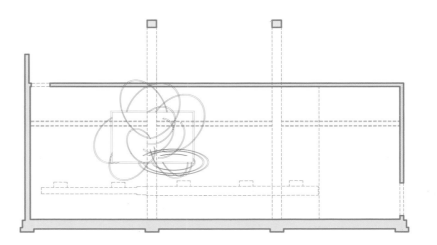

NATIONAL AERONAUTICS AND SPACE ADMINISTRATION (NASA)

National Aeronautics and Space Administration (NASA)
Public Communications Office
NASA Headquarters, Suite 5K39
Washington, D.C. 20546–0001
USA

Tel: +1 202 358 0001
Fax: +1 202 358 4338
Web: www.nasa.gov

The **NATIONAL AERONAUTICS AND SPACE ADMINISTRATION** (NASA) runs the space, aeronautics, and aerospace research of the United States government. Created in 1958, NASA was responsible for the Apollo missions to the moon, and, more recently, the Space Shuttle. It currently supports the International Space Station, as part of its goal to "pioneer the future in space exploration, scientific discovery, and aeronautics research." The agency currently employs about 18 000 people and has an annual budget in the range of $17.5 billion. Although former President George W. Bush declared that NASA should lead an effort to return to the moon and possibly go on to Mars, an ambition confirmed by the Administrator of NASA in 2007 who said the goal would be to reach Mars by 2037, President Barack Obama has sought to limit this plan and asked that NASA should place its focus on "space taxis" limited to trips to orbital stations such as the ISS (published here). The current Administrator of NASA is Charles Bolden, named by President Obama in 2009.

Die **NATIONAL AERONAUTICS AND SPACE ADMINISTRATION** (NASA) verantwortet die Raum- und Luftfahrtforschung der USA. Die 1958 gegründete NASA war zuständig für die Apollo-Missionen zum Mond sowie in jüngerer Zeit den Space Shuttle. Aktuell beteiligt sie sich an der Internationalen Raumstation (ISS) im Rahmen ihrer Zielsetzung, „die Zukunft der Weltraumforschung, wissenschaftlicher Erkenntnisse und Luftfahrtforschung als Pionier voranzutreiben". Gegenwärtig beschäftigt die Behörde 18 000 Mitarbeiter und verfügt über ein Jahresbudget von rund 17,5 Milliarden US Dollar. Während der ehemalige amerikanische Präsident George W. Bush noch erklärt hatte, die NASA solle ihre Bemühungen vorantreiben, auf den Mond zurückzukehren und möglicherweise auf dem Mars zu landen – ein Ziel, das 2007 vom Administrator der NASA bekräftigt wurde, der erklärte, man wolle bis 2037 auf den Mars – geht es Präsident Barack Obama darum, diese Pläne einzuschränken. Seiner Vorgabe nach soll sich die NASA darauf konzentrieren, „Space Taxis" zu betreiben, die ausschließlich darauf zugeschnitten sind, Stationen in der Erdumlaufbahn, wie die hier vorgestellte ISS, anzufliegen. Derzeitiger Administrator der NASA ist Charles Bolden, der 2009 von Präsident Obama ernannt wurde.

La NASA, **NATIONAL AERONAUTICS AND SPACE ADMINISTRATION**, gère la recherche spatiale, aéronautique et aérospatiale de l'État américain. Fondée en 1958, elle est responsable des missions Apollo vers la lune et, plus récemment, du programme de la navette spatiale. Elle gère actuellement la Station spatiale internationale dans le cadre de son programme « Ouvrir la voie au futur par l'exploration spatiale, les découvertes scientifiques et la recherche aéronautique ». L'agence emploie actuellement environ 18 000 personnes et bénéficie d'un budget annuel de 17,5 milliards de dollars. Bien que le président George W. Bush ait déclaré que la NASA devait retourner sur la lune et peut-être atteindre Mars – une ambition confirmée par l'administrateur de la NASA qui a déclaré que l'objectif d'atteindre Mars était fixé à 2037 –, le président Obama a cherché à limiter ces plans, et a demandé à la NASA de se concentrer sur des « taxis de l'espace » chargés d'aller-retour vers des stations orbitales comme l'ISS (publiée ici). L'administrateur actuel de la NASA est Charles Bolden, nommé par le président Obama en 2009.

INTERNATIONAL SPACE STATION

1998–2011 (ongoing)

Mass: 369 914 kg (2009). Length: 51 m. Width: 109 m.
Collaboration: National Aeronautics and Space Administration (NASA), European Space Agency (ESA), Russian Federal Space Agency (RKA),
Japanese Aerospace Exploration Agency (JAXA), and Canadian Space Agency (CSA)

Intended as an international research facility for the study of biology, chemistry, physics, astronomy, and meteorology, the **ISS** is by far the largest artificial satellite ever to have orbited the earth. There has been continual human presence on the ISS since October 31, 2000. The first module of the station was launched by Russia (Zarya, November 20, 1998), with the first US Space Shuttle visit occurring two weeks later. Work on the station was paused for two years due to the destruction of the Space Shuttle Columbia in 2003. By late 2009, 136 space walks had been necessary for the maintenance and assembly of the ISS. Traveling at approximately 27 750 kilometers per hour, the ISS orbits the earth 15.7 times per day. Because of the international organization required for the ISS, the obligations and rights of participants were established by the Space Station Intergovernmental Agreement (IGA, 1998). Because it is designed for the environment of outer space, the ISS has taken on a very particular form made up of modules conceived in different countries. There is no doubt that the ISS represents the most ambitious "space architecture" yet conceived and implemented. News about the ISS can be read on www.nasa.gov/mission_pages/station/main/index.html and www.nasa.gov/externalflash/ISSRG/index.html.

Die **ISS**, konzipiert als internationale Forschungseinrichtung für Biologie, Chemie, Physik, Astronomie und Meteorologie, ist der bei weitem größte künstliche Satellit, der sich je in der Erdumlaufbahn befunden hat. Seit dem 31. Oktober 2000 verfügt die ISS ununterbrochen über eine menschliche Besatzung. Das erste Modul der Station wurde von Russland in die Umlaufbahn gebracht (Sarja, 20. November 1998) und zwei Wochen später erstmals von einem amerikanischen Space Shuttle angeflogen. Nachdem das Space Shuttle Columbia 2003 beim Eintritt in die Erdatmosphäre auseinandergebrochen war, wurden die Arbeiten an der ISS zwei Jahre lang unterbrochen. Bis Ende 2009 waren 136 Außenbordeinsätze für Wartungs- und Montagearbeiten der ISS erforderlich. Bei einer Geschwindigkeit von rund 27 750 km/h umrundet die Station 15,7 Mal täglich die Erde. Aufgrund der internationalen Organisationsstruktur sind Rechte und Pflichten der Beteiligten durch das Intergovernmental Agreement für die ISS (IGA, 1998) geregelt. Bedingt durch ihr Umfeld im Weltraum hat die ISS eine spezifische modulare Bauform, deren einzelne Module in verschiedenen Ländern entwickelt werden. Zweifellos ist die ISS die ambitionierteste „Weltraumarchitektur", die je entwickelt und realisiert wurde. Aktuelle Meldungen zur ISS sind unter folgenden Adressen abrufbar: www.nasa.gov/mission_pages/station/main/index.html und www.nasa.gov/externalflash/ISSRG/index.html.

Station internationale destinée à des programmes de recherche de biologie, chimie, physique, astronomie et météorologie, l'**ISS** est de loin le plus gros satellite jamais lancé autour de la terre. Elle est en permanence habitée depuis le 31 octobre 2000. Le premier module a été lancé par la Russie (Zarya, 20 novembre 1998), la première navette américaine s'y arrimant deux semaines plus tard. Les travaux sur la station ont été arrêtés pendant deux ans à la suite de la destruction de la navette Columbia en 2003. Fin 2009, 136 sorties spatiales avaient déjà été comptabilisées pour assurer son assemblage et sa maintenance. Se déplaçant à une vitesse de 27 750 km/h environ, l'ISS fait le tour de la terre 15,7 fois par jour. Un accord intergouvernemental (IGA) signé en 1998 fixe les droits et obligations des États participants. Conçue pour l'environnement spatial et composée de modules construits par différents pays, l'ISS présente une forme très particulière. C'est sans aucun doute la plus ambitieuse « architecture spatiale » jamais conçue et mise en œuvre. Pour en savoir davantage : www.nasa.gov/mission_pages/station/main/index.html et www.nasa.gov/externalflash/ISSRG/index.html.

In a sense, the ISS is the ultimate piece of temporary architecture, with forms that are made to function only in space, dictated essentially by the laws of physics and engineering.

In gewisser Weise ist die ISS das ultimative Beispiel für temporäre Architektur: Ihre bauliche Form ist ausschließlich auf die Funktionalität im Weltraum zugeschnitten und wird im Grunde von physikalischen und bautechnischen Gesetzmäßigkeiten diktiert.

En un sens, l'ISS est l'exemple ultime de l'architecture temporaire. Ses formes sont exclusivement adaptées à l'espace, essentiellement dictées par les lois de la physique et de l'ingénierie.

IVÁN NAVARRO

Iván Navarro
Galerie Daniel Templon
30 Rue Beaubourg
Paris 75003
France

Tel: +1 42 72 14 10 / Fax: +1 42 77 45 36
E-mail: info@danieltemplon.com
Web: www.danieltemplon.com

IVÁN NAVARRO was born in Santiago, Chile, in 1972. He is an artist who lives and works in New York. He studied at the Pontificia Universidad Católica de Chile (1991–95). His recent solo exhibitions include "¿Dónde Están?," Centro Cultural Matucana 100 (Santiago, Chile, 2007); "Antifurniture," Galerie Daniel Templon (Paris, France, 2008); *Threshold*, Chilean Pavilion, Venice Biennale (Venice, Italy, 2009, published here); "Nowhere Man," Towner (Eastbourne, UK, 2009); "Nowhere Man," Galerie Daniel Templon (Paris, France, 2009); "No Man's Land," Centro de Arte Caja de Burgos (Burgos, Spain, 2010); and "Heaven or Las Vegas," Paul Kasmin Gallery (New York, USA, 2011). Navarro's work can be considered sculpture—he uses objects such as shopping carts or tables and frequently includes fluorescent lights, which has led to some comparisons with the work of Dan Flavin. His *White Electric Chair* (fluorescent light, metal fixtures, and electric energy, 2005) is in the collection of Charles Saatchi, whose web site states: "Iván Navarro views his work as building upon the unresolved aspects of minimalism, striving to engage viewer interaction and highlight the social and political factors that inherently lie within formal composition. Utilizing the aesthetic purity of florescent light bulbs, Iván Navarro's *White Electric Chair* reveals a chilling menace in its sensitivity as a design object. Modeled as fashionable furniture, Navarro's sculpture poses as desirable commodity…" (see www.saatchigallery.co.uk/artists/ivan_navarro_articles.htm).

IVÁN NAVARRO wurde 1972 in Santiago de Chile geboren. Der Künstler lebt und arbeitet in in New York. Er studierte an der Pontificia Universidad Católica de Chile (1991–95). Zu seinen jüngeren Einzelausstellungen zählen *¿Dónde Están?*, Centro Cultural Matucana 100 (Santiago, Chile, 2007), *Antifurniture*, Galerie Daniel Templon (Paris, Frankreich, 2008), *Threshold*, Chilenischer Pavillon, Biennale Venedig (Venedig, Italien, 2009, hier vorgestellt), *Nowhere Man*, Towner (Eastbourne, GB, 2009), *Nowhere Man*, Galerie Daniel Templon (Paris, Frankreich, 2009), *No Man's Land*, Centro de Arte Caja de Burgos (Burgos, Spanien, 2010) und *Heaven or Las Vegas*, Paul Kasmin Gallery (New York, USA, 2011). Navarros Werk kann als Skulptur verstanden werden – er arbeitet mit Objekten wie Einkaufswagen oder Tischen und integriert dabei häufig Leuchtstoffröhren, was zu Vergleichen mit dem Werk von Dan Flavin geführt hat. Seine Arbeit *White Electric Chair* (Leuchtstoffröhren, Metallfassungen und Strom, 2005) befindet sich in der Sammlung von Charles Saatchi, auf dessen Website es heißt: „Iván Navarro versteht seine Arbeit als ein Aufbauen auf den ungeklärten Aspekten des Minimalismus, wobei er die Interaktion mit dem Betrachter sucht und zugleich die sozialen und politischen Faktoren herausstreicht, die in formaler Komposition impliziert sind. Iván Navarros *White Electric Chair* enthüllt mit seiner Feinsinnigkeit als Designobjekt zugleich eine schaurige Drohung. Navarros Skulptur ist einem eleganten Möbelstück nachempfunden und präsentiert sich als erstrebenswertes Konsumgut…" (siehe www.saatchigallery.co.uk/artists/ivan_navarro_articles.htm).

Né à Santiago du Chili en 1972, **IVÁN NAVARRO** est un artiste qui vit et travaille à New York. Il a étudié à la Pontificia Universidad Católica de Chile (1991–95). Parmi ses récentes expositions personnelles figurent : « ¿Dónde Están? », centre culturel Matucana 100 (Santiago, Chili, 2007) ; « Antifurniture », Galerie Daniel Templon (Paris, 2008) ; « Threshold », Pavillon chilien, Biennale de Venise (Venise, 2009, publié ici) ; « Nowhere Man »,Towner (Eastbourne, GB, 2009) ; « Nowhere Man », Galerie Daniel Templon (Paris, 2009) ; « No Man's Land », Centro de Arte Caja de Burgos (Burgos, Espagne, 2010) et Heaven or Las Vegas (« Le paradis ou Las Vegas »), Galerie Paul Kasmin (New York, 2011). L'œuvre de Navarro peut être considérée comme de la sculpture. Il utilise, par exemple, des objets comme des chariots de supermarché, des tables et souvent des tubes fluorescents, ce qui a fait parfois comparer son travail avec celui de Dan Flavin. Sa *White Electric Chair* (« Chaise électrique blanche », lumières fluorescentes, accessoires de métal et énergie électrique, 2005) appartient à la collection de Charles Saatchi, dont le site web précise : « Iván Navarro voit son travail comme une élaboration de problématiques non résolues du minimalisme, s'efforçant de provoquer des interactions avec le spectateur et de souligner les facteurs sociaux et politiques qui font partie inhérente d'une composition formelle. Utilisant la pureté esthétique des éclairages fluorescents, la *White Electric Chair* d'Iván Navarro diffuse sa menace glaçante à travers une sensibilité d'objet de design. Réalisée comme un meuble élégant, la sculpture de Navarro se présente comme un objet de consommation désirable… » (cf. www.saatchigallery.co.uk/artists/ivan_navarro_articles.htm).

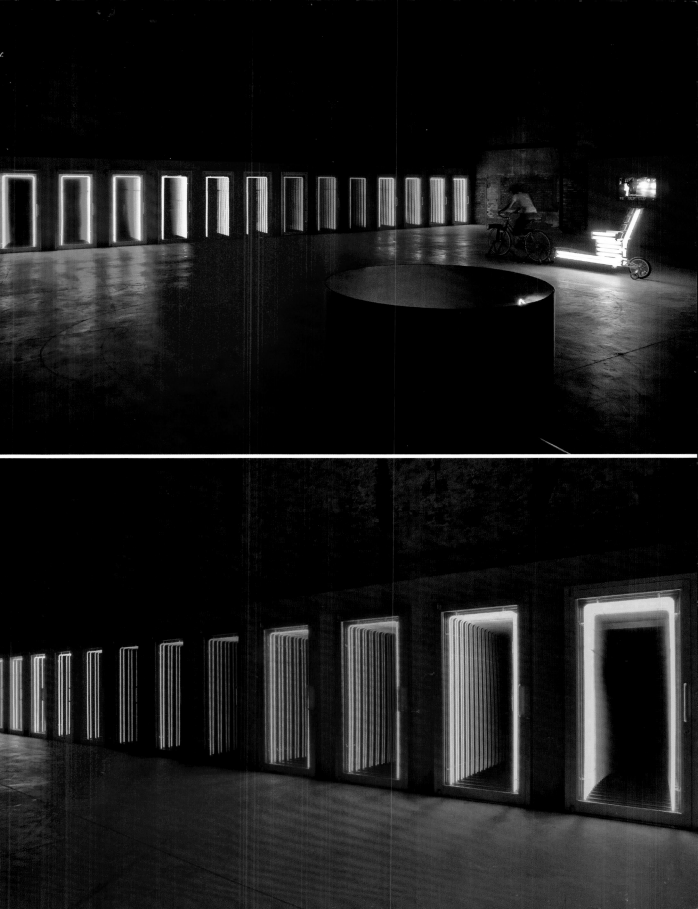

THRESHOLD, CHILEAN PAVILION

53rd Biennale of Venice, Venice, Italy, 2009

Area: 279 m². Client: not disclosed. Cost: not disclosed

A detail view of the work Death Row as seen at the 2009 Venice Biennale.

Detail der Installation Death Row auf der Biennale von Venedig 2009.

Vue détaillée de la pièce Death Row, à la Biennale de Venise 2009.

To the right, a drawing of the Threshold *project by the artist. Above, the work* Resistance *seen in Venice.*

Rechts eine Zeichnung des Künstlers für sein Projekt Threshold. *Oben eine Ansicht von* Resistance, *ebenfalls in Venedig ausgestellt.*

À droite, dessin de l'artiste du projet Threshold. *Ci-dessus, l'œuvre intitulée* Renaissance, *à Venise.*

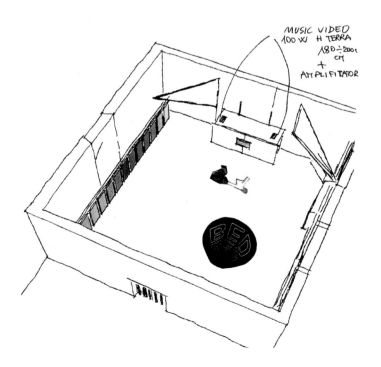

MUSIC VIDEO
100 W/ H TERRA
180÷200c
CM
+
AMPLIFITATOR

This installation in Venice included three works, called *Resistance*, *Death Row*, and *Bed*. The artist's own description of the works, which are clearly architectural, is more revealing than any commentary:

Resistance, 2009 Installation, variable dimensions. Sculpture (127 x 370.8 x 58.4 cm) and video (6:17 minutes). Fluorescent light, human-powered electric generator, metal fixtures, bicycle, cart, and electric energy. A bicycle is fixed with a single-seat carriage made of fluorescent lights. The lights are illuminated by a dynamo activated by human energy (pedaling the bicycle). A character rides the bicycle in Times Square, and the brightness of his vehicle depends on the degree of his physical exertion. The action is documented and edited into a six-minute video, accompanied by a new recording of a Chilean 80s anarchist rock anthem that speaks out against nationalism. *Death Row*, *2006–09* 218.4 x 1699.3 x 11.4 cm. Neon light, aluminum doors, mirror, one-way mirror, and electric energy. This installation is based on the Ellsworth Kelly painting *Spectrum V*. Each color panel of the original painting is represented by a single aluminum door whose interior contains a play of lights and a mirror, which creates the illusion of an endless tunnel through the wall. *Bed*, *2009* 82.6 x 181.6 cm (diameter). Neon light, plywood, mirror, one-way mirror, and electric energy. A word that is repeated in space is made of a neon light in the shape of half of each letter, which is then reflected by a mirror. In order to create this effect, the words must contain only letters that are absolutely symmetrical forms when divided horizontally. The mirror completes the formation of the word, and then repeats it endlessly in space.

Die Installation in Venedig bestand aus den drei Arbeiten *Resistance*, *Death Row* und *Bed*. Die Beschreibung der klar architektonischen Arbeiten durch den Künstler ist aussagekräftiger als jeder Kommentar:

Resistance, 2009 Installation, Maße variabel. Skulptur (127 x 370,8 x 58,4 cm) und Video (6:17 min). Leuchtstoffröhren, durch Menschenkraft betriebener Generator, Metallfassungen, Fahrrad, Anhänger, Strom. Ein Fahrrad ist mit einem einsitzigen Anhänger aus Leuchtstoffröhren versehen. Die Röhren leuchten mithilfe eines Dynamos, der durch Menschenkraft betrieben wird (Betätigen der Pedale). Eine Person fährt mit dem Fahrrad über den Times Square, wobei die Leuchtstärke des Gefährts der physischen Anstrengung des Fahrers entspricht. Die Aktion wurde dokumentiert und zu einem 6-minütigen Video geschnitten. Soundtrack ist die Neuaufnahme eines anarchistischen chilenischen Rocksongs der 1980er Jahre, dessen Text ein Appell gegen Nationalismus ist. *Death Row*, *2006–09* 218,4 x 1699,3 x 11,4 cm. Neonröhren, Aluminiumtüren, Spiegel, Einwegspiegel, Strom. Die Installation knüpft an Ellsworth Kellys Gemälde *Spectrum V* an. Die einzelnen Farbtafeln des Originals werden durch je eine Aluminiumtür repräsentiert, hinter der sich ein Spiel aus Licht und Spiegel verbirgt. So entsteht die Illusion eines endlosen Tunnels in die Wand hinein. *Bed*, *2009* 82,6 x 181,6 cm (Durchmesser). Neonröhren, Sperrholz, Spiegel, Einwegspiegel, Strom. Das sich endlos in den Raum hinein wiederholende Wort wird durch halbe Buchstaben aus Neonlicht und ihr Spiegelbild erzeugt. Um diesen Effekt zu erzeugen, muss das entsprechende Wort ausschließlich aus Buchstaben bestehen, die bei horizontaler Teilung streng symmetrisch sind. Der Spiegel vervollständigt die Konturen des Wortes und reflektiert es endlos in den Raum.

Cette installation réalisée pour Venise comprenait trois œuvres intitulées *Resistance*, *Death Row* et *Bed*. Le descriptif donné par l'artiste est plus révélateur que n'importe quel commentaire :

Resistance, 2009 Installation, dimensions variables. Sculpture (127 x 370,8 x 58,4 cm) et vidéo (6'17'). Éclairage fluorescent, générateur électrique manuel, accessoires métalliques, bicyclette, chariot et énergie électrique. Un chariot fait de tubes de néon est attaché à une bicyclette. Les tubes sont alimentés par une dynamo activée par le pédalage. Une personne utilise la bicyclette à Times Square et la brillance du véhicule dépend du degré de son effort physique. L'action a été filmée et produite en une vidéo de six minutes, accompagnée d'un nouvel enregistrement de l'hymne anarchiste chilien des années 1980, qui s'élève contre le nationalisme. *Death Row*, *2006–09* 218,4 x 1699,3 x 11,4 cm. Tubes néon, portes en aluminium, miroir, miroir sans tain et énergie électrique. Cette installation a été inspirée par une peinture d'Ellsworth Kelly intitulée *Spectrum V*. Chaque panneau de couleur de la peinture originale est représenté par une porte d'aluminium dans l'ouverture de laquelle ont été installés des tubes néon et un miroir qui crée l'illusion d'un tunnel sans fin percé à travers le mur. *Bed*, *2009* 82,6 x 181,6 cm (diamètre). Tubes néon, contreplaqué, miroir, miroir sans tain et énergie électrique. Le mot *Bed* est répété dans l'espace fait d'un tube néon pour chaque moitié de lettre, qui se reflète ensuite dans un miroir. Pour créer cet effet, les mots ne peuvent contenir que des lettres qui restent symétriques, une fois coupées horizontalement en deux. Le miroir complète la formation du mot qui se répète à l'infini dans l'espace.

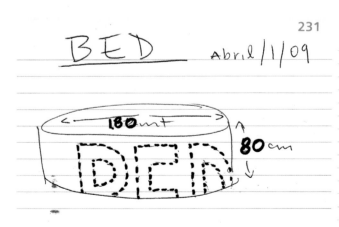

231

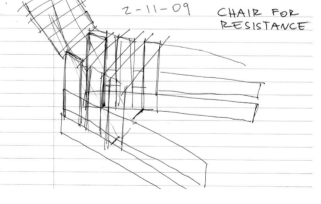

229

A drawing for the Bed project and two images of the installation to the right. A kind of well, this work gives the impression of an infinite progression of neon signs with the word "BED."

Eine Skizze für das Projekt Bed. Rechts zwei Ansichten der Installation. Die wie ein Brunnen konzipierte Arbeit lässt den Eindruck entstehen, eine endlose Flucht des Neonschriftzugs „BED" vor sich zu haben.

Un dessin et deux photos de l'installation du projet Bed, à droite. Cette œuvre en forme de puits donne l'impression d'une progression infinie de lettres de néon composant le mot « Bed ».

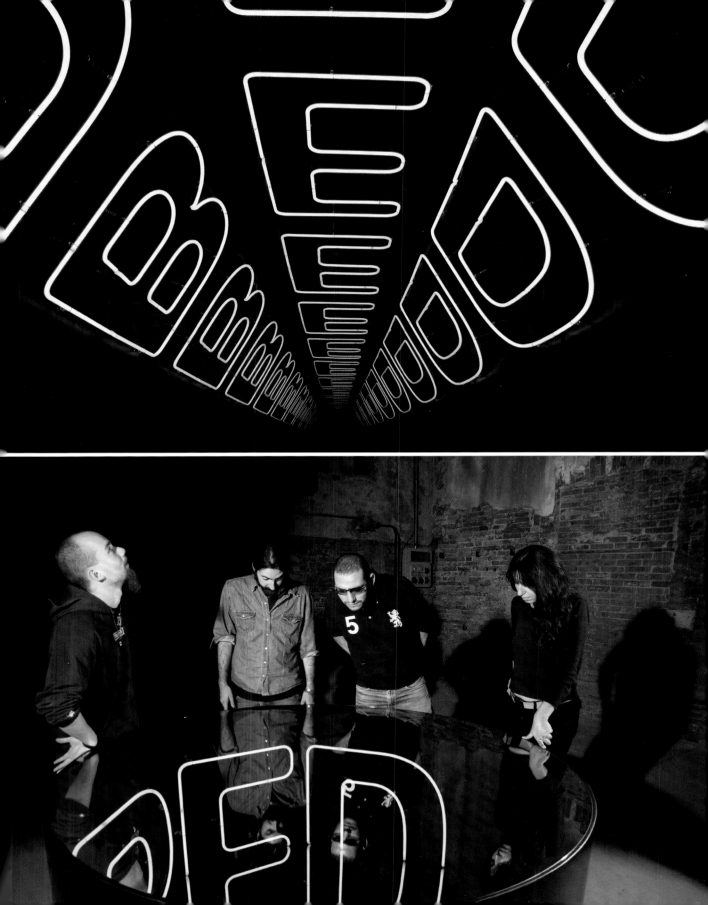

JEAN NOUVEL

Ateliers Jean Nouvel
10 Cité d'Angoulême / 75011 Paris / France
Tel: +33 1 49 23 83 83 / Fax: +33 1 43 14 81 10
E-mail: info@jeannouvel.fr / Web: www.jeannouvel.com

Born in 1945 in Fumel, France, **JEAN NOUVEL** studied in Bordeaux and then at the Paris École des Beaux-Arts (1964–72). From 1967 to 1970, he was an assistant of Claude Parent and Paul Virilio. In 1970, he created his first office with François Seigneur. Jean Nouvel received the RIBA Gold Medal in 2001 and the Pritzker Prize in 2008. His first widely noticed project was the Institut du Monde Arabe (Paris, 1981–87, with Architecture Studio). His major completed projects since 2000 are the Music and Conference Center (Lucerne, Switzerland, 1998–2000); the Agbar Tower (Barcelona, Spain, 2001–03); social housing at the Cité Manifeste (Mulhouse, France, 2004); the extension of the Reina Sofia Museum (Madrid, Spain, 1999–2005); the Quai Branly Museum (Paris, 2001–06); an apartment building in SoHo (New York, New York, USA, 2006); the Guthrie Theater (Minneapolis, Minnesota, USA, 2006); Les Bains des Docks (Le Havre, France, 2006–08); the Danish Radio Concert House (Copenhagen, Denmark, 2003–09); an office tower in Doha (Qatar, 2010); and he has just opened an office building in the City of London (UK), and a mixed-use building in Vienna (Austria). Published here is the Serpentine Pavilion, designed in 2010 (London, UK). Ongoing projects include two apartment buildings in Ibiza (Spain, 2006–11); the City Hall in Montpellier (France, 2008–11); a hotel in Barcelona (Spain, –2011); the new Philharmonic Hall in Paris (–2012); the Louvre Abu Dhabi (UAE, 2009–13); the Tour de Verre in New York (New York, USA); Frasers Broadway, a mixed-use high-rise building in Sydney (Australia, 2009–); the Tour Signal in Paris La Défense; the National Museum of Qatar (Doha, Qatar); and the Grand Paris project (with Jean-Marie Duthilleul and Michel Cantal-Dupart; Paris). Furthermore, Jean Nouvel is the architect-manager of all the projects for the Île Seguin in Boulogne-Billancourt (Paris, 2012–23).

JEAN NOUVEL, geboren 1945 in Fumel, Frankreich, studierte in Bordeaux und danach an der Pariser École des Beaux-Arts (1964–72). Von 1967 bis 1970 war er Assistent bei Claude Parent und Paul Virilio. 1970 gründete er sein erstes Büro mit François Seigneur. 2001 wurde er mit der RIBA-Goldmedaille ausgezeichnet, 2008 erhielt er den Pritzker-Preis. Sein erstes weithin bekannt gewordenes Projekt war das Institut du Monde Arabe (Paris, 1981–87, mit Architecture Studio). Seine bedeutendsten realisierten Projekte seit 2000 sind das Kultur- und Kongresszentrum Luzern (Schweiz, 1998–2000), der Agbar-Turm (Barcelona, 2001–03), Sozialbauwohnungen in der Cité Manifeste (Mulhouse, Frankreich, 2004), die Erweiterung der Reina Sofia (Madrid, 1999–2005), das Museum am Quai Branly (Paris, 2001–06), ein Apartmenthaus in SoHo (New York, USA, 2006), das Guthrie-Theater (Minneapolis, Minnesota, USA, 2006), Les Bains des Docks (Le Havre, Frankreich, 2006–08), das Konzerthaus für den Dänischen Rundfunk (Kopenhagen, 2003–09) und ein Bürohochhaus in Doha (Qatar, 2010). Soeben eröffnet wurden ein Bürogebäude in der Londoner City (GB) und ein Wohn- und Geschäftshaus in Wien (Österreich). Hier vorgestellt ist der Pavillon für die Serpentine Gallery, Entwurf 2010 (London, Großbritannien). Laufende Projekte sind u.a. zwei Apartmenthäuser auf Ibiza (Spanien, 2006–11), das Rathaus in Montpellier (Frankreich, 2008–11), ein Hotel in Barcelona (Spanien, –2011), die neue Philharmonie in Paris (–2012), der Louvre Abu Dhabi (VAE, 2009–13), der Tour de Verre in New York (New York, USA), Frasers Broadway, ein Wohn- und Geschäftshaus in Sydney (Australien, 2009–), der Tour Signal im Pariser Viertel La Défense, das Nationalmuseum von Qatar (Doha, Qatar) sowie das Grand Paris-Projekt (mit Jean-Marie Duthilleul und Michel Cantal-Dupart; Paris). Darüber hinaus ist Jean Nouvel leitender Architekt für sämtliche Bauvorhaben auf der Île Seguin in Boulogne-Billancourt (Paris, 2012–23).

Né en 1945 à Fumel, **JEAN NOUVEL** étudie à l'École des beaux-arts de Bordeaux, puis à celle de Paris (1964–72). De 1967 à 1970, il est assistant de Claude Parent et de Paul Virilio. En 1970, il crée une première agence avec François Seigneur. Il reçoit la médaille d'or du RIBA en 2001 et le prix Pritzker en 2008. Son premier projet, largement salué, est l'Institut du monde arabe (Paris, 1981–87), avec Architecture Studio. Parmi ses principaux projets depuis 2000 : le Centre de congrès et de musique de Lucerne (Suisse, 1998–2000) ; la tour Agbar (Barcelone, Espagne, 2001–03) ; les logements sociaux de la Cité Manifeste (Mulhouse, France, 2004) ; l'extension du musée Reina Sofia (Madrid, 1999–2005) ; le musée du quai Branly (Paris, 2001–06) ; un immeuble d'appartements à SoHo (New York, 2006) ; le théâtre Guthrie (Minneapolis, Minnesota, 2006) ; les Bains des Docks (Le Havre, France, 2006–08) ; la salle de concert de la radio danoise (Copenhague, 2003–09) ; une tour de bureaux à Doha (Qatar, 2010) ; un immeuble de bureaux dans la City de Londres ; un immeuble mixte à Vienne (Autriche) et le Pavillon 2010 de la Serpentine (Londres, 2010, publié ici). Il travaille actuellement sur deux immeubles d'appartements à Ibiza (Espagne, 2006–11) ; l'Hôtel de Ville de Montpellier (France, 2008–11) ; un hôtel à Barcelone (Espagne, –2011) ; une nouvelle salle philharmonique à Paris (–2012) ; le Louvre Abou Dhabi (EAU, 2009–13) ; la Tour de Verre à New York ; Frasers Broadway, un immeuble mixte de grande hauteur à Sydney (Australie, 2009–) ; la tour Signal à Paris La Défense ; le Musée national du Qatar (Doha, Qatar) et le projet du Grand Paris (avec Jean-Marie Duthilleul et Michel Cantal-Dupart). Par ailleurs, Jean Nouvel est l'architecte en chef de tous les projets architecturaux de l'île Seguin (Boulogne-Billancourt, France, 2012–23).

SERPENTINE PAVILION

Kensington Gardens, London, UK, 2010

Area: 500 m². Client: Serpentine Gallery. Cost: £750 000.
Collaboration: Gaston Tolila, Ute Rinnebach, Sophie Laromiguiere

"Red," says Jean Nouvel, "is the heat of summer. It is the complementary color of green. Red is alive, piercing. Red is provocative, forbidden, visible. Red is English like a red rose, like objects in London that one has to see: a double-decker bus, an old telephone booth, transitional places where one has to go." Nouvel's Pavilion in Hyde Park is indeed red. It is bold and geometric. It has retractable awnings but, most visibly, a freestanding 12-meter-high sloping wall. Some commentators have found that the structure may recall the Follies at the Parc de la Villette in Paris (Bernard Tschumi). Intended as a public space, the Pavilion was the venue for the Gallery's program of public talks and events, "Park Nights." Red outdoor ping-pong tables emphasize Nouvel's interest in play in this outdoor, park context. Edwin Heathcote wrote in the *Financial Times* (July 9, 2010): "His Pavilion is another step into something new. A series of theatrical red planes, bars and canopies, it stands somewhere between a hip Ibiza nightclub and Soviet constructivist agit-prop."

„Rot", so Jean Nouvel, „ist die Hitze des Sommers. Es ist die Komplementärfarbe zu Grün. Rot ist lebendig, durchdringend. Rot ist provokativ, verboten, offensichtlich. Rot ist englisch wie eine rote Rose, wie Londoner Wahrzeichen, die jeder gesehen haben muss: ein Doppeldeckerbus, eine alte Telefonzelle, Durchgangsorte, die man passieren muss." Nouvels Pavillon im Hyde Park ist unzweifelhaft rot. Er ist kühn und geometrisch. Er hat ausfahrbare Markisen, am auffälligsten ist jedoch seine freistehende, 12 m hohe schiefe Wand. Manche Kommentatoren erinnert der Bau an die Follies von Bernard Tschumi im Pariser Parc de la Villette. Der als öffentlicher Raum intendierte Pavillon diente als Veranstaltungsort für ein Programm aus öffentlichen Vorträgen und Events, die sogenannten Park Nights. Rote, für den Außenraum geeignete Tischtennisplatten unterstreichen Nouvels Interesse am Spiel in diesem Kontext im Park, unter freiem Himmel. Edwin Heathcote schrieb in der *Financial Times* (9. Juli 2010): „Sein Pavillon ist ein weiterer Schritt hin zu etwas Neuem. Mit zahlreichen dramatischen roten Ebenen, Bars und Markisen ist er irgendwo zwischen einem hippen Club in Ibiza und sowjetischem Agitprop anzusiedeln."

« Le rouge, dit Jean Nouvel, c'est la chaleur de l'été. C'est la couleur complémentaire du vert. Le rouge est vivant, perçant. Le rouge est provocateur, interdit, visible. Le rouge est anglais, comme une rose, comme ces objets que l'on voit à Londres : un bus à impériale, une vieille cabine téléphonique, des lieux de transition où l'on doit se rendre. » Le pavillon de Jean Nouvel à Hyde Park est certes très rouge. Audacieux et géométrique, il possède des auvents rétractables et un mur incliné de 12 m de haut qui impose sa présence. Certains commentateurs lui ont trouvé des points communs avec les Follies de Bernard Tschumi du parc de la Villette à Paris. Lieu public, le pavillon a accueilli le programme de débats publics et de manifestations de la Serpentine Gallery, les « Park Nights ». Des tables de ping-pong extérieures, rouges bien sûr, montrent la sensibilité de Jean Nouvel au contexte de détente du parc. Edwin Heathcote a écrit dans le *Financial Times* (9 juillet 2010) : « Son pavillon est un pas vers quelque chose de nouveau. Succession de plans, de barres et d'auvents rouges, il se situe quelque part entre un night-club hype d'Ibiza et une manifestation du constructivisme soviétique d'agit-prop. »

A plan (right), an image of the pavilion seen from a distance in Kensington Gardens (left), and an interior view (above) with the Serpentine Gallery in the background.

Ein Grundriss (rechts), eine Ansicht des Pavillons in Kensington Gardens aus größerer Entfernung (links) sowie eine Innenansicht (oben) mit dem Gebäude der Serpentine Gallery im Hintergrund.

Plan (à droite), image du pavillon dans les jardins de Kensington (à gauche) et vue intérieure (ci-dessus). On devine la Serpentine Gallery dans le fond.

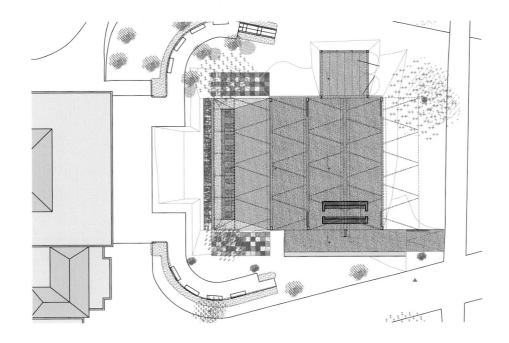

The ubiquitous use of an intense red for the pavilion colors passersby and presents a willful contrast with the green of the park itself.

Das allgegenwärtige intensive Rot des Pavillons taucht Passanten in rotes Licht und ist zugleich ein bewusst gewählter Kontrast zum Grün der Parklandschaft.

L'omniprésence du rouge se répercute jusque sur les passants et contraste vigoureusement avec la verdure du parc.

Above, a façade view, and below, two elevations with the high tilted wall that leans toward the Serpentine building.

Oben eine Ansicht der Fassade, unten zwei Aufrisse mit der hohen, schrägen Wand, die sich zum Galeriegebäude neigt.

Ci-dessus, vue de la façade et ci-dessous, deux élévations montrant le grand mur qui s'incline dans l'axe du toit de la Serpentine Gallery.

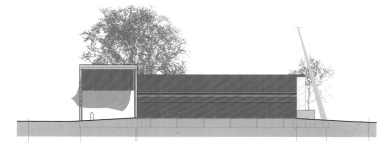

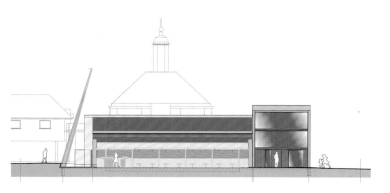

OBRA ARCHITECTS

OBRA Architects
315 Church Street 4FL
New York, NY 10013
USA

Tel: +1 212 625 3868
Fax: +1 212 625 3874
E-mail: press@obraarchitects.com
Web: www.obraarchitects.com

PABLO CASTRO was born in San Juan, Argentina, attended the Universidad Nacional de San Juan, Argentina (1987), and received his M.S. in Advanced Architectural Design from the Columbia University Graduate School of Architecture in 1989. He worked in the office of Richard Meier in New York (1989–92) and with Steven Holl (1995–2000), before cofounding OBRA Architects with Jennifer Lee in 2000. **JENNIFER LEE** attended Harvard College (1990) and received her B.Arch degree from the Cooper Union School of Architecture (New York, 1997). Their work includes Red+Housing, National Art Museum of China (Beijing, China, 2009, published here); and the Internationale Bauausstellung Smart Price Houses Competition (Hamburg, Germany, 2010). Current work includes the Villa of Captured Distance, ORDOS100 (Ordos, Inner Mongolia, China, under construction); Casa Osa (Cerro Osa, Osa Peninsula, Costa Rica, under construction); and the Chicago Children's Museum Town Square Exhibit (Chicago, Illinois, USA).

PABLO CASTRO wurde in San Juan, Argentinien, geboren, besuchte die Universidad Nacional de San Juan, Argentinien (1987) und absolvierte seinen M.S. in Advanced Architectural Design (Aufbaustudiengang Entwerfen) an der Architekturfakultät der Columbia University (1989). Er arbeitete im Büro von Richard Meier in New York (1989–92) und für Steven Holl (1995–2000), ehe er 2000 gemeinsam mit **JENNIFER LEE** das Büro OBRA Architects gründete. Jennifer Lee studierte am Harvard College (1990) und absolvierte ihren B.Arch an der Architekturfakultät der Cooper Union (New York, 1997). Zu ihren Projekten zählen Red+Housing, Chinesisches Nationalmuseum für Kunst (Peking, China, 2009, hier vorgestellt) und der Wettbewerbsbeitrag Internationale Bauausstellung Hamburg/Smart Price Houses (2010). Aktuelle Projekte sind u.a. Villa of Captured Distance, ORDOS100 (Ordos, Innere Mongolei, China, im Bau), Casa Osa (Cerro Osa, Halbinsel Osa, Costa Rica, im Bau) sowie das Town-Square-Projekt für das Children's Museum Chicago (Chicago, Illinois, USA).

PABLO CASTRO, né à San Juan, Argentine, a étudié à l'Universidad Nacional de San Juan (Argentine, 1987). Il a obtenu son M.S. en conception architecturale avancée à l'École d'architecture de l'université Columbia (1989). Il a travaillé dans les agences de Richard Meier à New York (1989–92) et de Steven Holl (1995–2000), avant de fonder OBRA Architects avec Jennifer Lee en 2000. **JENNIFER LEE** a étudié au Harvard College (1990) et passé son diplôme de B. Arch à l'École d'architecture de la Cooper Union (New York, 1997). À leur actif figurent un projet de logement d'urgence Red+Housing pour le Musée national d'art de Chine (Pékin, 2009, publié ici) et leur participation au concours des maisons à prix réduit de l'Internationale Bauausstellung (Hambourg, 2010). Ils travaillent actuellement à des projets comme la « Villa of Captured Distance », ORDOS100 (Ordos, Mongolie intérieure, Chine, en construction) ; la Casa Osa (Cerro Osa, péninsule d'Osa, Costa Rica, en construction) et l'exposition du Musée des enfants de Chicago (Town Square, Chicago, Illinois, États-Unis).

RED+HOUSING: ARCHITECTURE ON THE EDGE OF SURVIVAL

Beijing, China, 2009

Area: 45 m². Client: National Art Museum of China. Cost: estimated future production cost $5000.
Collaboration: Shin Kook Kang (Project Architect)

This project involved an emergency housing prototype commissioned as part of the exhibit "Crossing" which occurred one year after the Sichuan earthquake. "Emergency housing from the point of view of design," declare the architects, "is only an extreme form of architecture." The structure is intended to be economical, transportable, easy to assemble, made with renewable materials, and digitally prefabricated. The prototype shown in China was made of red parachute cloth and plywood. The architects further said: "We feel architecture can contribute not only to the physical but also emotional and psychological well-being of disaster victims." OBRA also created plywood furniture for the project.

Bei diesem Projekt ging es um den Entwurf eines Prototyps für Notunterkünfte im Rahmen der Ausstellung *Crossing*, die ein Jahr nach dem Erdbeben von Sichuan stattfand. „Notunterkünfte sind aus gestalterischer Sicht nichts weiter als eine extreme Form von Architektur", so die Architekten. Vorgesehen ist, die Konstruktion ökonomisch, transportabel und leicht montierbar zu halten und mit digitalen Methoden aus erneuerbaren Materialien vorzufertigen. Der in China vorgestellte Prototyp bestand aus roter Fallschirmseide und Sperrholz. Die Architekten führen weiter aus: „Wir glauben, dass Architektur nicht nur physisch, sondern auch emotional und psychologisch zum Wohlbefinden von Katastrophenopfern beitragen kann." OBRA entwarf darüber hinaus Möbel aus Sperrholz für das Projekt.

Ce projet portait sur un prototype de logement d'urgence proposé dans le cadre de l'exposition « Crossing », organisée un an après le tremblement de terre du Sichuan. « Du point de vue de la conception, expliquent les architectes, le logement d'urgence n'est qu'une forme extrême d'architecture. » La structure est économique, transportable, facile à assembler, faite de matériaux renouvelables, et est préfabriquée à l'aide de machines à commandes numériques. Le prototype exposé en Chine a été réalisé en toile de parachute rouge et en contreplaqué. « Nous pensons que l'architecture peut contribuer au bien-être non seulement physique, mais également émotionnel et psychologique des victimes d'une catastrophe », ont déclaré les architectes. OBRA a également créé des meubles en contreplaqué pour ce projet.

OBRA Architects took part in the first anniversary of the Sichuan earthquake through participation in "CROSSING: Dialogues for Emergency Architecture" at the National Art Museum of China.

Mit ihrem Entwurf beteiligte sich OBRA an der Ausstellung CROSSING: Dialoge zur Architektur von Notunterkünften am National Art Museum of China zum ersten Jahrestag des großen Erdbebens von Sichuan.

OBRA Architects a marqué le premier anniversaire du tremblement de terre du Sichuan par sa participation à la manifestation « CROSSING : dialogues pour une architecture d'urgence » au Musée national d'art de Chine.

A view of the installation in Beijing, and a series of drawings showing the assembly of the structures.

Ansicht der Installation in Peking und verschiedene Montagezeichnungen.

Vue de l'installation à Pékin, et dessins détaillant le principe de construction des logements.

Drawings and photos with the red parachute cloth giving a warm impression of the interiors of this emergency relief housing.

Zeichnungen und Fotos der mit roter Ballonseide bespannten Notunterkünfte vermitteln etwas von der Wärme des Innenraums.

Dessins et photos sur la mise en place de la toile de parachute rouge qui crée une atmosphère chaleureuse dans ces logements d'urgence.

A series of photos showing the assembly of the Red+Housing installation at the National Art Museum.

Eine Bildsequenz illustriert den Montageprozess der Red+Housing Notunterkünfte am National Art Museum.

Photos de l'installation de Red+Housing au Musée national d'art.

OFFICE OF MOBILE DESIGN

Office of Mobile Design
1725 Abbot Kinney Boulevard
Venice, CA 90291
USA

Tel: +1 310 439 1129
Fax: +1 310 745 0439
E-mail: info@designmobile.com
Web: www.designmobile.com

Born in 1965 in New York, **JENNIFER SIEGAL** obtained her M.Arch degree from the SCI-Arc in 1994. She was an apprentice and resident at Arcosanti (Codes Junction, Arizona, 1987) and then worked in the offices of Skidmore, Owings & Merrill in San Francisco (1988), Mark Mack (1992), and Hodgetts + Fung (1994–95). She has been the Principal of the Office of Mobile Design in Venice, California, since 1998. The work of OMD includes Swellhouse, a mass-customized/prefabricated eco-friendly house (Los Angeles, California, 2003); Portable House, a prefabricated eco-friendly mobile house (San Diego, California, 2003); and Seatrain Residence, a custom residence composed of two pairs of stacked ISO shipping containers sheltered under a 15-meter steel-and-glass roof membrane (Los Angeles, California, 2003). More recent work includes the Country School: Middle School (North Hollywood, California, 2008); Taliesin Mod.Fab (Scottsdale, Arizona, 2009, published here); the OMD Prefab Show House (Joshua Tree, California, 2006/2010, also published here); and the Big Sur Prefab Residence (Big Sur, California, 2010), all in the USA.

JENNIFER SIEGAL wurde 1965 in New York geboren und absolvierte ihren M.Arch 1994 am SCI-Arc. Sie war Auszubildende und Stipendiatin in Arcosanti (Codes Junction, Arizona, 1987). Davor hatte sie für Skidmore, Owings & Merrill in San Francisco (1988), Mark Mack (1992) und Hodgetts + Fung (1994–95) gearbeitet. Seit 1998 leitet sie das Office of Mobile Design in Venice, Kalifornien. Zu den Projekten von OMD zählen Swellhouse, ein umweltfreundliches, massengefertigtes, nach Kundenwunsch modifiziertes Fertighaus (Los Angeles, Kalifornien, 2003), Portable House, ein umweltfreundliches mobiles Fertighaus (San Diego, Kalifornien, 2003) sowie die Seatrain Residence, ein nach Kundenwunsch gefertigtes Haus aus zwei übereinandergestapelten ISO-Containern unter einem 15 m großen Schutzdach aus Glas und Stahl (Los Angeles, Kalifornien, 2003). Jüngere Projekte sind die Country School: Middle School (North Hollywood, Kalifornien, 2008), Taliesin Mod.Fab (Scottsdale, Arizona, 2009, hier vorgestellt), OMD Fertigbau-Musterhaus (Joshua Tree, Kalifornien, 2006/2010, ebenfalls hier vorgestellt) sowie das Big Sur Fertighaus (Big Sur, Kalifornien, 2010), alle in den USA.

Née en 1965 à New York, **JENNIFER SIEGAL** a obtenu son M. Arch au SCI-Arc (1994). Elle a été apprentie et résidente à Arcosanti (Codes Junction, Arizona, 1987) et a travaillé dans les agences Skidmore, Owings & Merrill à San Francisco (1988), Mark Mack (1992) et Hodgetts + Fung (1994–95). Elle dirige l'Office of Mobile Design à Venice, en Californie, depuis 1998. Les références d'OMD comprennent : la Swellhouse, une maison écologique personnalisée/préfabriquée (Los Angeles, 2003) ; la Portable House, maison écologique mobile préfabriquée (San Diego, 2003), et la Seatrain Residence, une résidence composée de deux paires de conteneurs ISO empilés abrités sous une toiture d'acier et de verre de 15 m de haut (Los Angeles, 2003). Plus récemment, elle a réalisé une école (Hollywood Nord, Californie, 2008) ; la maison modèle préfabriquée Taliesin Mod.Fab House (Scottsdale, Arizona, 2009, publiée ici) ; la maison d'exposition préfabriquée OMD Prefab Show House (Joshua Tree, Californie, 2006/2010, publiée ici) et la Big Sur Prefab Residence (Big Sur, Californie, 2010).

OMD PREFAB SHOW HOUSE

Joshua Tree, California, USA, 2006/2010

Address: Uphill Road, Joshua Tree, California, USA
Area: 70 m². Client: Chris Hanley. Cost: $150 000

This prototype house was originally located on Abbot Kinney Boulevard and was used to display the work of OMD. It is now placed in 32 hectares of wilderness land. The steel-frame structure measures 3.5 x 18 meters and has a 3.8-meter ceiling height inside. The design makes use of radiant heat ceiling panels and tankless water heaters, but also includes a central, luxurious Boffi kitchen. The architect states: "Whether briefly situated in an urban lot, momentarily located in the open landscape, or positioned for a more lengthy stay, the **JOSHUA TREE PREFAB** accommodates a wide range of needs and functions."

Dieser Hausprototyp stand ursprünglich am Abbot Kinney Boulevard und wurde von OMD zur Präsentation ihrer Projekte genutzt. Inzwischen steht es auf einem 32 ha großen Wüstengrundstück. Die Stahlrahmenkonstruktion misst 3,5 x 18 m und hat innen eine Deckenhöhe von 3,8 m. Ausgestattet ist der Bau mit einer Deckenheizung und Durchlauferhitzern, jedoch auch mit einer luxuriösen Boffi-Küche. Die Architektin erklärt: „Ob kurzfristig auf einem Stadtgrundstück, vorübergehend in der offenen Landschaft oder auch an einem langfristigeren Standort, das **JOSHUA TREE PREFAB** wird einer großen Bandbreite von Anforderungen und Funktionen gerecht."

Cette maison prototype a été dressée au départ sur Abbot Kinney Boulevard où elle servait à présenter le travail de l'agence. Elle est aujourd'hui installée dans un petit domaine naturel de 32 ha. La construction en acier de 3,5 m de large par 18 m de long bénéficie d'un plafond de 3,8 m de haut. Elle fait appel à des panneaux de chauffage radiant pour son plafond et des radiateurs à eau, mais comprend également une luxueuse cuisine Boffi. « Qu'elle soit brièvement installée sur une parcelle urbaine, momentanément installée dans un paysage dégagé en attendant une implantation plus durable, la **MAISON PRÉFABRIQUÉE DE JOSHUA TREE** répond à un grand nombre de besoins et de fonctions », a précisé l'architecte.

With a form that recalls that of shipping containers, the OMD Prefab Show House sits, above, in its location in Joshua Tree, California.

Von außen erinnert das OMD Prefab Show House an Seefrachtcontainer. Oben eine Ansicht des Baus vor Ort in Joshua Tree, Kalifornien.

La maison d'exposition préfabriquée OMD sur site, à Joshua Tree en Californie. Sa forme rappelle celle de conteneurs de transport.

Right, the house being transported on a flatbed truck. Below, it is seen installed in its wilderness site.

Rechts der Transport des Hauses auf einem Tieflader. Unten nach dem Aufbau auf dem Wüstengrundstück.

À droite, la maison transportée par camion. Ci-dessous son installation dans le désert.

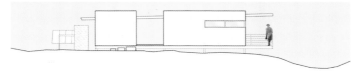

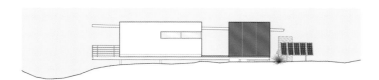

Elevation drawings and an image of the house in a more urban setting, where its long, thin design makes it fit readily into a small lot.

Aufrisse und eine Ansicht des Hauses in wesentlich urbanerem Kontext. Hier fügt sich die lange, schmale Gebäudeform problemlos in ein kleines Baugrundstück.

Ces élévations et la photo ci-dessous situent la maison dans son cadre urbain. Le plan en longueur est adapté à la petite taille de la parcelle.

A floor plan and interior views show the modern, generous spaces, with minimal walls reserved only for the enclosed toilet and kitchen areas.

Grundriss und Innenansichten der modernen großzügigen Räume. Die wenigen Innenwände umschließen lediglich Bad und Küchenbereich.

Le plan au sol et les vues de l'intérieur illustrent l'ampleur des volumes intérieurs, les seuls murs sont réservés à la séparation des sanitaires et de la cuisine.

TALIESIN MOD.FAB

Frank Lloyd Wright School of Architecture, Taliesin West, Scottsdale, Arizona, USA, 2009

*Address: Taliesin West, 12621 North Frank Lloyd Wright Blvd., Scottsdale, Arizona, USA
Area: 56 m². Client: Frank Lloyd Wright School of Architecture. Cost: not disclosed.
Collaboration: Michael P. Johnson, Design/Build students at Taliesin*

Jennifer Siegal points out that Frank Lloyd Wright created a scheme to build prefabricated houses early in the 20th century (American System of Housing). The **TALIESIN MOD.FAB** is a prototype for "simple, elegant, and sustainable living in the desert." The one-bedroom steel-frame residence can be transported on normal roads and makes use of passive and active (solar panels) energy saving measures. The project is a result of a design/build studio class on prefabricated construction co-taught by Jennifer Siegal and Michael Johnson. The prototype was built almost entirely by students with low-tech hand and power tools. The building sits cantilevered over a desert wash and is used as a guesthouse for visiting scholars.

Jennifer Siegal weist darauf hin, dass Frank Lloyd Wright bereits Anfang des 20. Jahrhunderts ein Fertighaussystem entwickelt hat (American System of Housing). Das **TALIESIN MOD.FAB** ist der Prototyp für „einfaches, elegantes und nachhaltiges Wohnen in der Wüste." Die 2-Zimmer-Stahlrahmenkonstruktion kann auf regulären Straßen transportiert werden und nutzt sowohl passive, als auch, durch Solarzellen, aktive Energiesparstrategien. Das Projekt entstand im Rahmen einer Studioklasse für Entwerfen und Bauen zum Thema Fertigbau unter Leitung von Jennifer Siegal und Michael Johnson. Der Prototyp wurde fast ausschließlich von Studierenden mit einfachen Hand- und Elektrowerkzeugen gebaut. Das Haus kragt über einen erosionsbedingten Wüstenabhang aus und wird als Gästehaus für Wissenschaftler genutzt.

Jennifer Siegal fait remarquer que Frank Lloyd Wright avait eu un projet de construction de maisons préfabriquées dès le début du XXᵉ siècle (« American System of Housing »). Le **TALIESIN MOD.FAB** est le prototype d'une « maison simple, élégante et durable pour vivre dans le désert ». Cette petite résidence de deux pièces à ossature en acier, transportable sur routes normales, fait appel à des dispositifs actifs et passifs d'économie d'énergie. Le projet est aussi l'aboutissement d'un programme d'enseignement en atelier sur la construction préfabriquée, donné par Jennifer Siegal et Michael Johnson. Ce prototype a été presque entièrement construit par des étudiants à l'aide d'un outillage classique. En porte-à-faux au-dessus d'un ravin dans le désert, il sert de maison d'hôtes pour des chercheurs invités.

Intended for desert living, the Taliesin Mod.Fab house harkens back in its references to schemes by Frank Lloyd Wright, but does not retain the older architect's organic approach to design.

Das Taliesin Mod.Fab Haus wurde für das Wüstenklima konzipiert und nimmt Bezug auf Wohnbauprojekte Frank Lloyd Wrights. Allerdings setzt es die organische Architekturauffassung des älteren Architekten nicht fort.

Conçue pour le désert, cette maison modèle préfabriquée Taliesin va chercher des références du côté de Frank Lloyd Wright, mais sans retenir l'approche organique du grand architecte.

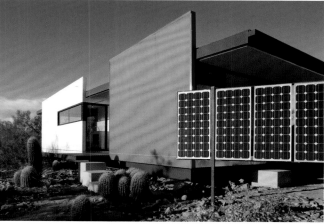

Prada Men and Women 2010 Sp
Summer Fashion S.

OMA

OMA
Heer Bokelweg 149 / 3032 AD Rotterdam / The Netherlands
Tel: +31 10 243 82 00 / Fax: +31 10 243 82 02
E-mail: office@oma.com / Web: www.oma.com

REM KOOLHAAS created the Office for Metropolitan Architecture in 1975, together with Elia and Zoe Zenghelis and Madelon Vriesendorp. Born in Rotterdam in 1944, Koolhaas worked as a journalist for the *Haagse Post* and as a screenwriter, before studying at the Architectural Association in London. He became well known after the 1978 publication of his book *Delirious New York*. OMA is currently led by seven partners: Rem Koolhaas, Ellen van Loon, Reinier de Graaf, Shohei Shigematsu, Iyad Alsaka, David Gianotten, and managing partner Victor van der Chijs. The work of Rem Koolhaas and OMA has won several international awards including the Pritzker Prize (2000); the Praemium Imperiale (Japan, 2003); the RIBA Gold Medal (UK, 2004); the Mies van der Rohe—European Union Prize for Contemporary Architecture (2005); and the Golden Lion Award for Lifetime Achievement at the 12th International Architecture Exhibition—La Biennale di Venezia (2010). OMA's built work includes the McCormick Tribune Campus Center at the Illinois Institute of Technology (Chicago, Illinois, USA, 2000–03); the Dutch Embassy in Berlin (Germany, 2003); and Seattle Central Library (Washington, USA, 2004). Other work includes Prada boutiques in New York (USA, 2001) and Los Angeles (USA, 2004); the 1850-seat Casa da Música (Porto, Portugal, 2005); the New City Center for Almere, for which the firm has drawn up the master plan (The Netherlands, 2007); Prada Men and Women 2010 Spring/Summer Fashion Shows, Fondazione Prada (Milan, Italy, 2009, published here); and design of the 575 000-square-meter Headquarters and Cultural Center for China Central Television (CCTV, Beijing, China, 2005–). Current work includes the Shenzhen Stock Exchange (China); Milstein Hall, an extension of the College of Architecture, Art, and Planning, Cornell University (New York, USA); new headquarters for Rothschild Bank London, UK); and De Rotterdam, the largest building in the Netherlands.

1975 gründete **REM KOOLHAAS** mit Elia und Zoe Zenghelis und Madelon Vriesendorp das Office for Metropolitan Architecture (OMA). Koolhaas, 1944 in Rotterdam geboren, arbeitete als Journalist für die *Haagse Post* und als Drehbuchautor, bevor er sein Studium an der Architectural Association in London aufnahm. Bekannt wurde er 1978 nach der Veröffentlichung seines Buchs *Delirious New York*. Heute wird OMA von sieben Partnern geführt: Rem Koolhaas, Ellen van Loon, Reinier de Graaf, Shohei Shigematsu, Iyad Alsaka, David Gianotten und Victor van der Chijs als geschäftsführendem Partner. Das Schaffen von Koolhaas und OMA wurde mit zahlreichen internationalen Preisen ausgezeichnet, dem Pritzker-Preis (2000), dem Praemium Imperiale (Japan, 2003), der RIBA-Goldmedaille (GB, 2004), dem Mies-van-der-Rohe-Preis der Europäischen Union für zeitgenössische Architektur (2005) und dem Goldenen Löwen für das Lebenswerk der 12. Internationalen Architekturbiennale Venedig (2010). Zu OMAs realisierten Bauten zählen das McCormick Tribune Campus Center am Illinois Institute of Technology (Chicago, Illinois, USA, 2000–03), die Niederländische Botschaft in Berlin (Deutschland, 2003) und die Seattle Central Library (Washington, USA, 2004). Weitere Projekte sind die Prada Stores in New York (USA, 2001) und Los Angeles (USA, 2004), die Casa Música in Porto mit 1850 Plätzen (Portugal, 2005), das neue Stadtzentrum von Almere, dessen Masterplan das Büro entwarf (Niederlande, 2007), die Prada-Modenschauen Men und Women Spring/Summer 2010, Fondazione Prada (Mailand, Italien, 2009, hier vorgestellt) und der Entwurf für die 575 000 m² große Zentrale mit Kulturzentrum für das chinesische Staatsfernsehen (CCTV, Peking, China, 2005–). Aktuelle Projekte sind u.a. die Börse in Shenzhen (China), Milstein Hall, der Erweiterungsbau des College of Architecture, Art, and Planning der Cornell University (New York, USA), eine neue Zentrale für die Rothschild Bank in London (GB) und De Rotterdam, das größte Gebäude der Niederlande.

REM KOOLHAAS a fondé l'OMA (Office for Metropolitan Architecture) en 1975 en compagnie d'Elia et Zoe Zenghelis et de Madelon Vriesendorp. Né à Rotterdam en 1944, il a débuté comme journaliste pour le *Haagse Post*, puis a été scénariste, avant d'étudier à l'Architectural Association de Londres. Il s'est fait connaître en 1978 par la publication de son livre *Delirious New York*. OMA est dirigée aujourd'hui par sept partenaires : Rem Koolhaas, Ellen van Loon, Reinier de Graaf, Shohei Shigematsu, Iyad Alsaka, David Gianotten, et Victor van der Chijs pour la gestion. Les réalisations d'OMA et de Rem Koolhaas leur ont valu plusieurs prix internationaux, dont le prix Pritzker (2000), le Praemium Imperiale au Japon (2003), la médaille d'or du RIBA au Royaume-Uni (2004), le prix de l'Union européenne pour l'architecture contemporaine Mies van der Rohe (2005) et le Lion d'or pour l'ensemble de son œuvre lors de la 12e Exposition internationale d'architecture à la Biennale de Venise (2010). Parmi les réalisations d'OMA : le Centre du campus McCormick Tribune à l'Institut de technologie de l'Illinois (Chicago, 2000–03) ; l'ambassade néerlandaise à Berlin (2003) ; la bibliothèque publique de Seattle (Washington, 2004) ; des boutiques Prada a New York (2001) et Los Angeles (2004) ; la salle de concert de Porto de 1850 places (Portugal, 2005) ; le nouveau centre-ville d'Almere pour lequel ils out conçu le plan directeur (Pays-Bas, 2007) ; le podium Hommes et Femmes Prada SS 2010 pour la Fondazione Prada (Milan, 2009, publié ici) et les 575 000 m² du siège et centre culturel de la Télévision centrale de Chine (CCTV, Pékin, 2005–). Plus récemment, on note la bourse de Shenzhen (Chine) ; le Milstein Hall, une extension du College of Architecture, Art, and Planning à l'université Cornell (New York) ; un nouveau siège pour la banque Rothschild à Londres et De Rotterdam, le plus grand bâtiment des Pays-Bas.

PRADA MEN AND WOMEN 2010 SPRING/ SUMMER FASHION SHOWS

Fondazione Prada, Milan, Italy, 2009

Area: 323 m². Client: Prada. Cost: not disclosed.
Collaboration: Ippolito Pestellini Laparelli, Shabnam Hosseini, Andreas Kofle

A major part of the fashion industry has to do with its ephemeral nature, and OMA has not shied away from being involved in the design of the **FASHION SHOWS OF PRADA**. The Men Show was entitled "A Secret Passage or Love for the Void," and consisted in a linear catwalk hidden between one edge of the existing room and a new seven-meter-high wall covered in wallpaper showing conversations between male film characters. A kind of secret passage for the audience behind a wall was revealed by a "slot of intense light." Another slot in the wall framed views of the fashion show. As the architects describe the inside space: "The imaginary of modern black-and-white movies informs the treatment of the show space. Multiple tones of grays appear on all surfaces, as the catwalk experience would be floating into the blurred memory of a movie." A floor made up of a grid of black and gray Plexiglas tiles was used to set up the order of the seating arrangement. The concept called for models to enter the room as though they were walking out of the conversations depicted on the wallpaper. For the Women Show, the audience was split along two sides of an "abstract wall" with seven doors set at regular intervals. Models walk in front of the wall and turn around it through its last opening. The wall divides two spaces with a Plexiglas checkerboard floor on one side and black metal squares creating a bigger checkerboard in combination with the plain concrete of the original room. Twelve projections of imaginary corridors create "mental spaces that combine grand hotels' rich and classic door frames, acid neon lights, trash, and abandoned atmospheres, or bright images of crowded beaches. The result is a sequence of indefinable settings that follow one another along the show, framing models into constantly changing backgrounds," according to the architects.

Ein entscheidender Aspekt der Modeindustrie ist ihre Flüchtigkeit. Nichtsdestotrotz scheute sich OMA nicht, sich bei der Gestaltung der **MODENSCHAUEN VON PRADA** einzubringen. Die Modenschau der Herrenkollektion trug den Titel „A Secret Passage or Love for the Void" (Ein geheimer Gang oder Die Liebe zur Leere). Ein schnurgerader Catwalk war zwischen einer bestehenden Wand der Location und einer neu hochgezogenen, sieben Meter hohen Wand verborgen, auf die Ausschnitte aus Dialogszenen mit männlichen Filmdarstellern auftapeziert worden waren. Der hinter der Wand verborgene „geheime Gang" war für das Publikum durch einen schmalen „Schlitz, durch den grelles Licht" fiel, einsehbar. Eine weitere Aussparung rahmte Durchblicke auf die eigentliche Modenschau. Die Architekten beschreiben den Innenraum wie folgt: „Die Gestaltung des Raums für die Schau ist von der Bildsprache moderner Schwarzweißfilme inspiriert. Eine Vielzahl von Grautönen zeigt sich auf sämtlichen Oberflächen, während das Catwalk-Erlebnis fließend zu einer vagen Erinnerung an einen alten Film wird." Die Anordnung der Sitzplätze orientierte sich an einem Bodenmuster aus schwarzen und grauen Plexiglasfliesen. Das Konzept sah vor, die Models in den Raum treten zu lassen, als würden sie direkt den Dialogszenen auf der Tapetenwand entspringen. Bei der Schau der Damenkollektion saß das Publikum zu beiden Seiten einer „abstrahierten Wand" mit sieben Türöffnungen, die in regelmäßigen Abständen positioniert waren. Die Models liefen vor der Wand entlang und durch die letzte Tür zurück. Die Wand gliederte den Raum in zwei Teile, mit einem Schachbrettboden aus Plexiglas auf der einen und schwarzen Metallfliesen auf der anderen Seite, die mit dem rohen Betonboden der Location ein größeres Schachbrettmuster bildeten. Zwölf Projektionen verwandelten den Catwalk in imaginäre Korridore, in „fiktive Räume, in denen die opulenten, klassizistischen Türrahmen alter Grandhotels neben grellem Neonlicht, Trash und verlassenen Orten oder flirrend-hellen Bildern von dicht bevölkerten Stränden" zu sehen waren. „Das Resultat ist eine Sequenz undefinierbarer Orte, die während der Schau aufeinander folgen und die Models vor permanent wechselnden Kulissen verorten", so die Architekten.

L'industrie de la mode est confrontée au caractère éphémère de ses produits et OMA n'a pas hésité à s'intéresser à la conception des **DÉFILÉS DE MODE DE PRADA**. Le défilé Homme était intitulé « Passage secret ou l'amour du vide ». Il consistait en un podium rectiligne installé entre le mur du fond d'une salle existante et un mur spécialement construit de 7 m de haut, tendu de papier peint illustrant des conversations entre des vedettes masculines de cinéma. Une sorte de passage secret destiné au public était indiqué par « une fente de lumière intense ». Une autre fente percée dans le mur permettait des vues cadrées du défilé. Pour l'architecte : « L'univers imaginaire des films modernes en noir et blanc nourrit le traitement de l'espace du défilé. De multiples tonalités de gris animent les surfaces, comme si ce podium flottait entre les souvenirs confus d'un film. » Les sièges étaient disposés selon le calepinage du sol tramé en carreaux de plexiglas noir et gris. Selon le concept, les mannequins entraient dans la salle comme s'ils sortaient des conversations représentées sur le papier peint. Pour le défilé Femmes, le public se répartissait des deux côtés d'un « mur abstrait » percé à intervalles réguliers de sept portes. Les mannequins défilaient devant le mur, puis revenaient de l'autre côté en sortant par la dernière porte. Le mur divisait l'espace en deux parties, dont le sol était d'un côté recouvert d'un damier de plexiglas, et de l'autre de carreaux de métal noir formant, avec la dalle d'origine en béton brut, un damier de dimensions plus importantes. Douze projections de corridors imaginaires créaient « des espaces mentaux combinant des embrasures de portes de grands hôtels au décor riche et ornementé, des éclairages au néon de couleurs acides, des atmosphères *trash* d'abandon, ou des images très colorées de plages bondées. Le résultat donnait une multiplicité de contextes indéfinissables se succédant tout au long du défilé, les mannequins défilant devant un décor de fond en changement permanent ».

Photos taken in the empty space and during a show reemphasize the large temporary wall added by the architects, and show the movie dialogues written on the walls.

Deutlich zu sehen auf Aufnahmen des leeren Raums und Fotos der Modenschau: die große temporäre, von den Architekten eingezogene Trennwand und Zitate aus Filmdialogen auf den Wänden.

Ces photos de l'espace avant et pendant un défilé font ressortir l'importance du mur temporaire élevé par les architectes et les dialogues de films inscrits sur les murs.

With its long slit opening and film dialogues on the walls, the installation for the Men show emphasizes the cinematographic nature of fashion.

Die Installation für die Herrenmodenschau mit ihrer langen Schlitzöffnung in der Wand und den dort aufgebrachten Filmdialogen unterstrich das kinematografische Element der Mode.

Par ses étroites ouvertures en bandeaux et l'inscription de dialogues de films sur les murs, la mise en scène du défilé met l'accent sur la nature cinématographique de la mode.

JOHN PAWSON

John Pawson
Unit B / 70–78 York Way / London N1 9AG / UK

Tel: +44 20 78 37 29 29
Fax: +44 20 78 37 49 49
E-mail: email@johnpawson.co.uk
Web: www.johnpawson.com

Born in Halifax in central England in 1949, **JOHN PAWSON** worked in his own family's textile mill before going to Japan for four years. On his return, he studied at the Architectural Association (AA) in London and set up his own firm in 1981. He has worked on numerous types of buildings, including the flagship store for Calvin Klein in New York, airport lounges for Cathay Pacific airlines at the Chek Lap Kok Airport in Hong Kong, and a small apartment for the author Bruce Chatwin. Pawson may be better known to the general public because of his 1996 book *Minimum*, which focused on such essential subjects as Light, Structure, Ritual, Landscape, and Volume. Some of his recent work includes Lansdowne Lodge Apartments (London, UK, 2003); Hotel Puerta America in Madrid (Spain, 2005); the Tetsuka House (Tokyo, Japan, 2003–06); Calvin Klein Apartment (New York, USA, 2006); the Sackler Crossing in the Royal Botanic Gardens (Kew, London, UK, 2006); work and renovation of a wing of the Monastery of Our Lady of Nový Dvůr (Czech Republic, 2004; second phase 2009); the Martyrs Pavilion Saint Edward's School (Oxford, UK, 2009); a church renovation concerning the Sacristy, Lateral and Chapels (Monastery of Our Lady of Sept-Fons, Burgundy, France, 2009); and a number of apartments in New York (Schrager Penthouse, 50 Gramercy Park North, Hoppe Apartment, etc., 2009). In 2010 he realized the House of Stone (Milan, Italy, published here); and his work was the object of a solo exhibition, "John Pawson Plain Space" in the Design Museum (London, UK). Current work includes the refurbishment of the Saint Moritz Church (Augsburg, Germany); renovation of the Former Commonwealth Institute (London, UK); as well as several houses in France, Greece, Portugal, Spain, the UK, and the USA.

JOHN PAWSON, 1949 in Halifax, England, geboren, arbeitete in der Textilfabrik seiner Familie, ehe er für vier Jahre nach Japan ging. Nach seiner Rückkehr studierte er an der AA in London und eröffnete 1981 sein eigenes Büro. Er war mit vielgestaltigen Projekten befasst, darunter dem Flagshipstore von Calvin Klein in New York, Flughafenlounges für Cathay Pacific am Flughafen Chek Lap Kok in Hongkong sowie einem kleinen Apartment für den Schriftsteller Bruce Chatwin. Der Allgemeinheit ist Pawson besser bekannt wegen seines 1996 erschienenen Buchs *Minimum*, in dem er sich mit so grundsätzlichen Themen wie Licht, Struktur, Ritual, Landschaft und Raum beschäftigt. Eine Auswahl jüngerer Projekte umfasst u.a.: Lansdowne Lodge Apartments (London, 2003), Hotel Puerta America in Madrid (2005), Haus Tetsuka (Tokio, 2003–06), Calvin Klein Apartment (New York, USA, 2006), Sackler Crossing-Brücke in Kew Gardens (Kew, London, GB, 2006), Neubauten und Sanierung eines Gebäudeflügels am Kloster Nový Dvůr (Tschechische Republik, 2004, zweite Bauphase 2009), Martyrs Pavilion für die Saint Edward's School (Oxford, 2009), Sanierung von Sakristei, Querschiff und Kapellen des Klosters Sept-Fons (Sept-Fons, Burgund, Frankreich) sowie mehrere Apartments in New York (Schrager Penthouse, 50 Gramercy Park North, Hoppe Apartment u.a., 2009). 2010 realisierte er das House of Stone (Mailand, 2010, hier vorgestellt). Im gleichen Jahr widmete ihm das Design Museum London die Einzelausstellung John Pawson Plain Space (London, GB). Zu seinen aktuellen Projekten zählen die Sanierung der St. Moritzkirche (Augsburg), die Sanierung des Former Commonwealth Institute (London, GB) sowie mehrere Privathäuser in Frankreich, Griechenland, Portugal, Spanien, Großbritannien und den USA.

Né à Halifax en Angleterre en 1949, **JOHN PAWSON**, travaille dans l'usine de textile familiale, avant de séjourner quatre ans au Japon. À son retour, il étudie à l'Architectural Association de Londres et crée son agence en 1981. Il est intervenu sur de nombreux types de projets, dont le magasin amiral de Calvin Klein à New York, les salons de la compagnie Cathay Pacific à l'aéroport de Chek Lap Kok à Hong Kong ou un petit appartement pour l'écrivain Bruce Chatwin. Il est surtout connu du grand public à travers le succès de son livre *Minimum* (1996) sur les thèmes de la lumière, de la structure, du rituel, du paysage et du volume. Parmi ses réalisations récentes : les Lansdowne Lodge Apartments (Londres, 2003) ; l'hôtel Puerta America à Madrid (2005) ; la maison Tetsuka (Tokyo, 2003–06) ; l'appartement de Calvin Klein (New York, 2006) ; le pont du Sackler Crossing dans les Jardins botaniques royaux (Kew, Londres, 2006) ; la rénovation d'une aile du monastère de Notre-Dame de Nový Dvůr (République tchèque, 2004, seconde phase en 2009) ; le pavillon des Martyrs de l'École Saint Edward (Oxford, 2009) ; la rénovation d'une église : sacristie, nef latérale et chapelles (monastère de Notre-Dame de Sept-Fons en Bourgogne, France), et un certain nombre d'appartements à New York (penthouse Schrager ; 50 Gramercy Park North ; appartement Hoppe ; etc., 2009). En 2010, il a réalisé la maison de pierre (Milan, publiée ici) et son œuvre a fait l'objet d'une exposition personnelle, « John Pawson Plain Space » au Design Museum de Londres. Il travaille actuellement à la rénovation de l'église Saint-Moritz (Augsburg, Allemagne) ; à celle de l'ancien Institut du Commonwealth à Londres et sur plusieurs projets de maisons en France, en Grèce, au Portugal, en Espagne, au Royaume-Uni et aux États-Unis.

HOUSE OF STONE

Milan, Italy, 2010

Area: 43 m². Client: Interni Think Tank. Cost: not disclosed.
Collaboration: Alfredo Salvatori S.r.l. (Sponsoring Partner)

In the course of the 2010 Milan Furniture Fair, the Interni Think Tank sponsored an event where architects and designers were assigned a manufacturing partner and asked to create installations for sites within the Università degli Studi. John Pawson was paired with Alfredo Salvatori S.r.l., maker of Lithoverde, a 100% recycled stone material. It is made with 99% scrap and 1% natural resin. The **HOUSE OF STONE** makes use of this material and takes into account the double-arcaded courtyard where it was set. The architect states: "In a defining gesture, the structure was sliced along its ridge and through its mid-section, opening the interior to the changing play of sunlight and the vagaries of the weather. At night, internal sources of illumination transformed the cuts into blades of light." The House of Stone is to be permanently installed in the park of the Milan Triennale.

Im Zuge der Mailänder Möbelmesse 2010 initiierte der Interni Think Tank als Sponsor ein Event, bei dem Architekten und Designer je einem Hersteller zugeteilt wurden und den Auftrag erhielten, Installationen auf dem Gelände der Università degli Studi zu realisieren. John Pawson wurde Alfredo Salvatori S.r.l. zugeteilt, dem Hersteller von Lithoverde, einem zu 100 % recycelten Mauerstein. Das Material besteht zu 99 % aus Steinabfällen und zu 1 % aus natürlichem Harz. Das **HOUSE OF STONE** nutzt dieses Material und ist dabei zugleich auf den Hof mit seinen Doppelarkaden abgestimmt, in dem es sich befindet. Der Architekt erklärt: „In einer charakteristischen Geste wurde der Bau entlang des Firsts sowie quer zerschnitten, wodurch der Innenraum für das Spiel des Sonnenlichts und die Launen des Wetters geöffnet wird. Nachts werden die Einschnitte durch eine Lichtquelle im Innern zu Klingen aus Licht." Das House of Stone soll dauerhaft im Park der Mailänder Triennale wieder errichtet werden.

À l'occasion du Salon du meuble de Milan 2010, le Think Tank du magazine *Interni* a sponsorisé un événement sur le thème de la collaboration entre architectes, designers et fabricants pour créer des installations temporaires à l'intérieur de l'Università degli Studi. John Pawson s'est associé avec Alfredo Alvadori S.r.l., fabricant de Lithoverde, un matériau à base de pierre 100 % recyclable, composé de 99 % de déchets de pierre et 1 % de résine naturelle. La **MAISON DE PIERRE** réalisée dans ce matériau a pris en compte son environnement, une cour à double arcade. « Dans un geste puissant, la structure a été tranchée selon l'axe de son faîte et en deux parties égales, permettant ainsi à l'intérieur de s'ouvrir au jeu de la lumière et des changements du temps. La nuit, des éclairages internes transforment ces découpes en lames de lumière », explique Pawson. La maison de pierre sera installée en permanence dans le parc de la Triennale de Milan.

Known precisely for his strict, mini-malist vocabulary, John Pawson uses a traditional house shape, but renders it original with its long slit openings in the ceiling and walls.

John Pawson, bekannt für seine strenge, minimalistische Formenspra-che, greift auf eine traditionelle Haus-form zurück, die er jedoch mit langen Schlitzen in Decke und Wänden unge-wöhnlich interpretiert.

Connu pour son vocabulaire architec-tural d'un minimalisme strict, John Pawson utilise ici la forme tradition-nelle d'une maison qu'il transforme par de longues ouvertures pratiquées dans les plafonds et les murs.

PHILIPPE RAHM

Philippe Rahm architectes
12 Rue Chabanais
75002 Paris
France

Tel: +33 1 49 26 91 55
E-mail: info@philipperahm.com
Web: www.philipperahm.com

PHILIPPE RAHM was born in 1967 and studied architecture at the EPFL in Lausanne and the ETH in Zurich. He created the firm Décosterd & Rahm associés with Gilles Décosterd in 1995 in Lausanne. They won a number of competitions in Switzerland and participated in numerous exhibitions in Europe and the United States, and later, in Japan. Amongst these were Archilab, Orléans, France, 2000, and the 2003 Biennal de Valencia, Spain. Décosterd & Rahm represented Switzerland in the 2002 Venice Architecture Biennale and received the Swiss Federal Art Prize in 2003. They worked on an atelier-residence for the artist Fabrice Hybert in the Vendée region of France, and on a project for a park in San Sebastien, Spain, with the landscape architects Gilles Clément and Joseph Andeuza. Rahm and Déscosterd ceased direct collaboration in 2005 and Philippe Rahm created his own firm, Philippe Rahm architects, in Paris. Since then, he has worked on the Grizedale Artfarm (Ambleside, Cumbria, UK, 2006); a pavilion for the École des Beaux-Arts (Nantes, France, 2006–07); Split-Time Café (Lebring, Austria, 2007); Floating Pavilions for the Voies Navigables de France (Paris, Lyon, France, 2008); Domestic Astronomy, Louisiana Museum (Humlebæk, Denmark, 2009, published here); White Geology, Grand Palais (Paris, France, 2009, also published here); and Digestible Gulf Stream (Paris region, France, 2008–10, for Dominique Gonzalez-Foerster).

PHILIPPE RAHM wurde 1967 geboren und studierte Architektur an der EPFL in Lausanne sowie der ETH Zürich. 1995 gründete er mit Gilles Décosterd das Büro Décosterd & Rahm associés in Lausanne. Das Team gewann mehrere Wettbewerbe in der Schweiz und war an zahlreichen Ausstellungen in Europa, den USA und später auch in Japan beteiligt. Hierzu zählten u.a. Archilab (Orléans, Frankreich, 2000) sowie die Biennale von Valencia 2003 (Spanien). 2002 vertraten Décosterd & Rahm die Schweiz auf der Architekturbiennale in Venedig und wurden 2003 mit dem Schweizer Kunstpreis des Bundes ausgezeichnet. Sie arbeiteten an einem Atelier und Wohnhaus für den Künstler Fabrice Hybert in der Vendée, Frankreich, und, gemeinsam mit den Landschaftsarchitekten Gilles Clément und Joseph Andeuza, an einem Parkprojekt für San Sebastian, Spanien. Rahm und Décosterd beendeten ihre direkte Zusammenarbeit 2005. Rahm gründete daraufhin sein eigenes Büro, Philippe Rahm architectes, in Paris. Seither arbeitet er an der Grizedale Art Farm (Ambleside, Cumbria, Großbritannien, 2006), einem Pavillon für die École des Beaux-Arts (Nantes, Frankreich, 2006–07), dem Split-Time Café (Lebring, Österreich, 2007), den schwimmenden Pavillons für die Voies Navigables de France (Paris und Lyon, Frankreich, 2008), Domestic Astronomy am Louisiana Museum (Humlebæk, Dänemark, 2009, hier vorgestellt), White Geology am Grand Palais (Paris, 2009, ebenfalls hier vorgestellt) sowie dem Digestible Gulf Stream (Region Paris, Frankreich, 2008–10, für Dominique Gonzalez-Foerster).

Né en 1967, **PHILIPPE RAHM** a étudié l'architecture à l'EPFL à Lausanne et à l'ETH à Zurich. Il a fondé l'agence Décosterd & Rahm Associés à Lausanne avec Gilles Décosterd en 1995. Ils ont remporté un certain nombre de concours en Suisse et participé à de nombreuses expositions en Europe, aux États-Unis et au Japon, dont Archilab (Orléans, France, 2000) et la Biennale 2003 de Valence (Espagne). Décosterd & Rahm ont représenté la Suisse à la Biennale d'architecture de Venise de 2002 et reçu le prix fédéral d'Art en 2003. Ils ont travaillé sur un projet de résidence-atelier pour l'artiste Fabrice Hybert en Vendée (France) et un parc à Saint-Sébastien (Espagne), avec les paysagistes Gilles Clément et Joseph Andeuza. Rahm et Décosterd ont cessé leur collaboration directe en 2005 et Philippe Rahm a créé sa propre agence à Paris, Philippe Rahm architectes. Depuis, il a travaillé sur le projet de la ferme d'art de Grizedale (Ambleside, Cumbria, GB, 2006) ; un pavillon pour l'École des beaux-arts (Nantes, France, 2006–07) ; le Split-Time Café (Lebring, Autriche, 2007) ; des pavillons flottants pour la société Voies Navigables de France (Paris et Lyon, France, 2008) ; le projet « Domestic Astronomy » pour le Louisiana Museum (Humlebæk, Danemark, 2009, publié ici) ; « White Geology », Grand Palais (Paris, 2009, également publié ici), et le projet « Digestible Gulf Stream » (Île-de-France, France, 2008–10, pour Dominique Gonzalez-Foerster).

DOMESTIC ASTRONOMY

Louisiana Museum, Humlebæk, Denmark, 2009

Area: 60 m². Client: Louisiana Museum
Cost: not disclosed

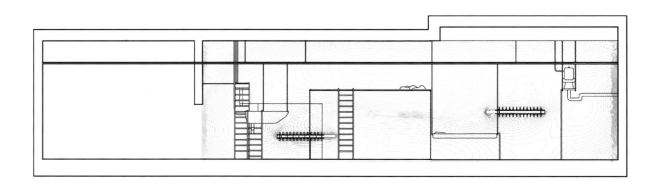

Above, a section of the exhibition in-stallation, which is both domestic in nature and experimental in concept.

Oben ein Querschnitt durch die Ins-tallation, die sich mit Wohnkonzepten befasst, dabei jedoch höchst experi-mentell ist.

Ci-dessus, une coupe de l'installation exposée, à la fois domestique dans sa nature et expérimentale dans son concept.

Presented in the context of Louisiana Museum's summer 2009 exhibition "Green Architecture for the Future," between June and September, **DOMESTIC ASTRONOMY** was a scheme for an apartment. According to Philippe Rahm: "Our proposal is to make allowances for these physical differences in the distribution of temperature in the space and to exploit them by changing the way of life; to replace a horizontal way of living with a vertical one where we can occupy different heat zones, different layers, different heights. And thus to create a global ecosystem like a kind of astronomy in the home, where combinations of temperature, lights, time, and place are reconfigured." Like much of the earlier work of the architect, this installation approaches art as much as it does architecture, and yet the ideas, concerning ne-glected areas of domestic felicity such as air or temperature, offer a real area of investigation for the built environment.

DOMESTIC ASTRONOMY war der Entwurf für eine Wohnung und im Rahmen der Sommerausstellung *Grüne Architektur für die Zukunft* am Louisiana Museum von Juni bis September 2009 zu sehen. Philippe Rahm erklärt: „Unser Vorschlag sieht vor, das physikalische Gefälle in der Temperaturverteilung im Raum zu berücksich-tigen und zu nutzen, indem wir das horizontal orientierte Wohnverhalten durch ein vertikales ersetzen, das erlaubt, verschiedene Wärmezonen zu besetzen, verschiedene Schichten, unterschiedliche Höhen. Und auf diese Weise ein globales Ökosystem zu schaffen, eine Art Astronomie im Haus, mit der sich neue Konstellationen aus Tempe-ratur, Lichtquellen, Zeit und Ort bilden lassen." Wie viele frühere Arbeiten des Architekten ist diese Installation ebenso in der Nähe der Kunst wie der Architektur anzusie-deln. Dennoch befasst sie sich mit vernachlässigten Aspekten heimischen Komforts, wie etwa Luftströmen oder Temperatur, und erschließt damit einen Forschungsbe-reich für die gebaute Umwelt.

Présenté dans le contexte de l'exposition du Louisiana Museum intitulée « Architecture verte pour le futur » de juin à septembre 2009, « **ASTRONOMIE DOMESTIQUE** » était un projet d'appartement. Comme l'explique Philippe Rahm : « Notre propos est aujourd'hui de prendre en compte les disparités physiques dans la répartition de la température dans l'espace et d'en profiter pour transformer la manière d'habiter l'espace, en quittant l'exclusivité d'un mode d'habitation horizontal en intérieur pour un mode d'habitation vertical où l'on peut habiter différentes zones thermiques, différentes strates, différentes altitudes. Nous proposons de construire en intérieur un écosystème global, comme une sorte de nouvelle astronomie d'intérieur, où la température, les lumières, le temps et l'espace se recombinent. » Comme une grande partie des travaux antérieurs de l'architecte, cette installation est aussi proche de l'art que de l'architecture, mais ses idées sur les zones négligées de la vie à la maison, comme l'air ou la température, ouvrent un nouveau domaine d'investigation.

Photographs of the installation make the distinction between top and bot-tom or horizontal and vertical very ambiguous, as intended by Philippe Rahm.

Ansichten der Installation belegen, wie unscharf die Grenzen zwischen oben und unten, horizontal und verti-kal sein können: Eine Wirkung, die von Philippe Rahm durchaus gewollt ist.

Comme le souhaitait Philippe Rahm, les photographies de l'installation rendent les notions de bas et de haut, d'horizontal et de vertical très ambi-gües.

WHITE GEOLOGY

Grand Palais, Paris, France, 2009

Area: 14 000 m². Client: French Ministry of Culture, Réunion des Musées nationaux (RMN)
Cost: €800 000

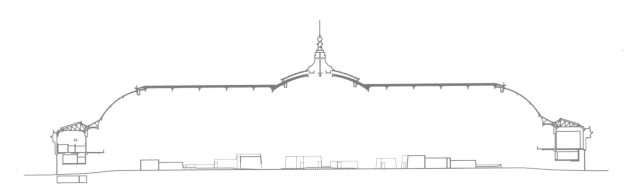

Any temporary art installation in the vast volume of the central hall of the Grand Palais in Paris is fraught with certain risks for the architect, but Philippe Rahm has used the space to the advantage of the art on display.

Die Realisierung einer temporären Kunstinstallation im mächtigen Pariser Grand Palais birgt unweigerlich Risiken für den Architekten, doch Philippe Rahm gelingt es, den Raum gewinnbringend für die ausgestellte Kunst zu interpretieren.

Toute installation artistique temporaire dans l'énorme volume du Grand Palais à Paris représente un risque pour un architecte, mais Philippe Rahm a réussi à utiliser l'espace au bénéfice des œuvres présentées.

This exhibition installation was created for "La Force de l'Art 02," the second triennial contemporary art exhibition at the Grand Palais in Paris. As Philippe Rahm describes the work: "Originally a white rectangle measuring 125 meters by 24 meters, it buckles, hollows, and swells under the geological forces that come into play in the formation of a landscape: tectonic shifts, distortion, pressure and depression, folding. Here, the movements and distortion of the territory are caused by the abstract forces in the art works." Philippe Rahm further elaborates on this entirely white installation: "It is… the opposite of exhibition design in the sense that it is not the work of art that fits into the architecture, but the architecture which yields to the demands of the work of art." The exhibits will work together to shape the landscape through the simultaneous play of pressure and checks and balances. In his other work, the architect is accustomed to working on forms of "emptiness" that might be the air, humidity, or temperature. In this instance, it is also the emptiness in the architectural design where the works of art make their place.

Die Ausstellungsarchitektur wurde für *La Force de l'Art 02* entworfen, die zweite Triennale für Zeitgenössische Kunst im Pariser Grand Palais. Philippe Rahm beschreibt die Installation wie folgt: „Was ursprünglich ein weißes Rechteck von 125 x 24 m war, biegt sich nun, wird ausgehöhlt und wirft sich auf wie unter dem Einfluss geologischer Kräfte, die bei der Entstehung von Landschaften ins Spiel kommen: tektonische Verschiebungen, Verwerfungen, Druck und Senkenbildungen, Faltungen. Hier werden die Bewegungen und Verwerfungen durch die geheimnisvollen Kräfte in den Kunstwerken ausgelöst." Philippe Rahm äußert sich weiter zu seiner ganz in Weiß gehaltenen Installation: „Sie ist das Gegenteil einer Ausstellungsarchitektur, denn hier müssen sich die Kunstwerke nicht in die Architektur einfügen; vielmehr reagiert die Architektur auf die Anforderungen der Kunstwerke." Gemeinsam definieren die Exponate durch das simultane Zusammenspiel von Druck, Barrieren und Gegendruck eine Landschaft. In seinen anderen Projekten arbeitet der Architekt häufig mit Formen von „Leere", die in Phänomenen wie Luft, Feuchtigkeit oder Temperatur zu finden sind. In diesem Fall sind es Leerräume im architektonischen Entwurf, in denen die Kunstwerke ihren Raum besetzen.

Cette scénographie d'un blanc immaculé a été créée pour « La Force de l'Art 02 », seconde exposition triennale d'art contemporain organisée au Grand Palais à Paris. Philippe Rahm décrit ainsi son intervention : « C'est d'abord une surface dans l'espace, un rectangle blanc de 125 x 24 m qui va commencer à se déformer, à se creuser, à enfler selon un jeu de forces propre au langage géologique de formation du paysage par mouvements tectoniques, déformations, pressions et dépressions, plissements. Ici, ce sont des forces abstraites qui sont à l'origine des mouvements et des déformations plastiques de ce territoire, celles des œuvres d'art elles-mêmes… C'est donc un appareil muséographique inversé qui est proposé, ce n'est pas l'œuvre d'art qui s'adapte à l'architecture, mais l'architecture qui se plie aux exigences de l'œuvre d'art. » Dans un jeu de mouvements mutuels de poussées et d'équilibres réciproques et simultanés, les œuvres vont ainsi, ensemble, provoquer le surgissement d'un paysage. Dans ses autres travaux, l'architecte travaille souvent sur des formes de « vide » qui peuvent être l'air, l'humidité ou la température. Ici, les œuvres d'art trouvent leur place dans le vide du projet architectural.

Using a careful orchestration of white volumes, the architect succeeds both in giving place to the works of art and in playing on the spectacular glazed roof of the Grand Palais.

Der Architekt orchestrierte die weißen Raumkörper bis ins Detail und gestaltete so erfolgreich eine Bühne für die Kunstwerke. Zugleich bezog er spielerisch die Wirkung des spektakulären Glasdachs des Grand Palais mit ein.

Par une habile orchestration de volumes peints en blanc, l'architecte offrait aux œuvres d'art la présentation qui leur convenait tout en jouant de l'effet de la spectaculaire verrière du Grand Palais.

A floor plan shows how the architect uses irregular volumes suited to the work of art to create a perfectly rectangular volume for the whole show.

Le plan au sol montre le développé de la composition de volumes irréguliers à l'intérieur d'un plan parfaitement rectangulaire.

Eine Grundriss illustriert, wie der Architekt mit unregelmäßigen Raumkörpern arbeitete. Dieser Ansatz wurde den Kunstwerken gerecht und bildete zugleich in der Gesamtanlage ein vollkommen ebenmäßiges Rechteck.

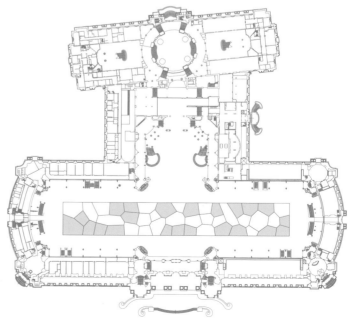

RAUMLABORBERLIN

Raumlaborberlin
Am Flutgraben 3
12435 Berlin
Germany

Tel: +49 30 27 58 08 82
Fax: +49 30 247 63 19
E-mail: info@raumlabor-berlin.de
Web: www.raumlabor-berlin.de

RAUMLABORBERLIN is a group of architects and urban designers based in Berlin, Germany, created in 1999. Working in "various interdisciplinary teams they investigate strategies for urban renewal." They have experimented in urban design and planning, architecture, interactive environments, research, and the design of public space and art installations. The group is made up of eight architects: Francesco Appuzzo (born in Naples, 1972), Markus Bader (born in Karlsruhe, 1968), Benjamin Foerster-Baldenius (born in Stuttgart, 1968), Andrea Hofmann (born in Osnabrück, 1969), Jan Liesegang (born in Cologne, 1968), Christof Mayer (born in Wangen im Allgäu, 1969), Matthias Rick (born in Versmold, 1965), and Axel Timm (born in Hanover, 1973). Recent work includes Moderato Cantabile (Graz, Austria, 2008, published here); the temporary transformation of the Eichbaum metro station located between Essen and Mülheim into an opera house (Germany, 2009); temporary Houses of Literature for Children (unbuilt, 2009); the Promising Land, an installation along the Liverpool-Leeds Canal (UK, 2009); Spacebuster (New York, New York, USA, 2009, also published here); *Soap Opera*, an installation for the opening ceremony of "Ruhr.2010 European Capital of Culture"(Essen, Germany, 2010); and Open House, a vertical village and social sculpture in Anyang for APAP 2010 (South Korea, 2010).

RAUMLABORBERLIN ist eine Gruppe von Architekten und Stadtplanern in Berlin und wurde 1999 gegründet. Die Mitglieder arbeiten in „verschiedenen interdisziplinären Teams, die Strategien für urbane Erneuerung entwickeln". Ihre Versuchsfelder sind Stadtentwurf und -planung, Architektur, interaktive Räume, Forschung sowie die Gestaltung von öffentlichem Raum und Kunstinstallationen. Die Gruppe besteht aus acht Architekten: Francesco Appuzzo (geboren 1972 in Neapel), Markus Bader (geboren 1968 in Karlsruhe), Benjamin Foerster-Baldenius (geboren 1968 in Stuttgart), Andrea Hofmann (geboren 1969 in Osnabrück), Jan Liesegang (geboren 1968 in Köln), Christof Mayer (geboren 1969 in Wangen im Allgäu), Matthias Rick (geboren 1965 in Versmold) und Axel Timm (geboren 1973 in Hannover). Zu ihren jüngeren Projekten zählen Moderato Cantabile (Graz, Österreich, 2008, hier vorgestellt), die temporäre Transformation der U-Bahnstation Eichbaum zwischen Essen und Mülheim in ein Opernhaus (Deutschland, 2009), temporäre Kinderliteraturhäuser (nicht realisiert, 2009), The Promising Land, eine Installation am Liverpool-Leeds-Kanal (Großbritannien, 2009), Spacebuster (New York, 2009, ebenfalls hier vorgestellt), Soap Opera, eine Installation für das Eröffnungsfest von „Ruhr.2010 Kulturhauptstadt Europas" (Essen, 2010) sowie Open House, vertikales Dorf und soziale Skulptur in Anyang für APAP 2010 (Südkorea, 2010).

RAUMLABORBERLIN est un groupe d'architectes et d'urbanistes basé à Berlin créé en 1999. Travaillant en « équipes interdisciplinaires de configurations variées, ils étudient des stratégies de renouveau urbain ». Ils interviennent dans les champs de la conception et de la programmation urbanistiques, l'architecture, les environnements interactifs, la recherche et la conception d'espaces publics et d'installations artistiques. Le groupe se compose de huit architectes : Francesco Appuzzo (né à Naples, 1972), Markus Bader (né à Karlsruhe, 1968), Benjamin Foerster-Baldenius (né à Stuttgart, 1968), Andrea Hofmann (né à Osnabrück, 1969), Jan Liesegang (né à Cologne, 1968), Christof Mayer (né à Wangen im Allgäu,1969), Matthias Rick (né à Versmold, 1965) et Axel Timm (né à Hanovre, 1973). Parmi leurs travaux récents : Moderato Cantabile (Graz, Autriche, 2008, publié ici) ; la transformation temporaire de la station de métro Eichbaum entre Essen et Mülheim en opéra (Allemagne, 2009) ; des maisons de la littérature pour enfants temporaires (non construites, 2009) ; *Terre promise*, une installation le long du canal Liverpool-Leeds (GB, 2009) ; Spacebuster (New York, 2009, publié ici) ; *Soap Opera*, une installation pour la cérémonie d'ouverture de « Ruhr.2010 capitale européenne de la culture » (Essen, Allemagne, 2010), et Open House (« Maison ouverte »), un village vertical et une sculpture sociale à Anyang pour l'APAP 2010 (Corée du Sud, 2010).

MODERATO CANTABILE

Graz, Austria, 2008

Area: 800 m². Client: Steirischer Herbst
Cost: not disclosed

This was a design for a festival center intended to be set in an empty Baroque museum building in the context of the Steirischer Herbst Festival. The theme of this festival was "misfortune avoidance strategies." Raumlabor designed a café, ticket office, exhibition space, and club, and an exterior pavilion. The architects explain: "We designed the pavilion in the form of an explosion; a shape and structure which develops a fascinating force at the exact moment of its dissolution. We reduced the colors of the interior walls, floors, and fixtures to a few gray tones so that only the shapes of the objects and visitors themselves stood out." This extrusion, which certainly resembles a work of contemporary sculpture, was made with various forms of "trash, including chairs and laundry drying machines."

Der Entwurf für das Festivalzentrum für den Steirischen Herbst wurde in einem leer stehenden Barockmuseum realisiert. Thema des Festivals war „Unglücksvermeidungsstrategien". Raumlabor gestaltete ein Café, einen Kassenschalter, Ausstellungsräume, einen Club sowie einen Pavillon. Die Architekten erklären: „Wir gestalteten den Pavillon als Explosion, eine Form und Struktur, die genau im Moment ihrer Auflösung eine faszinierende Kraft entwickelt. In den Innenräumen reduzierten wir die Farben sämtlicher Wände, Böden und Einbauten auf wenige Grautöne, sodass allein die Form der Gegenstände und die Besucher selbst hervortreten." Die Extrusion, die fraglos wie eine zeitgenössische Skulptur wirkt, wurde aus verschiedenen Arten von Sperrmüll gebaut, „darunter Stühle und Wäschetrockner".

Ce centre pour le Festival d'automne du Steiermark en Autriche, dont le thème était « Stratégies d'évitement du malheur », a été installé dans un musée vide, de style néobaroque. Raumlabor a conçu un café, une billetterie, un espace d'expositions, un club et un pavillon extérieur : « Nous avons imaginé le pavillon comme une explosion, une forme et une structure qui développent une puissance fascinante au moment précis de leur dissolution. Nous avons réduit les couleurs des murs intérieurs, des sols et des équipements à quelques tons de gris pour que seuls ressortent les visiteurs et les formes des objets. » Cette extrusion, qui faisait penser à une sculpture contemporaine, se composait de divers « déchets, dont des sièges et des sèche-linge ».

The architects state that the exterior pavilion added to a much more traditional building is intended to have "the form of an explosion"—a description justified by the images and drawing seen on this page.

Die Architekten nennen den Pavillonanbau an das alte Gebäude eine „Explosion" – eine Beschreibung, die dem Entwurf durchaus gerecht wird, wie Aufnahmen und Zeichnung auf dieser Seite belegen.

Pour les architectes, ce pavillon extérieur se projetant d'un bâtiment classique a « la forme d'une explosion », ce qu'illustrent les photographies et les dessins de cette page.

Interior views correspond well to the "explosive" impression given by the exterior pavilion.

Innenansichten, die dem „explosiven" Eindruck des Pavillons am Außenbau durchaus gerecht werden.

Les vues de l'intérieur rendent bien l'impression d'explosion donnée par l'extérieur du pavillon.

Above, on the ramp leading to the exterior pavilion, and below, a section showing the interior installation and the front "explosion."

Auf der Rampe zum Pavillonanbau (oben). Unten ein Querschnitt durch den Bau sowie die Installationen im Innern und die „Explosion" vor dem Gebäude.

Ci-dessus, la rampe conduisant au pavillon extérieur et ci-dessous, une coupe montrant l'installation intérieure et « l'explosion » de la partie extérieure.

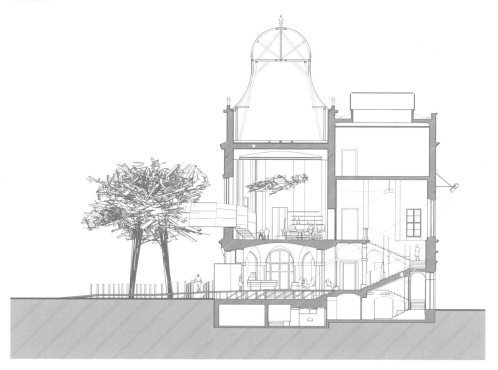

SPACEBUSTER

New York, New York, USA, 2009

Area: 100 m². Client: Storefront for Art and Architecture
Cost: not disclosed

SPACEBUSTER is intended to "transform architectural and social space." It is made up of a van and an inflatable space for up to 80 people that comes out of the back of the van. Visitors enter through the passenger door of the vehicle and enter the translucent bubble. The architects describe the membrane as a semi-permeable border between public and more private space and liken its use to public theater. Desks, chairs, or dining tables are added to the bubble space as required. Another advantage of the scheme is that the bubble can be squeezed into available space where the van parks. In 2009, the architects hosted nine consecutive evenings in Manhattan and Brooklyn. The inventors of the project explain: "As a research tool the Spacebuster disclosed peoples' relation to urban space and to quite a number of invisible borders within the city that shape the built and social space."

Ziel des SPACEBUSTERS ist es, den „architektonischen und sozialen Raum" zu verändern. Der Spacebuster besteht aus einem Kleinlaster mit einem aufblasbaren Raum für bis zu 80 Personen, der sich aus der Rückseite des Buses entfaltet. Besucher betreten den Raum durch die Beifahrertür des Wagens und treten hinaus in die transparente Blase. Die Architekten beschreiben die Membran als semipermeable Grenze zwischen öffentlichem und tendenziell privatem Raum und vergleichen deren Einsatz mit einer öffentlichen Theateraufführung. Je nach Bedarf wird die Blase mit Schreibtischen, Stühlen oder Esstischen ausgestattet. Ein weiterer Vorteil des Entwurfs ist, dass die Blase im verfügbaren Laderaum verstaut werden kann, wenn der Bus parkt. 2009 realisierten die Architekten eine Reihe von neun Abendveranstaltungen in Manhattan und Brooklyn. Die Erfinder des Projekts führen aus: „Als Forschungsinstrument entlarvt der Spacebuster die Beziehung von Menschen zum urbanen Raum und zu zahlreichen unsichtbaren Grenzen in der Stadt, die den gebauten und sozialen Raum definieren."

Le SPACEBUSTER se propose de « transformer l'espace architectural et social ». L'installation se compose d'une camionnette et d'une structure gonflable pouvant contenir jusqu'à 80 personnes qui se déploie de l'arrière du camion. Les visiteurs entrent par la portière passager du véhicule, puis pénètrent dans la bulle translucide. Les architectes présentent cette membrane comme une frontière semi-perméable entre l'espace public et un espace plus privatif qu'ils comparent à un théâtre. Des bureaux, des sièges ou des tables pour les repas sont installés dans la bulle selon les besoins. Celle-ci peut aussi se loger dans l'espace disponible lorsque la camionnette est stationnée. En 2009, les architectes ont organisé neuf manifestations consécutives en soirée à Manhattan et Brooklyn : « En tant qu'espace de recherche, le Spacebuster met en lumière les relations des gens avec l'espace urbain et un certain nombre de limites urbaines invisibles qui contribuent à la mise en forme de l'espace social et construit. »

A bulbous additional space expands from within the confines of the Spacebuster van, implying questions about the very nature of architectural space.

Aus der Enge des Hecks des Spacebuster-Busses wölbt sich eine Raumblase: Hier werden herkömmliche Vorstellungen von Architektur und Raum in Frage gestellt.

Le volume additionnel se déploie en forme de bulle à partir de la camionnette, posant au passage des questions sur la nature même de l'espace architectural.

In its expanded state, the Space-buster can accommodate up to 80 people in a completely ephemeral space that requires no structural adaptation other than a flat, empty area to expand into.

In aufgeblasenem Zustand bietet der Spacebuster Platz für bis zu 80 Personen. Der ephemere Raum erfordert keinerlei Stützkonstruktion, sondern lediglich eine ebene, freie Fläche, um sich zu entfalten.

Déployé, le Spacebuster peut recevoir jusqu'à 80 personnes dans un espace totalement éphémère qui ne demande rien d'autre qu'un lieu plat et dégagé pour être mis en place.

The beauty of the Spacebuster is that it can really be installed in any location—here under the arches of a bridge.

Der Reiz des Spacebusters liegt darin, dass der Aufbau tatsächlich an jedem Standort möglich ist – hier unter den Bögen einer Brücke.

L'intérêt du Spacebuster est qu'il peut vraiment s'installer n'importe où, ici sous les arches d'un pont.

Seen from the interior and from the exterior (left page, bottom), the Spacebuster has an undeniable modernity about it, a bit like the more durable "blob" structures created when computer-assisted design became popular.

Innen- und Außenansichten (linke Seite unten) vermitteln unbestreitbar Modernität – ähnlich wie bei dauerhafteren „Blob"-Bauten, die entstanden, als sich computerbasiertes Entwerfen durchzusetzen begann.

Vue de l'intérieur comme de l'extérieur, (page de gauche, en bas), le Spacebuster présente une indéniable modernité, un peu comme les structures en « blob » créées aux débuts de la conception assistée par ordinateur.

FRANCESC RIFÉ

Francesc Rifé
C/ Escoles Pies 25 bajos
08017 Barcelona
Spain

Tel: +34 93 414 12 88
Fax: +34 93 241 28 14
E-mail: f@rife-design.com
Web: www.rife-design.com

FRANCESC RIFÉ was born in Sant Sadurní d'Anoia (Barcelona, Spain) in 1969. He studied architecture at the Universidad Politécnica de Cataluña (Barcelona) and obtained a degree in Interior Design from the Escuela DIAC-Eiade / La Llotja (Barcelona) and another degree in Industrial Design from the same institution. He is currently a Professor at the Elisava School of Design, which is part of Pompeu Fabra University (Barcelona). He established his own studio in Barcelona in 1994. His projects range from interior to industrial design, for both commercial and private clients. His work includes the Hotel Blu Almansa (Albacete, 2007); Nino Alvarez (Barcelona, 2007); the Clínica Borrell (Sabadell, Barcelona 2007); the Gastromium Miguel Díaz (Seville, 2008); Optica XD (Sant Sadurní d'Anoia, Barcelona, 2008); Pomme Sucre (Oviedo, Asturias, 2009); and AB21 Stand, Hábitat Valencia 2009 Trade Fair (Valencia, 2009, published here). In 2010 he completed GDENT, a dental clinic (Vitoria); Arrop, Hotel Palacio Marqués de Caro Restaurant (Valencia); and the RD House (Sant Sadurní d'Anoia), all in Spain.

FRANCESC RIFÉ wurde 1969 in Sant Sadurní d'Anoia (Barcelona, Spanien) geboren. Er studierte Architektur an der Universidad Politécnica de Cataluña (Barcelona), absolvierte einen Abschluss in Innenarchitektur an der Escuela DIAC-Eiade / La Llotja (Barcelona) sowie einen Abschluss in Industriedesign an derselben Hochschule. Derzeit ist er Professor an der Elisava Fakultät für Design an der Universität Pompeu Fabra (Barcelona). Sein Büro gründete er 1994 in Barcelona. Er arbeitet in den Bereichen Innenarchitektur und Industriedesign, für gewerbliche wie für private Auftraggeber. Zu seinen Projekten zählen das Hotel Blu Almansa (Albacete, 2007), Nino Alvarez (Barcelona, 2007), die Clínica Borrell (Sabadell, Barcelona 2007), das Gastromium Miguel Díaz (Sevilla, 2008), Optica XD (Sant Sadurní d'Anoia, Barcelona, 2008), Pomme Sucre (Oviedo, Asturias, 2009) und einen Messestand für AB21 auf der Hábitat Valencia 2009 (Valencia, 2009, hier vorgestellt). 2010 konnte die Zahnklinik GDENT fertiggestellt werden (Vitoria), das Restaurant Arrop im Hotel Palacio Marqués de Caro (Valencia) sowie das Haus RD (Sant Sadurní d'Anoia), alle in Spanien.

FRANCESC RIFÉ, né à Sant Sadurní d'Anoia (Barcelone, 1969), a étudié l'architecture à l'Universidad Politécnica de Cataluña (Barcelone), puis a obtenu un diplôme d'architecture d'intérieur à la Escuela DIAC-Eiade / La Llotja (Barcelone) et un diplôme de designer industriel de la même institution. Il est actuellement professeur à l'École de design Elisava qui fait partie de l'université Pompeu Fabra (Barcelone). Il a créé son agence à Barcelone en 1994. Ses projets vont de l'architecture intérieure au design industriel pour des clients aussi bien commerciaux que privés. Parmi ses réalisations : l'hôtel Blu Almansa (Albacete, 2007) ; le magasin Nino Alvarez (Barcelone, 2007) ; la clinique Borrell (Sabadell, Barcelone, 2007) ; le Gastromium Miguel Díaz (Séville, 2008) ; le magasin Optica XD (Sant Sadurní d'Anoia, Barcelone, 2008) ; le magasin Pomme Sucre (Oviedo, Asturias, 2009) et le stand AB21, Salon Hábitat à la Foire de Valence 2009 (Valence, 2009, publié ici). En 2010, il a achevé la clinique dentaire GDENT (Vitoria) ; Arrop, le restaurant de l'hôtel Palacio Marqués de Caro (Valencia) et la maison RD (Sant Sadurní d'Anoia).

AB21 STAND

Hábitat Valencia 2009 Trade Fair, Valencia, Spain, 2009

Area: 160 m². Client: AB21 ALFOMBRAS
Cost: not disclosed

"The space," says the designer, "was conceived like an art gallery in which rug collections by several designers are distributed. Carpets are exposed as if they were true works of art (paintings) in the different areas of the stand." Francesc Rifé also says that the closed space is "suspended in the air." Using rather blank wooden surfaces, the designer maintains a minimalist tension throughout this stand, up to and including the geometric furniture. Lifting the smooth façade of the stand in certain places and slotting it in others, Rifé communicates an image of quality and simplicity in this fair stand.

„Der Raum", so der Architekt, „wurde wie eine Galerie konzipiert, in der Teppichkollektionen von verschiedenen Designern präsentiert wurden. Die Teppiche wurde in verschiedenen Bereichen des Stands so exponiert ausgestellt, als handle es sich tatsächlich Kunstwerke (Gemälde)." Francesc Rifé beschreibt den geschlossenen Raum außerdem als „schwebend". Indem der Architekt mit eher schmucklosen Holzflächen arbeitet, wahrt er eine minimalistische Spannung im gesamten Entwurf, bis hin zum geometrischen Mobiliar. Rifé löst die glatte Fassade des Stands an einzelnen Stellen vom Boden und versieht sie an anderen Stellen mit Schlitzen und vermittelt mit seinem Messestand so ein Bild von Qualität und Schlichtheit.

« Cet espace, explique le designer, a été conçu comme une galerie d'art dans laquelle aurait été répartie une collection de tapis signés de divers créateurs. Ils sont exposés comme de vraies œuvres d'art (peintures) dans les différentes zones du stand. » Francesc Rifé précise également que l'espace fermé est « suspendu dans l'air ». Par des cloisonnements de bois assez neutres, le designer a maintenu une tension minimaliste dans l'ensemble du stand, qui comprend également un mobilier géométrique. En soulevant du sol à certains endroits la façade lisse du stand et en la découpant à d'autres, il a donné à cette installation commerciale une intéressante image de qualité et de simplicité.

Both in its lighting and in the carefully orchestrated placement of its vertical surfaces, the stand does come across much like an art gallery, to the benefit of the carpets displayed.

Der Messestand wirkt dank Beleuchtung und sorgfältig orchestrierter Platzierung der vertikalen Flächen stark wie eine Kunstgalerie. Hiervon profitieren nicht zuletzt die präsentierten Teppiche.

À la fois dans son éclairage et dans sa composition savamment orchestrée de plans verticaux colorés, le stand se présente presque comme une galerie d'art, pour le plus grand bénéfice des tapis exposés.

Panels of different colors and varying heights form a continuous upper line, while allowing for openings at the bottom, making the entire stand permeable.

Unterschiedlich hohe und verschiedenfarbige Wandsegmente schließen oben in einer bündigen Linie ab. Unten ergeben sich Öffnungen, durch die der Stand durchlässig wird.

Des panneaux de couleurs et de hauteurs variées forment un cloisonnement continu en partie supérieure, même si les ouvertures pratiquées en partie basse rendent le stand perméable à son environnement.

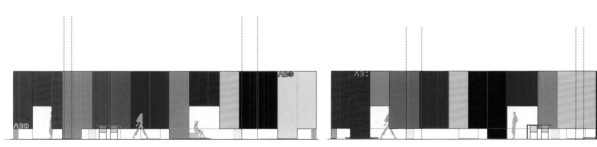

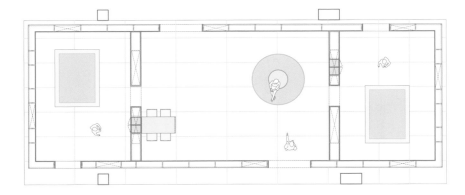

*The plan of the rectangular stand
is very simple, but its variety of
openings makes the space rich and
attractive (above).*

*Der Grundriss des rechteckigen
Stands ist denkbar schlicht; doch
durch die variablen Öffnungen gewinnt der Raum an Vielschichtigkeit
und Attraktivität (oben).*

*Si le plan au sol est très simple, la
variété des ouvertures réussit à
rendre cet espace séduisant et
surprenant (ci-dessus).*

In these photos, the idea of the stand, which is to say the presentation of rugs like works of art, is very clear.

Mehr als deutlich belegen diese Ansichten das Konzept des Stands – die Präsentation der Teppiche als Kunstwerke.

L'idée du stand – présenter les tapis comme des œuvres d'art – est particulièrement évidente ici.

ROJKIND ARQUITECTOS

Rojkind Arquitectos
Paseo de la Reforma #509, piso 7 oficinas A y B
Col. Cuauhtémoc
México D.F. 06500
Mexico

Tel: +52 55 280 8396
Fax: +52 55 280 8021
E-mail: info@rojkindarquitectos.com
Web: www.rojkindarquitectos.com

MICHEL ROJKIND was born in 1969 in Mexico City where he studied architecture and urban planning at the Universidad Iberoamericana. After working on his own for several years, he teamed up with Isaac Broid and Miquel Adria to establish Adria+Broid+Rojkind (1998–2002). In 2002, he established his own firm in Mexico City. With Arturo Ortiz, Derek Dellekamp, and Tatiana Bilbao, Michel Rojkind cofounded the non-profit MXDF Urban Research Center (2004). His built work includes Tlaxcala 190 Apartment building (Colonia Condesa, Mexico City, 2002); Mexico City National Videotheque (Mexico City, 2002); Falcon Headquarters (San Angel, Mexico City, 2004); Boska Bar (Mexico City, 2004); Nestlé Auditorium (Toluca, 2007); Nestlé Chocolate Museum (Phase I, Toluca, 2007); Philips Pavilion, "House of Simplicity" (Mexico City, 2007, published here); and Nestle Application Group (Querétaro, 2009). Other recent projects are the Tori Tori Restaurant (Mexico City, 2009); R432, mixed-use high-rise (Reforma, Mexico City, 2009); and Highpark, mixed-use building (Monterrey, Mexico City, 2010). Work in progress includes the renovation of the Hotel Del Angel (Mexico City, 2007–); and of the San Francisco Hotel (Mexico City, 2007–), all in Mexico.

MICHEL ROJKIND wurde 1969 in Mexico City geboren, wo er an der Universidad Iberoamericana Architektur und Stadtplanung studierte. Nachdem er einige Jahre allein gearbeitet hatte, schloss er sich mit Isaac Broid und Miquel Adria zu Adria+Broid+Rojkind zusammen (1998–2002). 2002 gründete er sein eigenes Büro in Mexico City. Gemeinsam mit Arturo Ortiz, Derek Dellekamp und Tatiana Bilbao gründete Michel Rojkind das gemeinnützige MXDF Urban Research Center (2004). Zu seinen realisierten Bauten zählen das Apartmenthaus Tlaxcala 190 (Colonia Condesa, Mexico City, 2002), die Nationalvideothek in Mexico City (2002), die Zentrale von Falcon (San Angel, Mexico City, 2004), die Bar Boska (Mexico City, 2004), das Nestlé Auditorium (Toluca, 2007), das Nestlé Schokoladenmuseum (1. Bauabschnitt in Toluca, 2007), der Philips-Pavillon „House of Simplicity" (Mexico City, 2007, hier vorgestellt) sowie die Nestlé Application Group (Querétaro, 2009). Andere jüngere Projekte sind u.a. das Restaurant Tori Tori (Mexico City, 2009), das Geschäfts- und Wohnhochhaus R432 (Reforma, Mexico City, 2009) und das Geschäfts- und Wohnhaus Highpark (Monterrey, Mexico City, 2010). Zu seinen laufenden Projekten zählen die Sanierung des Hotel Del Angel (Mexico City, 2007–) und des Hotel San Francisco (Mexico City, 2007–), alle in Mexiko.

Né en 1969 à Mexico, **MICHEL ROJKIND** a étudié l'architecture et l'urbanisme à l'Universidad Iberoamericana. Après avoir travaillé seul pendant plusieurs années, il s'est associé à Isaac Broid et Miquel Adria pour créer Adria+Broid+Rojkind (1998–2002), puis a fondé sa propre agence à Mexico en 2002. Avec Arturo Ortiz, Derek Dellekamp et Tatiana Bilbao, Michel Rojkind est cofondateur du Centre de recherches urbaines MXDF, association à but non lucratif (2004). Ses références comprennent l'immeuble d'appartements Tlaxcala 190 (Colonia Condesa, Mexico, 2002) ; la vidéothèque nationale du Mexique (Mexico, 2002) ; le siège de Falcon (San Angel, Mexico, 2004) ; le Boska Bar (Mexico, 2004) ; l'auditorium Nestlé (Toluca, Mexique, 2007) et le musée Nestlé du chocolat, phase I (Toluca, 2007) ; le pavillon Philips, House of Simplicity (« Maison de la simplicité », Mexico, 2007, publié ici), et le siège de Nestlé Application Group (Querétaro, 2009). Parmi ses projets récents figurent le restaurant Tori Tori (Mexico, 2009), l'immeuble de grande hauteur R432 (Reforma, Mexico, 2009) et Highpark, un immeuble mixte (Monterey, 2010). Il travaille actuellement à la rénovation de l'Hotel Del Angel (Mexico, 2007–) et du San Francisco Hotel (Mexico, 2007).

PHILIPS PAVILION, "HOUSE OF SIMPLICITY"

Mexico City, Mexico, 2007

Area: 94 m². Client: Philips. Cost: not disclosed.
Collaboration: Juan Carlos Vidals, Augustin Peyrera, Fermin Espinosa

Michel Rojkind explains: "The idea behind the **PHILIPS PAVILION 'HOUSE OF SIMPLICITY'** was to enhance the experience of a specific product for the exhibition, understanding that we wanted the visitors to enter a space inspired by sound waves, or to be more specific, by demonstrating the relationship between positive and negative spaces as discovered through the process of Boolean experimentation." Lighting is employed to create a "spatial sequence" of the pavilion, while the architect selected the blue coloring to serve as a backdrop to a special screen. The curving, superimposed wall configuration contributes to a sense of movement and modernity in the structure.

Michel Rojkind führt aus: „Die Idee hinter dem **PHILIPS-PAVILLON ‚HOUSE OF SIMPLICITY'** war die Absicht, das Erlebnis eines speziellen Produkts für die Messe besonders hervorzustreichen, davon ausgehend, dass die Besucher einen Raum betreten würden, der von Klangwellen inspiriert war – oder genauer gesagt von der Veranschaulichung der Beziehung von positivem und negativem Raum, wie man ihn durch die Versuche zur Booleschen Algebra entdeckt hatte." Die Lichtführung dient dazu, eine „räumliche Sequenz" im Pavillon zu schaffen; zugleich wählte der Architekt eine blaue Farbpalette als Hintergrund für einen speziellen Bildschirm. Die geschwungene, vorgehängte Wandkonfiguration trägt dazu bei, der Konstruktion Dynamik und Modernität zu geben.

Pour Michel Rojkind : « L'idée du **PAVILLON PHILIPS**, avec la **"MAISON DE LA SIMPLICITÉ"**, est d'enrichir l'expérience d'un produit spécifique de l'exposition, en faisant passer les visiteurs par un espace inspiré des ondes sonores ou, plus spécifiquement, en démontrant la relation entre les espaces positifs et négatifs observés dans les expérimentations booléennes. » L'éclairage sert à créer une « séquence spatiale » dans le pavillon, et l'architecte a choisi une coloration bleue qui sert de fond à un écran spécial. La configuration de ces murs incurvés en lamelles contribue à créer une forte impression de mouvement et de modernité.

Interior views give an almost surreal impression of space in movement in this temporary exhibition space.

Die Innenansichten des temporären Ausstellungsraums wirken geradezu surreal – der gesamte Raum scheint in Bewegung.

Les vues intérieures de ce lieu d'exposition temporaire laissent une impression quasi surréaliste d'espace en mouvement.

ROTOR

Rotor Vzw-Asbl
Laekensestraat 101
1000 Brussels
Belgium

Tel: +32 485 87 57 63
Fax: +32 22 19 20 11
E-mail: rotorasbl@gmail.com
Web: www.rotordb.org

The principals of the non-profit organization Rotor call it "a platform for the endorsement of industrial waste reuse. Rotor wants, among other things, to encourage contacts between producers of 'interesting' waste and potential reusers from the field of industry, design, or architecture." **MAARTEN GIELEN** was born in Aalst, Belgium, in 1984. He is a founding member of Rotor, created in 2005. **TRISTAN BONIVER** was born in Brussels in 1976 and his currently finishing his M.Arch in La Cambre Architecture Institute, Brussels. He is another founding member of the team. **LIONEL DEVLIEGER** was born in Rwamagana, Rwanda, in 1972. He obtained his Master in Architecture and Urbanism degree from Ghent University (1996) and a Ph.D. in Engineering Sciences—Architecture from the same university in 2005. He has been an active member of Rotor since 2006. **BENJAMIN LASSERRE** was born in Lille in 1985 and studied stage design at the Saint Luc Institute in Brussels. He became a member of Rotor after taking part in the KFDA09 project published here. **MELANIE TAMM** was born in West Berlin in 1974 and joined Rotor on a part-time basis in 2008. Their recent projects include RDF181, temporary offices (Brussels, Belgium, 2006–07); "Deutschland im Herbst" exhibition at the Ursula Blickle Stiftung (Kraichtal, Germany, 2008); the Festival Center for Kunstenfestivaldesarts 2009—KFDA09 (Brussels, Belgium, 2009, published here); and Usus/Usures, 12th International Architecture Biennale (Venice, Italy, 2010)..

Die Partner der gemeinnützigen Organisation Rotor definieren sich als „Plattform für die Wiederverwertung von Industriemüll. Rotor will, unter anderem, Kontakte zwischen den Produzenten ‚interessanter' Abfälle und potenziellen Wiederverwendern in Industrie, Design und Architektur fördern". **MAARTEN GIELEN** wurde 1984 in Aalst, Belgien, geboren. Er absolviert zur Zeit seinen M.Arch am Architekturinstitut der Kunsthochschule La Cambre in Brüssel. Auch er zählt zu den Gründungsmitgliedern des Teams. **LIONEL DEVLIEGER** wurde 1972 in Rwamagana, Ruanda, geboren. Er absolvierte seinen Master in Architektur und Stadtplanung an der Universität Gent (1996) und promovierte 2005 in Ingenieurwissenschaften/Architektur an derselben Universität. Er ist seit 2006 aktives Mitglied bei Rotor. **BENJAMIN LASSERRE** wurde 1985 in Lille geboren und studierte Bühnenbild am Institut Saint-Luc in Brüssel. Er wurde nach seiner Mitarbeit am hier vorgestellten Projekt KFDA09 Mitglied bei Rotor. **MELANIE TAMM** wurde 1974 West-Berlin geboren und schloss sich Rotor 2008 auf Teilzeitbasis an. Die jüngsten Projekte des Teams sind u.a. RDF181, temporäre Büros (Brüssel, 2006–07), *Deutschland im Herbst*, Ausstellung der Ursula Blickle Stiftung (Kraichtal, Deutschland, 2008), das Festivalcenter für das Kunstenfestivaldesarts 2009 – KFDA09 (Brüssel, 2009, hier vorgestellt) sowie Usus/Usures, 12. Internationale Architekturbiennale (Venedig, 2010).

Les dirigeants de Rotor présentent cette association à but non lucratif, créée en 2005, comme une « plate-forme pour la promotion de la réutilisation des déchets industriels. Rotor souhaite, entre autres, encourager les contacts entre les producteurs de déchets "intéressants" et leurs réutilisateurs potentiels dans les domaines de l'industrie, du design et de l'architecture ». **MAARTEN GIELEN**, né à Aalst (Belgique) en 1984, est membre fondateur de Rotor. **TRISTAN BONIVER**, né à Bruxelles en 1976, termine actuellement son M. Arch à l'Institut d'architecture de La Cambre à Bruxelles et a également participé à la fondation de Rotor. **LIONEL DEVLIEGER**, né à Rwamagana (Rwanda) en 1972, a obtenu son mastère en architecture et urbanisme à l'université de Gand (1996) et son Ph. D. en sciences de l'ingénierie-architecture à la même université en 2005. Il est membre actif de Rotor depuis 2006. **BENJAMIN LASSERRE** est né à Lille en 1985 et a étudié la scénographie à l'Institut Saint-Luc de Bruxelles. Il est devenu membre de Rotor après avoir participé au projet KFDA09, publié ici. **MELANIE TAMM** est née à Berlin-Ouest en 1974, et a rejoint Rotor à temps partiel en 2008. Leurs projets récents comprennent : RDF181, des bureaux temporaires (Bruxelles, 2006–07) ; « Deutschland im Herbst », exposition à la Fondation Ursula Blickle (Kraichtal, Allemagne, 2008) ; le Centre pour le festival Kunstenfestivaldesarts 2009 – KFDA09 (Bruxelles, 2009, publié ici) et Usus/Usures pour la XIIe Biennale internationale d'architecture de Venise (2010).

FESTIVAL CENTER FOR KFDA09

Brussels, Belgium, 2009

Area: 36 m² (mezzanine); Terrace: 180 m² (terrace); 212 m² (converted interior)
Client: KFDA09. Cost: not disclosed

Rotor was asked to revamp the interior of the Brigittines Arts Center for a three-week period with a modest budget. They added a mezzanine to the hall of the building. The architects state: "We opted for a design that took into account the future destination of the materials used in its creation. We worked with rented prefab elements used as formwork in the building industry and different kinds of wood waste for finishings. Melaminated chipboard from unmarketable furniture was used as flooring. In this way, the large structures erected for the festival left hardly any supplementary waste after their purposes were fulfilled." The use of scaffolding or manifestly temporary elements in this installation served to reinforce the lively, dynamic nature of the activities in the space.

Der Auftrag von Rotor lautete, die Innenräume des Kunstzentrums Les Brigittines für einen Zeitraum von drei Wochen im Rahmen eines bescheidenen Budgets umzugestalten. Sie realisierten daraufhin ein Mezzaningeschoss im Foyer des Gebäudes. Die Architekten führen aus: „Wir entschieden uns für ein Design, das die zukünftige Verwendung der eingesetzten Materialien von vornherein mit berücksichtigte. Wir arbeiteten mit gemieteten Fertigbauelementen, die in der Industrie als Schalungsmaterial zum Einsatz kommen sowie mit verschiedenen Arten von Holzabfällen für die Verkleidung. Melaminharzbeschichtete Spanplatten von unverkäuflichen Möbeln diente als Bodenbelag. Auf diese Weise hinterließen die für das Festival aufgebauten Großkonstruktionen kaum zusätzliche Abfälle, nachdem sie ihren Zweck erfüllt hatten." Der Einsatz von Gerüsten und augenscheinlich temporären Elementen für diese Installation trugen dazu bei, die Lebendigkeit und Dynamik der in den Räumen stattfindenden Aktivitäten hervorzustreichen.

On avait demandé à Rotor de redonner un style au Centre d'art contemporain des Brigittines, qui devait être utilisé pendant trois semaines par le festival. Le budget était modeste. L'équipe a créé une mezzanine dans le hall du bâtiment. « Nous avons opté pour un projet prenant en compte la future destination des matériaux utilisés dans sa création. Nous avons travaillé à partir d'éléments préfabriqués loués comme des coffrages de chantier de bâtiment et divers types de matériaux de récupération pour les finitions. Des planches d'aggloméré mélaminé, récupérées sur des meubles invendables, ont servi à faire les sols. Ainsi, les constructions de grandes dimensions érigées pour la durée du festival n'ont généré pratiquement aucun déchet supplémentaire une fois leur fonction remplie. » L'utilisation d'échafaudages ou d'éléments manifestement temporaires renforçait par ailleurs la dynamique et le caractère vivant des activités qui se déroulaient dans cet espace.

The architects specialize in attaching
new temporary spaces to existing
structures, using rough, available
materials.

Die Architekten haben sich darauf
spezialisiert, temporäre Anbauten an
bestehenden Gebäuden zu realisieren
und nutzen dafür verfügbare, oftmals
grobe Materialien.

Ces architectes se sont spécialisés
dans la création d'espaces temporaires rattachés à des constructions
existantes, réalisés à partir de matériaux bruts, souvent de récupération.

Below, spearing from the exterior like
a temporary wooden platform set up
on pipe scaffolding, the structure
embraces and expands on the older
building.

Die Konstruktion unten, eine temporäre Plattform aus Holz und Gerüststangen, ragt aus der Fassade heraus,
knüpft an das ältere Gebäude an und
erweitert es zugleich.

Ci-dessous, la plate-forme en bois
temporaire posée sur des tubes
d'échafaudage enveloppe et agrandit
le bâtiment ancien.

The use of pipe scaffolding emphasizes the temporary nature of the
space, which is seen in the drawings
on the right as the darker added
terrace space in the plan.

*Die Verwendung von Gerüststangen
unterstreicht die temporäre Natur des
Anbaus, der auf den Zeichnungen
rechts als dunklerer Terrassenbereich
zu erkennen ist.*

*L'utilisation d'éléments d'échafauda-
ge tubulaire matérialise la nature
temporaire de l'espace créé, présent
dans les plans à droite, au-dessus de
la zone ombrée délimitant la terrasse.*

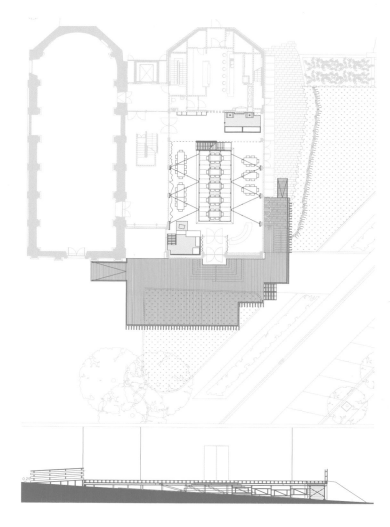

TOMÁS SARACENO

Studio Tomás Saraceno
Atelier Frankfurt / Hohenstaufenstr. 13–25
60327 Frankfurt am Main / Germany

Tel: +49 69 76 80 70 32
E-mail: info@t-saraceno.org
Web: www.cloudcities.org

TOMÁS SARACENO was born in 1973 in San Miguel de Tucumán, Argentina. He says that he "lives and works between and beyond the planet earth," which makes it clear that he is an artist. His actual place of residence is Frankfurt am Main, Germany. He received his degree as an architect from the Universidad Nacional de Buenos Aires, Argentina UBA (1992–99). He did postgraduate studies of art and architecture at the Escuela Superior de bellas Artes de la Nación Ernesto de la Cárcova (Buenos Aires, 1999–2000), at the Staatliche Hochschule für Bildende Künste Städelschule-Frankfurt am Main (2001–03), and at the IUAV, again in art and architecture (Venice, 2003–04). In the summer of 2009, he attended the International Space Studies Program (NASA Ames Research Center, Moffett Field, California). Winner of the 2009 Calder Prize, he has been a resident artist at the Calder Atelier (Saché, France, 2010), where he presented the exhibition "Tomás Saraceno—Cloud Cities" in which works published here could be seen. The art critic Rodrigo Alonso writes: "Tomás Saraceno's work defies traditional notions of space, time, gravity, consciousness and perception through architectural, social and communitarian means that are utopian and participatory in nature. The sky and the earth are interchangeable in his installations, in which gardens float and people achieve their longstanding desire to fly." A solo exhibition of his work, "Tomás Saraceno: 14 billions," was also presented in 2010 at the Bonniers Konsthall (Stockholm) and then at the Baltic Center for Contemporary Art (Gateshead, UK); two new solo shows are scheduled for 2011 in the Hamburger Bahnhof (Berlin, Germany) and in K21 (Dusseldorf, Germany).

TOMÁS SARACENO wurde 1973 in San Miguel de Tucumán, Argentinien, geboren. Nach eigener Aussage „lebt und arbeitet" er „zwischen und über den Planeten Erde hinaus" und stellt damit klar, dass er Künstler ist. Aktuell lebt er in Frankfurt am Main. Sein Studium der Architektur schloss er an der Universidad Nacional de Buenos Aires (UBA), Argentinien, ab (1992–99). Aufbaustudien in Kunst und Architektur absolvierte er an der Escuela Superior de bellas Artes de la Nación Ernesto de la Cárcova (Buenos Aires, 1999–2000), der Staatlichen Hochschule für Bildende Künste/Städelschule in Frankfurt am Main (2001–03) und der IUAV (Venedig, 2003–04). Im Sommer 2009 besuchte er das International Space Studies Program (NASA Ames Forschungszentrum, Moffett Field, Kalifornien). 2009 wurde er mit dem Calder-Preis ausgezeichnet, dem sich 2010 ein Künstleraufenthalt am Atelier Calder (Saché, Frankreich) anschloss, wo er die Ausstellung *Tomás Saraceno – Cloud Cities* präsentierte, bei der die hier vorgestellten Arbeiten zu sehen waren. Der Kunstkritiker Rodrigo Alonso schreibt: „Tomás Saracenos Werk entzieht sich allen konventionellen Vorstellungen von Raum, Zeit, Schwerkraft, Bewusstsein und Wahrnehmung – mithilfe architektonischer, sozialer und kommunitaristischer Mittel, die zugleich utopisch und partizipatorisch sind. Bei seinen Installationen sind Himmel und Erde austauschbar; dort gibt es schwebende Gärten, und Menschen verwirklichen den alten Traum vom Fliegen." 2010 war auch die Einzelausstellung des Künstlers, *Tomás Saraceno: 14 billions*, in der Bonniers Konsthall (Stockholm) und anschließend am Baltic Center for Contemporary Art (Gateshead, Großbritannien) zu sehen. Für 2011 sind zwei Einzelausstellungen im Hamburger Bahnhof (Berlin) und am K21 (Düsseldorf) geplant.

TOMÁS SARACENO est né en 1973 à San Miguel de Tucumán en Argentine. C'est en tant qu'artiste qu'il déclare « vivre et travailler sur et au-delà de la planète Terre ». Son lieu actuel de résidence est Francfort-sur-le-Main. Il est diplômé en architecture de l'Université nationale de Buenos Aires (UBA), (Argentine, 1992–99) et a effectué des études supérieures d'art et d'architecture à l'Escuela Superior de bellas Artes de la Nación Ernesto de la Cárcova (Buenos Aires, 1999–2000), à la Staatliche Hochschule für Bildende Künste – Städelschule (Francfort-sur-le-Main, 2001–03) et à l'IUAV (Venise, 2003–04). Pendant l'été 2009, il a suivi le programme d'études spatiales internationales de la Nasa (Nasa Ames Research Center, Moffett Field, Californie). Titulaire du prix Calder 2009, il a été artiste en résidence à l'atelier Calder (Saché, France, 2010), où il a présenté son exposition « Tomás Saraceno – Cloud Cities » dans laquelle figuraient des œuvres présentées ici. Le critique d'art Rodrigo Alonso a écrit : « Le travail de Tomás Saraceno remet en question les notions traditionnelles d'espace, de temps, de gravité, de conscience et de perception par des moyens architecturaux, sociaux et communautaires, de nature à la fois participative et utopiste. Le ciel et la terre sont interchangeables dans ses installations où l'on voit des jardins flotter et des personnes accomplir leur rêve très ancien de voler. » Une exposition personnelle de son œuvre, « Tomás Saraceno: 14 billions », a été présentée en 2010 à la Bonniers Konsthall (Stockholm) et au Centre « Baltic » pour l'art contemporain (Gateshead, GB) ; deux expositions personnelles sont prévues en 2011 à la Hamburger Bahnhof (Berlin) et au K21 (Düsseldorf, Allemagne).

CLOUD CITIES/AIR-PORT-CITY

Planet Earth, work in progress

Area: variable sizes. Client: not disclosed
Cost: not disclosed

The artist presented an exhibition at the Calder Atelier in Saché, France, under the title "Tomás Saraceno—**CLOUD CITIES**" (June 19–July 4, 2010). Saraceno describes the project as "a structure that seeks to challenge today's political, social, cultural, and military restrictions in an attempt to reestablish new concepts of synergy. Up in the sky there will be this cloud, a habitable platform that floats in the air, changing form and merging with other platforms, just as clouds do. It will fly through the atmosphere pushed by the winds, both local and global, in an attempt to equalize the (social) temperature and differences in pressure." Suspended above the ground, these works appear to float in space. Their architectural content is clearly significant for the artist even if, as such, Saraceno's mode of expression is art. It is rather an ambition for architecture that he presents, one in which a floating, temporary world might replace the immovable solidity of the city. Since 2008, there has been a permanent installation of the work *On Clouds (Air-Port-City)* at the Towada Arts Center (Towada, Japan).

Der Künstler präsentierte eine Ausstellung am Calder Atelier in Saché, Frankreich, unter dem Titel *Tomás Saraceno* – **CLOUD CITIES** (19. Juni–4. Juli 2010). Saraceno beschreibt das Projekt als „eine Struktur, die die heutigen politischen, sozialen, kulturellen und militärischen Beschränkungen hinterfragen will und versucht, neue Synergiekonzepte wieder zu etablieren. Hoch oben im Himmel wird es eine Wolke geben, eine in der Luft schwebende, bewohnbare Plattform, die ihre Form verändert und mit anderen Plattformen verschmilzt, gerade so, wie es Wolken tun. Sie wird durch die Atmosphäre fliegen, getrieben von Winden, lokalen ebenso wie globalen, im Streben danach, die (sozialen) Temperatur- und Druckgefälle zu harmonisieren." Die über dem Erdboden abgespannten Arbeiten scheinen frei im Raum zu schweben. Ihr architektonischer Gehalt ist für den Künstler zweifellos von Bedeutung, auch wenn sein Medium der Wahl die Kunst ist. Vielmehr ist es ein Ziel der Architektur, die er präsentiert, eine fließende, temporäre Welt zu imaginieren, die die unbewegliche Statik der Stadt ablöst. Seit 2008 befindet sich eine permanente Installation seiner Arbeit „On Clouds (Air-Port-City)" im Towada Arts Center (Towada, Japan).

C'est dans l'atelier de Calder à Saché, en France, que l'artiste a présenté son exposition intitulée « Tomás Saraceno – **CLOUD CITIES** » (19 juin–4 juillet 2010). Il décrit son projet comme « une structure qui cherche à remettre en cause les restrictions politiques, sociales, culturelles et militaires actuelles, afin de rétablir de nouveaux concepts de synergie. Dans le ciel, pourra ainsi se déplacer une plate-forme habitable de forme changeante, fusionnant à l'occasion avec d'autres plates-formes, comme le font les nuages. Elle se déplacera dans l'atmosphère, poussée par les vents locaux ou globaux, pour équilibrer les températures (sociales) et les différences de pression. » Suspendues au-dessus du sol, ces œuvres semblent flotter dans l'espace. Leur contenu architectural a du sens, même si Saraceno s'exprime sur un mode artistique. Il introduit une ambition nouvelle pour l'architecture dans laquelle un monde flottant et temporaire pourrait remplacer la masse statique de la cité. Depuis 2008, le Centre des arts de Towada (Towada, Japon) présente en permanence une installation de l'œuvre *On Clouds (Air-Port-City)*.

On this double page, images of Cloud Cities/Air-Port-City *installed at the Calder Atelier in Saché, France, during the artist's stay there in 2010.*

Auf dieser Doppelseite: Bilder von Cloud Cities/Air-Port-City, *einem Projekt, das der Künstler 2010 bei seinem Aufenthalt im Atelier Calder in Saché, Frankreich, realisierte.*

Sur ces pages, images de Cloud Cities/Air-Port-City *installée auprès de l'atelier Calder à Saché (France) pendant le séjour qu'y fit Saraceno en 2010.*

Below, right, Cumulonimbus/Air-Port-City, *part of the exhibition "How to Live Together," São Paulo Biennale, 2006.*

Unten rechts: Cumulonimbus/Air-Port-City, *ein Projekt im Rahmen der Ausstellung „How to Live Together", São Paulo Biennale 2006.*

Ci-dessous à droite, Cumulonimbus/Air-Port-City, *qui faisait partie de l'exposition « How to Live Together » (Comment vivre ensemble), Biennale de São Paulo 2006.*

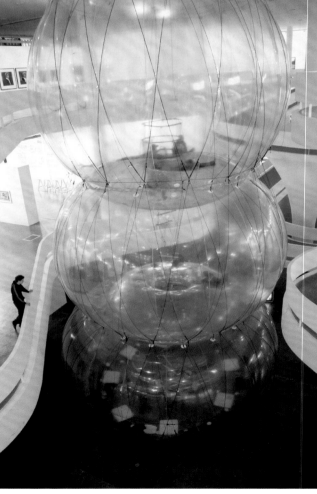

Biosphere, 2009. Exhibited at the Statens Museum for Kunst, Copenhagen. Another part of this work is seen on the left page (left).

Biosphere, 2009. Projekt im Statens Museum for Kunst, Kopenhagen. Gegenüber (links unten) ein anderer Teil der Arbeit.

Biosphere, 2009, exposée au Statens Museum for Kunst, Copenhague. Une autre partie de cette œuvre est visible page de gauche (à gauche).

Above, Observatory/Air-Port-City, *2008. Below*, 14 billions, *2010. Upper right*, Galaxies Forming along Filaments, like Droplets along the Strands of a Spider's Web, *2009, Venice Biennale. Lower right*, Biosphere MW32/Flying Garden/ Air-Port-City, *2007*.

Oben Observatory/Air-Port-City, *2008. Unten*, 14 billions, *2010. Oben rechts*, Galaxies Forming along Filaments, like Droplets along the Strands of a Spider's Web, *Biennale Venedig, 2009. Unten rechts*, Biosphere MW32/Flying Garden/ Air-Port-City, *2007*.

Ci-dessus, Observatory/Air-Port-City, *2008. Ci-dessous*, 14 billions, *2010. En haut à droite*, Galaxies Forming along Filaments, like Droplets along the Strands of a Spider's Web, *Biennale de Venise, 2009. En bas à droite*, Biosphere MW32/Flying Garden/Air-Port-City, *2007*.

Images taken at "Poetic Cosmos of the Breath," Airshow in Gunpowder Park, London, 2007.

Aufnahmen von Saracenos Arbeit Poetic Cosmos of the Breath *auf der Airshow in Gunpowder Park, London, 2007.*

Images de « Poetic Cosmos of the Breath », exposition aérienne au Gunpowder Park, Londres, 2007.

SOLID OBJECTIVES—IDENBURG LIU

Solid Objectives—Idenburg Liu
68 Jay Street #501
Brooklyn, NY 11201
USA

Tel: +1 718 624 6666
Fax: +1 718 624 6616
E-mail: office@so-il.org
Web: www.so-il.org

FLORIAN IDENBURG was born in 1975 in Heemstede, the Netherlands. He received an M.Sc. degree in Architectural Engineering from the Technical University of Delft (1999) and worked with SANAA in Tokyo from 2000 to 2007. **JING LIU** was born in 1980 in Nanjing, China. She received her M.Arch degree from Tulane University in 2004 and worked from 2004 to 2007 with KPF in New York. Recent work includes Upto35, student housing (Athens, Greece, competition winner 2009); The Hague Dance and Music Center (The Netherlands, competition 2010); Pole Dance, PS1 (Long Island City, New York, USA, 2010, published here); Kukje Gallery (Seoul, South Korea, 2009–11); a Park Pavilion (Amsterdam, The Netherlands, project 2010–11); Wedding Chapel (Nanjing, China, 2008–12); and a Housing Block (Athens, Greece, project 2010–12).

FLORIAN IDENBURG wurde 1975 in Heemstede, Niederlande, geboren. Er absolvierte einen M.Sc. in Versorgungstechnik an der TU Delft (1999) und war von 2000 bis 2007 für SANAA in Tokio tätig. **JING LIU** wurde 1980 in Nanjing, China, geboren. Sie absolvierten ihren M.Arch 2004 an der Tulane University und arbeitete von 2004 bis 2007 für KPF in New York. Zu ihren jüngeren Projekten zählen das Studentenwohnheim Upto35 (Athen, Siegerbeitrag für einen Wettbewerb 2009), das Dance and Music Center in Den Haag (Niederlande, Wettbewerbsbeitrag 2010), Pole Dance, PS1 (Long Island City, New York, USA, 2010, hier vorgestellt), Galerie Kukje (Seoul, 2009–11), ein Park-Pavillon (Amsterdam, Projekt 2010–11), eine Hochzeitskapelle (Nanjing, China, 2008–12) sowie ein Wohnblock (Athen, Projekt 2010–12).

FLORIAN IDENBURG, né en 1975 à Heemstede (Pays-Bas), a obtenu son M. Sc. en ingénierie architecturale de l'Université polytechnique de Delft (1999) et a travaillé chez SANAA à Tokyo de 2000 à 2007. **JING LIU**, née à Nankin (Chine) en 1980, a obtenu son M. Arch de la Tulane University (2004) et a travaillé de 2004 à 2007 chez KPF à New York. Parmi leurs activités récentes : Upto35, logements pour étudiants (Athènes, concours remporté en 2009) ; le Centre de la musique et de la danse de La Haye (Pays-Bas, concours 2010) ; *Pole Dance*, PS1 (Long Island City, New York, 2010, publié ici) ; la galerie Kukje (Séoul, Corée du Sud, 2009–11) ; un pavillon pour un parc (Amsterdam, projet 2010–11) ; une chapelle destinée aux mariages (Nankin, Chine, 2008–12) et un immeuble de logements (Athènes, projet 2010–12).

POLE DANCE

PS1, Long Island City, New York, USA, 2010

Area: 1329 m². Client: PS1 MoMA. Cost: $85 000

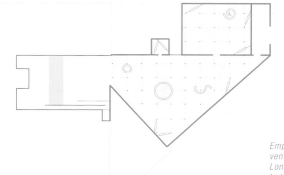

Mit minimalen Eingriffen gestalteten die Architekten einen spielerischen Raum im Innenhof des PS1 in Long Island City: auf diesen Aufnahmen Tänzer und Akrobaten.

Employing a minimal amount of intervention in the courtyard of PS1 in Long Island City, the architects created a playful space where dancers and acrobats were photographed, as here.

Intervenant a minima, les architectes ont créé dans la cour de PS1 à Long Island City cet espace ludique dans lequel ont été photographiés des danseurs et des acrobates.

Drawings show the simple support system for the netting, and an aerial image makes clear that very little additional material has been used to render the otherwise austere courtyard lively.

Zeichnungen veranschaulichen die einfache Stützkonstruktion für die Netze. Eine Luftaufnahme zeigt, wie wenig weiteres Material eingesetzt wurde, um den ansonsten strengen Hof zu beleben.

Le dessin de droite illustre la simplicité du système de soutien du filet. La vue aérienne montre que l'animation de cette cour austère n'a demandé que peu de matériaux.

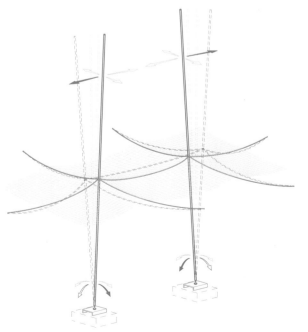

The architects start the description of this project with a bit of architectural philosophy: "Freed from the fascination of the finite, and confronted with new ecologies, economies, energies, flows, and fantasies, we can begin to comprehend, and depict, a new image of life on earth, that of a seemingly elastic cloud. Everything has become untethered. We bounce about, footloose, on a network of intersections and knots." With **POLE DANCE**, a temporary installation in the courtyard of MoMA's PS1 venue in Long Island City, they seek "to create sensorially charged environments rather than finite forms." They erected a 4.9-meter grid of 9.1-meter-high poles connected by bungee cords and covered by an open net. Any movement in part of this system engenders movement in the rest. Brightly colored balls, a pool, and an orange hammock add to the playful atmosphere of the installation. The architects have also added a sound generator to the work: "The small courtyard adjacent to the main space holds a surprise, an immersive, interactive courtyard where visitors can create and control a rich sound experience from within the installation. Eight poles contain accelerometers— electronic devices that measure the motion of the poles—connected to custom software that converts motion into tones specifically composed for the installation."

Die Architekten beginnen ihre Projektbeschreibung mit etwas Architekturphilosophie: „Befreit von der Faszination des Finiten und konfrontiert mit neuen Ökologien, Ökonomien, Energien, Flüssen und Fantasien können wir beginnen, ein neues Leben auf der Erde zu begreifen und beschreiben: das einer elastischen Wolke. Alles ist losgelöst. Wir bewegen uns frei und ungebunden durch den Raum, in einem Netzwerk aus Schnittstellen und Verknüpfungen." Mit **POLE DANCE**, einer temporären Installation im Hof der MoMA-Dependance PS1 in Long Island City, versuchen sie „sensorisch aufgeladene Umfelder statt finiter Formen" zu realisieren. Das Team errichtete ein 4,9 m breites Raster aus 9,1 m hohen Pfählen, die mit Bungeeseilen miteinander verbunden und mit einem offenen Netz überzogen waren. Jegliche Bewegung in einem Teil des Systems hatte Bewegung im Rest des Systems zur Folge. Bunte Bälle, ein Pool und eine orange Hängematte trugen zur spielerischen Atmosphäre der Installation bei. Darüber hinaus integrierten die Architekten einen Soundgenerator in die Arbeit: „Im kleinen, an den Hauptbereich angrenzenden Hof verbirgt sich eine Überraschung: ein immersiver, interaktiver Hof, in dem die Besucher ein vielschichtiges Klangerlebnis aus der Installation heraus erzeugen und steuern können. Acht Pfähle sind mit Beschleunigungssensoren ausgestattet – elektronischen Sensoren, die die Bewegung der Pfähle messen –, die wiederum mit einer eigens entwickelten Software verbunden sind, die die Bewegungen in Töne wandelt, die speziell für die Installation komponiert wurden."

Les architectes débutent la description de leur projet par quelques réflexions de philosophie architecturale : « Libérés de la fascination d'un monde fini, et confrontés à des écologies, des économies, des énergies, des flux et des visions nouvelles, nous pouvons commencer à appréhender et décrire une nouvelle image de la vie sur terre, qui serait celle d'un nuage d'apparence élastique. Tout s'est détaché. Nous rebondissons, sans entraves, sur un réseau d'intersections et de nœuds. » À travers **POLE DANCE**, cette installation temporaire dans la cour de PS1 à Long Island City, une institution qui dépend du MoMA, ils cherchent « à créer des environnements sensoriels plutôt que des formes finies ». Ils ont érigé une trame de 4,9 m matérialisée par des poteaux de 9,1 m de haut, réunis par des cordes élastiques et recouverts d'un filet. Tout mouvement se produisant dans une partie de cet ensemble déclenche des mouvements dans le reste de l'installation. Les architectes ont également ajouté un générateur de sons : « La petite cour adjacente à l'espace principal réserve une surprise, c'est une cour d'immersion interactive dans laquelle les visiteurs peuvent créer et contrôler toute une gamme d'expériences sonores de l'intérieur de l'installation. Huit poteaux contiennent des accéléromètres – appareils qui mesurent le mouvement des poteaux – connectés à un logiciel spécial qui convertit les mouvements en sons spécialement composés pour le projet. »

STUDIO TAMASSOCIATI

studio tamassociati
2731 Dorsoduro
30123 Venice
Italy

Tel: +39 041 522 69 74
E-mail: info@tamassociati.org
Web: www.tamassociati.org

RAUL PANTALEO was born in Milan, Italy, in 1962. He attended the IUAV in Venice, Italy, and holds an international certificate in Human Ecology obtained through postgraduate studies at the University of Padua. **MASSIMO LEPORE** was born in Udine, Italy, in 1960. He graduated from the IUAV University in Venice. He completed postgraduate studies in urban and environmental re-qualification at the "Taller de Arquitectura y Urbanismo" (Municipality of Lleida, Spain). **SIMONE SFRISO** was born in London in 1966. She also graduated from the IUAV University in Venice and now works as adviser and teaching assistant for courses in Urban Planning at the IUAV. They created studio tamassociati for "socially conscious design and communication" in 2001. Based in Venice, the firm works mainly for public institutions and NGOs. It is currently developing projects for public spaces and hospital projects for NGOs in the Sudan (Salam Center for Cardiac Surgery, Khartoum, 2006–07), Sierra Leone, Central African Republic, and Nicaragua. Their recent work includes a redesign of the Marconi Square (San Giorgio Piacentino, Italy, 2007); San Giacomo del Martignone urban park (Anzola Dell'Emilia, Italy, 2007); a project for a Children's Hospital (Bangui, Central African Republic, 2007); Emergency NGO housing for the Salam Center for Cardiac Surgery (Soba, Khartoum, Sudan, 2009, published here); and the Pediatric Center-Emergency (Nyala, Darfur, Sudan, 2010).

RAUL PANTALEO wurde 1962 in Mailand geboren. Er besuchte das IUAV (Istituto Universitario di Architettura di Venezia) in Italien und erwarb ein internationales Zertifikat in Ökologie im Zuge eines Postgraduiertenprogramms der Universität Padua. **MASSIMO LEPORE** wurde 1960 in Udine, Italien, geboren. Seinen Abschluss machte er am IUAV der Universität Venedig. Er absolvierte ein Postgraduiertenprogramm in urbaner und ökologischer Wiederaufbereitung an der „Taller de Arquitectura y Urbanismo" (Lleida, Spanien). **SIMONE SFRISO** wurde 1966 in London geboren. Auch sie machte ihren Abschluss am IUAV der Universität Venedig und ist inzwischen als Beraterin und Lehrassistentin für Stadtplanung am IUAV tätig. 2001 gründeten sie das studio tamassociati für „sozial verantwortliche Planung und Kommunikation". Die in Venedig ansässige Firma arbeitet hauptsächlich für öffentliche Träger und Nichtregierungsorganisationen (NGOs). Derzeit wird an Projekten für öffentliche Einrichtungen und Krankenhäuser von NGOs im Sudan (Zentrum für Herzchirurgie „Salam", Khartoum, 2006–07), in Sierra Leone, der Zentralafrikanischen Republik und Nicaragua gearbeitet. Aktuelle Projekte sind u.a. die Umgestaltung der Piazza Marconi (San Giorgio Piacentino, Italien, 2007), der Stadtpark in San Giacomo del Martignone (Anzola Dell'Emilia, Italien, 2007) sowie ein Kinderkrankenhausprojekt (Bangui, Zentralafrikanische Republik, 2007), eine Wohnsiedlung für die NGO Emergency am Zentrum für Herzchirurgie „Salam" (Soba, Khartoum, Sudan, 2009, hier vorgestellt) und eine Emergency-Kinderklinik (Nyala, Darfur, Sudan, 2010).

RAUL PANTALEO, né à Milan en 1962, a étudié à l'IUAV de Venise (Istituto Universitario di Architettura di Venezia) et, après des études supérieures à l'université de Padoue, a obtenu un certificat en écologie humaine. **MASSIMO LEPORE**, né à Udine (Italie) en 1960, est également diplômé de l'IUAV de Venise. Il a effectué des études supérieures en requalification urbaine et environnementale au « Taller de Arquitectura y Urbanismo » (Lleida, Espagne). **SIMONE SFRISO**, née à Londres en 1966, elle aussi diplômée de l'IUAV, travaille maintenant comme conseillère et assistante d'enseignement pour les cours d'urbanisme de l'IUAV. Ils ont créé ensemble l'agence studio tamassociati pour la « conception et communication socialement responsables » en 2001. Basée à Venise, elle travaille principalement pour des institutions publiques et des ONG. Actuellement, elle met au point des projets de lieux publics et d'hôpitaux pour des ONG au Soudan (Centre de chirurgie cardiaque Salam, Khartoum, 2006–07), en Sierra Leone, en République centrafricaine et au Nicaragua. Parmi leurs récentes interventions : la rénovation de la place Marconi (San Giorgio Piacentino, Italie, 2007) ; le parc urbain San Giacomo del Martignone (Anzola Dell'Emilia, Italie, 2007) ; un projet d'hôpital pour enfants (Bangui, République centrafricaine, 2007) ; des logements pour l'ONG Emergency pour le Centre de chirugie cardiaque Salam (Soba, Khartoum, Soudan, 2009, publiés ici) et le Centre de pédiatrie Emergency (Nyala, Darfour, Soudan, 2010).

EMERGENCY NGO HOUSING FOR THE SALAM CENTER FOR CARDIAC SURGERY

Soba, Khartoum, Sudan, 2009

Area: 1668 m². Client: Emergency NGO. Cost: €1.332 million.
Collaboration: Emergency Technical Office

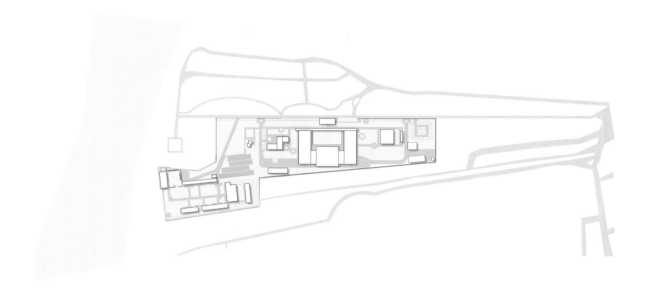

Built for and run by the Italian NGO Emergency, the Salam Center is located 20 kilometers south of Khartoum. The challenge posed for the architects was to design a quality environment with limited resources in a climate where there are frequent sandstorms and temperatures often range above 40°. Inspired by the number of discarded containers left near the construction site of the Salam Center, they decided to reuse them for the required international staff-housing conpound. Set near the hospital, not far from the Nile, the housing is located in a mango grove. Ninety-five 20 ft containers were used for housing and seven 40 ft containers were converted into the cafeteria. Each lodging measures 20 square meters and is made up of a bedroom, bathroom, and small veranda. The architects explain: "Special care has been dedicated to insulation and energy saving. The containers are insulated with a 'layer system.' Inside the container five-centimeter insulating panels have been placed. The outside 'skin' is realized with a second insulated roof and a bamboo *brise-soleil* panel system. In this way the rays of the sun never hit the containers. An innovative air-conditioning system has been tested using solar panels and chilling machines. This system involves a huge energy saving. Solar panels also supply hot water for the entire compound."

Das von der italienischen NGO Emergency erbaute und betriebene Salam Center liegt 20 km südlich von Khartoum. Die Herausforderung für die Architekten bestand darin, ein hochwertiges Umfeld mit begrenzten Ressourcen zu entwerfen, und das in einem Klima mit häufigen Sandstürmen und Temperaturen, die oft über 40°C liegen. Inspiriert von mehreren entsorgten Containern unweit der Baustelle des Salam Center beschlossen sie, diese für eine benötigte Wohnsiedlung für Mitarbeiter aus aller Welt umzunutzen. Die Wohnanlage in der Nähe des Krankenhauses liegt in einem Mangohain unweit des Nils. Fünfundneunzig 20-Fuß-Container wurden als Wohnquartiere genutzt, sieben 40-Fuß-Container wurden zur Cafeteria umfunktioniert. Jede Wohnung hat 20 m² und besteht aus Schlafzimmer, Bad und einer kleinen Veranda. Die Architekten erklären: „Besondere Aufmerksamkeit galt der Dämmung und Energieeinsparung. Die Container wurden mit einem ‚Schichtsystem' isoliert. In den Containern wurden 5 cm starke Dämmplatten angebracht. Die Außen-‚Haut' besteht aus einem zweiten gedämmten Dach und einem System aus *brise-soleil*-Paneelen aus Bambus. Auf diese Weise treffen die Sonnenstrahlen nie direkt auf die Container. Ein innovatives Klimaanlagensystem aus Solarpaneelen und Kühlelementen wurde getestet. Das System bedeutet eine enorme Energieersparnis. Solarpaneele versorgen die gesamte Wohnanlage außerdem mit heißem Wasser."

Construit et géré par l'ONG italienne Emergency, le Centre Salam est situé à 20 km au sud de Khartoum. Le défi lancé aux architectes était de concevoir un environnement d'une certaine qualité dans un climat difficile caractérisé par de fréquentes tempêtes de sable et des pointes de température dépassant souvent 40°. Intéressés par les conteneurs d'expédition abandonnés près du chantier du Centre Salam, ils ont décidé de les réutiliser pour les logements du personnel international. Cet ensemble résidentiel est implanté dans une mangrove, près de l'hôpital et non loin du Nil. Quatre-vingt-quinze conteneurs de 20 pieds de long ont été utilisés pour les logements, et 7 conteneurs de 40 pieds pour une cafétéria. Chaque logement mesure 20 m² et se compose d'une chambre, d'une salle de bains et d'une petite véranda. Comme l'expliquent les architectes : « Un soin particulier a été consacré à l'isolation et aux économies d'énergie. Les conteneurs sont isolés thermiquement par un système multistrate. À l'intérieur, ont été fixés des panneaux isolants de 5 cm d'épaisseur. La peau extérieure comprend une seconde toiture isolée et un système de brise-soleil en panneaux de bambou. Ainsi, les rayons du soleil ne touchent jamais directement les conteneurs. Un système de climatisation de l'air innovant à base de panneaux solaires et de système de refroidissement a été testé. Il permet d'importantes économies d'énergie. Les panneaux solaires fournissent l'eau chaude à l'ensemble de ces logements. »

On the left page, a plan of the facility. On this page, below, elevations and above, a photo of the completed structure.

Links ein Lageplan der Anlage. Auf dieser Seite unten Aufrisse sowie oben eine Aufnahme des realisierten Baus.

Page de gauche, un plan des installations. Ci-dessous, élévations et ci-dessus, photo du bâtiment achevé.

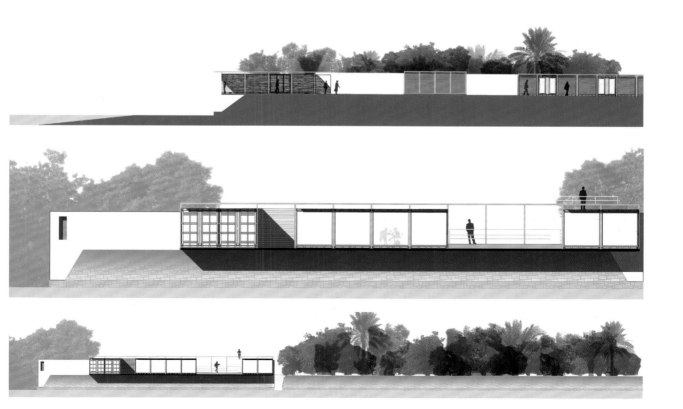

The facility makes use of open spaces such as the one below to encourage cooling breeze. Section drawings show the scale of the structure vis-à-vis the users: it is both human and inviting.

Der Komplex bindet offene Bereiche ein (unten), um kühlende Winde zu nutzen. Querschnitte veranschaulichen das Größenverhältnis von Gebäude und Nutzern, das ebenso auf den Menschen abgestimmt wie einladend wirkt.

Le bâtiment multiplie les espaces ouverts pour mieux profiter de la ventilation naturelle. Les coupes donnent une idée de l'échelle, humaine et accueillante.

Interior spaces are bright and airy. Drawings show such details as the bamboo sun baffles and solar collectors on the roof that add to the energy efficiency of the facility.

Die Innenräume sind hell und luftig. Zeichnungen zeigen Details wie Sonnenblenden aus Bambus oder Sonnenkollektoren auf dem Dach, die zur Energieeffizienz des Komplexes beitragen.

Les volumes intérieurs sont lumineux et aérés. Les éclatés montrent des détails comme les écrans de bambous utilisés pour la protection solaire et les panneaux photovoltaïques en toiture qui contribuent à l'efficacité énergétique des installations.

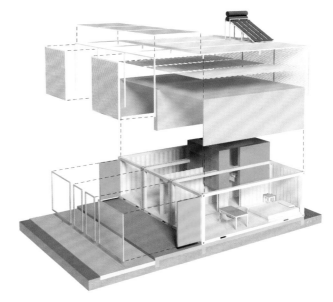

JAVIER TERRADOS CEPEDA

Javier Terrados Cepeda
C/ Rosario Vega, 2 Bajo derecha
41010 Seville
Spain

Tel: +34 954 00 14 20
Fax: +34 954 00 14 21
E-mail: estudio@javierterrados.com
Web: www.javierterrados.com

Born in 1963, **JAVIER TERRADOS CEPEDA** graduated from the School of Architecture of Seville (ETSAS). In 1989 he received a fellowship to study in the Master of Architectural Design Program at Cornell University (New York). Since returning to Spain, he has taught Architectural Design at the ETSAS while running his own architecture office in Seville. He has worked mostly in the area of public architecture (social housing, schools, health centers, theaters, offices, and public spaces) along with some private homes, and including the project published here, Kit Housing for Seasonal Workers (Cartaya, Huelva, 2006). Recently he has been the design principal behind the proposal of the University of Seville for an International Exhibition called "Solar Decathlon Europe 2010." Recent work includes an extension of the Faculty of Chemistry at the University of Seville (2010); a number of health centers in Cordoba and Seville; and Los Yesos, a private house in Sorvilan, all in Spain.

JAVIER TERRADOS CEPEDA, geboren 1963, schloss sein Studium an der Technischen Hochschule für Architektur in Sevilla (ETSAS) ab. 1989 erhielt er ein Stipendium für das Masterprogramm in architektonischem Entwerfen der Cornell University (New York). Seit seiner Rückkehr nach Spanien lehrt er als Dozent für Entwerfen an der ETSAS und betreibt sein eigenes Architekturbüro in Sevilla. Er ist primär tätig im Bereich öffentlicher Bauten (Sozialbauten, Schulen, Gesundheitszentren, Theater, Büros und öffentliche Einrichtungen), entwarf jedoch auch einzelne private Wohnbauten sowie das hier vorgestellte Fertighaussystem für Saisonarbeiter (Cartaya, Huelva, Spanien, 2006). In jüngster Zeit engagierte er sich als Chefdesigner für einen Wettbewerbsbeitrag der Universität Sevilla zum *Solar Decathlon Europe 2010*. Kürzlich realisierte Arbeiten sind auch ein Erweiterungsbau der Fakultät für Chemie der Universität Sevilla (2010). Aktuelle Projekte sind u.a. eine Reihe von Gesundheitszentren in Cordoba und Sevilla sowie Los Yesos, ein Privathaus in Sorvilan, alle in Spanien.

Né en 1963, **JAVIER TERRADOS CEPEDA** est diplômé de l'École d'architecture de Séville (ETSAS). Il a reçu en 1989 une bourse pour un programme de mastère de conception architecturale à l'université Cornell (New York). Depuis son retour en Espagne, il a enseigné la conception architecturale à l'ETSAS, tout en gérant son agence d'architecture à Séville. Il a principalement travaillé dans le domaine des bâtiments publics (logement social, écoles, dispensaires, théâtres, bureaux et lieux publics), mais a aussi réalisé quelques résidences privées, dont le projet, publié ici, de logement en kit pour travailleurs saisonniers (Cartaya, Huelva, 2006). Récemment, il a été le responsable d'une initiative d'exposition internationale organisée par l'université de Séville, intitulée « Solar Decathlon Europe 2010 ». Il a également construit une extension de la faculté de chimie de l'université de Séville (2010) ; plusieurs centres de remise en forme à Cordoue et Séville et la maison Los Yesos à Sorvilan (Espagne).

KIT HOUSING FOR SEASONAL WORKERS

Cartaya, Huelva, Spain, 2006

Area: 75 m². Client: Consejería de Obras Públicas y Transportes, Junta de Andalucía
Cost: €60 000

An overall view with the brightly colored façades of the structures and their breeze-catching towers.

Eine Gesamtansicht der leuchtend bunten Fassaden des Gebäudes mit den Windfänger-Türmen.

Vue d'ensemble des façades de couleurs vives des maisons et de leurs tours de ventilation.

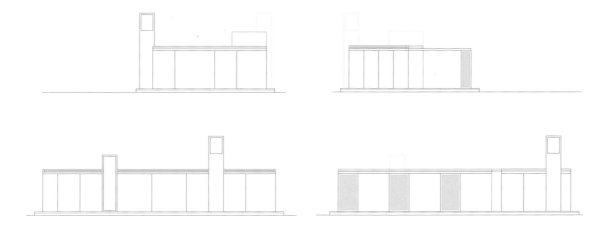

Living conditions in Huelva, in particular for immigrant workers for the strawberry harvest, posed numerous problems. This was a research project that aimed to resolve the difficulties by building a prototype or model house. The architect proposed to rethink the prefabricated house according to daily functions (e.g., eating, sleeping, watching TV, showering, storing clothes). "Thus," he states, "the house is conceived more as a comfortable and attractive assembly of furniture than an addition of walls and roof." The concept consisted in creating collective housing located near the greenhouses. A 32-worker module was developed with four wings, as was an eight-person unit in an L-shaped configuration with an exterior porch. The proposed kit included "climatic furniture"—four pieces of furniture that capture the breeze in the warm climate of southern Spain. The modular, lightweight prefabrication system allows the structures to be easily dismantled.

Die Lebensbedingungen in Huelva, insbesondere für Arbeitsmigranten, die zur Erdbeerernte kommen, haben zahlreiche Probleme aufgeworfen. Das hier vorgestellte Forschungsprojekt wollte diese Probleme lösen, indem es einen Prototyp beziehungsweise ein Musterhaus realisierte. Der Architekt schlägt vor, das Prinzip Fertighaus entsprechend täglicher Funktionen neu zu überdenken (Essen, Schlafen, Fernsehen, Duschen, Kleidung verstauen etc.). „In der Folge", so der Architekt, „wird das Haus eher als wohnliche und attraktive Zusammenstellung von Mobiliar entwickelt, statt als Kombination von Wänden und Dach." Das Konzept sah vor, Gemeinschaftswohnquartiere in der Nähe der Gewächshäuser zu bauen. Entwickelt wurde ein Modul für 32 Arbeiter mit vier Flügeln sowie ein L-förmiges Quartier für acht Personen mit Terrasse. Zum Fertighaussystem gehörten „Klima-Möbel" – vier Türme, in denen sich der Wind des warmen südspanischen Klimas fängt. Das Fertigbausystem aus modularen Leichtbauelementen ermöglicht, die Bauten auch problemlos zu demontieren.

Les conditions de vie à Huelva, en particulier pour les travailleurs migrants venus pour la récolte des fraises, posent de nombreux problèmes. Ce projet de recherche portait sur un prototype de maison. L'architecte a proposé de repenser le principe de maison préfabriquée à partie des fonctions quotidiennes (manger, dormir, regarder la télévision, faire sa toilette, ranger ses vêtements, etc.). « Ainsi, explique-t-il, la maison est davantage conçue comme un assemblage confortable et séduisant de mobilier que comme l'addition d'un toit aux murs. » Le concept propose également de créer des logements collectifs à proximité des serres. Un module pour 32 ouvriers a été mis au point. Il se présente sous la forme de quatre ailes, pour 8 personnes chacune, d'une configuration en L, avec un porche. Le kit comprend « un mobilier climatique » constitué de quatre meubles qui captent les brises bienvenues sous ce climat chaud. Le système de préfabrication modulaire, léger, permet par ailleurs un démontage facile de ces logements.

The interiors of the houses are airy and agreeable. Rooms provide sleeping space for four in the form of bunk beds.

Das Interieur der Häuser wirkt luftig und angenehm. Die Zimmer mit Etagenbetten bieten Schlafplatz für je vier Personen.

L'intérieur des maisons est aéré et agréable. Chaque chambre contient quatre lits superposés.

Below, drawings show the construction sequence of the building. A long, hollow brick base is covered with galvanized steel framing and a plywood floor. A system of plug-in furniture is used.

Zeichnungen (unten) illustrieren den Montageprozess des Gebäudes. Auf einem länglichen Fundament aus Hohlziegeln wird ein Gitter aus verzinktem Stahl sowie ein Sperrholzboden aufgebracht. Zum Einsatz kommt außerdem ein System aus Moduleinbaumöbeln.

Ci-dessous, dessins représentant la séquence de la construction. Un socle allongé en brique creuse est recouvert d'un plancher en acier galvanisé et d'un sol en contreplaqué. Les meubles s'accrochent aux parois.

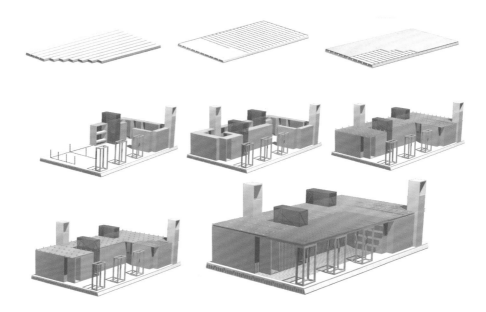

"The Theater of Immanen⚫

UNSTUDIO

UNStudio
Stadhouderskade 113
1073 AX Amsterdam
The Netherlands

Tel: +31 20 570 20 40
Fax: +31 20 570 20 41
E-mail: info@unstudio.com
Web: www.unstudio.com

BEN VAN BERKEL was born in Utrecht, the Netherlands, in 1957 and studied at the Rietveld Academy in Amsterdam and at the Architectural Association (AA) in London, receiving the AA Diploma with honors in 1987. After working briefly in the office of Santiago Calatrava in 1988, he set up his practice in Amsterdam with **CAROLINE BOS**. Bos studied the History of Art at Birkbeck College (University of London). She co-founded Van Berkel & Bos Architectuur Bureau in 1988, and UNStudio in 1999. As well as the Erasmus Bridge in Rotterdam (1996), Van Berkel & Bos Architectural Bureau has built the Karbouw and ACOM (1989–93) office buildings, and the REMU Electricity Station (1989–93), all in Amersfoort; and housing projects and the Aedes East Gallery for Kristin Feireiss in Berlin, Germany. Projects include the Möbius House (Naarden, 1993–98); Het Valkhof Museum (Nijmegen, 1998); and NMR Laboratory (Utrecht, 2000), all in the Netherlands; a Switching Station (Innsbruck, Austria, 1998–2001); an Electricity Station (Innsbruck, Austria, 2002); VilLA NM (Upstate New York, USA, 2000–06); the Mercedes-Benz Museum (Stuttgart, Germany, 2003–06); and the Arnhem Station (The Netherlands, 1986–). Recent work includes a Teahouse (Groot Kantwijk, Vreeland, The Netherlands, 2005–07); a Music Theater (Graz, Austria, 1998–2008); a Research Laboratory at Groningen University (Groningen, The Netherlands, 2003–08); Star Place (Kaohsiung, Taiwan, 2006–08); and Burnham Pavilion (Chicago, Illinois, USA, 2009).

BEN VAN BERKEL wurde 1957 in Utrecht geboren und studierte an der Rietveld-Akademie in Amsterdam sowie der Architectural Association (AA) in London, wo er 1987 das Diplom mit Auszeichnung erhielt. Nach einem kurzen Arbeitseinsatz 1988 bei Santiago Calatrava gründete er mit **CAROLINE BOS** sein eigenes Büro in Amsterdam. Bos studierte Kunstgeschichte am Birkbeck College (University of London). Sie begründete 1988 Van Berkel & Bos Architectuur Bureau mit und im folgenden Jahr UNStudio. Neben der 1996 eingeweihten Erasmusbrücke in Rotterdam baute Van Berkel & Bos Architectural Bureau in Amersfoort die Büros für Karbouw und ACOM (1989–93) sowie das Kraftwerk REMU (1989–93), alle in Amersfoort, und realisierte in Berlin Wohnbauprojekte sowie die Galerie Aedes East für Kristin Feireiss. Zu den Projekten des Teams zählen das Haus Möbius (Naarden, 1993–98) und das Museum Het Valkhof (Nijmegen, 1998), das NMR-Labor in Utrecht (2000), ein Umspannwerk (Innsbruck, 1998–2001), ein Elektrizitätswerk (Innsbruck, 2002), die VilLA NM (bei New York, 2000–06), das Mercedes-Benz-Museum (Stuttgart, 2003–06) sowie der Bahnhof Arnhem (Arnhem, 1986–). Jüngere Arbeiten sind u.a. ein Teehaus (Groot Kantwijk, Vreeland, Niederlande, 2005–07), ein Musiktheater in Graz (1998–2008), ein Forschungslabor an der Universität Groningen (2003–08), Star Place (Kaohsiung, Taiwan, 2006–08) sowie der Burnham-Pavillon (Chicago, 2009).

BEN VAN BERKEL, né à Utrecht en 1957, a étudié à la Rietveld Academie d'Amsterdam, ainsi qu'à l'Architectural Association de Londres (AA), dont il est sorti diplômé avec mention en 1987. Après avoir brièvement travaillé pour Santiago Calatrava en 1988, il a ouvert son agence à Amsterdam, en association avec **CAROLINE BOS**. Bos a fait ses études d'histoire d'art au Birkbeck College (University of London). Ella a fondé Van Berkel & Bos Architectuur Bureau en 1988, et UNStudio en 1999. En dehors du pont Érasme à Rotterdam (inauguré en 1996), Van Berkel & Bos Architectural Bureau a construit, à Amersfoort, les immeubles de bureaux Karbouw et ACOM (1989–93) ; la station électrique REMU (1989–93) ainsi que des logements et l'Aedes East Gallery de Kristin Feireiss à Berlin. Parmi ses projets plus récents : la maison Moebius (Naarden, 1993–98) ; le musée Het Valkhof (Nimègue, 1998) ; le laboratoire NMR (Utrecht, 2000), tous aux Pays-Bas ; une plate-forme d'échanges intermodaux (Innsbruck, Autriche, 1998–2001) ; une station d'électricité (Innsbruck, 2002) ; la VilLA NM (État de New York, 2000–06) ; le musée Mercedes-Benz (Stuttgart, Allemagne, 2003–06) et la gare d'Arnhem (Pays-Bas, 1986–). Plus récemment, l'agence a réalisé une maison de thé (Groot Kantwijk, Vreeland, Pays-Bas, 2005–07) ; une salle de concert (Graz, Autriche, 1998–2008) ; un laboratoire de recherche pour l'université de Groningue (Pays-Bas, 2003–08) ; le centre commercial Star Place (Kaohsiung, Taïwan, 2006–08) et le pavillon Burnham (Chicago, Illinois, États-Unis, 2009).

"THE THEATER OF IMMANENCE"

Portikus, Frankfurt am Main, Germany, 2007

Area: 11 x 8 x 3.5 m. Client: Portikus. Cost: not disclosed.
Collaboration: Johan Bettum, Luis Etchegorry, MESO Digital Interiors

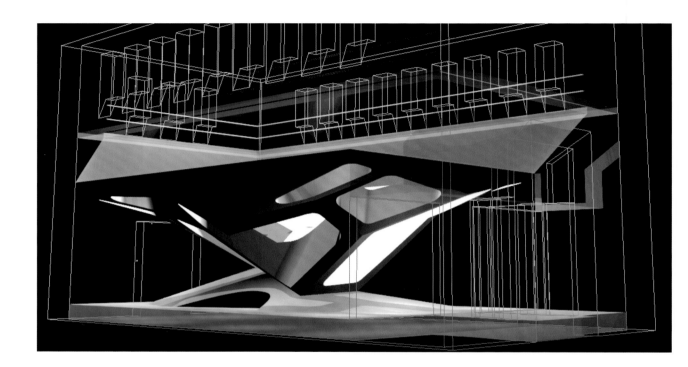

"BEN VAN BERKEL & THE THEATER OF IMMANENCE" was a combined art and architecture exhibition in which the different parts in the show "are synthesized into a complete whole." The theme of this installation was one of communication between visitors and the exhibited works and between the virtual and the real. Ben van Berkel's architectural installation was called The Thing and was designed with the help of the Frankfurt-based design group MESO, responsible for a "dynamic embellishment" of the architectural surfaces, in "an attempt to create a reactive surface of extraordinary spatial complexity." The upper level of The Thing was conceived as a theater and the lower level as an exhibition space, with the two spaces connected by a number of open holes. On the lower level, the exhibition presented a group of works by artists and architects who have participated in a one-year-long experimental project, entitled "The Space of Communication," organized by the Städelschule Architecture Class (SAC). The exhibiting participants in this project were the architects Asterios Agkathidis, Brennan Buck & Igor Kebel, Holger Hoffmann, Jonas Runberger, and Gabi Schillig, and the artists Florencia Colombo and Dani Gal.

BEN VAN BERKEL & THE THEATER OF IMMANENCE war eine Ausstellung für Kunst und Architektur, bei der die verschiedenen Bereiche „zu einer Gesamtheit vereint" wurden. Thema der Installation war die Kommunikation zwischen Besuchern und ausgestellten Werken sowie dem Virtuellen und Realen. Ben van Berkels Architekturinstallation trug den Titel *The Thing* und wurde in Zusammenarbeit mit der Frankfurter Designgruppe MESO realisiert. MESO war für die „dynamische Gestaltung" der architektonischen Oberflächen verantwortlich, die „Versuch, eine reaktive Oberfläche von außergewöhnlicher räumlicher Komplexität zu schaffen". Die obere Ebene von *The Thing* wurde als Theater konzipiert, die untere als Ausstellungsraum. Beide Ebenen waren durch eine Reihe von Öffnungen miteinander verbunden. Auf der unteren Ebene waren die Arbeiten einer Gruppe von Künstlern und Architekten zu sehen, die an einem einjährigen experimentellen Projekt der Architekturklasse der Städelschule (SAC), *The Space of Communication*, teilgenommen hatten. Die dort präsentierten Teilnehmer des Projekts waren die Architekten Asterios Agkathidis, Brennan Buck & Igor Kebel, Holger Hoffmann, Jonas Runberger, Gabi Schillig sowie die Künstler Florencia Colombo und Dani Gal.

« **BEN VAN BERKEL ET LE THÉÂTRE DE L'IMMANENCE** » est une exposition combinant art et architecture dans laquelle les différentes parties du spectacle « sont synthétisées en un tout complet ». Le thème de cette installation était celui de la communication entre les visiteurs et les œuvres exposées, entre le virtuel et le réel. L'installation architecturale de van Berkel, intitulée *The Thing* (« La chose »), avait été conçue avec l'assistance du groupe de design MESO basé à Francfort, en charge de « l'embellissement dynamique » des surfaces architecturales dans une « tentative de créer une surface réactive d'une complexité spatiale extraordinaire ». La partie supérieure de *The Thing* était conçue comme un théâtre et sa partie inférieure comme une galerie d'exposition, les deux espaces étant reliés par un certain nombre d'orifices ouverts. L'exposition présentait des œuvres d'artistes et d'architectes qui avaient participé à un projet expérimental d'une année, intitulé « L'Espace de la communication », organisé par la classe d'architecture de la Städelschule (SAC). Les participants et exposants étaient les architectes Asterios Agkathidis, Brennan Buck & Igor Kebel, Holger Hoffmann, Jonas Runberger, Gabi Schillig et les artistes Florencia Colombo et Dani Gal.

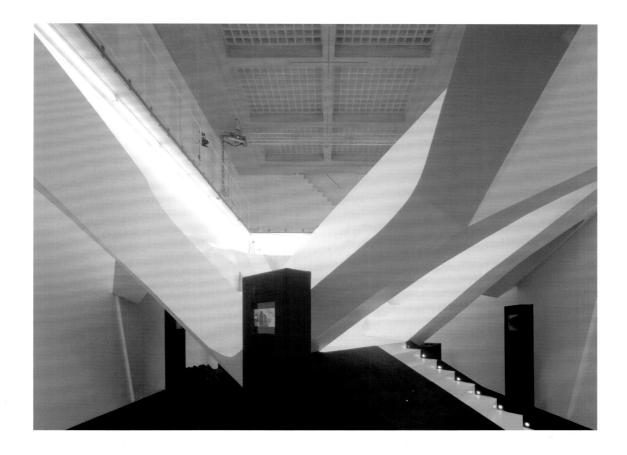

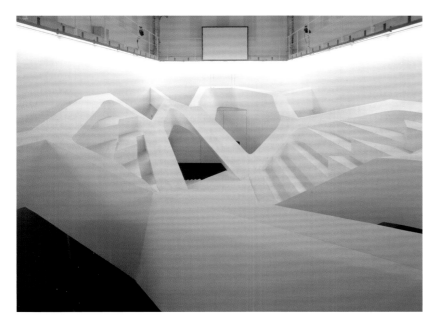

The complex surfaces of the exhibition are very much in keeping with the aesthetic vocabulary of UNStudio.

Die komplexen Oberflächen des Ausstellungsraums spiegeln deutlich die ästhetische Formensprache von UNStudio.

La complexité des plans est dans l'esprit du vocabulaire esthétique d'UNStudio.

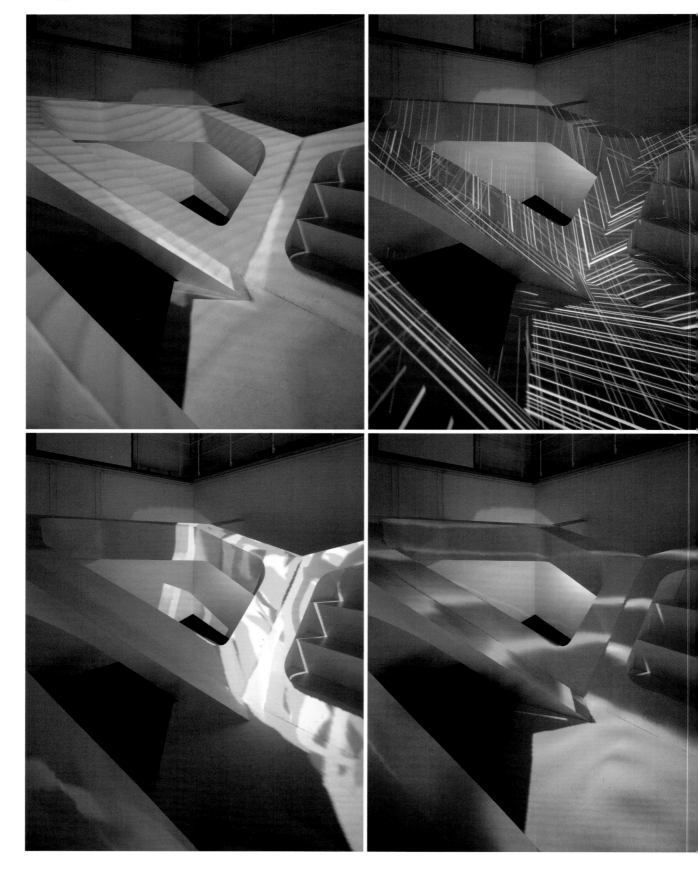

The architects seek to make the boundary between the real and the virtual difficult to ascertain. In this way computer-designed reality makes the leap from the screen into three dimensions.

Den Architekten geht es darum, Grenzen zwischen Realität und Virtualität verschwimmen zu lassen. Hier gelingt der computergenerierten Realität der Sprung vom Monitor in die Dreidimensionalität.

Les architectes ont cherché à rendre la frontière entre le réel et le virtuel difficile à percevoir. La virtualité de l'écran de l'ordinateur se transfère ici dans la réalité en trois dimensions.

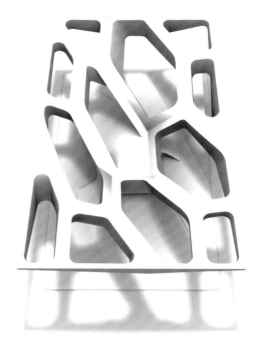

HELENA WILLEMEIT

Helena Willemeit
AIRSCAPE
Brunnenstr. 40
10115 Berlin
Germany

Tel: +49 174 707 72 44
E-mail: info@air-scape.de
Web: www.air-scape.de

HELENA WILLEMEIT was born in 1975 in Lilongwe, Malawi. She was raised in Malawi, Zimbabwe, and Germany and studied architecture at the Universität der Künste (Berlin, 1994–2001) and at the University of New South Wales (Sydney, 1999–2000). She worked in several offices, including those of Daniel Libeskind (Berlin, 2003) and Graft (Berlin and Los Angeles, 2004). In 2004, she participated in the creation of a firm called NYANGA (conception, design, and construction of architecture, surfaces, and furniture from concrete and wood) and, in 2008, the company Airscape, dedicated to "nomadic living," temporary architecture, and furniture: see the project published here, Airscape (Berlin, Germany, 2008).

HELENA WILLEMEIT wurde 1975 in Lilongwe, Malawi, geboren. Sie wuchs in Malawi, Zimbabwe, und Deutschland auf und studierte Architektur an der Universität der Künste Berlin (1994–2001) und der Universität von New South Wales (Sydney, 1999–2000). Sie war in verschiedenen Büros tätig, darunter für Daniel Libeskind (Berlin, 2003) und Graft (Berlin und Los Angeles, 2004). 2004 war sie an der Gründung des Büros NYANGA beteiligt (Konzeption, Entwurf und bauliche Realisierung von Architektur, Oberflächen und Möbeln aus Beton und Holz) sowie 2008 an der Gründung von Airscape, einem Büro, das sich „nomadischen Wohnformen", temporärer Architektur und dem Möbeldesign verschrieben hat, siehe auch das hier vorgestellte Projekt Airscape (Berlin, 2008).

HELENA WILLEMEIT, née en 1975 à Lilongwe (Malawi), a été élevée au Malawi, au Zimbabwe et en Allemagne. Elle a fait ses études d'architecture à l'Université des arts (Universität der Künste, Berlin, 1994–2001) et à l'université de la Nouvelle-Galles du Sud (Sydney, 1999–2000). Elle a travaillé dans plusieurs agences, dont celle de Daniel Libeskind (Berlin, 2003), et Graft (Berlin et Los Angeles, 2004). En 2004, elle a participé à la création de l'agence NYANGA (conception, design et construction d'architectures, surfaces et mobiliers en bois et béton) et, en 2008, à celle de la société Airscape qui se consacre à la « vie nomade », l'architecture temporaire et le mobilier – voir son projet publié ici, Airscape (Berlin, 2008).

AIRSCAPE
Berlin, Germany, 2008

Area: 70 m². Client: Helena Willemeit
Cost: not disclosed

Airscape is essentially an inflatable arch that can serve as a shelter. The structure can be articulated in different ways and combined with other Airscape elements.

Airscape, ein aufblasbarer Bogen, lässt sich als schützender Unterstand nutzen. Die Struktur kann zu verschiedenen Formen konfiguriert und mit weiteren Airscape-Elementen kombiniert werden.

Airscape est tout simplement un arc gonflable qui peut servir d'abri. Il peut s'articuler de différentes façons et se combiner avec d'autres éléments identiques.

AIRSCAPE tents are "amorphous and mobile architectural spaces" that can be inflated within a few minutes. "With their sensual arched roofs," says Helena Willemeit, "the structures can enclose a floor space of 70 square meters to over 300 square meters. The outstanding characteristic of the modular system is its creative potential: whether a solitary sculpture is presented as a distinct, eye-catching structure, or tents are combined in groups to create a landscape of flowing spaces—the range of applications is wide open." She suggests that the tents can be used for private or corporate events and emphasizes the correspondence between this initiative and the increasingly "nomadic" lifestyle of developed countries. In this sense she seems to be returning in a more modern way to her African upbringing. Airscape tents were used for the 2010 Nintendo Wii City summer tour (Potsdam).

Die **AIRSCAPE**-Zelte sind „amorphe und mobile architektonische Räume", die sich innerhalb weniger Minuten aufblasen lassen. „Mit ihren sinnlich geschwungenen Dächern", so Helena Willemeit, „können die Konstruktionen eine Grundfläche von 70 bis zu über 300 m² haben. Das hervorstechendste Merkmal des modularen Systems ist sein kreatives Potenzial: Ob nun eine einzelne Skulptur als individuelle, plakative Struktur präsentiert wird oder Zelte zu Gruppen und damit zu einer Landschaft aus fließenden Räumen kombiniert werden – das Spektrum der Anwendungsmöglichkeiten ist denkbar breit." Willemeit weist darauf hin, dass die Zelte sowohl für private als auch für Firmenveranstaltungen eingesetzt werden können und hebt insbesondere die Ähnlichkeiten zwischen ihrer Aktion und dem zunehmend „nomadenhaften" Lebensstil entwickelter Länder hervor. In diesem Sinne scheint sie auf zeitgenössische Weise an ihre Kindheit in Afrika anzuknüpfen. Die Airscape-Zelte kamen unter anderem bei der Nintendo-Wii-Sommertour City 2010 zum Einsatz (Potsdam).

Les tentes **AIRSCAPE** sont des « espaces amorphes et mobiles » gonflables en quelques minutes. « Sous leur forme arquée, sensuelle, explique Helena Willemeit, ces structures peuvent recouvrir un espace de 70 à plus de 300 m². La caractéristique la plus remarquable de ce système modulaire est son potentiel créatif : d'une sculpture surprenante et solitaire à des combinaisons en groupe pour créer un paysage d'espaces en flux, la gamme de ses applications est grande ouverte. » Elle suggère des utilisations pour des manifestations privées ou d'entreprise, et insiste sur la correspondance entre cette initiative et le style de vie de plus en plus « nomade » dans les pays développés. En ce sens, elle semble revenir, mais de façon moderne, à ses racines africaines. Les tentes Airscape ont été utilisées pour la tournée 2010 du Nintendo Wii City (Potsdam).

Drawings show the relative scale of the inflatable arches and a number of the ways in which they might be combined to form more complex structures.

Zeichnungen veranschaulichen die Größenverhältnisse der aufblasbaren Bögen und verschiedene Kombinationsmöglichkeiten zu komplexeren Strukturen.

Les dessins montrent des arcs gonflables à différentes échelles et un certain nombre de combinaisons permettant de constituer des structures plus complexes.

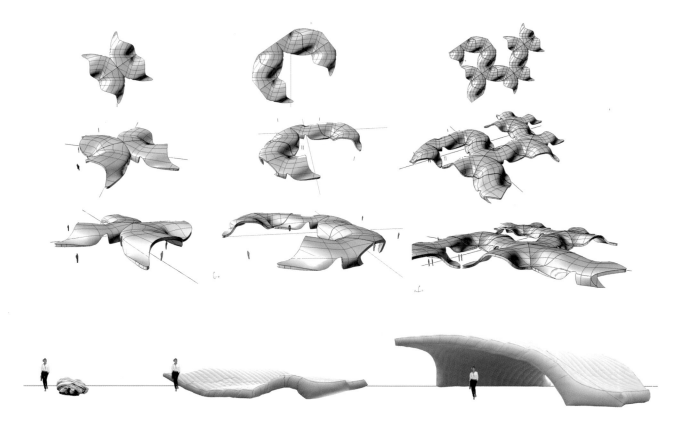

Configured as a simple, low arch, the Airscape can readily be installed or moved according to needs.

In seiner Konfiguration als einfacher niedriger Bogen lässt sich Airscape problemlos aufbauen und nach Bedarf bewegen.

En forme d'arc simple surbaissé, Airscape s'installe et se déplace aisément, selon les besoins.

In these images, children give some sense of the way in which users can appropriate the structures themselves, going beyond the immediate intentions of the architect.

Diese Aufnahmen mit Kindern vermitteln, wie sich Nutzer die Strukturen aneignen und dabei durchaus von den ursprünglichen Absichten der Architektin lösen können.

Ici, des enfants montrent certaines utilisations d'Airscape, qui dépassent peut-être les intentions de l'architecte.

TOKUJIN YOSHIOKA

Tokujin Yoshioka Design
9–1 Daikanyama-cho
Shibuya-ku
Tokyo 150–0034
Japan

Tel: +81 3 5428 0830
Fax: +81 3 5428 0835
E-mail: tyd@tokujin.com
Web: www.tokujin.com

TOKUJIN YOSHIOKA was born in 1967 in Saga, Japan. He graduated from the Kuwasawa Design School and worked under the celebrated designer Shiro Kuramata (1987) and then with Issey Miyake from 1988. He established his own studio, Tokujin Yoshioka Design, in 2000 in Tokyo. His work for Issey Miyake over a period of 20 years included extensive shop design and installations. His work is represented at the Museum of Modern Art (MoMA) in New York, the Centre Pompidou in Paris, the Victoria and Albert Museum in London, Cooper Hewitt National Design Museum in New York, and Vitra Design Museum in Germany. He has collaborated with companies such as Hermès, BMW, and Toyota. Among other objects, he designed Yamagiwa's lighting ToFU (2000); the paper chair Honey-pop (2000–01); Driade's Tokyo-pop (2002); Water Block made of special glass (2002); Media Skin cell phone (2005); Stardust chandelier for the Swarovski Crystal Palace (2005); PANE Chair (2003–06); Waterfall (Tokyo, Japan, 2005–06); VENUS–Natural crystal chair (2008); and the Swarovski Flagship Store in Ginza (Tokyo, Japan, 2006–08). Tokujin Yoshioka recently completed PLEATS PLEASE Issey Miyake Aoyama (Tokyo, Japan, 2009); Camper To&ether (London, UK, 2009); and the Rainbow Church, MUSEUM Beyondmuseum (Seoul, South Korea, 2010, published here).

TOKUJIN YOSHIOKA wurde 1967 in Saga, Japan, geboren. Sein Studium schloss er an der Kuwasawa Design School ab. Er arbeitete für den bekannten Designer Shiro Kuramata (1987) und ab 1988 für Issey Miyake. Sein eigenes Studio, Tokujin Yoshioka Design, gründete er 2000 in Tokio. Zu seinen im Laufe von rund 20 Jahren entstandenen Arbeiten für Issey Miyake zählen zahlreiche Ladengestaltungen und Installationen. Zu sehen ist sein Werk auch im Museum of Modern Art (MoMA) in New York, dem Centre Pompidou in Paris, dem Victoria and Albert Museum in London, dem Cooper Hewitt National Design Museum in New York sowie dem Vitra Design Museum in Deutschland. Tokujin kooperierte mit Firmen wie Hermès, BMW oder Toyota. Er gestaltete unter anderem die Leuchte „ToFU" für Yamagiwa (2000), die Stühle „Honey-pop" aus Papier (2000–01), „Tokyo-pop" für Driade (2002) und „Water Block" aus Spezialglas (2002), das „Media Skin" Mobiltelefon (2005), den Kronleuchter „Stardust" für den Swarovski Crystal Palace (2005), den Stuhl „PANE" (2003–06), Waterfall (Tokio, 2005–06), den Stuhl „VENUS" aus Kristall (2008) sowie den Swarovski-Flagshipstore im Ginza-Viertel (Tokio, 2006–08). Tokujin Yoshioka realisierte unlängst die Boutique PLEATS PLEASE für Issey Miyake in Aoyama (Tokio, Japan, 2009), Camper To&ether (London, 2009) sowie die Rainbow Church, für das MUSEUM Beyondmuseum (Seoul, Südkorea, 2010, hier vorgestellt).

TOKUJIN YOSHIOKA, né en 1967 à Saga (Japon), est diplômé de l'École de design Kuwasawa et a travaillé auprès du célèbre designer Shiro Kuramata (1987), puis avec Issey Miyake à partir de 1988. Il a fondé son agence, Tokujin Yoshioka Design, en 2000 à Tokyo. Ses réalisations pour Issey Miyake pendant plus de vingt ans comprennent de multiples projets de magasins et des installations. Son œuvre est présente au Musée d'art moderne de New York (MoMA), au Centre Pompidou à Paris, au Victoria and Albert Museum à Londres, au Musée national du design Cooper Hewitt à New York et au Vitra Design Museum en Allemagne. Il a travaillé pour des entreprises comme Hermès, BMW et Toyota. Entre autres projets, il a conçu la lampe ToFU pour Yamagiwa (2000) ; le siège en papier Honey-pop (2000–01) ; le canapé Driade, Tokyo-pop (2002) ; le siège Water Block en verre spécial (2002) ; le téléphone cellulaire Media Skin (2005) ; le lustre Stardust pour le Swarovski Crystal Palace (2005) ; le siège PANE (2003–06) ; le bar Waterfall (Tokyo, 2005–06) ; le siège en cristal VENUS (2008) et le magasin amiral de Swarovski à Ginza (Tokyo, 2006–08). Récemment, Tokujin Yoshioka a achevé le magasin PLEATS PLEASE Issey Miyake Aoyama (Tokyo, 2009) ; la boutique Camper To&ether (Londres, 2009) et l'église de l'arc-en-ciel (Rainbow Church), MUSEUM Beyondmuseum (Séoul, Corée du Sud, 2010, publiée ici).

RAINBOW CHURCH

MUSEUM Beyondmuseum, Seoul, South Korea, 2010

Area: 9.2 m (height of stained glass), 1.6 m (width), 100 m² (gallery area)
Client: MUSEUM. Cost: not disclosed

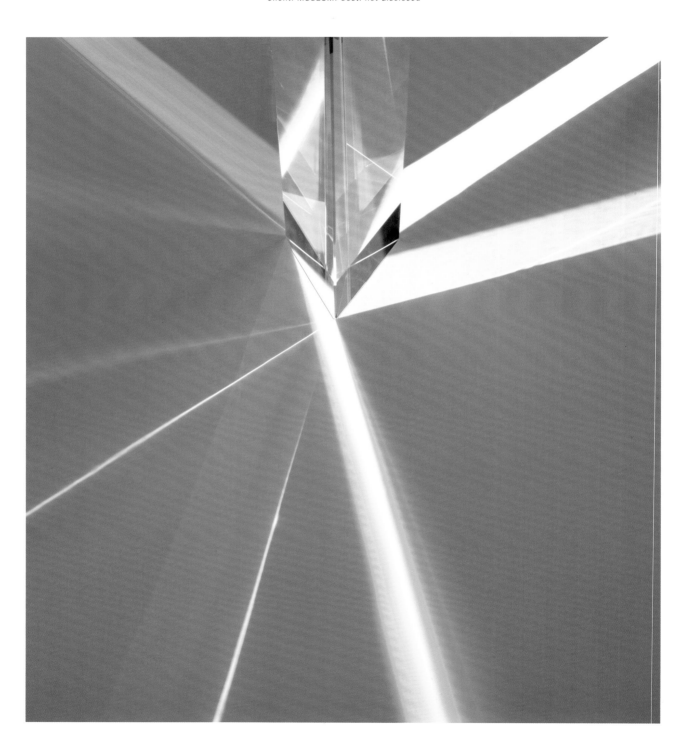

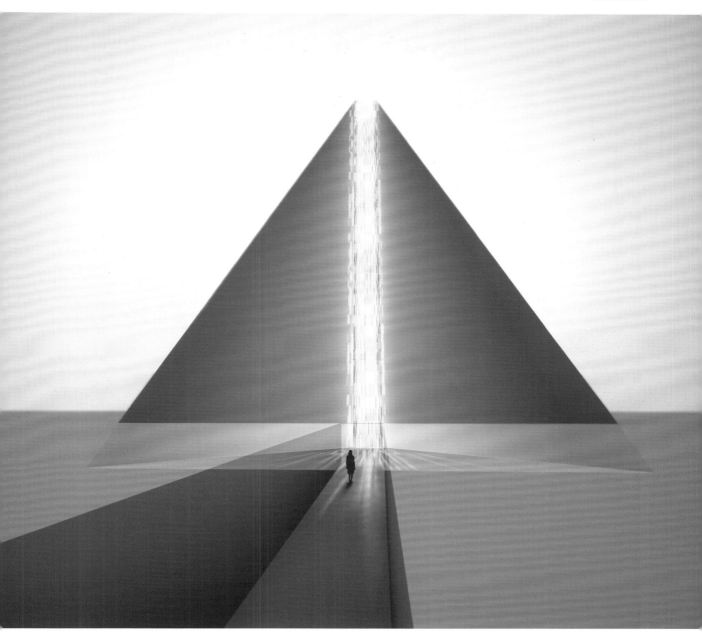

The designer has made use of 500 crystal prisms that refract and diffuse light throughout the space. The simplicity of the design, intended only for an exhibition, verges on the spiritual in the image above.

Der Designer arbeitet mit 500 Kristallprismen, die das Licht brechen und im Raum streuen. Auf der Ansicht oben wirkt der für eine Ausstellung entwickelte Entwurf fast spirituell.

Le designer a utilisé 500 prismes de cristal qui réfractent et diffusent la lumière dans l'espace. La simplicité de ce projet, prévu pour une exposition unique, frôle le spirituel (image ci-dessus).

Seoul was designated World Design Capital for 2010, and an exhibition was organized at the MUSEUM Beyondmuseum on that occasion, opening May 1, 2010. A part of this exhibition is the **RAINBOW CHURCH**. The designer explains that the idea for this work dates back to when he was in his early 20s. He visited the Chapelle du Rosaire (Vence, France, 1943–49) by the artist Henri Matisse: "I was engrossed in the beauty of the light that the chapel created," says Yoshioka. "Since then," he continues, "I have been dreaming of designing an architecture where people can feel the light with all senses." The installation is made up of 500 crystal prisms arranged in a nine-meter-high "stained-glass" arrangement "filling the space with rainbow colors as the light shines on it." The idea of light and color as tangible elements of space has been explored by artists such as James Turrell, and here takes on a particularly architectural feeling, despite the fact that this is more an art installation than it is in any sense a building.

Als Seoul zur Weltdesignhauptstadt 2010 ernannt wurde, fand zu diesem Anlass eine Ausstellung am MUSEUM Beyondmuseum statt, die am 1. Mai 2010 eröffnet wurde. Teil dieser Ausstellung war die **RAINBOW CHURCH** (Regenbogenkirche). Der Designer berichtet, die Idee des Projekts reiche zurück in eine Zeit, als er Anfang zwanzig war. Damals besuchte er die Chapelle du Rosaire (Vence, Frankreich, 1943–49) von Henri Matisse: „Ich war gebannt von der Schönheit des Lichts in der Kapelle", erzählt Yoshioka. „Seither", fährt er fort, „habe ich davon geträumt, eine Architektur zu gestalten, in der die Menschen das Licht mit allen Sinnen spüren können." Die Installation besteht aus 500 Kristallprismen, die zu einer 9 m hohen „Glasfenster"-Konstellation angeordnet wurden, „die den Raum mit Regenbogenfarben füllt, sobald das Licht auf sie fällt". Das Prinzip von Licht und Farbe als greifbare, raumkonstituierende Elemente wurde unter anderem von Künstlern wie James Turrell ausgelotet. Hier gewinnt die Idee eine besonders architektonische Qualität, obwohl dies eher eine Kunstinstallation als ein Gebäude ist.

Séoul a été désignée Capitale mondiale du design 2010, et, à cette occasion, une exposition a été organisée au MUSEUM Beyondmuseum, qui a ouvert ses portes le 1ᵉʳ mai 2010. L'Église de l'arc-en-ciel (**RAINBOW CHURCH**) fait partie de cette manifestation. Le designer a expliqué que l'idée de cette intervention remonte à ses vingt ans. Il avait visité la chapelle du Rosaire (Vence, France, 1943–49) d'Henri Matisse : « J'étais captivé par la beauté de la lumière créée par cette chapelle… Depuis, je rêve de concevoir une architecture dans laquelle les gens pourraient sentir la lumière par tous leurs sens. » Cette installation compte 500 prismes de cristal, disposés en une « composition de vitrail » de 9 m de haut, « remplissant l'espace des couleurs de l'arc-en-ciel, lorsque la lumière le touche ». L'idée de lumière et de couleurs, éléments tangibles de l'espace, a été explorée par des artistes comme James Turrell, et prend des résonances architecturales particulières dans le cas de Yoshioka, même s'il s'agit davantage d'une installation que d'une construction.

Detailed photos show the ways in which the crystal prisms are arrayed, forming a regular, articulated surface that makes light into the main object of the exhibition space.

Detailaufnahmen zeigen die Anordnung der Kristallprismen zu einer regelmäßig strukturierten Oberfläche, durch die das Licht zum zentralen Blickpunkt des Ausstellungsraums wird.

Photos de détails montrant la disposition des prismes de cristal constituant une surface régulière articulée qui fait de la lumière l'objet principal de l'exposition.

INDEX OF BUILDINGS, NAMES, AND PLACES

INDEX OF BUILDINGS, NAMES, AND PLACES

CREDITS